Advancements in Computer Vision Applications in Intelligent Systems and Multimedia Technologies

Muhammad Sarfraz
Kuwait University, Kuwait

A volume in the Advances in Computational
Intelligence and Robotics (ACIR) Book Series

Published in the United States of America by
    IGI Global
    Engineering Science Reference (an imprint of IGI Global)
    701 E. Chocolate Avenue
    Hershey PA, USA 17033
    Tel: 717-533-8845
    Fax: 717-533-8661
    E-mail: cust@igi-global.com
    Web site: http://www.igi-global.com

Library of Congress Cataloging-in-Publication Data

Names: Sarfraz, Muhammad, editor.
Title: Advancements in computer vision applications in intelligent systems
  and multimedia technologies / Muhammad Sarfraz, editor.
Description: Hershey, PA : Engineering Science Reference, an imprint of IGI
  Global, [2020] | Includes bibliographical references and index. |
  Summary: "This book discusses innovative developments in computational
  imaging for solving real-life issues and problems and addresses their
  execution in various disciplines"-- Provided by publisher.
Identifiers: LCCN 2019060146 (print) | LCCN 2019060147 (ebook) | ISBN
  9781799844440 (hardcover) | ISBN 9781799852049 (paperback) | ISBN
  9781799844457 (ebook)
Subjects: LCSH: Computer vision. | Digital video. | Multimedia systems. |
  Intelligent control systems.
Classification: LCC TA1634 .A288 2020 (print) | LCC TA1634 (ebook) | DDC
  006.3/7--dc23
LC record available at https://lccn.loc.gov/2019060146
LC ebook record available at https://lccn.loc.gov/2019060147

This book is published in the IGI Global book series Advances in Computational Intelligence and Robotics (ACIR) (ISSN: 2327-0411; eISSN: 2327-042X)

British Cataloguing in Publication Data
A Cataloguing in Publication record for this book is available from the British Library.

All work contributed to this book is new, previously-unpublished material. The views expressed in this book are those of the authors, but not necessarily of the publisher.

For electronic access to this publication, please contact: eresources@igi-global.com.

Advances in Computational Intelligence and Robotics (ACIR) Book Series

Ivan Giannoccaro
University of Salento, Italy

ISSN:2327-0411
EISSN:2327-042X

MISSION

While intelligence is traditionally a term applied to humans and human cognition, technology has progressed in such a way to allow for the development of intelligent systems able to simulate many human traits. With this new era of simulated and artificial intelligence, much research is needed in order to continue to advance the field and also to evaluate the ethical and societal concerns of the existence of artificial life and machine learning.

The **Advances in Computational Intelligence and Robotics (ACIR) Book Series** encourages scholarly discourse on all topics pertaining to evolutionary computing, artificial life, computational intelligence, machine learning, and robotics. ACIR presents the latest research being conducted on diverse topics in intelligence technologies with the goal of advancing knowledge and applications in this rapidly evolving field.

COVERAGE

- Natural Language Processing
- Artificial Life
- Artificial Intelligence
- Evolutionary Computing
- Cyborgs
- Adaptive and Complex Systems
- Agent technologies
- Neural Networks
- Algorithmic Learning
- Computational Logic

IGI Global is currently accepting manuscripts for publication within this series. To submit a proposal for a volume in this series, please contact our Acquisition Editors at Acquisitions@igi-global.com or visit: http://www.igi-global.com/publish/.

Titles in this Series

For a list of additional titles in this series, please visit:
http://www.igi-global.com/book-series/advances-computational-intelligence-robotics/73674

Artificial Intelligence and the Journey to Software 2.0 Emerging Research and Opportunities
Divanshi Priyadarshni Wangoo (Indira Gandhi Delhi Technical University for Women, India)
Engineering Science Reference • © 2021 • 150pp • H/C (ISBN: 9781799843276) • US $165.00

Applications of Artificial Intelligence for Smart Technology
P. Swarnalatha (VIT University, India) and S. Prabu (VIT University, India)
Engineering Science Reference • © 2020 • 300pp • H/C (ISBN: 9781799833352) • US $215.00

Practical Applications and Use Cases of Computer Vision and Recognition Systems
Chiranji Lal Chowdhary (Vellore Institute of Technology, India) and B.D. Parameshachari (GSSS Institute of Engineering and Technology for Women, India)
Engineering Science Reference • © 2020 • 300pp • H/C (ISBN: 9781799849247) • US $195.00

Machine Learning Applications in Non-Conventional Machining Processes
Goutam Kumar Bose (Haldia Institute of Technology, Haldia, India) and Pritam Pain (Haldia Institute of Technology, India)
Engineering Science Reference • © 2020 • 300pp • H/C (ISBN: 9781799836247) • US $195.00

Handbook of Research on Smart Technology Models for Business and Industry
J. Joshua Thomas (UOW Malaysia KDU Penang University College, Malaysia) Ugo Fiore (University of Naples Parthenope, Italy) Gilberto Perez Lechuga (Autonomous University of Hidalgo State, Mexico) Valeriy Kharchenko (Federal Agroengineering Centre VIM , Russia) and Pandian Vasant (Universiti Teknologi PETRONAS, Malaysia)
Engineering Science Reference • © 2020 • 400pp • H/C (ISBN: 9781799836452) • US $295.00

Applications of Artificial Neural Networks for Nonlinear Data
Hiral Ashil Patel (Ganpat University, India) and A.V. Senthil Kumar (Hindusthan College of Arts and Science, India)
Engineering Science Reference • © 2020 • 300pp • H/C (ISBN: 9781799840428) • US $245.00

Handbook of Research on Natural Language Processing and Smart Service Systems
Rodolfo Abraham Pazos-Rangel (Tecnológico Nacional de México, Mexico & Instituto Tecnológico de Cd. Madero, Mexico) Rogelio Florencia-Juarez (Autonomous University of Juarez City, Mexico) Mario Andrés Paredes-Valverde (Tecnológico Nacional de México, Mexico & Instituto Tecnológico de Orizaba, Mexico) and Gilberto Rivera (Autonomous University of Juarez City, Mexico)
Engineering Science Reference • © 2020 • 350pp • H/C (ISBN: 9781799847304) • US $295.00

701 East Chocolate Avenue, Hershey, PA 17033, USA
Tel: 717-533-8845 x100 • Fax: 717-533-8661
E-Mail: cust@igi-global.com • www.igi-global.com

Table of Contents

Detailed Table of Contents

Chapter 1

Sanjida Nasreen Tumpa, University of Calgary, Canada
K. N. Pavan Kumar, University of Calgary, Canada
Madeena Sultana, University of Calgary, Canada
Gee-Sern Jison Hsu, National Taiwan University of Science and Technology, Taiwan
Orly Yadid-Pecht, University of Calgary, Canada
Svetlana Yanushkevich, University of Calgary, Canada
Marina L. Gavrilova, University of Calgary, Canada

Smart societies of the future will increasingly rely on harvesting rich information generated by day-to-day activities and interactions of its inhabitants. Among the multitude of such interactions, web-based social networking activities became an integral part of everyday human communication. Flickr, Facebook, Twitter, and LinkedIn are currently used by millions of users worldwide as a source of information, which is growing exponentially over time. In addition to idiosyncratic personal characteristics, web-based social data include person-to-person communication, online activity patterns, and temporal information, among others. However, analysis of social interaction-based data has been studied from the perspective of person identification only recently. In this chapter, the authors elaborate on the concept of using interaction-based features from online social networking platforms as a part of social behavioral biometrics research domain. They place this research in the context of smart societies and discuss novel social biometric features and their potential use in various applications.

Chapter 2

Mohit Dua, National Institute of Technology, Kurukshetra, India
Abhinav Mudgal, National Institute of Technology, Kurukshetra, India
Mukesh Bhakar, National Institute of Technology, Kurukshetra, India
Priyal Dhiman, National Institute of Technology, Kurukshetra, India
Bhagoti Choudhary, National Institute of Technology, Kurukshetra, India

In this chapter, a human detection system based on unsupervised learning method K-means clustering followed by deep learning approach You Only Look Once (YOLO) on thermal imagery has been proposed. Generally, images in the visible spectrum are used to conduct such human detection, which are not suitable for nighttime due to low visibility, hence for evaluation of our system. Hence, long wave infrared (LWIR) images have been used to implement the proposed work in this chapter. The system follows a two-step approach of generating anchor boxes using K-means clustering and then using those anchor boxes in 252 layered single shot detector (YOLO) to predict proper boundary boxes. The dataset of such images is provided by FLIR company. The dataset contains 6822 images for training purposes and 757 images for the validation. This proposed system can be used for real-time object detection as YOLO can achieve much higher rate of processing when compared to traditional method like HAAR cascade classifier in long wave infrared imagery (LWIR).

Chapter 3

Stanislav Krajčovič, Comenius University, Slovakia
Roman Ďurikovič, Comenius University, Slovakia
Jiří Šilha, Comenius University, Slovakia

The partial goal of the transformation of a newly acquired telescope into a professional observation device was a design and development of an image processing pipeline. The pipeline can process an acquired raw image of space debris into object observations in time (tracklets), and further correlate and identify them with selected catalogues. The system contains nine image processing elements (IPEs) in total that are further described in this chapter and have already been deployed and tested on real space debris data.

Chapter 4

Amal Bouti, Department of Computer Sciences, Sidi Mohamed Ben Abdellah University, Morocco
Mohamed Adnane Mahraz, Sidi Mohamed Ben Abdellah University, Morocco
Jamal Riffi, Department of Computer Sciences, Sidi Mohamed Ben Abdellah University, Morocco
Hamid Tairi, Department of Computer Sciences, Sidi Mohamed Ben Abdellah University, Morocco

In this chapter, the authors report a system for detection and classification of road signs. This system consists of two parts. The first part detects the road signs in real time. The second part classifies the German traffic signs (GTSRB) dataset and makes the prediction using the road signs detected in the first part to test the effectiveness. The authors used HOG and SVM in the detection part to detect the road signs captured by the camera. Then they used a convolutional neural network based on the LeNet model in which some modifications were added in the classification part. The system obtains an accuracy rate of 96.85% in the detection part and 96.23% in the classification part.

Chapter 5

Andrew Jong, San Jose State University, USA
Melody Moh, San Jose State University, USA
Teng-Sheng Moh, San Jose State University, USA

This chapter elaborates on using generative adversarial networks (GAN) for virtual try-on applications. It presents the first comprehensive survey on this topic. Virtual try-on represents a practical application of GANs and pixel translation, which improves on the techniques of virtual try-on prior to these new discoveries. This survey details the importance of virtual try-on systems and the history of virtual try-on; shows how GANs, pixel translation, and perceptual losses have influenced the field; and summarizes the latest research in creating virtual try-on systems. Additionally, the authors present the future directions of research to improve virtual try-on systems by making them usable, faster, more effective. By walking through the steps of virtual try-on from start to finish, the chapter aims to expose readers to key concepts shared by many GAN applications and to give readers a solid foundation to pursue further topics in GANs.

Chapter 6

Formula One races provide a wealth of data worth investigating. Although the time-varying data has a clear structure, it is pretty challenging to analyze it for further properties. Here the focus is on a visual classification for events, drivers, as well as time periods. As a first step, the Formula One data is visually encoded based on a line plot visual metaphor reflecting the dynamic lap times, and finally, a classification of the races based on the visual outcomes gained from these line plots is presented. The visualization tool is web-based and provides several interactively linked views on the data; however, it starts with a calendar-based overview representation. To illustrate the usefulness of the approach, the provided Formula One data from several years is visually explored while the races took place in different locations. The chapter discusses algorithmic, visual, and perceptual limitations that might occur during the visual classification of time-series data such as Formula One races.

Chapter 7

Shadows occur very frequently in digital images while considering them for various important applications. Shadow is considered as a source of noise and can cause false image colors, loss of information, and false image segmentation. Thus, it is required to detect and remove shadows from images. This chapter addresses the problem of shadow detection in high-resolution aerial images. It presents the required main concepts to introduce for the subject. These concepts are the main knowledge units that provide for the reader a better understanding of the subject of shadow detection and furthering the research. Additionally, an overview of various shadow detection methods is provided together with a detailed comparative study. The results of these methods are also discussed extensively by investigating their main features used in the process to detect the shadows accurately.

    Samsul Ariffin Abdul Karim, Universiti Teknologi PETRONAS, Malaysia
    Nur Atiqah Binti Zulkifli, Universiti Teknologi PETRONAS, Malaysia
    A'fza Binti Shafie, Universiti Teknologi PETRONAS, Malaysia
    Muhammad Sarfraz, Kuwait University, Kuwait
    Abdul Ghaffar, Ton Duc Thang University, Vietnam
    Kottakkaran Sooppy Nisar, Prince Sattam bin Abdulaziz University, Saudi Arabia

This chapter deals with image processing in the specific area of image zooming via interpolation. The authors employ bivariate rational cubic ball function defined on rectangular meshes. These bivariate spline have six free parameters that can be used to alter the shape of the surface without needed to change the data. It also can be used to refine the resolution of the image. In order to cater the image zomming, they propose an efficient algorithm by including image downscaling and upscaling procedures. To measure the effectiveness of the proposed scheme, they compare the performance based on the value of peak signal-to-noise ratio (PSNR) and root mean square error (RMSE). Comparison with existing schemes such as nearest neighbour (NN), bilinear (BL), bicubic (BC), bicubic Hermite (BH), and existing scheme Karim and Saaban (KS) have been made in detail. From all numerical results, the proposed scheme gave higher PSNR value and smaller RMSE value for all tested images.

    Ichrak Khoulqi, Faculty of Sciences and Technics, Sultan Moulay Slimane University,
        Morocco
    Najlae Idrissi, Faculty of Sciences and Technics, Sultan Moulay Slimane University,
        Morocco
    Muhammad Sarfraz, Kuwait University, Kuwait

Breast cancer is one of the significant issues in medical sciences today. Specifically, women are suffering most worldwide. Early diagnosis can result to control the growth of the tumor. However, there is a need of high precision of diagnosis for right treatment. This chapter contributes toward an achievement of a computer-aided diagnosis (CAD) system. It deals with mammographic images and enhances their quality. Then, the enhanced images are segmented for pectoral muscle (PM) in the Medio-Lateral-Oblique (MLO) view of the mammographic images. The segmentation approach uses the tool of Gaussian Mixture Model-Expectation Maximization (GMM-EM). A standard database of Mini-MIAS with 322 images has been utilized for the implementation and experimentation of the proposed technique. The metrics of structural similarity measure and DICE coefficient have been utilized to verify the quality of segmentation based on the ground truth. The proposed technique is quite robust and accurate, it supersedes various existing techniques when compared in the same context.

    Peilin Li, University of South Australia, Australia

In literature, the initial parameters are critical for K-means function. By seedling randomly or ad hoc approach, the results are not optimal. This chapter details an estimation method using the principal component analysis (PCA) solution based on the connection between PCA solution and membership of clusters from K-means from research. All the mathematical justification is provided. The evaluation has been done empirically with a comparative study. The validation results show the significant feasibility of the proposed method to initialize parameters.

Chapter 11

Detecting corner points for the digital images is based on determining significant geometrical locations. Corner points lead and guide for providing significant clues for shape analysis and representation. They actually provide significant features of an object, which can be used in different phases of processing. In shape analysis problems, for example, a shape can be efficiently reformulated in a compact way and with sufficient accuracy if the corners are properly located. This chapter selects seven well referred algorithms from the literature to review, compare, and analyze empirically. It provides an overview of these selected algorithms so that users can easily pick an appropriate one for their specific applications and requirements.

Chapter 12

In this chapter, the authors have given a detailed review on optical character recognition. Various methods are used in this field with different accuracy levels. Still there are some difficulties in recognizing handwritten characters because of different writing styles of different individuals even in a particular language. A comparative study is given to understand different types of optical character recognition along with different methods used in each type. Implementation of neural network in different forms is found in most of the works. Different image processing techniques like OCR with CNN, RNN, combination of CNN and RNN, etc. are observed in recent research works.

Chapter 13

The main difficulty in developing a successful optical character recognition (OCR) system lies in the confusion between the characters. In the case of Amazigh writing (Tifinagh alphabets), some characters have similarities based on rotation or scale. Most of the researchers attempted to solve this problem by combining multiple descriptors and / or classifiers which increased the recognition rate, but at the expense of processing time that becomes more prohibitive. Thus, reducing the confusion of characters and their recognition times is the major challenge of OCR systems. In this chapter, the authors present an off-line OCR system for Tifinagh characters.

Chapter 14
A Perceptually Optimized Foveation Wavelet Visible Difference Predictor Quality Metric Based
on Psychovisual Properties of the Human Visual System (HVS): Region of Interest Image Coding
Abderrahim Bajit, National School of Applied Sciences, Ibn Toufail University, Morocco

Region of interest (ROI) image and video compression techniques have been widely used in visual communication applications in an effort to deliver good quality images and videos at limited bandwidths. Foveated imaging exploits the fact that the spatial resolution of the human visual system (HVS) is highest around the point of fixation (foveation point) and decreases dramatically with increasing eccentricity. Exploiting this fact, the authors have developed an appropriate metric for the assessment of ROI coded images, adapted to foveation image coding based on psycho-visual quality optimization tools, which objectively enable us to assess the visual quality measurement with respect to the region of interest (ROI) of the human observer. The proposed metric yields a quality factor called foveation probability score (FPS) that correlates well with visual error perception and demonstrating very good perceptual quality evaluation.

Preface

Computer Vision and Imaging (CVI) are significant areas of study in the discipline of computing today. Although these are considered distinct as areas of study among the community worldwide, but at the same time are closely related fields too. They provide the latest industry findings which are extremely useful to academicians, researchers, practitioners and professionals. There are numerous latest developments going on in the current time and age which are leading towards innovations in science and technology. Due to vital importance, effectiveness and usefulness, extensive advances and discoveries are needed for better future perspectives. One can find huge community worldwide contributing in these fields. In particular, CVI play significant roles in the development of Intelligent Systems and Multimedia Technologies (ISMT) in real life applications. Such applications are not just needed to solve various important problems in the recent scenarios of the international world, but also continuously needed to improve past and current practices. There is also a severe need to discover new state of the art methodologies and systems for every day challenging life. Due to a high need of the time, it is desired to explore innovations and methods in the area. A compilation of latest advances may be a source revolutionizing for facilitating and enhancing the exchange of information among researchers involved in both the theoretical and practical aspects. This book is specifically dedicated to the advances in CVI while working towards ISMT applications.

This book consists of original and innovative findings in the field of Computer Vision and Imaging for Intelligent Systems and Multimedia Technologies. It is intended to focus on theories and methods from various dimensions. It would look at trends and needs in the modern perspective of present and future. It is also intended to address a variety of disciplines including image processing, computer vision, computer graphics, pattern recognition, information retrieval, machine learning, artificial intelligence, soft computing communication science, human-computer interaction, information systems, intelligent systems, and multimedia. The book integrates interdisciplinary and multidisciplinary needs to the significant issues in this age of science, technology and communication. It focuses on theories, approaches, methods, tools, experiences and state-of-the-art technologies for solving real life issues and problems.

The book is targeted to computing community, communication and multimedia experts, system engineers, scientists, researchers, practitioners, academicians, and related professionals. It will aim at the latest advances for an in-depth discussion on CVI, ISMT and their applications. The chapters in this comprehensive reference explore the latest developments, methods, approaches and applications in a wide variety of fields and endeavors. This book is compiled with a view to provide readers of backgrounds and methods with an in-depth discussion of the latest advances. It consists of fifteen chapters from different disciplines of life.

Tumpa, Kumar, Sultana, Hsu, Yadid-Pecht, Yanushkevich and Gavrilova begin the book with a discussion upon Social Behavioral Biometrics in Smart Societies. They describe that Smart societies of the future will increasingly rely on harvesting rich information generated by day to day activities and interactions of its inhabitants. Among the multitude of such interactions, web-based social networking activities became an integral part of everyday human communication. Flickr, Facebook, Twitter, and LinkedIn are currently used by millions of users worldwide as a source of information which is growing exponentially over time. In addition to idiosyncratic personal characteristics, Web-based social data include person to person communication, online activity patterns, and temporal information among others. However, analysis of social interaction-based data has been studied from the perspective of person identification only recently. In this chapter, the authors elaborate on the concept of using interaction based features from online social networking platforms as a part of Social Behavioral Biometrics research domain. They place this research in the context of smart societies and discuss novel social biometric features and their potential use in various applications.

Dua, Mudgal, Bhakar, Dhiman and Choudhary, in Chapter 2 of the book, follow with a discussion of "K-means and DNN based Novel Approach to Human Identification in Low Resolution Thermal Imagery." They propose a human detection system based on unsupervised learning method K-means clustering which is followed by deep learning approach "You Only Look Once (YOLO)" on Thermal Imagery. Generally, images in visible spectrum are used to conduct human detection that are not suitable for night time due to low visibility. Therefore, the authors have used Long Wave Infrared (LWIR) images for the evaluation of their proposed system. It follows a 2-step approach of generating anchor boxes using K-means clustering and then using those anchor boxes in 252-layered single shot detector (YOLO) to predict proper boundary boxes. The dataset of such images is provided by FLIR company, it contains 6822 images for training purposes and 757 images for the validation. The proposed system can be used for real-time object detection as YOLO can achieve much higher rate of processing when compared to traditional method like HAAR cascade classifier in Long Wave Infrared Imagery (LWIR).

This follows the chapter on "Masking and Tracklet Building for Space Debris and NEO Observations: The Slovak Image Processing Pipeline" introduced by Krajčovič, Ďurikovič and Šilha. It highlights that the partial goal of the transformation of a newly acquired telescope into a professional observation device is a design and development of an image processing pipeline. The pipeline can process an acquired raw image of space debris into object observations in time (tracklets), and further correlate and identify them with selected catalogues. The authors proposed a system which contains 9 Image Processing Elements (IPEs) in total, that are further described in this chapter. A modular pipeline for space debris observations, Image Processing System (IPS), has been introduced and two of its nine complex IPEs were described in detail. It has been largely developed by the Faculty of Mathematics, Physics and Informatics (FMPI) of the Comenius University in Bratislava, Slovakia. The pipeline has been tested and validated on real examples taken by the AGO70 telescope. The fact that every IPE performs its operation in real time ensures that IPS can process large number of data fast.

Traffic Sign Detection and Recognition (TSDR) has been very popular in recent years. This is due to the large number of applications that such a system can provide. These applications include maintenance of signs, signs inventory, driving assistance and smart autonomous vehicles. Bouti, Mahraz, Riffi, Tairi, and Liian, in Chapter 4 of the book, follow with a discussion on "A Robust System for Road Sign Detection and Classification Using LeNet Architecture Based on Convolutional Neural Network." Their work reports a system for detection and classification of road signs. This system consists of two parts. The first part detects the road signs in real time. The second part classifies the German traffic signs (GTSRB) dataset and makes the prediction using the road signs detected in the first part to test the effectiveness. The authors have used histogram of oriented gradients (HOG) and support vector machine (SVM) in the detection part to detect the road signs captured by the camera. Then authors used a convolutional neural network based on the Convolutional Neural Networks (CNN) architecture LeNet model in which some modifications were added in the classification part. The proposed system obtains an accuracy rate of 96.85% in the detection part and 96.23% in the classification part.

In the next chapter, Andrew Jung, Melody Moh and Teng-Sheng Moh make a taxonomical survey of Virtual Try-on with Generative Adversarial Networks (GANs). This chapter elaborates on using Generative Adversarial Networks for virtual try-on applications. Virtual try-on represents a practical application of GANs and pixel translation, which improves on the techniques of virtual try-on prior to these new discoveries. This survey details the importance of virtual try-on systems and the history of virtual try-on. It shows how GANs, pixel translation, and perceptual losses have influenced the field, and summarized the latest research in creating virtual try-on systems. Additionally, the authors present the future directions of research to improve virtual try-on systems by making them usable, faster, more effective. By walking through the steps of virtual try-on from start till the end, the chapter aims to expose readers to key concepts shared by many GAN applications, and gives the reader a solid foundation to pursue further topics in GANs in the future.

Formula One data has a dynamic nature, it consists of event-based data and shows various differences when observing it from the drivers' perspectives. Inspecting the data between different time intervals might lead to the detection of several temporal stages in a race, for example, lap by lap, but also between arbitrarily identified race phases. Lots of outside distractions play a crucial role for the identified dynamic race patterns, being it weather conditions, accidents, bad performing cars, or drivers that behave not equally well supposed the race conditions change from time to time. Formula One races provide a wealth of data worth investigating. Although the time-varying data has a clear structure, it is pretty challenging to analyze it for further properties. Chapter 6 is devoted to "Visual Classification of Formula One Races by Events, Drivers, and Time Periods" by Lampprecht, Salb, Mauser, Wetering, Burch and Kloos. They focus on a visual classification for events, drivers, as well as time periods. As a first step, the Formula One data is visually encoded based on a line plot visual metaphor reflecting the dynamic lap times. Finally, a classification of the races based on the visual outcomes gained from these line plots, is presented. The visualization tool is web-based and provides several interactively linked views on the data. However, it starts with a calendar-based overview representation. To illustrate the usefulness of the approach, the provided Formula One data from several years is visually explored while the races took place in different locations. This book chapter discusses algorithmic, visual, and perceptual limitations that might occur during the visual classification of time-series data such as Formula One races.

Chapter 7 on "An Overview of Feature Based Shadow Detection Methods" by Musleh, Sarfraz and Raafat provides tools and techniques on aerial images have shadows. Shadow is a phenomenon that occurs when light is occluded by a solid object. Shadow presence in digital images is useful for some computer applications to estimate buildings height for example, but shadow-free images are of high demand for many other computer applications to complete their tasks successfully, such as image segmenting and object tracking. The detection and removal processes play a significant role in improving the accuracy of many applications as they recover many distorted information in the target image. Shadows occur very frequently in digital images while considering them for various important applications. Shadow is considered as a source of noise and can cause in false image colors, loss of information, and false image segmentation. This chapter highlights on the subject of how to detect and remove shadows from images. It addresses the problem of shadow detection in high-resolution aerial images and presents the required main concepts to introduce for the subject. These concepts are the main knowledge units that provide for the reader a better understanding of the subject of Shadow detection and furthering the research. Additionally, an overview of various shadow detection methods is provided together with a detailed comparative study. The results of these methods are also discussed extensively by investigating their main features used in the process to detect the shadows accurately.

The technology of medical image processing is vigorously growing in the industry as the demand increases from time to time. It is highly demanding in film scanners, ultrasound, Magnetic Resonance Imaging (MRI), Computed Tomography (CT), Positron Emission Tomography (PET), Single Positron Emission Computed Tomography (SPECT), Digital Subtraction Angiography (DSA), and Magnetic Source Imaging (MSI), etc. The image within the patient's body have different kind of film digitizers such as, laser scanner, solid-state camera, drum scanner, and video camera that capable to convert X-ray films into digital format for image processing. Therefore, image zooming on the selected parts are important especially when the expert want to detect any anomalies at the body parts. Binti Zulkifli, Abdul Karim, Binti Shafie, Sarfraz, Abdul Ghaffar and Nisar have contributed Chapter 8 on "Medical Image Zooming by Using Rational Bicubic Ball Function". This chapter deals with image processing in the specific area of image zooming via interpolation. The authors employ bivariate rational cubic Ball function defined on rectangular meshes. These bivariate splines have six free parameters that can be used to alter the shape of the surface without needed to change the data. It can also be used to refine the resolution of the image. In order to cater the image zooming, the chapter proposes an efficient algorithm by including image downscaling and upscaling procedures. To measure the effectiveness of the proposed scheme, the performance is compared based on the value of Peak Signal-to-Noise Ratio (PSNR) and Root Mean Square Error (RMSE). Comparison with existing schemes such as nearest neighbour (NN), bilinear (BL), bicubic (BC), bicubic Hermite (BH) and scheme by Karim and Saaban (KS) have been made in details. From all numerical results, the proposed scheme gave higher PSNR value and smaller RMSE value for all tested images.

Chapter 9, by Khoulqi, Idrissi and Sarfraz, continues on medical imaging. It addresses the "Segmentation of Pectoral Muscle in Mammogram Images using Gaussian Mixture Model-Expectation Maximization." Breast cancer is one of the significant issues in medical sciences today. Specifically, women are suffering most worldwide. Early diagnosis can result to control the growth of the tumor. However, there is a need of high precision of diagnosis for right treatment. This chapter contributes toward an achievement of a computer-aided diagnosis (CAD) system. It deals with mammographic images and enhances their quality. Then, the enhanced images are segmented for pectoral muscle (PM) in the Medio-Lateral-Oblique (MLO) view of the mammographic images. The segmentation approach uses the tool of Gaussian Mixture Model-Expectation Maximization (GMM-EM). A standard database of Mini-MIAS with 322 images has been utilized for the implementation and experimentation of the proposed technique. The metrics of Structural Similarity measure and DICE Coefficient have been utilized to verify the quality of segmentation based on the ground truth. The proposed technique is quite robust and accurate, it supersedes various existing techniques when compared in the same context.

In clustering literature, the initial parameters are critical for the clustering function to converge to the proper local optima. For example, K-means function uses Euclidean metric to find the valid data clusters with the given initial centroids of ellipsoids. However, it is difficult to provide the priori due to the local optima by the multivariate function. Currently, the initial parameters are chosen randomly or with some ad hoc approaches. The function either converges into different local optima or slowly. Recently, research found that the principal component analysis (PCA) solution indicates the membership of the clusters from K-means function. Based on the case of two classes of data set, Chapter 10 "Use of PCA solution in hierarchy and case of two classes of data sets to initialize parameters for clustering function" by Li proposes an estimation method using PCA solution in hierarchy to estimate the parameters for K-means function. Here, PCA solution is employed to find the eigenvectors of the centered covariance matrix of each data subset. Then the image data is split with global thresholding on the projected data in the maximal eigenvector subspace. Each data subset is evaluated for the initial cluster under the termination criterion of geometric ellipsoidal form. The connection between PCA solution and the clusters' membership for K-means function is verified mathematically for two classes of data sets in this approach with confidence. The estimation method is evaluated against another two classical methods with some different data bank. The validation results show that the proposed method can effectively provide the core parameters for models in clustering function.

Chapter 11 presents a study on "Some Algorithms on Detection of Corner Points for Digital Images" by Sarfraz. Detecting corner points for the digital images is based on determining significant geometrical locations. Corner points lead and guide for providing significant clues for shape analysis and representation. They actually provide significant features of an object which can be used in different phases of processing. In shape analysis problems, for example, a shape can be in an efficiently reformulated in a compact way and with sufficient accuracy if the corners are properly located. This chapter selects seven well referred algorithms, from the literature, to review, compare and analyze empirically. It provides an overview of these selected algorithms so that users can easily pick an appropriate one for their specific applications and requirements.

Das and Mohanty, in the next chapter, make a use of Deep Neural Network for Optical Character Recognition. They have given a detailed review on optical character recognition. Various methods are used in this field with different accuracy levels. Still there is some difficulties in recognizing handwritten characters because of different writing styles of different individuals even in a particular language. A comparative study is given to understand different types of optical character recognition along with different methods used in each type. Implementation of neural network in different forms is found in most of the works. Different image processing techniques like OCR with CNN, RNN, combination of CNN and RNN etc., are observed in recent research works.

Second last chapter of the book is entitled "Search based Classification for Offline Tifinagh Alphabets Recognition" and authored by Erritali, Chouni and Ouadid. The authors state that the main difficulty in developing a successful Optical Character Recognition (OCR) system lies in the confusion between the characters. In the case of Amazigh writing (Tifinagh alphabets), some characters have similarities based on rotation or scale. Many of the researchers attempted to solve this problem by combining multiple descriptors and / or classifiers which increased the recognition rate. But, it was done at the expense of processing time that becomes more prohibitive in practice. Thus, reducing the confusion of characters as well as their recognition times are the major challenges for OCR systems. This chapter presents an off-line OCR system for Tifinagh characters. It proposes a key point extraction algorithm which divides the character skeleton into several segments. The length and orientation of every segment are stored into a feature vector, then the relationship between these segments are represented by a graph in the form of an incidence matrix. Classification is done by searching for similarity between test images and their counterparts in the reference database by comparing their incidence matrix. When search provides multiple classes, feature vectors are compared and input image is assigned to the closest class. Based on experiments done on 3300 images, an accuracy of 99% is achieved.

Final chapter of the book is on "A Perceptually Optimized Foveation Wavelet Visible Difference Predictor Quality Metric Based on Psychovisual Properties of the Human Visual System HVS" which is contributed by Bajit, Nahid, Tamtaoui and Benbrahim. This chapter describes that region of interest (ROI) image and video compression techniques have been widely used in visual communication applications in an effort to deliver good quality images and videos at limited bandwidths. Foveated imaging exploits the fact that the spatial resolution of the human visual system (HVS) is highest around the point of fixation (foveation point) and decreases dramatically with increasing eccentricity. Exploiting this fact, the authors have developed an appropriate metric for the assessment of ROI coded images, adapted to foveation image coding based on psychovisual quality optimization tools. It objectively enable to assess the visual quality measurement with respect to the region of interest (ROI) of the human observer. The proposed metric yields a quality factor called foveation probability score (FPS) that correlates well with visual error perception, and demonstrating very good perceptual quality evaluation. Thus, the authors have avoided the traditional subjective criteria called mean opinion score (MOS), which involves human observers. They believe, such criteria are inconvenient, time-consuming, and influenced by environmental conditions. Widely used pixelwise measures such as the mean square error (MSE) and the peak signal to noise ratio (PSNR) cannot capture the artifacts like blurriness or blockiness. The proposed model therefore called the Foveated Wavelet Visible Difference Predictor (FWVDP), is based both on traditional psychometric function and the Daly model visible difference predictor (VDP), it integrates various psychovisual models (foveation, luminance and contrast masking). Experiments show that FWVDP integrates foveation filtering with foveated image coding and demonstrate very good performance in terms of foveated image quality measurement.

Muhammad Sarfraz
Kuwait University, Kuwait

Chapter 1
Social Behavioral Biometrics in Smart Societies

Sanjida Nasreen Tumpa
ⓘD https://orcid.org/0000-0003-3024-4420
University of Calgary, Canada

K. N. Pavan Kumar
ⓘD https://orcid.org/0000-0002-7893-0588
University of Calgary, Canada

Madeena Sultana
University of Calgary, Canada

Gee-Sern Jison Hsu
ⓘD https://orcid.org/0000-0003-2631-0448
National Taiwan University of Science and Technology, Taiwan

Orly Yadid-Pecht
University of Calgary, Canada

Svetlana Yanushkevich
ⓘD https://orcid.org/0000-0003-4794-9849
University of Calgary, Canada

Marina L. Gavrilova
University of Calgary, Canada

ABSTRACT

Smart societies of the future will increasingly rely on harvesting rich information generated by day-to-day activities and interactions of its inhabitants. Among the multitude of such interactions, web-based social networking activities became an integral part of everyday human communication. Flickr, Facebook, Twitter, and LinkedIn are currently used by millions of users worldwide as a source of information,

DOI: 10.4018/978-1-7998-4444-0.ch001

which is growing exponentially over time. In addition to idiosyncratic personal characteristics, web-based social data include person-to-person communication, online activity patterns, and temporal information, among others. However, analysis of social interaction-based data has been studied from the perspective of person identification only recently. In this chapter, the authors elaborate on the concept of using interaction-based features from online social networking platforms as a part of social behavioral biometrics research domain. They place this research in the context of smart societies and discuss novel social biometric features and their potential use in various applications.

INTRODUCTION

The biometric authentication system can be referred to as an identification technique based on the physical, and behavioral attributes of an individual (Jain et al., 2008). Biometric systems use pattern recognition processes to identify a person by matching the feature vectors obtained from their physiological or behavioral characteristics (Jain et al., 2006).

Traditionally, two types of biometrics: physiological and behavioral, have been considered (Jain et al., 2008). Physiological biometrics relies on physical attributes of individuals, such as face, palm, fingerprint, iris, ear, etc. Behavioral biometrics are based on human activities dictated by person's behaviour, such as handwriting, gait, signature and voice, which also afford discriminability among individuals. Behavioral biometrics are more volatile to changes an individual may undergo through their life but have the advantages of being non-intrusive and cost effective over physiological biometrics (Yampolskiy & Govindaraju, 2008). It is gaining an increasing demand for person identification and verification purposes to reduce security threats, especially in the cyber worlds. Another application where behavioral biometrics show significant potential is in combination with smart devices. One of the obvious benefits is combining behavioral characteristics with the mobile devices, in order for example to keep track of an individual's health status (i.e. heart rate, body temperature), or to remind to change the posture during an exercise based on the gait. Huge benefits can be also obtained in using such information during an emergency response, while providing service for those seeking admission to the homeless centre, or in providing an assistance to an elderly person if a fall is detected by sensors in a smart building.

In a highly interconnected society, people spend a lot of time interacting with each other on social media or in online virtual worlds. Users leave their virtual footprints expressed as shared thoughts, writing style, interaction patterns, in online communities, virtual worlds and as recorded by smart devices. It is possible to observe repetitive patterns in a user's social interactions via online since they are driven by human behaviours and habits. A person's social connections can be obtained by analysing whom the user most frequently and consistently communicates over time.

In this chapter, we first classify the existing behavioral biometrics into two main categories: *machine-independent* human behaviour and *machine-dependent* human behaviour. Machine independent behavioral biometrics are well established in the community, with most of the early works falling under this category. For example, person identification from his/her unique signature, gait or walking style, or from a piece of drawing are being studied over last decade (Monwar & Gavrilova, 2013; Bazazian & Gavrilova, 2015; Al-Zubi et al., 2003). The latter category is emerging compared to the former and more demanding field of research due to increasing number of cybersecurity threats. Due to the wide range of applications of computing devices and software, users can interact with computers and each other in many ways.

We classify machine dependent human behaviours further into the following three sub-categories based on the type of communication with the machine: *interaction-based, skill-based, and intelligence-based*. First subcategory is based on human interaction with input device that does not consider any knowledge or intelligence of the user. Some examples are keystroke dynamics, mouse dynamics, touch-screen interaction, etc. (Bakelman et al., 2013; Jorgensen & Yu, 2011; Bo et al., 2013; Frank et al., 2012). Second subcategory takes into account the style or preference of a user during interaction with the computer. Coding style of a programmer, browsing style or handshaking style would fall under this category (Spafford & Weeber, 1993; Olejnik & Castelluccia, 2013; Guo et al., 2013). Finally, the third subdivision includes human intelligence, knowledge, and skills into account during interaction with software such as game playing strategy, car driving skill, hobby or habits, for instance (Yampolskiy & Govindaraju, 2010; Igarashi et al.,2004; Jiang et al., 2013).

Human activities that involve machine or sensor interaction are not limited to programming, computing, gaming or typing. Now, in the era of social networking and internet-of-things, human identity as well as everyday activities have been naturally extended into web-based and sensor-based dimensions (Eastwood et al., 2015; Dattner & Yadid-Pecht, 2011). Our first hypothesis is that, similarly to a physical world, behavioral patterns and habits are present in the daily activities of virtual world users. Patterns can be found in different online Social Networking Service (SNS) activities such as: tweets, status updates, 'likes', URLs, photo and video tagging, uploads, comments, communications and so on. Our second hypothesis is that a person can be identified based on his activities and information which accumulates through online social networking platforms. Therefore, in this chapter we are introducing the fourth subcategory of machine dependent behavioral biometrics: *web-based social biometrics*. We also investigate the feasibility of using users' web-based social networking activities as novel behavioral biometrics to identify a person in virtual domain.

In this chapter, we introduce *web-based social and sensor data as behavioral biometric features*. The concept of how these features can be used for person identification will also be analyzed. Some existing works based on relevant web-based social data are reviewed in the background study. Some state-of-the-art web-based biometric features are analyzed thereafter to understand the significance of the novel biometric. The key challenges and applications are also identified to discover the potential directions for the future research. This chapter is an updated version of the book chapter "Online User Interaction Traits in Web-based Social Biometrics", that appeared in Computer Vision, Image Processing, Intelligent Systems Multimedia Technologies book in 2014 (Sultana et al., 2014c).

Social Behavioral Biometrics

Biometric traits or identifiers can be classified into the following categories: physiological biometrics, behavioral biometrics and social behavioral biometrics. Figure 1 represents those categories of biometric traits.

Physiological biometrics are unique physical attributes of individuals. These traits remain consistent over time. The physiological traits can be divided into different subcategories according to their respective position in the human body, such as hand-based attributes, facial based attributes, ocular and periocular region attributes, and medico-chemical attributes (Unar et al., 2014; Hsu et al., 2017a; Hsu et al., 2017b; Hsu et al., 2018).

Behavioral biometrics are based on the analysis of human activities. Behavioral biometrics includes typing styles (keystroke dynamics), vocal characteristics (voice), signature dynamics and humans walking style (gait) (Jain et al., 2008). It analyses dynamic behavioral patterns rather than permanent physiological characteristics (Jain et al., 2016). Behavioral biometrics are quite sensitive to change over time and the environment. Thus, makes the behavioral biometrics more dynamic than static physiological one and difficult to imitate for fraud activities. As behavioral biometrics depends on a person's behaviour, it can be classified into activity-based biometrics, skill and intelligence-based biometrics, biological signal-based biometrics, Human-Computer Interaction (HCI)-based biometrics, and habit and preference-based biometrics. Such classification can be highly useful in security applications, for instance in design of e-border authentication systems (Lai et al, 2017; Yanushkevich et al., 2004).

Social interactions are inseparable parts of human behaviour. Every person possesses different social behaviour than others. The existing biometric person authentication systems mainly depend on physical and behavioral traits, some researchers incorporating personality traits such as preference, interest, and habit as biometric modalities (Delgado-Gómez et al., 2010; Azam & Gavrilova, 2017). However, the vital part of human behaviour, social interaction remained almost unexplored in the biometric domain. *Social Behavioral Biometrics (SBB) is formally defined as* (Sultana et al., 2014a):

"Social Behavioral Biometrics is an identification of an actor (person or avatar) based on their social interactions and communication in different social settings."

Social Behavioral biometrics can be divided into two categories, namely *Offline Social Context* and *Online Social Context*. Offline social interactions are face to face interactions that can be manifested in any physical place of social gatherings. Some researchers are interested in Social Signal Processing (SSP), which can be generated from body posture, facial expression, gesture, voice, head tilt, eye movement, interactions, etc. Social biometric features can be extracted from these activities to identify a person. Another one is based on online social contexts. People's interaction with each other on online social platforms are considered in this type. For example, individual's social behavior can be dug from their interactions in blogs, posts, discussion forums, online games, virtual worlds, social networks, multimedia sharing sites, etc. In this research, this subdivision of biometrics will be the main interest. Analysis of social data obtained from networking sites may reveal valuable information about the individuals which can be used in biometric authentication.

Biometric authentication using physical and behavioral traits is a well-researched domain. The physiological traits of a person are permanent over time, robust and acceptable. However, the problem arises when these traits are compromised. Thus, the importance of behavioral biometric emerges, which is more dynamic than physiological traits and also can assist in capturing fraudulent activities. Human behavior is strongly dominated by an individual's skill, intelligence, and interest (Oak, 2018). Therefore, a person can be identified by their working skills and communication styles in additional to traditionally accepted behavioral biometrics such as voice or gait. For example, researchers identified real-time drivers by their driving characteristics (Jeong et al., 2018). Yampolskiy & Govindaraju (2010) exploited behavioral biometrics for player authentication from a game tactic. Similarly, a vast amount of behavioral information exists in the virtual world. Based on the user web browsing style, it is possible to identify them (Olejnik & Castelluccia, 2013). A significant amount of information can be mined from the interactive behavior of users via online social networks or with their smart devices. Thus, incorporating such interactions into biometric identification and smart cities planning can be a highly promising new avenue for research.

Figure 1. Generalized taxonomy of biometrics

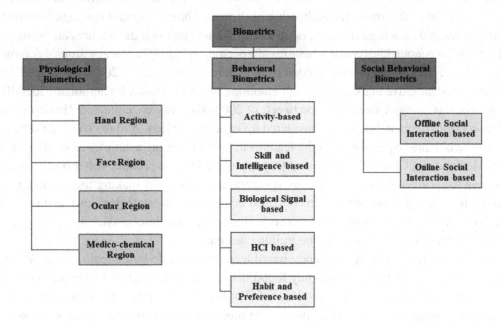

The concept of Social Behavior Biometrics was originally introduced by Sultana et al. (2014b). The authors discussed the social communications in different contexts namely, offline social context and online social context. Authors proposed unimodal and multimodal framework to identify the person using profile information, network information and communicative information obtained from online social networks. Authors mined Twitter data to obtain personal characteristics of a user that can eventually be used as personal biometric trait (Sultana et al., 2014b, 2015). Authors have generated five networks from the online social interactions of a person, such as reply network, retweet network, URL network, hashtag network, close friend network and the topic of interest. Matching techniques on training and test set have been applied to these networks for person authentication. A further study has been done by Sultana and Gavrilova (2018), where temporal patterns were successfully used for the first time to identify online users. Another work by the same authors identified a set of social behavioral features from the online social interactions of 241 Twitter users. They proposed a framework to utilize these features for automated user recognition and discovered that only ten recent tweets are enough to recognize 58% of users at rank-1 (Sultana et al., 2017b).

Aside from the above works, human behavior and communication style expressed through online SNSs have not being investigated from the biometric perspective. However, they have been extensively studied from the point of view of authorship attribution. In this rest of the section, we discuss the approaches to author identification from micro-blogs (e.g. tweets) as well as the differences between the web-based social biometrics and author identification.

Shalhoub et al. (2010) studied the feasibility of applying stylistic features or stylometry for author identification from Twitter. They considered a case where a user's writing profile has to be generated from his books, blogs or other writings. Then this profile would be matched to a writing profile created from tweets. In the same year, Layton et al. (2010) published the very first work of author identification from microblogs on Twitter. About 200 tweets from each of the 14000 users were collected, then 50 potential authors were selected for experimentation. Source Code Authorship Profile (SCAP) and n-gram methods were applied to determine the authorship of the text. Three important findings from this paper are: a) 140 characters do not limit the authorship identification process if the features are being selected efficiently, b) tweets contain idiosyncratic features of a person, and c) 27% accuracy drops if commination to other users i.e. replies in tweets are excluded from feature set. Silva et al. (2011) introduced 3 type of stylistic features: quantitative markers, marks of emotions, and punctuation for authorship identification from tweets. For this research, over 4 million tweets of 200,000 users were collected. However, only 120 "prolific" users from the initial set were considered for experimentation. Authors showed that good performance can be obtained by applying all the features to a set of training examples as small as 60 tweets per author. Macleod and Grant (2012) showed that aggregated tweets produce better results than single tweets. During experimentation they aggregated several messages thus making their training samples longer and then extracted a number of features based on grammatical style, lexicons, and punctuations from the aggregated message. As one would expect, for a set of 20 authors maximum accuracy has been obtained by aggregating 10 messages as one training sample.

An interesting analysis of using frequency-based features and style-based features has been accomplished by Green and Sheppard (2013). They found that length constraint of 140 characters of tweets limits the effectiveness of vocabulary-based Bag-Of-Words (BOW) method. However, context free style markers such as capitalization, punctuations etc. are much more informative for author identification than traditional BOW method.

All of the above-mentioned works are intended for smart cities cyber forensic applications thus have major limitations:

1. Small closed set of candidates is being used for experimentation and might not be adequate as identified behaviours have to be applicable for all users of SNS to maintain the desired universality property of a good biometric trait.
2. Author identification from microblogs is a well studies area of a web-based user identification. Features that indicates communication behaviour of the user such as replies, hashtags, retweets, links (URLs), and temporal features have been recently successfully used as part of social behavioral biometric identification. However, user personality styles have been largely ignored in those works. Further investigation is thus warranted to leverage this information for a more accurate identification.
3. Finally, multi-modal system architecture has been only partially explored in previous works. However, combination of multiple modalities (content-based, linguistic, temporal, personality style) and sensor-based data has not yet been considered.

The rest of this chapter is devoted to a closer look at the remedies to those identified deficiencies.

OVERVIEW OF BEHAVIORAL BIOMETRICS

One major advantage of behavioral biometric over traditional biometric is it is very difficult to fake. For example, it might be possible to prepare a fake fingerprint but imitating the walking style of a person (i.e. gait) is quite difficult. For this reason, behavioral biometric is becoming a popular alternative to well-established physiological biometrics, such as fingerprints. Many new behavioral biometrics have been proposed over past decade. A comprehensive summary of common behavioral biometrics can be found in the research conducted by Yampolskiy (2011). Some recent behavioral biometrics are listed below:

Continuous Keystroke Dynamics

Bours (2012) used keystroke dynamics as a behavioral biometric for continuous authentication of a user instead of ordinary static authentication. The concept of continuous authentication is the following. The current user is continuously verified by matching his/her typing pattern to the stored template. Continuous matching does not mean that if the user does any typing mistake the system would be locked out instantly. Only the confidence or trust level of genuine user would decrease, and it may increase again if the user's typing matches with the stored template. The system would only be locked out if the trust level decreases below a certain threshold. Thus, typing behavior of the user would serve as a biometric to authenticate the user continuously.

Context Based Gait Biometric

Bazazian and Gavrilova (2015) proposed a novel context-based gait biometrics for person identification. In this work, additional information about behavioral patterns of users and the context are fused with gait biometrics to enhance the recognition rate. This work demonstrates that the performance of existing gait recognition systems can be improved up to 100% by fusing distinctive context-based behavioral features of users even at a very low cost.

Touch Based Biometrics

Frank et al. (2012) identified 30 behavioral touch features from raw touchscreen logs of smartphones and named these novel biometric features as *Touchalytics*. This study demonstrates that different users has distinct pattern of navigation and this behavioral pattern exhibits consistency over time. However, *Touchalytic* is not enough for being used as a standalone continuous authentication system for long term, it could be utilized for short term authentication or as a part of a multimodal biometric authentication system. Bo et al. (2013) showed that considering the fine details of touch pattern improves the uniqueness of the touch-based biometrics. As a result, the user identification rate could reach as high as 99% based solely touch based micro and large-scale movements on smart phones.

Handshaking Biometrics

Handshaking is a specific set of human actions needed to unlock the screen of the smartphone of a user. Guo et al. (2013) collected 200 users' handshaking actions with their smart phones. They observed unique, stable, and distinguishable idiosyncratic patterns in shaking behaviors of users. Based on these findings, the authors designed four shaking functions to fetch the unique pattern of user's handshaking actions which can be used to authenticate a user of a smartphone.

Hobby Driven Biometrics

Jiang et al. (2013) proposed a novel behavioral biometric called hobby driven biometric. They presented a comprehensive study on habitual behaviors driven by hobbies. Considering the decorating and tidying style of a room as hobby-driven behavior they conducted a survey on 225 people of different ages and professions. They observed unique and steady characteristics based on style, color, position, and habitual operating order of the object for different persons. Their study demonstrates that the novel hobby-driven habitual behavioral biometric-based authentication system is feasible.

Browsing Style

Olejnik and Castelluccia (2013) proposed another novel biometric trait based on web browsing habits of users. Authors investigated the potential of this novel biometric based on the browsing data of 4,578 users. Their empirical analysis demonstrates that the idiosyncratic web browsing patterns of users can obtain low False Acceptance Rate and high False Rejection Rate for person authentication. Person authentication, anomaly, and fraud detections etc. could be the potential applications of browsing style based novel behavioral biometric trait.

From the above summary it is pertinent that idiosyncratic patterns can be found in every aspect of human actions ranging from walking style in real world to browsing style in cyber world. Therefore, human activities on web-based SNSs have unique patterns that can be used as behavioral biometric features for person authentication.

BIOMETRIC FEATURES FROM SOCIAL NETWORKS

Behavioral biometric refers to identifying individuals from their very own behavioral characteristics (Yampolskiy & Govindaraju, 2008). The daily activities in SNSs leave a large number of behavioral footprints which are very difficult to fake. However, to identify a set of consistent idiosyncratic activities is the biggest challenge for establishing SNS interactions based social biometrics. Therefore, our first task is to identify a set of consistent features from the wide ranges of social activities and information from web-based SNSs.

Twitter is one of the most popular social media platforms where millions of people exchange their ideas and thoughts with their virtual community. Regardless of the geographic location, Twitter has approximately 554.7 million active users around the globe who post 58 million tweets per day and 9100 tweets per second (Murthy, 2018). Twitter is a convenient platform for studying behavioral patterns of user as is it a popular platform with publicly available information that provides real-time microblogging, which is a rich source of human communication activities. Twitter user profiles contain rich source of information about the user and his/her network. In the following section we would discuss what kind of information can be obtained from a user profile in Twitter and the significance of the information in formation of the proposed web-based social biometrics.

In general, following information can be obtained from Twitter: Profile information, Network information, Tweets (Sultana et al., 2014c, 2017a, 2017b). The summary of main observations presented in those works is provided below.

Profile Information

Information is very crucial to profile the behavior of a person. In general, the following information can be obtained from a typical user profile in Twitter:

- **Personal information:** real name, Twitter handle, URL for his personal web page, additional information provided by the user e.g. profession, interests etc.
- **Temporal information:** location, profile creation date etc.

All the above information can be used as metadata for profiling user's online social networking behavior for further authentication.

Network Information

Twitter also provides information about how and to whom the user is connected. Twitter maintains two types of connection between users: follower and following (Glossary, 2019). A connection can be one way or both ways. For example, if user A wants to get status updates from user B then A can add user B as a following. In this case user B would see user A as a follower. Again, both way connection may exist between user A and B. In this case, user A would be a follower of B and B would be a follower of A.

Information of the followers and following can be obtained from Twitter. From this information, a social networking graph can be generated to understand the pattern of connection of the user. More inference can be drawn from the analysis of the network. For example, which community the user belongs to, close friend list and so on.

Tweets

Tweets are real time microblogs posted by the users in Twitter. Though it is limited to 140 characters still is a rich source of information about the user and his communication behavior. Idiosyncratic pattern of tweets of a user can be explored by analyzing the following features:

- **Text:** The writing style of users, use of special characters, punctuation symbols, emoticons, spelling mistakes, abbreviations can be analyzed to extract discriminant feature set for the user. For this purpose, many well-known text mining approaches such as bag-of-words, n-grams, style markers analysis, frequency analysis can be utilized.
- **Hashtags:** Hashtag are used to mark keywords or topics in a Tweet and preceded by # symbol (Glossary, 2019). Just like bag-of-words bag-of-hashtags can be analyzed to as feature set to identify the user.
- **Retweets:** Retweeting is the act of sharing other user(s) Tweets to all of the followers a user (Glossary, 2019). Analysis of retweets would be useful to build user's behavioral profile in Twitter. Social networking analysis can be applied to analyze the correlation between friends and retweets of the users.
- **Reply:** Replies are Tweets of the users posted in reply to another user's message in his/her timeline (Glossary, 2019). Analyzing replies would provide us important behavioral information such

as – to whom the user replies most, any specific pattern or style followed by the user to reply to a specific person and so on.

- **URLs:** The most frequent URL(s) posted by the user, URL shorteners are being used or not etc. can be included based on the frequency analysis of the posted URLs in user's timeline.
- **Other information:** Timestamp, geo-location (if present) etc. of tweets can also be used as either soft biometrics or creating behavioral profile for person identification (Jain et al., 2004).

A profile can be created based on the above information of the user to represent as a novel biometric trait feature called web-based social biometric (Sultana et al., 2014c, 2017a). Two main challenges of such data analysis would be:

1) Extraction of features from large apparently random dataset.
2) Selection of a small and consistent behavioral feature set to be used for the identification purpose.

SOCIAL BEHAVIORAL MODELING

Social interactions of humans vary from person to person. Tweets are restricted to 280 characters, which make users write many abbreviations and shorten terms to express their thoughts within this character limit (Gouws et al., 2011; Gligorić et al., 2018). However, tweets are overloaded with information about the users and their social communication. Usually, the following types of information can be extracted from the users' profile and tweets (Sultana et al., 2014c, 2017a, 2017b; Sultana & Gavrilova, 2018):

- Spatio-temporal information collected across both time and space such as users' geo-location, time-zone, timestamp, travel information, profile creation date, log, schedule, devices used to access social media, etc.
- Content of the tweets such as vocabulary, lexicons, abbreviations, capitalization, punctuation, structure of sentences, misspelled words, etc.
- Context of the text such as hashtag, shared weblinks or URLs, emoticons, etc.
- Interpersonal communication data such as like, mention, comment, check-in, reply, retweet, etc.
- Community and social relationship data such as followings, followers, community, marital/relationship status, etc.

In this section, a new methodology based on the concept of social behavioral biometric is proposed. In order to model a person's social behaviour via Online Social Network (OSN), we suggest combining four types of information obtained from tweets, namely Content-based, Contextual, Spatio-temporal and Social Interpersonal Communication.

Pre-Processing of Data

The crawled data obtained from Twitter needs to be processed to obtain the required information. The tweets, list of replied, mentioned, retweeted acquaintances, hashtags, and URLs along with the corresponding frequency of occurrences and timestamps will be parsed for every user in each session. The timestamps of the posts in every session will be extracted for every user. All other identity-related information such as location, DOB, time zone, personal web link, etc. must be discarded. Overlapped data from different sessions are also needed to be removed.

Social Behavioral Biometrics User Profile Creation

Four types of profile will be created from the data, namely, Content-based profile, Context-based profile, Friendship profile, and Temporal profile. Figure 2 presents the flowchart of the proposed system. The detail description of the proposed framework is given below:

Content-Based Profile

The linguistic features of tweets contribute in biometric identification of a person. The content-based profile will be generated combining each of the following features which express user's writing style.

N-grams:

N-grams is a language model in Natural Language and Processing (NLP). The approach assigns probability on *n* consecutive units of text together for processing. Depending on the unit N-gram can be categorized as character-based, word-based and bit/binary based. N-grams uses the sliding window principle to create the n-sequential terms where the window size is *n*. Generally, a new window considers next *n* adjoining units for processing. The windows can be overlapping or non-overlapping with each other (Gómez-Adorno et al., 2018). In our proposed model, the overlapping Word-based N-grams model will be considered. In word-based N-grams, a single word from the tweet will be considered as a unit. From word-based n-grams, the user's writing style is expected to be extracted for generating the profile. Some common N-grams will be filtered to reduce the number of grams.

Lexical Features:

Lexical features contain a set of lexical items such as words or characters extracted from the text. The set includes the frequency of characters including upper case, lower case, vowels, white space, digits and special characters (Neal et al., 2018). Also, the previously mentioned N-grams technique is used to generate word-based 3-grams and 4-grams as lexical features.

Some other features will be extracted for each sample such as, number of words in the tweet, average sentence length in terms of words, average word length, frequency of short words (1-3 characters), frequency of long words (more than 6 characters), average syllable per word, and M-number of most frequently used words per user. The lexical richness will be measured by the number of hapax legomena, dis legomena and tris legomena present in the sample, which refers to a word occurring only once, twice or thrice in a text, respectively (Tweedie & Baayen, 1998).

Syntactic Features:

Syntactic features extract sentence structure in terms of punctuation, parts-of-speech and function words to represent the user's writing style (Li et al., 2017; Argamon et al., 2003). The usage of parts-of-speech and function words demonstrate the writing style of the user, even in short messages (Rocha et al., 2016). Sometimes, users put consecutive punctuation marks after a tweet regardless of the correctness, such as "Can anyone help me to solve this???", "I am bored...", "What a pleasant surprise!!!!!", etc. This also indicates the writing style of a user. The number of punctuation marks, number of each punctuation marks (single quotes, double quotes, commas, periods, colons, semi-colons, question marks, and exclamation marks), number of each Unicode punctuation marks, number of each parts-of-speech tags, number of articles, etc. will be extracted as Syntactic features.

Social Network-specific Features:

This feature set includes characteristics related to Twitter posts as well as short messages. The icons and emoticons help to express better the user's mood through the tweets as they are the graphical representation of facial expression (Orebaugh & Allnutt, 2009). Thus, features related to emoticons include the number of Twitter special characters, number of text-based icons, number of Unicode-emoticons, number of Unicode-miscellaneous symbols, number of M consecutive same emoticons, number of M consecutive mixed emoticons, etc. Besides, features extracted from paragraph structure will also be considered such as topic words, number of miss of an uppercase letter when starting a sentence, number of miss of a period or other punctuation to end a sentence, number of sentences per sample, the average number of characters, average number of words and average number of sentences, etc. (Li et al., 2017).

The lexical features will help to understand the linguistic characteristics of the tweets, the syntactic features will help to understand user's writing style and the social network-specific features mostly helps to understand the tweet writing style of the users. After extracting the features from the content of the tweets, a content-based profile will be created for each user by combining all or selected features. To keep the most discriminating features for every individual, feature selection algorithms, namely Chi-square test, Principle Component Analysis, etc. can be used.

Friendship Profile

The concept of generating friendship profile is similar to Sultana et al. (2017b). The friendship profile of users will be created based on their active interactions, such as reply, mention, and retweet. A small set of friendships is mined from the active interactions of users on Twitter and a relationship has been assigned between them. The proposed friendship profile consists of two features: reply/mention network and retweet network.

Reply and Mention Network:

In this network, nodes and edges will be used to represent the network. Nodes are the user and the other users s/he replies. The process includes three major steps: listing all persons that the user replied to, counting the replies to each person, and finally applying a threshold. A threshold is applied on the counts of the replies for each individual the user replied to, as we are interested to include persons in the network whom the user replies frequently. For example, if a user replies to hundreds of his friends in a day, then we may be interested to find the persons whom the user replies frequently or regularly. A person is added to the reply network if and only if the count of reply is greater than a certain threshold.

Retweet Network:

Figure 2. System flowchart of the social profiles-based identification system

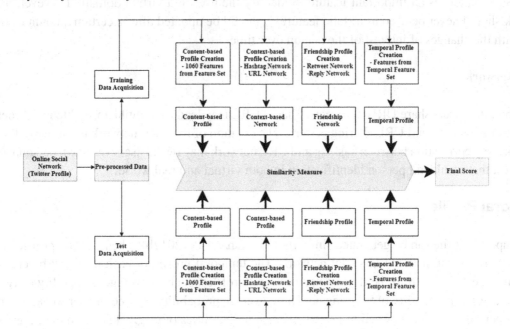

A retweet network is generated to find the most frequent retweeted persons in the user's timeline. The retweets are categorized based on the direction: retweeting and retweeted. Retweeting refers that a person is posting tweets of other users in his/her timeline. On the other hand, retweeted means the person's tweet is retweeted by some other users. Both are related to the proposed retweet network with the differences of direction only. Further behavioral patterns can be found by measuring the similarity of the reply and retweet networks. For example, weight of person in the users' friend list could be increased if that person exists on both retweet and reply networks. Such analysis may provide further information on the community that the user belongs to, which eventually could be used as auxiliary biometric features.

Contextual Profile

The concept of generating contextual profile is adopted from Sultana et al. (2017b). Contextual profile depends on the two networks, namely hashtag network and URL network.

Hashtag Network:

Bag-of-hashtags can be analyzed as a feature set using method similar to bag-of-words (Feng et al., 2015). Unlike in a reply or retweet network, a pre-processing step is required to reduce the number of hashtags on similar topics. The primary goal of the hashtag network is to identify personal interest of the user. Therefore, assigning a general topic of interest as a node would be more meaningful instead of using all hashtags as nodes. For this purpose, all similar or related hashtags could be categorized as one topic of interest and could be weighted based on their frequency. Then, a weighted hashtag network can be generated to explore some behavioral patterns of the user. For example, if some hashtags appear regularly in the tweets of a user over long time period, then the user is consistently interested about that issue. Such pattern is an important feature to identify the user in a virtual domain. However, hashtag network should never be used as a static feature, it should be updated after a certain amount of time to cope with the changes of interest of the person over time.

URL Network:

Sometimes, users share URLs in tweets. Shared URL may lead us to build a weighted URL network of the user's interests and URL sharing pattern. The creation of the URL network is similar to the reply network. Any correlation between hashtag and URL network may reveal users very own personal choice or interest that would aid person identification in both virtual and real world.

Temporal Profile

The temporal profile can be generated similarly to Sultana et al. (2017b). The temporal profile of users reveals their posting patterns in social network. The temporal profile of each user will be created by extracting the features from the timestamps of users' profiles, such as average probability of tweeting per Day, average probability of tweeting per Hour, average probability of tweeting per week, seven days interval period, seven days tweeting period, average probabilities of original tweet, retweet, and reply/mention per day, etc. (Sultana & Gavrilova, 2018).

Similarity Measure and Final Score

Similarity measure techniques are applied to each type of profile in order to find similarities between testing and training profiles of users. Four individual similarity measures will be obtained after all matching. Classical machine learning methods will be used to obtain the result. Finally, a final score will be generated basing on these four similarity measures to identify the person from Social Behavioral Biometrics (SBB).

Interested reader can find details on implementation of the above concepts and performance analysis in the articles on the subject that introduce concept of Social Behavioral Biometrics and a multi-modal biometric fusing social behavior with traditional physiological modalities (Sultana et al., 2014c, 2017a, 2017b; Sultana & Gavrilova, 2018).

PERSONALITY TRAIT AS A SOCIAL BIOMETRIC FEATURE

The latest developments in a wide variety of domains such as cybersecurity, digital surveillance, clinical psychology, economic modelling, policymaking, and advertising started to incorporate personality trait information (Russell et al., 2017). Personality traits have strong influences on important aspects of life such as success in the workplace, political temperament, and general emotional stability (Judge et al., 1999). Digital footprints left behind by users of social networking sites, specifically, Twitter, allow to ascertain the identity of the authors (Sultana et al., 2015). Moreover, computer-based personality assessments from passive mining of information on microblogging sites have shown to be more reliable and accurate than judgments made by people close to the subject. Analysis of language used on Twitter provides behavioral cues about the authors that allow for reliable estimation of an individual's personality traits. Accurately predicting personality traits from digital footprints however have not been considered as a social behavioral biometric trait. We thus hypothesize that it has unique characteristics that can be successfully used for online user recognition. In addition, it may serve as a rapid, cost-effective, and scalable alternative to surveys, which can benefit academic research and inform mental healthcare initiatives.

In this subsection, we introduce a personality traits classification system that incorporates distinctive language characteristics used by individuals on social networks, building on previous works in the domain of social behavioral biometrics. Figure 3 represents the overall architecture of personality trait detection system.

The prediction model discussed here is based on the Myers-Briggs Type Indicator (MBTI) personality scale (Orebaugh & Allnutt, 2009). It is an assessment of personality based on Carl Jung's theory of types. It continues to be the most frequently administered personality test today and commonly available public datasets consist of MBTI type indicators: Introversion-Extroversion (I/E), Sensing-Intuitive (S/N), Thinking-Feeling (T/F), Judging-Perceiving (J/P). We find that by analyzing a section of the last 50 tweets alone, we can reliably predict certain personality trait labels (ex: INTP) with high fidelity. We show that recent word-embedding techniques combined with existing machine learning methods can perform reasonably well at this task. Rather than constructing handcrafted linguistic and stylistic features or hierarchical dependencies, which requires considerable domain knowledge, our approach is to use easily interpretable count-based vectorization and emerging word-embedding techniques as input. Classification models that can leverage the high-dimensional and relational information encoded in word-embeddings are used to learn useful and meaningful patterns from the vectored representations.

Feature Extraction

The tweets are first can be filtered for URLs using regular expressions. Following this, the filtered set of words are lemmatized to their root forms, and the tweets are converted to a document-term matrix using a count-based vectorization (TF-IDF). The TF-IDF document-term matrix represents a user's most indicative and frequently used terms, whereas GloVe embedding of a word is its low-level representation learnt within a deep neural network trained on word-word co-occurrence statistics from 27 billion tweets (Pennington et al., 2014). Each tweet can be vectorized by summing the underlying GloVe embedding vector for each word weighted by its TF-IDF value. A concatenated representation of all 50 tweets is then analyzed by the classification model to obtain the personality trait label across each of the four MBTI dimensions.

Multi-Class Text Classification Using XGBoost and SVM

The TF-IDF document-term matrix and the concatenated GloVe embedding of all the posts by a user is used to build decision-tree ensembles consisting of classification and regression trees (CART), additively, based on a fitness measure to optimize the objective function. Our model is represented as follows:

$$\hat{y}_i = \sum_{k=1}^{K} f_k\left(x_i\right), f_k \in F.$$

where *K* is the number of trees, *f* is a function in the functional space ℱ and ℱ is the set of all possible CARTs. The objective function to be optimized is given by:

$$obj\left(\theta\right) = \sum_{i}^{n} l(y_i, \hat{y}_i^{(t)}) \; + \sum_{k-1}^{K} \Omega\left(f_k\right)$$

where the first term represents the training loss function denoted by the true label y_i and the prediction value $\hat{y}_i^{(t)}$ at step *t*. The second term is the regularization term that refers to the complexity of the tree at each time step. Softmax objective function is used with number of trees to fit (n_estimators) = 300, learning rate = 0.6, and max depth = 2 for base learning estimators. The optimal set of parameters is found using grid-search method.

As there are only very few irrelevant features when it comes to text classification, even the lowest-ranked features still contain relevant information and can prove to be useful. Since it seems unlikely that even the worst features in terms of information gain are completely redundant, the proposed framework builds a classification framework that combines the features extracted for all words within all tweets for each user. Consequently, the vectored tweet representation has high dimensionality, is sparse and contains a linearly separable sub-structure. Support Vector Machines (SVM) are well-suited for this setting as their ability to learn discernible patterns from the feature representation is independent of the dimensionality of the feature space. As a result, generalizability is preserved even in the presence of many features. The hinge-loss function with the L2 penalty and penalty parameter C=10 is used, where the optimal parameters are found using the grid-search method.

Dataset Description

The Twitter MBTI Personality Dataset was collected through the PersonalityCafe forum, which provides a large selection of people and their MBTI personality type, as well as what they have written. It was made available on Kaggle.com with user consent for academic research (Briggs & Myers, 2017). It contains information collected from 8675 people and on each row is a person's four-letter MBTI personality trait label and a section of each of their latest 50 tweets. We choose to evaluate our methodology on the Twitter MBTI dataset as it is one of the largest publicly available collection of tweets labelled with the author's personality traits. The dataset is imbalanced and requires some pre-processing for efficient learning. To address this issue, we use the SMOTE (synthetic minority oversampling) technique to balance the classes using a combination of oversampling and undersampling (Chawla et al., 2002).

Preliminary Results

In our preliminary experiments, it was observed that the dataset is unbalanced to contain significantly more instances of writings provided by INFP, INFJ, INTP and INTJ (»1000 each) types as compared to ESTP, ESFP, ESTJ and ESFJ (» 200 each) types. The correlation measures among each of the dimensions are calculated from the feature representations to ascertain that the dataset is clinically valid. Since each type comprising the MBTI scale is a distinct dimension used to describe a person's characteristics, it was observed that they are not correlated (maximum being 0.16 between IE and JP dimensions). Stratified cross-fold validation (k=4) is employed to measure the performance of each classifier model. It is observed that the classification works best for the INFP, INTP, INFJ, ENFP types and this may be attributable to the fact that there are 5 times as many examples of these classes in the dataset. We see that the XGBoost classifier outperforms the Linear SVM classifier by a small margin for all cases except the J-P dimension. With our ensemble prediction system, we can reliably predict the personality trait label across the Extraversion-Introversion and Sensation-Intuition dimensions (F1-score = 0.87 and 0.92 respectively). The Thinking-Feeling dimension can be classified with moderate accuracy and the Judging-Perceiving personality trait proves to be the hardest to classify. A much more detailed description of the underlying model, experiments, and results can be found in the research conducted by Kumar and Gavrilova (2019).

Figure 3. Language-based personality traits analysis using Social Behavioral Biometrics

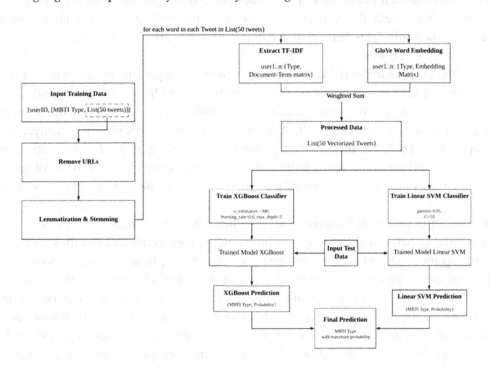

FUTURE RESEARCH DIRECTIONS

Although behavioral biometrics alone are not unique enough to identify a person with the capacity of real-world applications, they can obtain high verification rate and enhance recognition rate of multimodal biometric systems (Yampolskiy, 2011). Such a system takes into consideration more than one single biometric trait, and thus achieves a better recognition rate and ensures tolerance to noise. The proposed online social biometric features can be used to identify person in many ways such as:

- **Fraud or Anomaly Detections**: Continuous authentication is another promising application of the proposed web- based social biometric features. For example, instead of static or one time authentication SNSs can authenticate users continuously based on some social biometric features such as posted URLs, lexicons, replies, retweets etc. If the trust level of the current user drops significantly the system can generate alerts. This application would facilitate anomaly or fraud detection in virtual domain.

- **Multimodal Biometric Systems:** The proposed biometric features can be integrated with other behavioral or traditional biometric traits as multimodal system to identify a person in both virtual and real world. For example, tweeting pattern can be integrated with keystroke dynamics as a multimodal system to enhance the verification rate of users.

- **Forensic Applications:** It is known that author identification often needed for law enforcement and forensic applications of the investigations of cybercrimes. The proposed SNS based biometric features can be utilized for author identification of microblogs.

- **Cybersecurity:** Identifying users from social interaction plays a significant role to identify fake users. If the credential of an online account accidentally compromises, with the help of the proposed biometric system, the online social network system will be able to identify suspicious activities automatically. This benefits the online network users to secure their accounts through continuous authentication.

- **Personality Trait Detection:** The study of computer-based personality assessment systems is a very promising direction of research. The reliability and validity of personality estimation made by passive assessment of personality can be further studied. The interactive nature of social media coupled with its ever-increasing utilization provides a unique opportunity to analyze user emotion, opinion, and behavior through content that is made publicly available. Future study of human personality traits based on online activity using a naturally occurring, immense, ecologically valid dataset may capture the inclinations of individuals and their multifarious interactions on online social networks.

- **Smart Societies and Risk Management:** Another future research direction that can harvest the full potential of behavioral biometrics is investigating their combination with smart devices for risk management. One of the obvious benefits is combining behavioral characteristics with the mobile devices is, for example, to keep track of an individual's health status (i.e. heart rate, body temperature). Other benefits can be also obtained in using such information during an emergency response, while providing service for those seeking admission to the homeless centre, or in providing an assistance to an elderly person if a fall is detected by sensors in a smart building. Collecting application specific datasets that can combine user specific smart data with their online social behaviour would be highly beneficial to advance this emerging research direction.

CONCLUSION

In this chapter, the concept of social biometrics based on online social communications has been extensively discussed. The authors explained motivation behind using web-based social networking sites as a source of mining personal characteristics and behavioral patterns. Different types of social biometric features were introduced, discussed and presented as part of a multi-modal social biometric system. Previous research demonstrated that the proposed biometric features are strong enough to be utilized in security-critical applications, and that they can be used for verification or continuous authentication of users in the virtual domains and on-line communities. In addition, performance of existing physiological biometric authentication system can be enhanced by using the proposed personal characteristics as auxiliary biometrics. Therefore, revealing such idiosyncratic characteristics from web-based social interactions and their subsequent use as auxiliary biometrics would aid person identification in both real and virtual domain. The presented social behavioral system was augmented by the emerging research on personality traits detection from online social networks. Future research directions that include broad range of on-line social environment, cybersecurity, forensic, healthcare and civil applications were outlined. Investigating proposed web-based social biometric features in combination with personality traits research for all the above applications would open new doors for further research towards smart society.

ACKNOWLEDGMENT

Authors are grateful to partial support for this project provided by NSERC Strategic partnership Grant "MOST: Biometric-enabled Identity Management and Risk Assessment for Smart Cities", NSERC Discovery grant "Machine Intelligence for Biometric Security" and IDEaS AutoDefense Network funding.

REFERENCES

Al-Zubi, S., Brömme, A., & Tönnies, K. (2003). Using an active shape structural model for biometric sketch recognition. In *Joint Pattern Recognition Symposium* (pp. 187-195). Springer Berlin Heidelberg. 10.1007/978-3-540-45243-0_25

Argamon, S., Šarić, M., & Stein, S. S. (2003). Style mining of electronic messages for multiple authorship discrimination: first results. In *Proceedings of the Ninth ACM SIGKDD International Conference on Knowledge Discovery and Data Mining* (pp. 475-480). ACM. 10.1145/956750.956805

Azam, S., & Gavrilova, M. (2017). Person identification using discriminative visual aesthetic. In *Canadian Conference on Artificial Intelligence* (pp. 15-26). Springer.

Bakelman, N., Monaco, J. V., Cha, S. H., & Tappert, C. C. (2013). Keystroke biometric studies on password and numeric keypad input. In *Proceedings of Intelligence and Security Informatics Conference (EISIC)* (pp. 204-207). IEEE. 10.1109/EISIC.2013.45

Bazazian, S., & Gavrilova, M. (2015). A hybrid method for context-based gait recognition based on behavioral and social traits. In M. Gavrilova, C. Tan, K. Saeed, N. Chaki, & S. Shaikh (Eds.), *Transactions on Computational Science XXV* (Vol. 9030, pp. 115–134). Springer. doi:10.1007/978-3-662-47074-9_7

Bo, C., Zhang, L., Li, X. Y., Huang, Q., & Wang, Y. (2013). SilentSense: Silent user identification via touch and movement behavioral biometrics. In *Proceedings of the 19th Annual International Conference on Mobile Computing & Networking* (pp. 187-190). ACM. 10.1145/2500423.2504572

Bours, P. (2012). Continuous keystroke dynamics: A different perspective towards biometric evaluation. *Information Security Technical Report, 17*(1), 36–43. doi:10.1016/j.istr.2012.02.001

Briggs, K. C., & Myers, I. B. (2017). *Myers–Briggs Type Indicator (MBTI) Myers-Briggs Personality Type* [Dataset]. https://www.kaggle.com/datasnaek/mbti-type

Chawla, N. V., Bowyer, K. W., Hall, L. O., & Kegelmeyer, W. P. (2002). SMOTE: Synthetic minority over-sampling technique. *Journal of Artificial Intelligence Research, 16*, 321–357. doi:10.1613/jair.953

Dattner, Y., & Yadid-Pecht, O. (2011). High and low light CMOS imager employing wide dynamic range expansion and low noise readout. *IEEE Sensors Journal, 12*(6), 2172–2179. doi:10.1109/JSEN.2011.2179290

Delgado-Gómez, D., Sukno, F., Aguado, D., Santacruz, C., & Artés-Rodriguez, A. (2010). Individual identification using personality traits. *Journal of Network and Computer Applications, 33*(3), 293–299. doi:10.1016/j.jnca.2009.12.009

Eastwood, S. C., Shmerko, V. P., Yanushkevich, S. N., Drahansky, M., & Gorodnichy, D. O. (2015). Biometric-enabled authentication machines: A survey of open-set real-world applications. *IEEE Transactions on Human-Machine Systems, 46*(2), 231–242. doi:10.1109/THMS.2015.2412944

Feng, W., Zhang, C., Zhang, W., Han, J., Wang, J., Aggarwal, C., & Huang, J. (2015). STREAMCUBE: Hierarchical spatio-temporal hashtag clustering for event exploration over the twitter stream. In *Proceedings of the 31st International Conference on Data Engineering* (pp. 1561-1572). IEEE. 10.1109/ICDE.2015.7113425

Frank, M., Biedert, R., Ma, E., Martinovic, I., & Song, D. (2012). Touchalytics: On the applicability of touchscreen input as a behavioral biometric for continuous authentication. *IEEE Transactions on Information Forensics and Security, 8*(1), 136–148. doi:10.1109/TIFS.2012.2225048

Gligorić, K., Anderson, A., & West, R. (2018). How constraints affect content: The case of Twitter's switch from 140 to 280 characters, In *Twelfth International AAAI Conference on Web and Social Media* (pp. 596–599). AAAI.

Glossary. (2019). https://help.twitter.com/en/glossary

Gómez-Adorno, H., Posadas-Durán, J. P., Sidorov, G., & Pinto, D. (2018). Document embeddings learned on various types of n-grams for cross-topic authorship attribution. *Computing, 100*(7), 741–756. doi:10.100700607-018-0587-8

Gouws, S., Metzler, D., Cai, C., & Hovy, E. (2011). Contextual bearing on linguistic variation in social media. In *Proceedings of the Workshop on Languages in Social Media* (pp. 20-29). ACM.

Green, R. M., & Sheppard, J. W. (2013). Comparing frequency-and style-based features for Twitter author identification. In *Proceedings of the Twenty-Sixth International FLAIRS Conference* (pp. 64–69). AAAI.

Guo, Y., Yang, L., Ding, X., Han, J., & Liu, Y. (2013). OpenSesame: Unlocking smart phone through handshaking biometrics. In Proceedings IEEE INFOCOM (pp. 365-369). IEEE.

Hsu, G. S. J., Ambikapathi, A., & Chen, M. S. (2017). Deep learning with time-frequency representation for pulse estimation from facial videos. In *Proceedings of International Joint Conference on Biometrics (IJCB)* (pp. 383-389). IEEE. 10.1109/BTAS.2017.8272721

Hsu, G. S. J., Cheng, Y. T., Ng, C. C., & Yap, M. H. (2017). Component biologically inspired features with moving segmentation for age estimation. In *Proceedings of IEEE Conference on Computer Vision and Pattern Recognition Workshops (CVPRW)* (pp. 540-547). IEEE. 10.1109/CVPRW.2017.81

Hsu, G. S. J., Huang, W. F., & Kang, J. H. (2018). Hierarchical network for facial palsy detection. *IEEE/CVF Conference on Computer Vision and Pattern Recognition Workshops (CVPRW)* (pp. 693-699). IEEE.

Igarashi, K., Miyajima, C., Itou, K., Takeda, K., Itakura, F., & Abut, H. (2004). Biometric identification using driving behavioral signals. In *Proceedings of the International Conference on Multimedia and Expo (ICME)* (Vol. 1, pp. 65-68). IEEE.

Jain, A. K., Dass, S. C., & Nandakumar, K. (2004). Soft biometric traits for personal recognition systems. In *Biometric Authentication* (pp. 731–738). Springer Berlin Heidelberg. doi:10.1007/978-3-540-25948-0_99

Jain, A. K., Flynn, P., & Ross, A. A. (2008). *Handbook of Biometrics*. Springer Science & Business Media. doi:10.1007/978-0-387-71041-9

Jain, A. K., Nandakumar, K., & Ross, A. (2016). 50 years of biometric research: Accomplishments, challenges, and opportunities. *Pattern Recognition Letters*, *79*, 80–105. doi:10.1016/j.patrec.2015.12.013

Jain, A. K., Ross, A., & Pankanti, S. (2006). Biometrics: A tool for information security. *IEEE Transactions on Information Forensics and Security*, *1*(2), 125–143. doi:10.1109/TIFS.2006.873653

Jeong, D., Kim, M., Kim, K., Kim, T., Jin, J., Lee, C., & Lim, S. (2018). Real-time driver identification using vehicular big data and deep learning. In *International Conference on Intelligent Transportation Systems* (pp. 123-130). IEEE. 10.1109/ITSC.2018.8569452

Jiang, W., Xiang, J., Liu, L., Zha, D., & Wang, L. (2013). From mini house game to hobby-driven behavioral biometrics-based password. In *Proceedings of the 12th International Conference on Trust, Security and Privacy in Computing and Communications* (pp. 712-719). IEEE. 10.1109/TrustCom.2013.86

Jorgensen, Z., & Yu, T. (2011). On mouse dynamics as a behavioral biometric for authentication. In *Proceedings of the 6th ACM Symposium on Information, Computer and Communications Security* (pp. 476-482). ACM. 10.1145/1966913.1966983

Judge, T. A., Higgins, C. A., Thoresen, C. J., & Barrick, M. R. (1999). The big five personality traits, general mental ability, and career success across the life span. *Personnel Psychology*, *52*(3), 621–652. doi:10.1111/j.1744-6570.1999.tb00174.x

Kumar, K. P., & Gavrilova, M. L. (2019). Personality Traits Classification on Twitter. In *Proceedings of International Conference on Advanced Video and Signal Based Surveillance (AVSS)* (pp. 1-8). IEEE.

Lai, K., Kanich, O., Dvořák, M., Drahanský, M., Yanushkevich, S., & Shmerko, V. (2017). Biometric-enabled watchlists technology. *IET Biometrics*, *7*(2), 163–172. doi:10.1049/iet-bmt.2017.0036

Layton, R., Watters, P., & Dazeley, R. (2010). Authorship attribution for twitter in 140 characters or less. In *Cybercrime and Trustworthy Computing Workshop (CTC)* (pp. 1-8). IEEE. 10.1109/CTC.2010.17

Li, J. S., Chen, L. C., Monaco, J. V., Singh, P., & Tappert, C. C. (2017). A comparison of classifiers and features for authorship authentication of social networking messages. *Concurrency and Computation*, *29*(14), e3918. doi:10.1002/cpe.3918

Macleod, N., & Grant, T. (2012). Whose Tweet? Authorship analysis of micro-blogs and other short-form messages. In *International Association of Forensic Linguists' Tenth Biennial Conference* (pp. 210–224). Academic Press.

Monwar, M. M., & Gavrilova, M. (2013). Markov chain model for multimodal biometric rank fusion. *Signal, Image and Video Processing, 7,* 137–149. doi:10.100711760-011-0226-8

Murthy, D. (2018). *Twitter.* Polity Press.

Neal, T., Sundararajan, K., Fatima, A., Yan, Y., Xiang, Y., & Woodard, D. (2018). Surveying stylometry techniques and applications. *ACM Computing Surveys, 50*(6), 86. doi:10.1145/3132039

Oak, R. (2018). A literature survey on authentication using behavioral biometric techniques. In *Proceedings of Intelligent Computing and Information and Communication* (pp. 173–181). Springer. doi:10.1007/978-981-10-7245-1_18

Olejnik, L., & Castelluccia, C. (2013). Towards web-based biometric systems using personal browsing interests. In *Proceedings of International Conference on Availability, Reliability and Security* (pp. 274-280). IEEE. 10.1109/ARES.2013.36

Orebaugh, A., & Allnutt, J. (2009). Classification of instant messaging communications for forensics analysis. *International Journal of Forensic Computer Science, 1,* 22–28. doi:10.5769/J200901002

Pennington, J., Socher, R., & Manning, C. (2014). Glove: Global vectors for word representation. *In Proceedings of the 2014 Conference on Empirical Methods in Natural Language Processing (EMNLP)* (pp. 1532-1543). ACL. 10.3115/v1/D14-1162

Rocha, A., Scheirer, W. J., Forstall, C. W., Cavalcante, T., Theophilo, A., Shen, B., & Stamatatos, E. (2016). Authorship attribution for social media forensics. *IEEE Transactions on Information Forensics and Security, 12*(1), 5–33. doi:10.1109/TIFS.2016.2603960

Russell, J. D., Weems, C. F., Ahmed, I., & Richard, G. G. III. (2017). Self-reported secure and insecure cyber behaviour: Factor structure and associations with personality factors. *Journal of Cyber Security Technology, 1*(3-4), 163–174. doi:10.1080/23742917.2017.1345271

Shalhoub, G., Simon, R., Iyer, R., Tailor, J., & Westcott, S. (2010). Stylometry system–use cases and feasibility study. *Forensic Linguistics, 1*(8).

Silva, R. S., Laboreiro, G., Sarmento, L., Grant, T., Oliveira, E., & Maia, B. (2011). 'Twazn me! Automatic authorship analysis of micro-blogging messages. In *Natural Language Processing and Information Systems* (pp. 161–168). Springer. doi:10.1007/978-3-642-22327-3_16

Spafford, E. H., & Weeber, S. A. (1993). Software forensics: Can we track code to its authors? *Computers & Security, 12*(6), 585–595. doi:10.1016/0167-4048(93)90055-A

Sultana, M., & Gavrilova, M. (2018). Temporal pattern in tweeting behavior for persons' identity verification. In *Proceedings of International Conference on System, Men and Cybernetics (SMC)* (pp 2468-2473). IEEE. 10.1109/SMC.2018.00424

Sultana, M., Paul, P. P., & Gavrilova, M. (2014). A concept of social behavioral biometrics: motivation, current developments, and future trends. In *Proceedings of International Conference on Cyberworlds* (pp. 271-278). IEEE. 10.1109/CW.2014.44

Sultana, M., Paul, P. P., & Gavrilova, M. (2014). Mining social behavioral biometrics in Twitter. In *International Conference on Cyberworld* (pp. 293-299). IEEE.

Sultana, M., Paul, P. P., & Gavrilova, M. (2015). Social behavioral biometrics: An emerging trend. *International Journal of Pattern Recognition and Artificial Intelligence*, *29*(08), 1556013. doi:10.1142/S0218001415560133

Sultana, M., Paul, P. P., & Gavrilova, M. L. (2014). Online user interaction traits in web-based social biometrics. In M. Sarfraz (Ed.), *Computer Vision and Image Processing in Intelligent Systems and Multimedia Technologies* (pp. 177–190). IGI Global. doi:10.4018/978-1-4666-6030-4.ch009

Sultana, M., Paul, P. P., & Gavrilova, M. L. (2017). Social behavioral information fusion in multimodal biometrics. *IEEE Transactions on Systems, Man, and Cybernetics. Systems*, *48*(12), 2176–2187. doi:10.1109/TSMC.2017.2690321

Sultana, M., Paul, P. P., & Gavrilova, M. L. (2017). User recognition from social behavior in computer-mediated social context. *IEEE Transactions on Human-Machine Systems*, *47*(3), 356–367. doi:10.1109/THMS.2017.2681673

Tweedie, F. J., & Baayen, R. H. (1998). How variable may a constant be? Measures of lexical richness in perspective. *Computers and the Humanities*, *32*(5), 323–352. doi:10.1023/A:1001749303137

Unar, J. A., Seng, W. C., & Abbasi, A. (2014). A review of biometric technology along with trends and prospects. *Pattern Recognition*, *47*(8), 2673–2688. doi:10.1016/j.patcog.2014.01.016

Yampolskiy, R. V. (2011). Behavioral, cognitive and virtual biometrics. In A. Salah & T. Gevers (Eds.), *Computer Analysis of Human Behavior* (pp. 347–385). Springer. doi:10.1007/978-0-85729-994-9_13

Yampolskiy, R. V., & Govindaraju, V. (2008). Behavioral biometrics: A survey and classification. *International Journal of Biometrics*, *1*(1), 81–113. doi:10.1504/IJBM.2008.018665

Yampolskiy, R. V., & Govindaraju, V. (2010). Game playing tactic as a behavioral biometric for human identification. In L. Wang & X. Geng (Eds.), *Behavioral Biometrics for Human Identification: Intelligent Applications* (pp. 385–413). IGI Global. doi:10.4018/978-1-60566-725-6.ch018

Yanushkevich, S. N., Stoica, A., Srihari, S. N., Shmerko, V. P., & Gavrilova, M. L. (2004) Simulation of biometric information: the new generation of biometric systems, in *Proceedings of International Workshop Modeling and Simulation in Biometric Technology*, 87-98.

ADDITIONAL READING

Yanushkevich, S., Gavrilova, M., Wang, P., & Srihari, S. (2007). Image pattern recognition: Synthesis and analysis in biometrics. *Artificial Intelligence*, *67*.

KEY TERMS AND DEFINITIONS

Auxiliary Biometrics: Auxiliary biometrics are some personal features which themselves are not enough to represent standalone biometric traits but can provide additional information about the characteristics of person to aid the person identification process.

Behavioral Biometrics: Behavioral biometrics refer to some behavioral characteristics of human beings which can be used to identify a person.

Biometric Recognition: Recognizing a person by measuring the similarity of some biometric traits of the person stored biometric samples or templates in the system.

Biometric Verification: Verifying the identity of a person that he/she claims to be based on some biometric traits.

Multimodal Biometrics: Use of more than one biometric trait to identify a person.

Social Behavioral Biometrics: Social behavioral biometrics refer to social behaviors or interactions which possess some discriminant characteristics for being used to identify a person.

Unimodal Biometric: Use of a single physiological or behavioral biometric trait to identify a person.

Chapter 2
K–Means and DNN–Based Novel Approach to Human Identification in Low Resolution Thermal Imagery

Mohit Dua

https://orcid.org/0000-0001-7071-8323

National Institute of Technology, Kurukshetra, India

Abhinav Mudgal

National Institute of Technology, Kurukshetra, India

Mukesh Bhakar

National Institute of Technology, Kurukshetra, India

Priyal Dhiman

National Institute of Technology, Kurukshetra, India

Bhagoti Choudhary

National Institute of Technology, Kurukshetra, India

ABSTRACT

In this chapter, a human detection system based on unsupervised learning method K-means clustering followed by deep learning approach You Only Look Once (YOLO) on thermal imagery has been proposed. Generally, images in the visible spectrum are used to conduct such human detection, which are not suitable for nighttime due to low visibility, hence for evaluation of our system. Hence, long wave infrared (LWIR) images have been used to implement the proposed work in this chapter. The system follows a two-step approach of generating anchor boxes using K-means clustering and then using those

DOI: 10.4018/978-1-7998-4444-0.ch002

anchor boxes in 252 layered single shot detector (YOLO) to predict proper boundary boxes. The dataset of such images is provided by FLIR company. The dataset contains 6822 images for training purposes and 757 images for the validation. This proposed system can be used for real-time object detection as YOLO can achieve much higher rate of processing when compared to traditional method like HAAR cascade classifier in long wave infrared imagery (LWIR).

1. INTRODUCTION

With the increased interest in automation, a lot of work has been done in the field of self-driving cars (autonomous vehicle systems), security surveillance systems or autonomous search and rescue missions to detect a human/pedestrian. Researchers have proposed many algorithms for human detection using RGB images (Spinello et al., 2011; Vondricket al., 2013). However, detecting a high rate of true positives on RGB images is still a challenging task due to low resolution, moving objects, changing backgrounds or real time requirements using the visual images. Hence, instead of using RGB images, infrared (IR) images are a better option for the task of pedestrian detection in uneven scenarios. IR cameras capture the brightness intensity corresponding to the temperature and radiated heat of the object in the image. They are susceptible to illumination variations, occlusions or background noises. Hence, in the proposed work of this chapter, an additional source of information - IR images or thermal images captured through thermal cameras or sensors to get a gray scale mapping corresponding to a particular location have been used.

Substantial amount of work has been done in the field of human detection (Davis et al..2015; Spinello et al., 2011; Qi et al., 2014). Majority of work has been done in tracking people in well controlled surroundings like detection of hotspots by applying Maximally Stable Extremal Regions (MSER) on the Long-Wave Infrared (LWIR) images (Teutsch et al.,2014). MSER follows the assumption that the temperature of the human body is much greater than that of the background. Hence, MSER detects humans in a better manner than background subtraction or sliding window techniques. Human detection is done through the features that are observed in a person in an image. However, factors such as clothings, background, body temperature and illumination also affect the appearance of the person, that directly affects the feature descriptor. (Bin et al.,2014) proposed a Scattered Difference of Directional Gradients Descriptor (SDDG) which uses local gradient distribution information of thermal image to describe an object in certain directions. SDDG has demonstrated comparable performance (in comparison with Histogram Oriented Gradient (HOG) and HAAR wavelets).

For real-time detection, a cluttered environment must also be considered. Since ages, works have been done for real-time object detection taking every possible aspect into consideration like Histogram Oriented Gradient (HOG) technique and Support Vector Machine (SVM) classifier is used in research proposed in (Kachouane et al., 2012). The idea used behind HOG descriptors is that the intensity distribution of gradients and the direction of contours can describe the shape of an object. Image is divided into small connected regions and for each region histogram of gradient direction is computed. The combination of these histograms is the HOG descriptor. The final classification is done by using the linear kernel function of the SVM classifier. HOG descriptors are invariant to geometric and photometric descriptors and hence, this technique has shown good results in the field of robotics. An extension in HOG approach used in (Foong et al.,2006) has been proposed on thermal images in (Rujikietgumjorn, S., & Watcharapinchai, N. 2017), which takes foreground segmentation and human shape similarity into account with significant reduction in processing time and can perform in real-time on a Raspberry Pi embedded system while maintaining high accuracy in results (Foong et al.,2006).

Classifiers used in pattern matching algorithms fail in classifying humans in aerial images as they are captured at different angles and those techniques are not robust in dealing with such cases. To deal with such issues, a three-step approach has been used in (Portmann et al., 2014). Firstly, background subtraction is done in order to get all the bright connected regions as they are the actual regions of interest (ROIs). Various detectors like HOG detector, Local Binary Pattern(LBP) cascade, HAAR feature cascade based Body Parts Detector (BPD) are then applied in the pipeline to get every minute detail and these details are then passed to the tracker as guidance. The research work proposed in (De Oliveira et al.,2016) combines the thermal images and deep learning methods such as Convolutional Neural Network (CNN) to cope up with complex camera related problems faced during aerial imagery. Experimental results proved that a higher rate of correct classification with much higher precision can be achieved through deep learning. In (John et al.,2015), pedestrians are detected using adaptive fuzzy C-means clustering and convolutional neural networks. Clustering helps in segmenting the thermal images and retrieving candidate pedestrians. In fuzzy C-means clustering there is a need to specify the number of clusters. The proposed work uses the image intensity information to adaptively estimate the cluster number. Combining adaptive clustering with deep learning helped in achieving better detection accuracy.

Redmon et al. proposed a single shot detector- You Only Look Once (YOLO) which processes image in real-time at 155 frames per second. Unlike other classifiers, YOLO works on a single pass of an image. It divides an image into grids and if the center of the object falls in the grid then that grid is responsible for detection of the object. It maintains higher average precision. Redmon et al., (2016) YOLO is fast because it divides the image into s*s grid and it processes each grid only once. In the era of deep learning, old school methods of Image Processing like Histograms oriented gradients (HOG) (Kachouane et al., 2012) or MSER (Teutsch et al., 2014) are needed to be trained manually using their own feature set which is a cumbersome and error-friendly task. Deep learning models like CNN in (De Oliveira et al., 2016) removes this manual feature selection and identifies relevant features through the network but has a drawback of being extremely slow due to the need of passing a single image 2000x times to the network. YOLO architecture by Redmon et al., (2016) undermines both the problems. YOLO trains its own feature set like any other deep learning network but also really quickly using a single convolutional layer network and single pass of image.

Motivated by the above discussed methods and approaches, the proposed work in this chapter implements a two-step approach based on deep learning and unsupervised learning for real-time human recognition by using thermal images. The thermal dataset has been provided by FLIR company which consists of around 6000 images. To detect humans, YOLO has been used which is a deep learning, single pass, layered object detector. YOLO is one of the fastest technology of object detection and it uses convolutional neural networks for its implementation.

An enhancement that the chapter aims to do is to use K-means clustering algorithm to determine good anchor candidates for the training on a modified YOLO model consisting of 252 layers (additional layers replicated for improvement) rather than having the default anchor boxes. The clustering is based on the dataset and hence better anchor boxes could be identified to be used for training which may help in getting fast and better results. Hence, better results, in terms of true positives, have been achieved using the proposed approach.

The remainder of the chapter is organized as: Section 2 discusses the fundamentals of K-means clustering and YOLO model, Section 3 describes the details of proposed architecture, Section 4 gives the details of the setup used for the implementation of the chapter, Section 5 shows how different modules work to create the desired architecture and the results obtained after implementing it, Section 6 concludes the proposal and shows the possibility of further enhancements.

2. PRELIMINARIES

2.1 K-Means Clustering

Clustering is an unsupervised machine learning technique which divides the dataset into a number of clusters where data points are similar to each other in the same cluster and dissimilar to other clusters (Radford et al., 2015; Snoek et al., 2012). So, in general clusters are the collection of the data points on the basis of the similarity and dissimilarity between them. The data in every cluster make a meaningful structure, grouping inherent and feature generative. Rosenberger, C., & Chehdi, K., (2000) in his work proposed an unsupervised method called MLGB (modified LGB) based upon the clustering algorithm has been proposed, the method selects the number of clusters automatically by calling into question an intermediate result. This method also enables to improve the k-means algorithm. Unsupervised learning has a phenomenal wide range of applications and is very useful to solve real world problems such as anomaly detection, recommending systems, documents grouping, or finding customers with common interests based on their purchases. Chen et al., (2015) in their works suggested cluster based retrieval of images by unsupervised learning(CLUE). There are many clustering algorithms K-means clustering, Hierarchical clustering, Density based scan clustering and Gaussian clustering model. Out of these methods, K-means is the easiest clustering algorithm to understand and implement and it is very efficient computationally, that is why k-means is a very popular clustering algorithm. It gives the best result when data is distinct and well separated. In the proposed approach of this chapter, K-means clustering has been used because real time object detection is desired in this algorithm and k-means is that much faster. The main aim of the K-means clustering is to find out the K (it is defined by the user) number of groups of related data points. The similarity of the data points depends on distance between the data points. A centroid is the imaginary or real location representing the center of the cluster. Every data point is allocated to each of the clusters through reducing the in-cluster sum of squares. Here distance metric Intersection Over Union (IOU) (Nowozin et al., 2014) is used.

2.2 YOLO

YOLO (Ng et al., 2006; Al-masni et al., 2018) stands for You Only Look Once. It is a deep learning approach for detecting the object in a given image as an input (Han et al., 2018). Basically, YOLO is the CNN network and is very fast as compared to the image processing techniques and other object detection methods. Because of its faster computation, it has been used for the proposed approach. Yolo is targeted to real time processing like 24/7 surveillance and self-driving car assistance. YOLO can be trained end-to-end to improve accuracy.

When an image is passed through the YOLO model, it divides the image into s*s grid. Each grid is responsible to predict only one object and a fixed number of boundary boxes. However, the one-object rule limits how close detected objects can be. The purpose of each grid cell is:

- To predict B boundary boxes and each box with confidence score
- To detect only one object
- To predicts C conditional class probabilities

Each boundary box has five elements: x,y,w,h and box confidence score, where x and y are offsets to the corresponding cell, w is the width of the cell and h is the height of the cell. Conditional class probability is probability that tells the detected object belongs to a particular class. YOLO performs a linear regression using two fully connected layers to make 7×7×2 boundary box predictions (the middle picture below). To make a final prediction, we keep those with high box confidence scores (greater than 0.25) as final predictions. Class confidence score for each box is computed as:

$$\text{Class confidence} = \text{Conditional class probability} \times \text{Box confidence score} \tag{1}$$

YOLO (Redmon et al., 2016) is having 24 CNN layers followed by 2 fully connected layers. The YOLO model can predict multiple bounding boxes per grid cell to compute the loss for the true positive and that is responsible for the object. For object prediction purposes the highest IOU with ground is selected. YOLO uses sum-squared error between the predictions and the ground truth to calculate the loss. The total loss function is summation of classification loss, localization loss and confidence loss.

3. PROPOSED ARCHITECTURE

This section discusses the architecture of the proposed system. The proposed system uses K-means clustering to identify good anchor candidates. Using these anchor boxes further training is done over a single convolutional network i.e. YOLO to predict multiple bounding boxes simultaneously and show class probabilities for these boxes. YOLO trains on full images and directly optimizes detection performance. This model has various benefits over traditional methods of object detection due to its faster, easier and simplified way of implementation. As described by Figure 1, merger, K-means clustering, YOLO neural network and predictor class are the key components of the proposed architecture. The following subsections discuss these key components.

3.1 Merger

Initially, we had annotations files in JavaScript Object Notation (JSON) format corresponding to the thermal images carrying information about the positions of humans in the image. Merging process creates a train.txt file which contains data in the following format:

<Image_path> <Co-ordinates_of_image> <Category_Id>

This is used to be fed into the layered architecture that is to be trained. Originally, for a human detection system we need to get to all the image dataset separately, traverse its JSON file and find the ground truth boundary boxes every time. However, the proposed system includes a merger phase before the feature extraction and model training phase, due to which the model can be run over just one file. Hence, the proposed system does the whole process only once and stores it in a file for future use. The K-means clustering phase and YOLO training phase both use the same file for their execution to speed up the work.

3.2 K-Means Clustering

Using the train.txt file, created through a merging process, unsupervised K-means clustering is performed in order to get anchor boxes for the dataset according to the true boundary boxes of the dataset. In a foundational piece (Ng et al., 2006), YOLO model worked on default anchor boxes and not decided on the basis of the ground truth boundary boxes of the dataset, hence itself making it more difficult to train. However, it will be more beneficial to perform model training on the anchor boxes according to its dataset. First training would be faster and better. Second, accuracy will increase as the model is to be used under the same surrounding environment only, as in our case it is to be used during night time and on self-driving cars to predict pedestrians and cars. This clustering preprocessing is a must. Hence, in order to get better results, we used K-means clustering to find out our own set of anchor boxes. This helped with our training process to be faster and smoother. Through K-means clustering we are now able to get a set of nine clusters. Nine clusters obtained through K-means clustering for our dataset are:

Figure 1. Proposed System Architecture

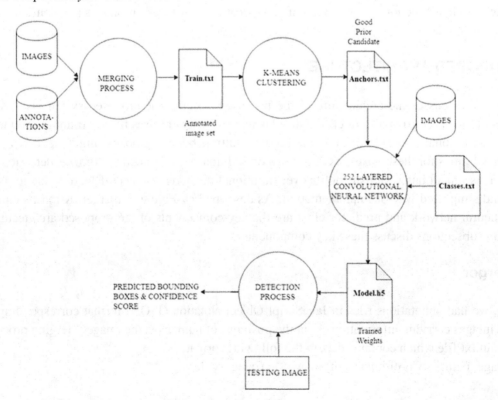

(10×13), (16×30), (33×23), (30×61), (62×45), (59×119), (116 × 90), (156 × 198), (373 × 326). These nine clusters are used with the YOLO network to identify correct boundary boxes based on the offset differences.

3.3 YOLO-Convolutional Neural Network

The Yolo-Convolutional Neural network used in the proposed system has been modified with a total of 252 layers. This subsection discusses the working of this layered architecture.

252-Layered Architecture: The proposed system uses modified YOLO architecture which consists of 252 layers where additional layers have been replicated and added for better results. The model has simply extended the number of layers and the same pattern is followed for the lower layers, as it is seen that due to low resolution of the images available in thermal spectrum, a more extended model could help us achieve a higher and better accuracy. Although the training will take much longer, the model is accurate enough to be used for predictions later on. Here, the classes and anchors file are given as input along with images to the 252-layered YOLO model and the model is trained on these inputs. After training we get a weights file and the predictive model is ready to be tested. For testing purposes the predictive model takes an image as input and predicts the boundary boxes and confidence score for the same.

Identify Class of an Object: For each box, class to which the object belongs is predicted using multi-label classification. Independent logistic classifiers are used for such classification. During training, YOLO uses binary cross entropy loss for the class predictions. As described earlier by Figure 1 the proposed system follows a two-step architecture, where the second step includes a 252 layered Convolutional Neural Network. The layers are a mix of Conv2D, Batch Normalization and Leaky Relu layers as described by Figure 2.

Figure 2. Different Layers in architecture

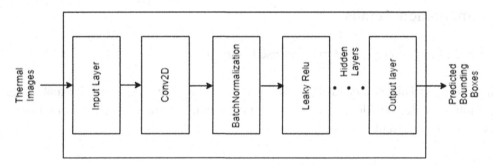

Convolution Layers perform linear operation involving the product of the set of weights and input. Batch Normalization Layers actually normalize the output of the previous activation layer by taking the mean of the batch and subtracting it and then dividing by the batch standard deviation. This actually helped us avoid using max pool layer or any other down sampling layer. Leaky Relu Layers are just for activation and classification knowledge purposes of the network.

Bounding Box Prediction: In YOLO bounding boxes are predicted using dimension clusters as anchor boxes. Predictions of boxes are made at three different scales by concatenating the layers. For each bounding box four coordinates are predicted. Logistic regression is used to predict objectness score corresponding to each bounding box. If this score is 1 then the bounding box prior overlaps a ground truth object by more than any other bounding box prior as depicted in the overall architecture to make final predictions.

3.4 Predictor Class

The outcome from the output layer is the coordinates of the boundary boxes. There is a possibility of getting multiple boundary boxes predicted for the same object. The Intersection Over Union (IOU), i.e the measure how much the predicted boundary overlaps with the ground truth (actual object contour), is used to separate out and filter only the most relevant of the boundary boxes out of many selected boundary boxes for the same object. The proposed model uses a predefined IoU threshold taken as 0.4, decided by hit and trials on the FLIR dataset in classifying whether the prediction is a True Positive (TP) or a False Positive (FP). From those coordinates, bounding boxes are drawn on the image along with the class scores derived from the tensor values threshold to be displayed on the screen.

4. EXPERIMENTAL SETUP AND RESULTS

For the implementation of this chapter, a dataset consisting of thermal images is provided by FLIR company which contains a set of around 6000 images. The model is trained on this dataset by using a Supercomputer named PARAM SHAVAK that has 2 multicore CPUs each with minimum 12 cores, 2 numbers of accelerator cards and 3 Tera-Flops peak computing power with 8 TB of storage. Around 4500 images are used for training purposes and among those 4500 images, 450 images are kept for validation. For testing, a set of 1500 images is used. This system requires the knowledge of Python and deep learning for implementation.

4.1 Implementation Details

Following is the brief description of modules used in the project:

Our_annotations.py: This module takes the annotations file in json format and thermal images, merge them into a single text file named as train.txt containing all the information in following format for every image present in the dataset-

Path to image box_co-ordinates category_id.

Model.py: This module creates the Yolo architecture containing convolutional, batch_normalization and LeakyRelu layers composed together to form 252 layered neural networks.

Train.py: This module uses the created model and takes classes as well as anchor boxes to feed and compile the model and start training in batches of 32 for 100 epochs.

K_means.py: This module takes the train.txt file, identifies and returns the optimal anchor boxes as per the data into result.txt file. This result.txt. file is used further in training rather than default anchors.

Yolo.py: This module creates a class yolo that loads the trained model and pre-process the image to detect it. Further it uses utils.py to draw onto and visualize the bounding boxes and confidence onto the output image.

Detect.py: This module is the driver module to take our image and model as arguments and then further call the rest of the required modules to return the results.

Utils.py: This module contains extra additional helping code necessary to perform pre and post processing.

4.2 Results

The Human Detection model predicts the boundary boxes and confidence score in a thermal image. To estimate the accuracy of the model for the variety of relevant classes to be distinguished, we have calculated the mean average precision (mAp). For that we first need to calculate Average Precision (AP) which is nothing but finding the area under the precision-recall curve as:

$$AP = \int_0^1 p(r)\,dr \tag{2}$$

where p is precision and r is recall values defined as:

$$Precision(p) = \frac{TP}{TP + FP} \tag{3}$$

$$Recall(r) = \frac{TP}{TP + FN} \tag{4}$$

where TP refers to true positive, FP refers to false positive, and FN refers to False negative. Figure 3 gives the results obtained for the four cases used to test the proposed system.

Case 1: The moving objects as well as the stationary objects have been clearly detected using the model. Interleaving humans in groups are also identified distinctively. And the humans that are a little behind and are smaller due to their distance from the camera along and are interleaved together as well are detected by the model.

Case 2: The cars hidden behind some other cars losing their complete curvature are also being identified using the model with great precision up to 0.88. Even the car far ahead from the camera is easily detected with a confidence score of 0.42.

Case 3: The model is able to identify a few far people as well with great precision. Interestingly, it is also able to de-capture a false bicycle printed on road unlike RGB Models which are going to classify it as a bicycle.

Case 4: The model is able to identify people nearby and very close to the camera with a very high confidence score of 0.99. It is also able to identify people of smaller scale that are very far distant from the camera but with a lesser precision as 0.41 can be seen in this case.

Figure 3. Different Case Studies of Model

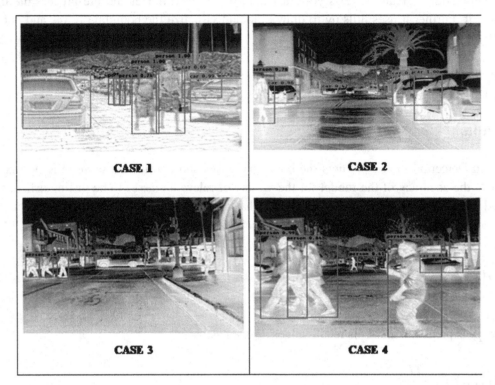

Figure 4 shows the mean average precision (Mann, W., 1953) for the three classes i.e person, car and bicycle taking average after considering all of the images in testing data. The mAP of the proposed model is 44.17%. AP is averaged over all the categories and plotted in Figure 4, as for person class AP = 0.5, for car class AP = 0.49 and for bicycle class AP= 0.33 for the YOLO model on FLIR data. Hence, mAP of model will be 0.51 + 0.49 + 0.33 / 3 = 0.44

Figure 4. mean Average Precision of the model

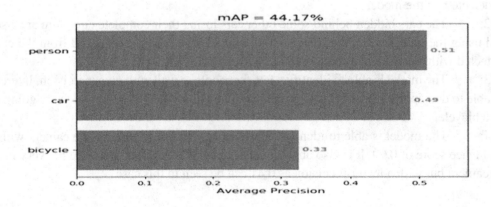

4.3 Comparative Analysis

The Table 1 gives the comparative analysis of the proposed system with various techniques proposed by researchers for making real-time detection of a person in thermal images. Different techniques with their precision in detecting objects or people are mentioned in the table and it can be observed that the proposed approach has shown better results in detecting humans even in worse surroundings.

Table 1. Analysis and comparison with earlier proposed works

Approach	Techniques Used	Testing Dataset	TP	FP	Precision
Michael Teutsch et al., 2014	MSER	695	610	85	0.8576
Diulhio & Marco, 2016	HAAR Cascade	100	59	31	0.6555
Diulhio & Marco, 2016	LBP Cascade	100	70	48	0.5932
Diulhio & Marco, 2016	CNN	100	94	22	0.8103
Sitapa & Nattachai, 2017	Conventional HOG: Atrium-red dataset Atrium-orange dataset	6923 6803	3348 2615	3363 1415	0.4989 0.6489
Proposed Approach	K-means Clustering + Yolo	3458	3042	416	0.8797

6. CONCLUSION AND FUTURE WORKS

A fast and accurate estimation of humans in low resolution or night time can help us solve various real time problems like identification of intruders in night time or the detection of pedestrians for a self-driving car/ unmanned vehicles. Usage of Long-wave infrared imagery instead of traditional RGB images to train a very unique and new model YOLO (You only look once) helped us capture better features in such scenarios. We achieved the mean average precision of 44.17% for thermal images which is considerably a decent result compared with 50-60% in RGB scenarios. The identification of better anchor boxes for training played a very helpful part in the predictions. The YOLO model has a clear cut upper hand in terms of speed due to its only one-time traversal of image concept. Due to this success over the old traditional detectors like HOG or MSER or even old deep learning models like R-CNN, Fast R-CNN etc, single shot detectors achieved decent accuracy at much faster pace. This model can be further researched to advance our efforts in the field of long/short-wave infrared imagery detections with modern deep learning tools. Also, the idea can be used to try different techniques as well, different clustering methods can be applied on the modified YOLO model to make better predictions. This can be a major achievement in the future to save lots of human beings by operating such systems in self-driving cars.

REFERENCES

Al-masni, M. A., Al-antari, M. A., Park, J. M., Gi, G., Kim, T. Y., Rivera, P., Valarezo, E., Choi, M.-T., Han, S.-M., & Kim, T. S. (2018). Simultaneous detection and classification of breast masses in digital mammograms via a deep learning YOLO-based CAD system. *Computer Methods and Programs in Biomedicine, 157*, 85–94. doi:10.1016/j.cmpb.2018.01.017 PMID:29477437

Chen, Y., Wang, J. Z., & Krovetz, R. (2005). CLUE: Cluster-based retrieval of images by unsupervised learning. *IEEE Transactions on Image Processing, 14*(8), 1187–1201. doi:10.1109/TIP.2005.849770 PMID:16121465

Davis, J. W., & Keck, M. A. (2005, January). A two-stage template approach to person detection in thermal imagery. In *Seventh IEEE Workshops on Applications of Computer Vision (WACV/MOTION'05)-Volume 1* (Vol. 1, pp. 364-369). IEEE.

De Oliveira, D. C., & Wehrmeister, M. A. (2016, May). Towards real-time people recognition on aerial imagery using convolutional neural networks. In *IEEE 19th International Symposium on Real-Time Distributed Computing (ISORC)* (pp. 27-34). IEEE.

Han, J., Zhang, D., Cheng, G., Liu, N., & Xu, D. (2018). Advanced deep-learning techniques for salient and category-specific object detection: A survey. *IEEE Signal Processing Magazine, 35*(1), 84–100. doi:10.1109/MSP.2017.2749125

John, V., Mita, S., Liu, Z., & Qi, B. (2015, May). Pedestrian detection in thermal images using adaptive fuzzy C-means clustering and convolutional neural networks. In *14th IAPR International Conference on Machine Vision Applications (MVA)* (pp. 246-249). IEEE. 10.1109/MVA.2015.7153177

Kachouane, M., Sahki, S., Lakrouf, M., & Ouadah, N. (2012, December). HOG based fast human detection. In *2012 24th International Conference on Microelectronics (ICM)* (pp. 1-4). IEEE. 10.1109/ICM.2012.6471380

Mann, W. R. (1953). Mean value methods in iteration. *Proceedings of the American Mathematical Society, 4*(3), 506–510. doi:10.1090/S0002-9939-1953-0054846-3

Ng, H. P., Ong, S. H., Foong, K. W. C., Goh, P. S., & Nowinski, W. L. (2006, March). Medical image segmentation using k-means clustering and improved watershed algorithm. In *IEEE Southwest Symposium on Image Analysis and Interpretation* (pp. 61-65). IEEE. 10.1109/SSIAI.2006.1633722

Nowozin, S. (2014). Optimal decisions from probabilistic models: the intersection-over-union case. In *Proceedings of the IEEE Conference on Computer Vision and Pattern Recognition* (pp. 548-555). 10.1109/CVPR.2014.77

Portmann, J., Lynen, S., Chli, M., & Siegwart, R. (2014, May). People detection and tracking from aerial thermal views. *IEEE International Conference on Robotics and Automation*, ●●●, 1794–1800. doi:10.1109/ICRA.2014.6907094

Qi, B., John, V., Liu, Z., & Mita, S. (2014, October). Pedestrian detection from thermal images with a scattered difference of directional gradients feature descriptor. In *17th International IEEE Conference on Intelligent Transportation Systems (ITSC)* (pp. 2168-2173). IEEE. 10.1109/ITSC.2014.6958024

Radford, A., Metz, L., & Chintala, S. (2015). *Unsupervised representation learning with deep convolutional generative adversarial networks.* arXiv preprint arXiv:1511.06434

Redmon, J., Divvala, S., Girshick, R., & Farhadi, A. (2016). You only look once: Unified, real-time object detection. In *Proceedings of the IEEE conference on computer vision and pattern recognition* (pp. 779-788). 10.1109/CVPR.2016.91

Rosenberger, C., & Chehdi, K. (2000). Unsupervised clustering method with optimal estimation of the number of clusters: Application to image segmentation. In *Proceedings 15th International Conference on Pattern Recognition. ICPR-2000* (Vol. 1, pp. 656-659). IEEE. 10.1109/ICPR.2000.905473

Rujikietgumjorn, S., & Watcharapinchai, N. (2017, August). Real-time hog-based pedestrian detection in thermal images for an embedded system. In *14th IEEE International Conference on Advanced Video and Signal Based Surveillance (AVSS)* (pp. 1-6). IEEE. 10.1109/AVSS.2017.8078561

Snoek, J., Larochelle, H., & Adams, R. P. (2012). Practical bayesian optimization of machine learning algorithms. In Advances in neural information processing systems (pp. 2951-2959). Academic Press.

Spinello, L., & Arras, K. O. (2011, September). People detection in RGB-D data. In *IEEE/RSJ International Conference on Intelligent Robots and Systems* (pp. 3838-3843). IEEE.

Teutsch, M., Muller, T., Huber, M., & Beyerer, J. (2014). Low resolution person detection with a moving thermal infrared camera by hot spot classification. In *Proceedings of the IEEE Conference on Computer Vision and Pattern Recognition Workshops* (pp. 209-216). 10.1109/CVPRW.2014.40

Vondrick, C., Khosla, A., Malisiewicz, T., & Torralba, A. (2013). Hoggles: Visualizing object detection features. In *Proceedings of the IEEE International Conference on Computer Vision* (pp. 1-8). IEEE.

Wang, W., Zhang, J., & Shen, C. (2010, September). Improved human detection and classification in thermal images. *IEEE International Conference on Image Processing* (pp. 2313-2316). IEEE. 10.1109/ICIP.2010.5649946

Chapter 3
Masking and Tracklet Building for Space Debris and NEO Observations:
The Slovak Image Processing Pipeline

Stanislav Krajčovič
Comenius University, Slovakia

Roman Ďurikovič
Comenius University, Slovakia

Jiří Šilha
Comenius University, Slovakia

ABSTRACT

The partial goal of the transformation of a newly acquired telescope into a professional observation device was a design and development of an image processing pipeline. The pipeline can process an acquired raw image of space debris into object observations in time (tracklets), and further correlate and identify them with selected catalogues. The system contains nine image processing elements (IPEs) in total that are further described in this chapter and have already been deployed and tested on real space debris data.

INTRODUCTION

Comenius University in Bratislava has acquired a 70 cm Newton telescope (see Figure 1) to set up in its Astronomical and Geophysical Observatory in Modra, Slovakia (further AGO), to observe space debris and other near-Earth objects. The set-up of this observational device consisted of many critical steps such as transportation of the telescope, installation in the cupola, installation of the telescope, acquisition of the necessary computing hardware, such as control unit, encoders, and other equipment,

DOI: 10.4018/978-1-7998-4444-0.ch003

and the development of software (Šilha et al., 2018). As of writing of this chapter, it contains 9 Image Processing Elements (further IPEs):

- star field identification,
- image reduction,
- background estimation and subtraction,
- objects search and centroiding,
- astrometric reduction,
- masking,
- tracklet building,
- object identification and
- data transformation.

The focus of this chapter will be on the description of two specific IPEs – masking and tracklet building.

BACKGROUND

The term space debris encompasses all man-made objects which no longer serve any purpose on the Earth's orbit (Klinkrad, 2006). Large objects orbiting around the Earth belong to this category, such as defunct satellites, rocket bodies used as heavy duty propellers, gloves lost by astronauts during planned

Figure 1. AGO70 telescope set up in its dome at Astronomical and Geophysical Observatory in Modra, Slovakia, belonging to the Comenius University Bratislava

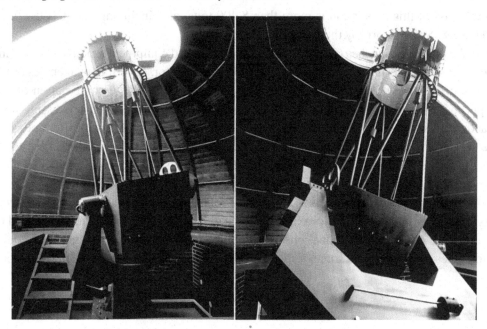

spacewalks and other; small objects such as paint flakes, Westford needles, fuel slag, or other (Klinkrad, 2006).

The risk of space debris has risen the moment humanity has become active in space exploration.

The spacecrafts rarely returned back to the Earth. It was more cost-effective to provide fuel only for the outbound journey and leave the unmanned satellites on their former orbit or move them to farther orbits at the end of its life (such as the graveyard orbit). In the same manner, rocket bodies decoupled at higher altitudes are not being actively "cleaned up." As a result, this led to the increase of space debris population which poses risk to the currently ran missions (ISS manoeuvres to move it out of the trajectory of incoming space debris) as well as for the future missions. Likewise, in the event of re-entry, a sufficiently large object which does not burn up in the atmosphere poses a danger to human lives – should it impact a populated area. Even though many objects are designed to burn up in the atmosphere or re-enter it at the end of their mission due to new regulations, the first step in understanding of the existing space debris is knowing where it comes from.

The biggest contributor of the space debris are fragmentation events which produce debris of various sizes (millimetres to metres). Reasons for fragmentation might be explosions of a satellite because of leftover fuel, damaged pressure tanks, collision with other satellite/debris or even deliberate destruction (Klinkrad, 2006). On the other side of the spectrum, each taking around 10% of the whole population, there is mission-related debris (such as the aforementioned gloves, a screwdriver, and other equipment) and the rocket bodies. An interesting, however small, subset of space debris population is anomalous debris – objects which usually have high area to mass ratio and their origin is not yet known.

As of time of writing of this chapter, statistical models currently estimate:

- 34,000 objects with sizes larger than 10cm,
- 900,000 objects with sizes larger than 1cm,
- more than 128,000,000 objects with sizes larger than 1mm (see Chart 1).

The total mass of this population is more than 8,400 tons (also including about 1,950 functioning satellites) ("ESA: Space debris by the numbers", 2019).

For the sake of future launches (for both safety of humans and equipment) and the monitoring of the rising danger of space debris, many entities—either in private sector, government agencies or academia all over the world—have developed optical or radar based systems (or the combination of two) with different purposes. No matter the type of observational device, there is a lot of processing being done between acquiring the raw data and understanding the information contained inside. For optical systems, the consecutive steps are best done in a pipeline with the raw image as an input and the information wanted as the output. While this might seem simple enough, the steps incorporated inside of each processing system are far beyond trivial.

Considering all this data together with the interest of contributing to the European space safety efforts, Comenius University in Bratislava, Slovakia, has purchased a 70cm Newtonian telescope and obtained funds to transform it into a professional observational device capable of observing space debris. The next section takes a closer look at some of the other, already established solutions for this problem.

Table 1. Image debris population by size

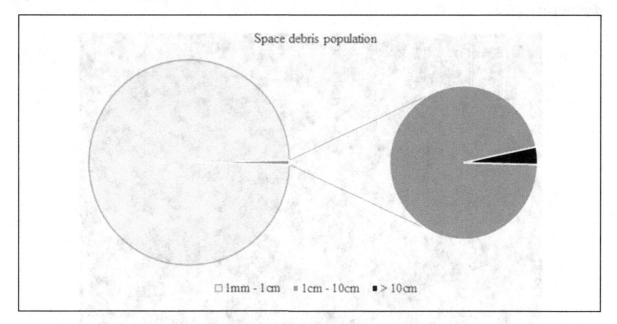

MAIN FOCUS OF THE CHAPTER

Issues, Controversies, Problems

The main problem of obtaining the necessary data for further space debris cataloguing is that they have to be read from raw astronomical images with various degrees of quality that depends on both the external environmental conditions and the quality of cameras used by the system.

Firstly, the geographical location of observational systems (or telescopes) needs to be carefully selected in order to accommodate the chosen system and its type of observation. For optical systems, location with very low light pollution is ideal. If the light pollution rises above the determined limit of camera's sensitivity, the observed objects, which are almost always displayed as white (high pixel intensity) points/dots, will blend with the background (polluted by the light coming from a nearby city, etc.) and will no longer be able to be extracted in later stages of processing. Additionally, the higher the telescope, the higher the atmospheric extinction—meaning photons from the observed objects are less absorbed and scattered during their passage through atmosphere and the object, therefore, has higher brightness.

A location with overall good weather conditions (good cloud conditions, preferably dry air) throughout the year must be chosen as well. Even if all these conditions are ensured and the environmental conditions are close to perfect—or even are perfect—successfully getting the positions of observed objects, and thus identifying them, can prove to be challenging.

The quality of cameras varies from manufacturer to manufacturer and from model to model, and will not be further discussed in this chapter. On the other hand, a quality image processing system is capable to extract the data even from the worse cameras.

Figure 2 shows an example of a Flexible Image Transport System (FITS) image, the conventionally used format for astronomical images. The details of this format will be discussed later in the chapter.

Figure 2. Example of a raw astronomical image containing stars depicted as points and a tracked object depicted as a streak

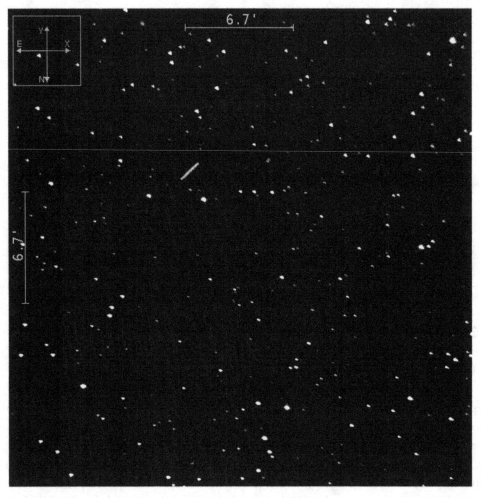

The image shows stars, which are depicted as white spots each having different intensity; the black background, an occasional hot pixel that might be a highly charged particle hitting the camera (cosmic radiation); the traced object as a white streak in the upper part of the image (because of its high velocity); deep black vertical artefacts (with intensity close or equal to 0) which are either the result of defect in the camera or an error in digitalisation of the camera data. Note that also faint objects (with lower signal intensity to noise ratio) must be processed. System's detectability of fainter objects means higher overall efficiency of the system. On the contrary, besides using them as for astrometric/photometric calibration and reduction, stars are irrelevant in space debris surveys and should be removed as soon as possible. In general, removingas much redundant information as possible in the earliest possible phase of processing reduces the complexity of the following phases of the processing algorithm and makes it more efficient.

There are several computer graphics approaches that refine the raw astronomical image and help extracting as much data as possible. A comprehensive overview of three established observational systems' processing pipelines is discussed in the following paragraphs.

OWL-net

OWL-net is a Korean network of optical telescopes situated all over the world with its main focus on observing Korean LEO and GEO satellites (Park et al., 2018). The authors start their image processing with removing additive and multiplicative errors by performing bias, dark and flat field corrections.

The details behind the corrections are explained later in the chapter, even though, in some cases, the corrections are not performed. The next step is to find the background satellites and satellite trajectories (because of the wide aperture of OWL-net, it is able to capture a relatively large part of the object's trajectory along the sky) and measure their position. To achieve this, the authors use an established tool, SExtractor (Bertin & Arnouts, 1996, pp. 393-406), to find coordinates of the midpoint of each trajectory/streak and correlate the data with time records. On the other hand, selected stars are compared with those stars catalogued in astronomical star charts to obtain a World coordinate system (further WCS) solution using WCSTools (Mink, 1997). Then, by using several data reduction algorithms (Park et al., 2016), real position of satellites and the corresponding time are stored in ASCII form and transmitted for further research. More details about the network can be found in the paper by Park et al. (2018).

SLR SmartNET™

The main objective of SmartNET™ is to exchange tracklets, between contributing actors who can then use the data to build their own catalogues, products, etc. Though at the same time, the network contains observation-capable telescopes which use a sophisticated processing chain named Backbone Catalogue of Relational Debris Information (BACARDI) (Weigel et al., 2015). It is important to note that BACARDI already works with created tracklets that are the finished product in this context and also the input into the processing chain. However, SmartNET™'s own processing system is currently under development. Nevertheless, at the time of writing of this chapter, telescopes belonging to the network are positioned at the most crucial longitude to observe GEO objects. SmartNET™ is, therefore, capable of providing essential service concerning orbit identification and orbit determination. For more details, see Fiedler (2017, 2018).

APEX II

On the contrary to the previous systems which were, in fact, networks that used image processing to yield the data, APEX II is a software package aimed at data reduction (Kouprianov, 2008). This means that any entity with relevant hardware, specifically an optical telescope, which is interested in data reduction/image processing might use APEX II as the processing software. Therefore, APEX II is not tied to a specific hardware and the resulting limitations. It is important to note, however, that the authors of the paper mention the pipeline working in the context of GEO objects. The APEX II pipeline consists of the following optional elements after an image has been loaded: bias/dark/flat field correction, sky background flattening, image filtering and enhancement. The next step, this time a mandatory one, is global thresholding which produces a bit mask that is further used to filter out noise and to reduce the probability of a false detection in another optional step, logical filtering. Segmentation, a mandatory step, serves as the identification of objects above the threshold used in the global thresholding step. Next in the pipeline is yet another optional step called deblending, which is generally used for objects that overlap.

The following steps in the pipeline are all mandatory and are either self-explanatory or more details can be found in the cited paper, such as isophotal analysis, Point Spread Function (PSF) fitting, rejection of *spurious* detections, astrometric catalogue matching, differential astrometry, differential photometry and finally, the report generation.

Considering the presented solution and their uniqueness, and to have full control over the processing algorithms, it was decided to create a new image processing pipeline. This is due to the facts that OWL-net is focused at Korean satellites which do not have to be debris yet. Moreover, the OWL-net authors use the conventional licensed software that has no possibility of enhancement. In a potential case, where the conventional software would not be able to yield satisfactory results, there is no way to extend it beyond its current function. Additionally, as it sometimes happens in software development, the projects which have no professional backing/funding have a higher probability of being abandoned, leaving the users with versions that might be incomplete, buggy, or worse. SmartNET™ does not solve this problem either but, instead, relies on the individual entities in their network that already have the necessary tools to produce tracklets. Furthermore, joining a network to improve orbit determination makes no sense if the telescope and the associated software have no capability to process high amount of data and create tracklets in an automated way. This is one of the largest influences in the architecture of the Image Processing Pipeline presented in the following sections and currently deployed, as the processing system at Astronomical and Geophysical Observatory in Modra, Slovakia, is APEX II.

SOLUTIONS AND RECOMMENDATIONS

Image Processing System (IPS) for space debris had been purposefully divided into multiple parts – Image Processing Elements (IPEs). This decision had been made to achieve modularity of the system which allows the operators to freely substitute any IPE (should the situation demand it such as, in the case, of a bad performing module). The modularity of the IPS is its biggest benefit – the ability to remove, add or substitute an IPE – makes the system responsive to changes in hardware, or to changing requirements. Additionally, the modularity had allowed for a quick development because each IPE could have been developed parallelly (by different people). On the other hand, the main negative of the modular architecture is the need in properly defining the input and the output for each of the IPEs and then ensuring the communication between them. At the time of writing of this chapter, the IPS is not yet fully automatic and requires human interaction. There are 9 IPEs in total, each performing a crucial step that ensures the image processing is done as accurately with as much detections as possible.

FITS format is an established system for the exchange of scientific images, especially the astronomic data.

A valid, "simple" FITS file usually contains a single header containing metadata about the image data itself. The metadata might include the name of the observer, camera model, pixel size, resolution, etc. The data itself is stored as a table of values, for example integers or float numbers. In the case of astronomical images, the values represent the intensity – brightness of each pixel. In the case of AGO70, the authors use the simplest and the most straightforward form of FITS images, even though, FITS is capable of storing multi-dimensional information with several headers (Wells et al., 1981).

Equatorial coordinate system (ECS) is a celestial coordinate system used to precisely specify positions of celestial objects in relation to the Earth. ECS using spherical coordinates (right ascension (α) and declination (δ)) is the most used coordinate system for astronomical purposes. Right ascension (also

RA) is equivalent with an axis in an ordinary two-dimensional plane, starting from the vernal equinox and increasing along the celestial equator eastwards. It is measured in minutes, hours and seconds, and comes from the interval. Declination (also DEC) is perpendicular to RA, equal to directly at the celestial equator and rises to above to north celestial pole and below to south celestial pole. RA\DEC system can exactly pinpoint location of space debris, stars and other celestial objects. It is also easy to convert between Cartesian coordinates and ECS coordinates.

Star Field Identification

Star field identification (IPE-SI) is a wrapper on the well-known Astrometry.net (Lang et al., 2010) routines which calculate the necessary information for astrometric and photometric purposes, such as plate constants. In the case of IPS, IPE-SI is called right after a new image is taken and is used to append the header of the FITS file by centre of field-of-view in right ascension (α) and declination (δ), and the beforementioned plate constants. Therefore, the input and output of this IPE are the same – the only difference is in the image headers which contain additional information when compared to the raw image. For more information, please see Šilha (2019).

Image Reduction

Image reduction (IPE-IR) is responsible for correcting additive and multiplicative errors which are caused by heating of the CCD camera, while gathering the data from the camera, by the electrical current on diodes which transmit energy from hitting photons, etc. Additive errors are removed by subtracting a dark frame (taken at a specific exposure time to capture the dark currents of the camera in pixels), or by subtracting a bias frame (taken at zero exposure time with the camera shutter closed). Multiplicative errors are corrected by dividing the raw image by a flat field frame (taken at dusk or dawn, close to zenith on an evenly illuminated field). As implied, the input is the image enriched by the additional header information from the previous IPE and the output is a corrected/modified image. For more information, see Šilha (2019).

Background Estimation and Subtraction

Background estimation and subtraction (IPE-BE) removes noise which the previous module, IPE-IR, could not do. Such noise comes from a nearby high brightness celestial object (a nebula, star, or the Moon), or imperfect observation conditions, such as stray light, reflections from the dome or the telescope itself. This IPE uses subsequent sigma clipping to estimate the background noise before it is removed from the image. IPE-BE takes the IPE-IR modified image as the input and produces the estimated background image and the input image corrected by this background image. For more information, please see Šilha (2019).

Objects Search and Centroiding (Segmentation)

The abbreviation for objects' search and centroiding is IPE-SC, and it is one of the more algorithmically complex elements of the IPS. The first step is the search algorithm which finds a pixel whose intensity exceeds a predefined threshold (which is calculated depending on the image's SNR). The pixel is saved and used in the next step – the centroiding algorithm. To measure the frame object's position and total intensity, the centroiding algorithm finds the object's centroid (centre-of-mass). The third, and the last part of this composite is the touch-down algorithm, which refines the centroid found in the previous step.

IPE-SC is also the last critical element which works with images – the output is a *.tsv* (tab separated values) text file containing each detected frame object on each row of the file. The columns implicitly created by tab separators hold important information for each object, such as *x* and *y* position of the centroid, its SNR, etc. (Šilha, 2019).

Astrometric Reduction

The second IPE which relies on the routines in the Astrometry.net (Lang et al., 2010) package, IPE-AR, reads the *(x, y)* coordinates of the *.tsv* file produced in the previous module (IPE-SC) and transforms them into equatorial coordinates *(α, δ)*. These values are calculated for each object and are then appended at the very end of each object's line. The information is crucial because it represents the location of an object on the celestial sphere. The output is therefore the same *.tsv* file as input, but with additional information.

Masking

By this point in the IPS, we only work with the *.tsv* files provided by the IPE-SC module, two steps back in the pipeline. The length of the file, and therefore the size, depends on the quality of a particular image and IPE-SC processing algorithms – there is a direct proportion between the number of detections and the length of the file in lines. In the case of AGO70 and a *regular* image (no dense fields with hundreds of stars), from experience, the files usually contain one to two hundred of objects. Typically, each space debris object is observed continuously during a set time period and this process results in a series of images. Additionally, as AGO70 tracks relatively slow space debris objects, the star background behind the currently tracked object remains unchanged for the most part of it. However, there are rare cases when a star visible in one image in the series can be shadowed by a different, less bright object (or by a cloud) in the second image of the series. It can then become visible again in the third image and so on. Nevertheless, IPE-MR is used to remove objects if they appear in the approximately same position in at least two different images of the series.

Despite it seeming like an easy solution to a frequent problem, there are several problems with this approach:

- What if we track an especially slow space debris or near-Earth asteroid which appears not to be moving?
- Comparing each image in the series with every other can computationally prove to be expensive and time consuming.
- How do we determine whether two observations of an object from two images in the same series actually belong to the same object?

All of these, and many more obstacles are solved and described in detail in the next paragraphs. Naturally, the first step is to read all the provided *.tsv* files from the same series. Since this module is preceded by other IPEs, which have modified the images and even the series themselves, it is safe to assume that the input text files are from the correct series and are clean. However, as this IPE is the first one in contact with the freshly created *.tsv* files (files), their validity is ensured by checking each line and an exception is raised if the columns are missing or redundant. At this point in the algorithm, we have read all the files and have frame objects in memory, where the variable represents the number of files in the series and the variable represents the number of objects in a file. can be calculated as

$$M = \sum_{i=1}^{N} m_i,$$

where m_i is the number of objects in the ith file.

It is important to define which objects represent the same celestial space debris object. As mentioned before, there can be many disruptions—either external or internal—while tracking an object. We, therefore, define a threshold σ_m [arcsec] which is a radius of a circle around an image object. The next part determines whether a different image object falls below this threshold. To do this, we calculate angular distance θ_{ij} [arcsec] of the two image objects o_i and o_j by using the cosine rule as follows:

$$\theta_{ij} = \cos^{-1}\left[\sin\delta_i \sin\delta_j + \cos\delta_i \cos\delta_j \cos\left(\alpha_j - \alpha_i\right)\right].$$

Therefore,

$$o_i = o_j \Leftrightarrow \theta_{ij} < \sigma_m.$$

For a visual example of this mechanism, refer to Figure 3 below.

Figure 3. A graph representing angular distance. The ellipse around object number 1 represents the area of interest.
Object number 2 falls in this region, is considered to be identical to object number 1 and is removed. Object number 3 is considered to be a different object and is preserved.

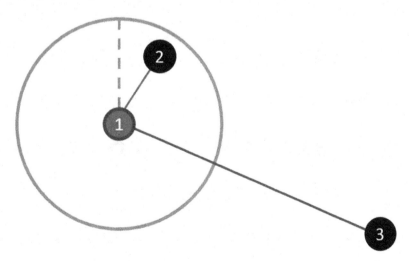

For example, if two frame objects have $\theta_{ij} < 1$ arcsec/s, they are ruled as the same celestial object and are removed from the memory. The value of σ_m can be changed freely. For slow celestial objects, it is better to set it to a lower value than for faster celestial objects. Generally, the value needs to be slightly lower than the velocity of the tracked celestial object between frames. Based on our experience from the data acquired by AGO70, the ideal value of σ_m is 6 arcsec/s.

Therefore, when the algorithm can identify the identical objects, it needs to check every image object against every other image object and compare them by using the aforementioned cosine rule. Naively comparing every object from one image with every object from other images can prove ineffective and the complexity is at best, where is the number of images. To mitigate this problem, the algorithm ignores the origin of the object – it is unimportant which file the object comes from.

This reduces the time complexity to $O(n^2)$. Furthermore, it is nonsensical to compare two frame objects which are too far apart from each other – there is no chance that the object in the left top corner could be the same as the object in the right bottom corner. The key to this problem is to sort the frame objects according to their right ascension α. As depicted in Figure 4 we ignore the δ dimension (y axis) and look only at α (x axis). The algorithm iterates over the objects in such a manner that it takes o_u as the first object of interest and looks at the closest object o_v in the list. The following property must be met if it is allowed to proceed: $|\alpha_u - \alpha_v \langle \sigma_m|$. This characteristic optimizes the algorithm – there is no point in determining θ_{uv} if the difference between α_u and α_v is larger than σ_m. The time complexity after this step has been reduced to $O(n^2)$ in the worst-case scenario.

Figure 4. Ignoring δ dimension puts all the objects in one line and simplifies the problem. For visualization purposes, all the δ values have been "normalized" to an arbitrary value (in this case, 3).

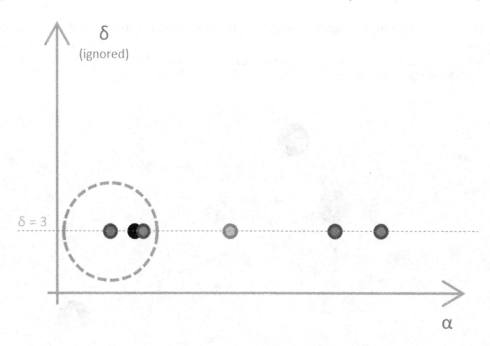

Tracklet Building

Space debris, or other commonly observed celestial objects, orbit around the Earth. This can be simplified by the fact that the field-of-view in the case of the most used telescopes is so small that the celestial object appears to be moving according to the laws of linear motion (Oda et al., 2014). Several algorithms which are commonly used in these types of problems were considered – such as Hough transform (Duda & Hart, 1972), linear regression, etc. In the end, Simple Linear Regression (further SLR) which is a statistical concept modelling a relationship between a dependent variable, commonly denoted as y and an independent variable, commonly denoted as x, was chosen. In principle, SLR models a line that describes a trend in the data, or, when concerning AGO70 observations, the predicted, imaginary trajectory of a celestial object, as shown below in Figure 5.

Figure 5. One of many possible representations of a tracklet. Darker objects/objects which are closest to the line are the objects that represent a tracklet.

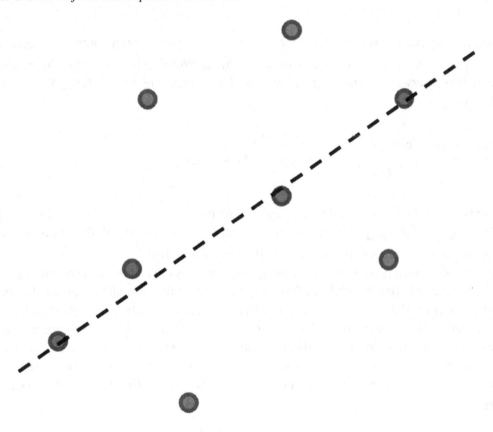

The first step in applying SLR to the data is to take a frame object $p_{1i}\left(\alpha_{1i}, \delta_{1i}, t_{1i}\right)$ from the first image and a frame object $p_{2i}\left(\alpha_{2i}, \delta_{2i}, t_{2i}\right)$ from the second image, where t stands for epoch at which the object was observed. Then, a line l_{1i2j} such that $p_{1i} \wedge p_{2j} \in l_{1i2j}$ is created. At the same time, baseline/ground truth values for:

- apparent angular velocity $\omega_{\alpha\delta,1i,2j}$ and
- position angle $PA_{\alpha\delta,1i,2j}$ are calculated.

This is done for all combinations of all frame objects contained in the first frame c and in the second frame d and yields $c_N d_N$ lines in total. The algorithm considers each object for each line, which means that the time complexity in the worst-case scenario is exponential.

The main computational core of the algorithms lies in the determination whether the next object $p_{3k}\left(\alpha_{3k},\delta_{3k},t_{3k}\right)$ belongs to the currently constructed tracklet. Its distance from the previously created line given by equation $ax_0 + by_0 + c = 0$ is calculated by using the standard Euclidean distance formula, $\dfrac{\left|ax_0 + by_0 + c\right|}{\sqrt{a^2 + b^2}}$. If the distance is lower than a predefined threshold σ_{tD}, i.e.

$$\frac{\left|a\alpha_0 + b\delta_0 + c\right|}{\sqrt{a^2 + b^2}} < \sigma_{tD}$$

the algorithm calculates apparent angular velocity $\omega_{\alpha\delta,2j,3k}$ by calculating angular distance with the formula mentioned in the previous section, divides it by $\Delta t*86400$ (where ∇t is the difference in time between the two observations/objects), and compares it to another pre-set threshold $\sigma_{t\omega}$.

In other words,

$$\frac{\cos^{-1}\left[\sin\delta_i \sin\delta_j + \cos\delta_i \cos\delta_j \cos\left(\alpha_j - \alpha_i\right)\right]}{"t}*86400 \geq \sigma_{t\omega}.$$

If these two conditions are met, the last value compared with yet another threshold σ_{tPA}, is position angle $PA_{\alpha\delta,2j,3k}$ i.e. $PA_{\alpha\delta,2j,3k} < \sigma_{tPA}$. It is very important to stress out that all three of these conditions must be satisfied in order to accept the considered object/observation.

The process described in the previous paragraph is iteratively done with all the remaining frame objects in all the remaining frames, while the frame objects, which fall below all the defined thresholds, are added to the tracklet and the line is corrected in such a manner that it reflects the new data. It is possible that several frame objects are considered at one step of the iteration. To clearly distinguish which frame object has the bigger possibility of belonging to the tracklet, weights w_i, w_j were introduced into the SLR.

These weights are calculated by comparing the calculated values of D_i (as in distance), ω_i and PA_i with thresholds σ_{iD}, $\sigma_{t\omega}$ and σ_{tPA}, and assigning bigger weights to those for which the absolute difference is smaller:

$$w_i > w_j \Leftrightarrow \left(\left|D_i - \sigma_{tD}\right| < \left|D_j - \sigma_{tD}\right|\right) \wedge \left(\left|\omega_i - \sigma_{t\omega}\right| < \left|\omega_j - \sigma_{t\omega}\right|\right) \wedge \left(\left|PA_i - \sigma_{tPA}\right| < \left|PA_j - \sigma_{tPA}\right|\right).$$

At the end of this IPE, we are left with a complex data structure containing ground truths, the line, successfully filtered frame objects, their values and weights. See Figure 6 below for a visualization of this data structure. Furthermore, the objects which have the biggest fit need to be passed into the tracklet for the next step. This is done by writing the tracklet into a text file. However, even though the previously mentioned complex data structure is 2-dimensional, the second dimension is ignored, which means that we effectively erase the additional frame objects which also fulfilled all the conditions but had lower weights.

Figure 6. A weighted tracklet example. Object candidates which are at the top are considered the most probable to be the object the observer is looking for.

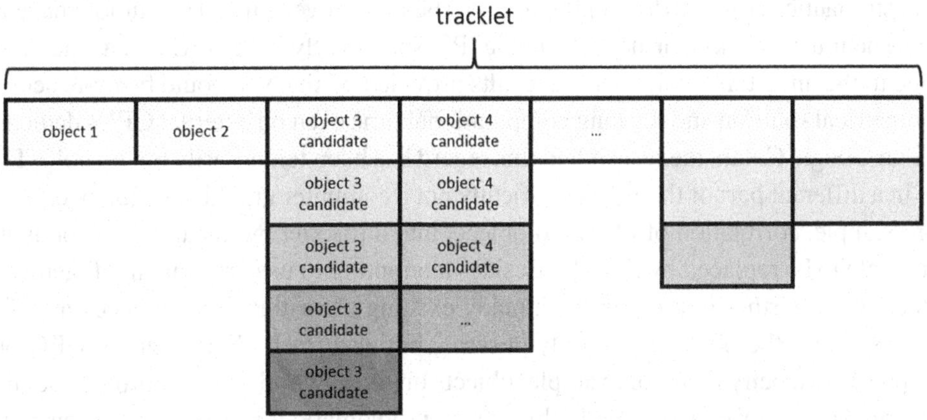

Object Identification

The next step, IPE-OI, has been developed to correlate a created tracklet from the previous step, with a space debris catalogue to find out which object was observed. The three parameters, angular distance θ, position angle *PA* and angular velocity ω, used throughout the two previous IPEs, Masking and Tracklet building, are calculated for both the tracklet and each catalogue object (by using Simplified General Perturbations model (Vallado et al., 2006) and Two-Line Element data (Vallado et al. 2006)) and compare the values. The output of this IPE is the object for which the difference between the two vectors of values was lower than the predefined thresholds.

Data Format Transformation

The conversion of astrometric positions from the internal tracklet format (Figure 6) to Consultative Committee for Space Data Systems (CCSDS) (Kummer, 1987), Tracking Data Message (TDM) ("Consultative Committee for Space Data Systems: Pink Book", 2017), Astronomical Institute of University of Bern's OBS, Minor Planet Center (MPC) format ("Minor Planet Center: Format For Astrometric Observations Of Comets, Minor Planets and Natural Satellites", 2019) and Interagency Space Debris Coordination Committee (IADC) light curves formats is done in this IPE.

FUTURE RESEARCH DIRECTIONS

Due to the heterogenous nature of IPS in the context of the many different algorithms used, there is always a room for future improvements in each of the algorithms. One of the more suitable modules, in this regard, is IPE-SC. Image segmentation that is done as a part of IPE-SC is a prime candidate for artificial intelligence, more specifically neural networks or machine learning. The recent advancements in neural networks' applications on computer vision and computer graphics enable and justify this direction.

There are currently attempts to use neural networks or machine learning to help with computational problems in astronautics (Liu, 2019) and the use will be rising over time. The authors have already attempted to use neural networks (further NN) in the IPS, specifically in the IPE-SC, as mentioned above. However, due to the uncertainty whether the results provided by the NN would be more accurate than a classical geometrical solution and the long computational time even on external GPUs dedicated for NN applications on Google Colab, the research in this regard has been temporarily put on hold. The application of NNs in a different part of the IPS, specifically not a computer graphics/vision one, is considered, as well. For example, correlation of observed objects into a tracklet by linear regression is yet another suitable candidate to be replaced by the NN. Besides attempting to use artificial intelligence in the IPS, it is vital to continue further improving the already existing algorithms where necessary. The current state of the IPS allows the observer not only observe, but also track objects on the GEO orbit which have lower apparent velocity than, for example, objects on the LEO orbit which orbit closer to the Earth and therefore appear to move faster. While this is also problematic for the hardware configuration and therefore out of scope for this chapter, faster running time of the IPS allows the observer to determine which other objects are worth tracking next. To guarantee fast processing times for each of the IPEs, the existing algorithms in computer graphics need to be parallelised, or even completely substituted with better alternatives from more recent research.

CONCLUSION

A modular pipeline for space debris observations, IPS, was introduced and two of its nine complex Image Processing Elements were described in detail. It has been largely developed by the Faculty of Mathematics, Physics and Informatics (FMPI) of the Comenius University in Bratislava, Slovakia. The pipeline has been tested and validated on real examples taken by the AGO70 telescope. The fact that every IPE performs its operation in real time ensures that IPS can process large number of data fast. See Figure 7 for results of IPE-TB (tracklet building) which shows an exponential relationship between the average number of frame objects and number of found tracklets. This result was expected – larger number of frame objects leads to more initial combinations, and therefore to more created initial lines. At the same time, resolution of the images does not change which means that higher number object frames have higher density of objects. Conversely to the implied nature of *linear* regression as the main algorithm behind the module, IPE-TB, due to corrections made to the line because of the new objects, can correlate even objects with hundreds of observations. With this number of observations, the observed object does no longer appear as if it was moving on a line – the trajectory is clearly curved. This behaviour was expected and is welcome, even though such huge observation series are rare at AGO. Additionally, there is no need to extend this IPE for curved trajectories in the future, in the case AGO70 would have been upgraded.

Figure 7. Tracklet building results across tens of tracklets. Number of found tracklets is a function of average number of frame objects per frame.

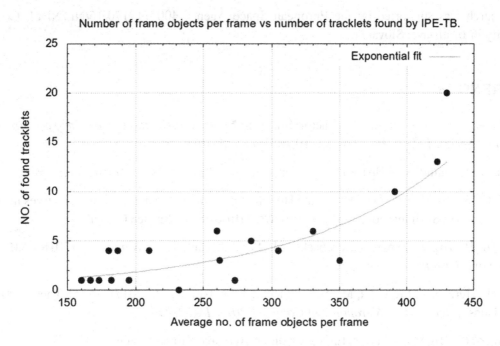

Table 1 shows a table containing results of masking of several tested objects on different orbits. The number of images per series ranged from 7 to 17 and the number of frame objects in each frame ranged between approx. 800 to approx. 2200. As can be seen in the 5th column from the left, IPE-MR was able to remove at least 70% of all frame objects in all cases. Out of all the known and identified stars in the images, IPE-MR was able to remove at least 84.5% and 99.3% at most. This success is diminished by the fact that from the two last series, one observation of a real object was removed. While this behaviour is obviously undesirable, the 7/8 observations from the first series and the 16/17 observations from the seconds series, is still enough to produce a tracklet and gain valuable data about the observed objects. Orbit types mentioned in the Table 1 below are further explained in the section "Key terms and definitions."

Table 1. A small excerpt of all the tested cases. A few interesting cases, namely the two observations of real objects

Object	Orbit type	No. of images/ frames	No. of frame objects	No. of removed frame objects [%]	No. of stars	No. of removed stars [%]	No. of real objects after removal
2018 CB	NEA	7	1383	**71.7**	737	**84.5**	7/7
11036A	GNSS	8	939	**80.6**	264	**95.5**	8/8
E10277A	eGEO	8	814	**77.0**	139	**99.3**	8/8
E14328A	Molniya	11	1139	**79.6**	209	**99.0**	7/8
E15204A	GEO	17	2160	**74.9**	772	**96.0**	16/17

ACKNOWLEDGMENT

This research was supported by the European Space Agency[4000117170/16/NL/NDe]; Comenius University in Bratislava, Slovakia.

REFERENCES

Bertin, E., & Arnouts, S. (1996). SExtractor: Software for source extraction. *Astronomy & Astrophysics. Supplement Series, 117*(2), 393–404. doi:10.1051/aas:1996164

Consultative Committee for Space Data Systems. (2018). *Tracking Data Message*. Pink Book.

Duda, R. O., & Hart, P. E. (1971). Use of the Hough transformation to detect lines and curves in pictures (No. SRI-TN-36). Sri International Menlo Park Ca Artificial Intelligence Center.

Fiedler, H., Herzog, J., Hinze, A., Prohaska, M., Schildknecht, T., & Weigel, M. (2018). *SMARTnet-Evolution and Results*. Academic Press.

Fiedler, H., Herzog, J., Prohaska, M., Schildknecht, T., & Weigel, M. (2017). SMARTnet (TM)-Status and Statistics. *International Astronautical Congress 2017, IAC 2017.*

Klinkrad, H. (2010). Space debris. Encyclopedia of Aerospace Engineering.

Kouprianov, V. (2008). Distinguishing features of CCD astrometry of faint GEO objects. *Advances in Space Research, 41*(7), 1029–1038. doi:10.1016/j.asr.2007.04.033

Kummer, H. (1987). The consultative committee for space data systems (CCSDS) planned and potential use of the recommendations. *Acta Astronautica, 16*, 199–205. doi:10.1016/0094-5765(87)90106-8

Lang, D., Hogg, D. W., Mierle, K., Blanton, M., & Roweis, S. (2010). Astrometry. net: Blind astrometric calibration of arbitrary astronomical images. *The Astronomical Journal, 139*(5), 1782–1800. doi:10.1088/0004-6256/139/5/1782

Liu, D., Chin, T., & Rowntree, T. (2019). Optical Detection of Geostationary Objects Using End-To-End Deep Learning. *Proceedings of International Astronautical Conference 2019.*

Mink, D. J. (1998, September). WCSTools: An image astrometry toolkit. *Bulletin of the American Astronomical Society, 30*, 1144.

Minor Planet Center. (2019). *Format for Astrometric Observations Of Comets, Minor Planets and Natural Satellites*. Retrieved from https://minorplanetcenter.net/iau/info/ObsFormat.html

Oda, H., Yanagisawa, T., Kurosaki, H., & Tagawa, M. (2014, September). Optical observation, image-processing, and detection of space debris in geosynchronous Earth orbit. *Proceedings of the Advanced Maui Optical and Space Surveillance Technologies Conference.*

Park, J. H., Yim, H. S., Choi, Y. J., Jo, J. H., Moon, H. K., Park, Y. S., Bae, Y.-H., Park, S.-Y., Roh, D.-G., Cho, S., Choi, E.-J., Kim, M.-J., & Choi, E. J. (2018). OWL-Net: A global network of robotic telescopes for satellite observation. *Advances in Space Research, 62*(1), 152–163. doi:10.1016/j.asr.2018.04.008

Park, S. Y., Choi, J., Roh, D. G., Park, M., Jo, J. H., Yim, H. S., Park, Y.-S., Bae, Y.-H., Park, J.-H., Moon, H.-K., Choi, Y.-J., Cho, S., & Choi, Y. J. (2016). Development of a data reduction algorithm for optical wide field patrol (OWL) II: Improving measurement of lengths of detected streaks. *Journal of Astronomy and Space Sciences, 33*(3), 221–227. doi:10.5140/JASS.2016.33.3.221

Šilha, J. (2019). Slovak optical telescope and image processing pipeline for the space debris and NEA observations and research. ESA NEO and Debris Conference.

Vallado, D., Crawford, P., Hujsak, R., & Kelso, T. S. (2006, August). Revisiting spacetrack report #3. In AIAA/AAS Astrodynamics Specialist Conference and Exhibit (p. 6753). Academic Press.

Weigel, M., Meinel, M., & Fiedler, H. (2015, October). Processing of optical telescope observations with the space object catalogue BACARDI. In *25th International Symposium on Space Flight Dynamics ISSFD* (*Vol. 19*, p. 23). Academic Press.

Wells, D. C., & Greisen, E. W. (1979). FITS - A Flexible Image Transport System. In Image Processing in Astronomy (p. 445). Academic Press.

ADDITIONAL READING

Kouprianov, V. (2012). Apex II+ FORTE: data acquisition software for space surveillance. *39th COSPAR Scientific Assembly 2012*, 14-22.

Schildknecht, T. (2007). Optical surveys for space debris. *The Astronomy and Astrophysics Review, 14*(1), 41–111. doi:10.100700159-006-0003-9

Šilha, J. (2019). Small telescopes and their application in space debris research and space surveillance tracking. *Contributions of the Astronomical Observatory Skalnaté Pleso, 49*(2), 307–319.

Tóth, J., Kornoš, L., Zigo, P., Gajdoš, Š., Kalmančok, D., Világi, J., ... Galád, A. (2015). All-sky Meteor Orbit System AMOS and preliminary analysis of three unusual meteor showers. *Planetary and Space Science, 118*, 102–106. doi:10.1016/j.pss.2015.07.007

Zigo, M., Šilha, J., & Krajčovič, S. (2019). BVRI Photometry of Space Debris Objects at the Astronomical and Geophysical Observatory in Modra. *In Proceedings* of *Advanced Maui Optical and Space Surveillance Technologies Cenference (AMOS)*, Conference, Maui, Hawaii, USA.

KEY TERMS AND DEFINITIONS

AGO: Astronomical and Geophysical Observatory in Modra, Slovakia, belonging to the Comenius University in Bratislava, Slovakia; it contains known telescopes such as All-Sky Meteor System (AMOS), AGO70, or a 60-cm telescope.

AGO70: A 70-cm Newton mount telescope with a CCD camera and BVRI filters capable of deep sky as well as low-Earth orbit observations.

Astrometry: Scientific discipline to measure and compute celestial objects' positions and movements.

FITS: Flexible image transport system; an image format used to transfer images/data between different entities.

GEO: Geostationary orbit; orbit on which the satellites match their orbit velocities with Earth's rotation.

GNSS: Global navigation satellite system; an established orbit used for GPS satellites.

IPE: Image processing module, a single self-sufficient and modular unit for partial space debris observations processing.

IPS: Image processing system, the whole space debris observations processing software package uniting all IPEs to work in coordinated way.

Molniya: A highly elliptical orbit used for telecommunication, weather monitoring, and other purposes used historically mainly by Russian Molniya satellites (hence the name).

NEA: Near-Earth asteroids; asteroids which have their orbits placed closed to Earth.

Tracklet: Collection of at least four consecutive observations in time.

Chapter 4

A Robust System for Road Sign Detection and Classification Using LeNet Architecture Based on Convolutional Neural Network

Amal Bouti

Department of Computer Sciences, Sidi Mohamed Ben Abdellah University, Morocco

Mohamed Adnane Mahraz

https://orcid.org/0000-0002-0966-9654

Sidi Mohamed Ben Abdellah University, Morocco

Jamal Riffi

Department of Computer Sciences, Sidi Mohamed Ben Abdellah University, Morocco

Hamid Tairi

Department of Computer Sciences, Sidi Mohamed Ben Abdellah University, Morocco

ABSTRACT

In this chapter, the authors report a system for detection and classification of road signs. This system consists of two parts. The first part detects the road signs in real time. The second part classifies the German traffic signs (GTSRB) dataset and makes the prediction using the road signs detected in the first part to test the effectiveness. The authors used HOG and SVM in the detection part to detect the road signs captured by the camera. Then they used a convolutional neural network based on the LeNet model in which some modifications were added in the classification part. The system obtains an accuracy rate of 96.85% in the detection part and 96.23% in the classification part.

DOI: 10.4018/978-1-7998-4444-0.ch004

I. INTRODUCTION

Detection and recognition of signs is an automobile equipment that reads and interprets permanent and temporary signs located at the edge or over the road, in order to inform the driver in case he could not see them. Speed limitation and over-ride signs are particularly concerned. Signs detection and recognition works through a camera mounted behind the interior rearview mirror. It detects signs located the left, right or over the road and compares it with an internal dataset. Once the sign is recognized, the driver is notified of the situation through a visual on the GPS or instrumentation. It is a useful aid for the driver who, in the ambient traffic, will not necessarily have seen the sign. Depending on the system, the car goes up to compare its speed with the current limitation and alert the driver if he is overspending. In the long term, we can also imagine that the optical reading of the signs can communicate with the adaptive cruise control. It is the vehicle that would automatically decide how fast to drive.

Traffic Sign Detection and Recognition (TSDR) has been very popular in recent years. This is due to the large number of applications that such a system can provide:

- Maintenance of signs.
- Signs inventory.
- Driving assistance.
- Smart autonomous vehicles.

A. Road Sign Detection:

Methods of detection of road signs are divided into three classes. Methods based on color, shape or machine learning. The dominant colors of most road signs are red, blue or yellow. Many authors (Lillo-Castellano, et al., 2015; Ellahyani, et al., 2016) use this property to detect signs. An associated component segmentation based on a color model is used. The regions of interest are then validated by a recognition algorithm or an appearance model. These methods are usually fast and invariant to translation, rotation, and scaling. Since color can be easily affected by lighting conditions, the main difficulty of color-based methods is how to be invariant to different lighting conditions. These methods tend to follow a common pattern: the image is transformed into a color space and then thresholded. The two spaces HSV and HSI are very used by researchers because they are based on human perception of colors and encode color information in one channel instead of three (Ardianto, et al., 2017).

For shape-based methods, the contours of the image are analyzed by a structural or global approach. These methods are generally more robust than color-based ones because they handle the gradient of the image and can handle grayscale images. These methods are very sensible to occlusions and deformation, that affects considerably their performances. To overcome this problem some researchers proposed to detect circular road signs using the circle detection algorithm EDCircles (Kaplan, et al., 2016) and other authors proposed to detect circular and triangular signs using HOG and Linear SVM (Zaklouta and Stanciulescu, 2014). systems that adopt shape-based methods to minimize color change due to lighting and climate change face the problem of detecting occluded and damaged signs that require color-based methods.

Finally, for methods based on machine learning, a classifier (cascade, SVM, neural networks) is trained based on examples. It is applied on a sliding window that traverses the image on several scales. These methods combine geometry and photometry but can be a costly step in computing time. They require the constitution of a learning base by type of signs, tedious step when the number of objects to be detected is large. Many researchers (Ellahyani, et al., 2016; Brkić, et al., 2010; Chen and Lu, 2016; Yi, et al., 2016; Bouti, et al., 2017) adopt this approach of combination between color-based methods and shape-based methods that can help to minimize the rate of false positives and increase the rate of true positives.

B. Road Sign Classification:

The methods of classification of road signs are divided into two classes. Learning methods based on hand-crafted features and in-depth learning methods. The basic idea of learning methods based on hand-crafted features is to design an algorithm to extract the characteristics of the image and form a classifier over it. Indeed, the overall accuracy of traditional methods depends primarily on the feature extraction algorithm because there are powerful classifiers, such as SVM or Random Forest, that can accurately learn nonlinear decision boundaries. However, if classes overlap in the feature space, classifiers will not be able to discriminate classes accurately (Habibi, et al2016; Zaklouta, et al., 2011; Chaiyakhan, et al., 2015). SVM classifier with HOG represents also one of the most used techniques for the classification of textual information in road signs.

As shown in many researches in the literature (Chaiyakhan, et al., 2015; Yang, et al., 2018), in-depth learning methods such as convolutional neural networks learn a highly non-linear function to project the raw image into a function space where classes are linearly separable and non-overlapping (Habibi, et al., 2016).

Our system consists of two main phases, detection and classification. In the detection phase we used HOG and linear SVM to detect road signs. Although deep learning approaches have proven their superiority in similar image detection problem, it is interesting to find out how a traditional computer vision approach performs in a situation like this. The representation of the HOG features and SVM greatly improves the results obtained and shows good results in terms of accuracy. The linear SVM not only achieves high accuracy but also costs least compared with another kernel function (Ma and Huang, 2015). In the classification phase we used the Convolutional Neural Networks (CNN) technique which has a formidable capacity to solve this kind of problem (i.e. image classification). We used an already existing CNN architecture LeNet and make some modifications to have the best performance and trained it to recognize signs using a dataset called German Traffic Sign Recognition Benchmark (GTSRB).

To do this, we have structured our article in 3 sections: In the first section, we will present the different methods used in our system among them the convolutional neural networks as well as their interests in the field of classification of images. In the second section, we will describe our system. Finally, in the third section we will show the different results obtained with a small comparison with other systems and in the end, we finish with a general conclusion.

II. MATERIALS AND METHODS

A. Histogram of Oriented Gradients (HOG):

The HOG feature descriptors were introduced by Dalal and Triggs (2005), researchers at INRIA Grenoble, at the CVPR conference in June 2005 in their pedestrian detection work. The essential idea behind the histogram of oriented gradients is that the local appearance and the object shape in an image that can be described by the intensity distribution of the gradients or the direction of the contours. The implementation of these descriptors can be obtained by dividing the image into small connected regions, called cells, and for each cell a histogram of the gradient directions or contour orientations for the pixels in the cell is calculated. The combination of these histograms then represents the descriptor. For best results, the local histograms are normalized in contrast, calculating a measure of intensity over wider areas than cells, called blocks, and using this value to normalize all cells in the block. This normalization allows a better resistance to the changes of illuminations and shadows

1. Gradient Computation:

A pre-processing step can be performed before the gradient is calculated, so that the colors of the image are normalized, and gamma correction correct. This step was finally not necessary, the standardization of the descriptor itself being enough. The first step of the method is the gradient calculation, the most common method for doing this is to apply a 1-D centered derivative filter in the horizontal and vertical directions. The following masks are used for this: $[-1, 0, 1]$ and $[-1, 0, 1]^T$. In the case of color images, the gradient is calculated separately for each component, and for each pixel the gradient of the largest standard is retained.

2. Histogram Construction:

The second step is the creation of histograms of gradient orientation. This is done in small square cells (4x4 to 12x12 pixels). Each pixel of the cell then votes for a class of the histogram, depending on the gradient orientation at that point. The vote of the pixel is weighted by the intensity of the gradient at this point. The histograms are uniform from 0 to 180 ° (unsigned case) or from 0 to 360 ° (signed case).

3. Descriptor Block:

An important step is the standardization of descriptors to avoid disparities due to illumination variations. This step also introduces redundancy into the descriptor. For this purpose, authors group several cells in a block, which is the unit on which the normalization is performed. The blocks overlap, so the same cell participates several times in the final descriptor, as a member of different blocks. Two types of block geometry are available: rectangular (R-HOG) or circular (C-HOG). The experiments done by Dalal and Triggs (2005) showed that the best performance was obtained for rectangular blocks containing 3x3 cells of 6x6 pixels each. A minor performance improvement is achieved by weighting the pixels by a Gaussian window on the block, decreasing the contribution of the pixels to the edges.

4. Block Normalization

Dalal and Triggs (2005) explored four different methods for block normalization. Let v be the non-normalized vector containing all histograms in a given block, $\| v \|_k$ be its k-norm for k = 1, 2 and e be some small constant. Then the normalization factor can be one of the following:

- L2-norm: $f = \dfrac{v}{\sqrt{\|v\|_2^2 + e^2}}$ (Eq. 1)

- L2-hys: L2-norm followed by clipping (limiting the maximum values of v to 0.2) and renormalizing.

- L1-norm: $f = \dfrac{v}{\|v\|_1 + e}$ (Eq.2)

- L1-sqrt: $f = \sqrt{\dfrac{v}{\|v\|_1 + e}}$ (Eq.3)

In addition, the scheme L2-hys can be computed by first taking the L2-norm, clipping the result, and then renormalizing. In their experiments, Dalal and Triggs (2005) found the L2-hys, L2-norm, and L1-sqrt schemes provide similar performance, while the L1-norm provides slightly less reliable performance; however, all four methods showed very significant improvement over the non-normalized data.

5. Classification:

The final step in the object detection process is the use of HOG descriptors to drive a supervised classifier. This step is not part of the definition of the HOG descriptor itself and different types of classifiers can be used. Dalal and Triggs (2005) voluntarily choose a simple classifier, a linear kernel SVM, to essentially measure HOG input. They specify that it would be interesting to develop a cascade-based method such as the Viola and Jones method, using HOGs. They specify that the use of a Gaussian kernel improves performance by 3%, for a false positive rate per window of 10^{-4} but a much higher computational cost.

B. Support Vector Machine (SVM):

Support Vector Machine (SVM) is a supervised machine learning algorithm initially defined for discrimination, that is, predicting a binary qualitative variable. They were then generalized to the forecast of a quantitative variable. In the case of discrimination of a dichotomous variable, they are based on finding the optimal margin hyperplane, where possible, classifies or separates the data correctly while being as far as possible from all observations. The principle is therefore to find a classifier, or a function of discrimination, whose capacity of generalization (quality of forecasting) is the greatest possible. SVM can be used for classification, regression SVR and detection outlets. However, it is mostly used in classification problems. It can solve linear and non-linear problems and work well for many practical problems.

A version of SVM for regression was proposed in 1996 by Vapnik et al. (Drucker, et al., 1996). This method is called support-vector regression (SVR) has been developed to solve nonlinear forecasting problems. Unlike ANN models, the SVR model can avoid over-learning, local minima, and dimension disaster problems (Hong, et al., 2019).

The first part of the process is to create a model from the dataset. This is the learning of the class. The dataset is broken down into a set of positive elements (containing one element of the class) and a set of negative elements (not containing any element of the class). A hyperplane separating the elements of each of the two sets is calculated in order to maximize the margin (Figure 1), that is, the resistance between the samples and the hyperplane. For this, the study space is transcribed on a larger space where the existence of a linear separator is possible. Finally, the set of positive examples is on one side of the hyperplane while the set of negative examples is on the other side. In the second part of the process, this model allows decision. If the vector is e of the hyperplane relative to the positive examples, then it is an element of the class. In the opposite case, it is not an element of the class. It may be noted that the distance of the characteristic vector to the hyperplane gives an evaluation of the reliability of the decision. Indeed, if this distance is very small, the decision will be less sharp because the example is very close to the two classes.

The advantages of support vector machines are:

- Effective in high dimensional spaces.
- Still effective in cases where number of dimensions is greater than the number of samples.
- Uses a subset of training points in the decision function (called support vectors), so it is also memory efficient.
- Versatile: different Kernel functions can be specified for the decision function. Common kernels are provided, but it is also possible to specify custom kernels.

C. Deep Learning:

This family of algorithms has made significant progress in the areas of image classification and language processing.

The Deep Learning models are built on the same model as the MLP multilayer perceptron. However, it should be emphasized that the various intermediate layers are more numerous. Each of the intermediate layers will be subdivided into sub-part, dealing with a sub-problem, simpler and providing the result to the next layer, and so on.

There are different algorithms of Deep Learning. We can cite:

- Deep Neural Networks: These networks are like MLP (Multilayer Perceptron) networks but with more hidden layers. The increase in the number of layers, allows a network of neurons to detect slight variations of the learning model, favoring over-learning or over-fitting.
- Convolutional Neural Networks (CNN): The problem is divided into subparts, and for each part, a cluster of neurons will be created to study this specific portion. For example, for a color image, it is possible to divide the image over width, height and depth (colors).
- Deep Belief Network Machine: These algorithms work in a non-supervised first phase, followed by supervised classical training. This unsupervised learning step, furthermore, facilitates super-vised learning.

D. Convolutional Neural Network (CNN):

Convolutional neural networks are currently the most efficient models for classifying images. Designated by the acronym CNN, they have two distinct parts. In input, an image is provided in the form of a matrix of pixels. It has 2 dimensions for a grayscale image. The color is represented by a third dimension, of depth 3 to represent the fundamental colors (Red, Green, Blue).

The first part of a CNN is the actual convolutive part. It functions as a feature extractor of images. An image is passed through a succession of filters, or convolution kernels, creating new images called

Figure 1. Illustration of the principle of operation of SVMs for a simple linear case. The elements of a class (white circles) are separated from elements of another class (black circles) by the separating hyperplane (solid line) which maximizes the margin (dotted lines).

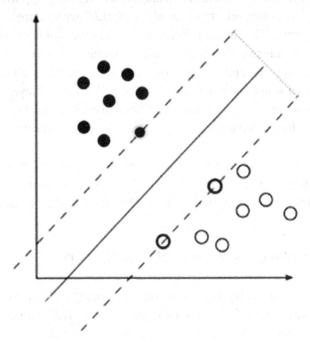

convolution maps. Some intermediate filters reduce the resolution of the image by a local maximum operation. Finally, the convolution maps are laid flat and concatenated into a feature vector, called the CNN code. This CNN code at the output of the convolutive portion is then connected to the input of a second portion, consisting of fully connected layers (multilayer perceptron). The role of this part is to combine the characteristics of the CNN code to classify the image.

The output is a final layer with one neuron per category. The numerical values obtained are generally normalized between 0 and 1, of sum 1, to produce a probability distribution on the categories. Creating a new convolutional neural network is expensive in terms of the expertise, material, and amount of annotated data needed.

It is first about fixing the architecture of the network, the number of layers, their sizes and the matrix operations that connect them. The training then consists of optimizing the network coefficients to minimize the output classification error. This training can take several weeks for the best CNNs, with many GPUs working on hundreds of thousands of annotated images.

Research teams specialize in improving CNN. They publish their technical innovations, as well as the details of networks driven on databases of references.

CNN architecture is formed by a stack of independent processing layers:

- Convolutional layer is the key component of convolutional neural networks and is still at least their first layer. Its purpose is to locate the presence of a set of features in the images received as input.

- Pooling layer: This type of layer is often placed between two convolution layers: it receives several feature maps as input and applies the pooling operation to each of them. The pooling operation consists of reducing the size of the images, while preserving their important characteristics.
- Correction layer (ReLU), often referred to as abuse 'ReLU' with reference to the activation function (linear grinding unit). The function ReLU designates the real nonlinear function defined by: $F(x) = \max(0, x)$ This function forces the neurons to return positive values.
- Fully connected layer is a perceptron type layer and is always the last layer of a neural network, convolutional or not - it is not characteristic of a CNN. This type of layer receives an input vector and produces a new output vector. For this, it applies a linear combination then possibly an activation function to the values received at the input. The last fully connected layer classifies the input image of the network
- Loss Layer specifies how network training penalizes the difference between the expected and actual signal. It is normally the last layer in the network. Various loss functions suitable for different tasks can be used. The 'Softmax' function is used to calculate the probability distribution on the output classes.

1. Typical Architecture of a Convolutional Neural Network:

A CNN is simply a stack of multiple layers of convolution, pooling, ReLU correction and the fully connected layer. Each image received as input will therefore be convolved, reduced and corrected several times, to finally form a vector. In the classification problem, this vector contains the probability of belonging to classes.

2. Setting the Layers:

A convolutional neural network is distinguished from another by the way the layers are stacked, but also parameterized. In fact, the convolution and pooling layers have hyper parameters, parameters whose value you must first define. The size of the feature maps at the output of the convolution and pooling layers depends on the hyper parameters. Each image (or feature map) has dimensions $W \times H \times D$, where W is its width in pixels, H is its height in pixels and D is the number of channels (1 for a black and white image, 3 for an image in colors).

The convolution layer has four hyperparameters:

- The number of filters K.
- The size F of the filters: each filter has dimensions $F \times F \times D$ pixels.
- The step S with which we slide the window corresponding to the filter on the image. For example, a step of 1 means that the window is moved one pixel at a time.
- The zero-padding P: we add to the input image of the layer a black outline of thickness P pixels. Without this outline, the output dimensions are smaller. Thus, the more one stack of convolution layers with $P = 0$, the more the input image of the network shrinks. So, we lose a lot of information quickly, which makes the task of extracting features difficult.

For each image of size W × H × D at the input, the convolution layer returns a matrix of dimensions $W_C \times H_C \times D_C$, where $W_C = \dfrac{W - F + 2P}{S} + 1$, $H_C = \dfrac{H - F + 2P}{S} + 1$ and $D_C = K$.

Choosing $P = \dfrac{F-1}{2}$ and $S = 1$ thus makes it possible to obtain feature maps of the same width and height as those received as input.

The pooling layer has only two hyper parameters:

- The size F of the cells: the image is divided into square cells of size F × F pixels.
- Step S: the cells are separated from each other by S pixels.

For each image size W×H×D at the input, the pooling layer returns a matrix of $W_P \times H_P \times D_P$ dimensions, where $W_P = \dfrac{W - F}{S} + 1$, $H_P = \dfrac{H - F}{S} + 1$ and $D_P = D$.

Like stacking, the choice of hyper parameters is done according to a classical scheme:

- For the convolution layer, the filters are small and dragged on the image one pixel at a time. The zero-padding value is chosen so that the width and height of the input volume are not changed at the output. In general, we choose F=3, P=1, S=1 or F=5, P=2, S=1.
- For the pooling layer, F=2 and S=2 is a wise choice. This eliminates 75% of the input pixels. We can also find F=3 and S=2: in this case, the cells overlap. Choosing larger cells causes too much loss of information and performs poorly in practice.

3. Learning Transfer:

To train a convolutional neural network is very expensive: the more layers stack up, the higher the number of convolutions and parameters to be optimized. The computer must be able to store several gigabytes of data and efficiently perform the calculations. That's why hardware manufacturers are stepping up their efforts to provide high-performance graphics processors (GPUs) that can quickly drive a deep neural network by paralleling calculations.

Transfer Learning allows you to do Deep Learning without having to spend a month of calculations. The principle is to use the knowledge acquired by a network of neurons when solving a problem in order to solve another similar. This is a transfer of knowledge, hence the name.

4. LeNet 5:

LeNet-5 is Yann LeCun's latest convolutional network designed for handwritten and printed character recognition. It is a convolutional neural network with enough input to receive multiple objects and multiple outputs called Space Displacement Neural Networks (SDNN), capable of recognizing strings in a single pass without segmentation prior. Sparse convolutional layers and max pooling are at the heart of the LeNet family of models. Although the exact details of the model vary considerably (Figure 2).

Figure 2. A graphical representation of a model LeNet.

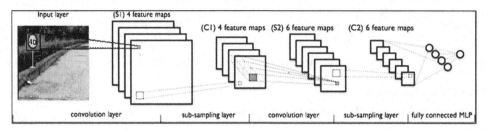

The lower layers are composed of convolution layers and max pool. The upper layers are however fully connected and correspond to a traditional MLP (hidden layer + logistic regression). The entry of the fully connected first layer is the set of all feature cards in the lower layer.

From the point of view of implementation, this means that the lower layers operate on the 4D tensors. These are then flattened into a 2D matrix of rasterized feature maps, to be compatible with the previous MLP implementation.

III. PROPOSED SYSTEM

In this paper, we report our built system which is based essentially on two steps: detection and classification. In the detection phase, we used the HOG algorithm to describe the distribution of image gradients in different orientations and to capture shape and aspect characteristics in detecting signs. Then the SVM classifier was used to filter false positives. For the classification phase, we have used convolutional neural networks based on Yann LeCun's model (Lecun, et al., 1998), and by adding some modifications to improve the model, to classify the German traffic signs into predefined classes then we will make a prediction by using the signs obtained in the detection part to check the efficiency of our classifier (Figure 3).

Figure 3. The proposed system for the detection and classification of road signs.

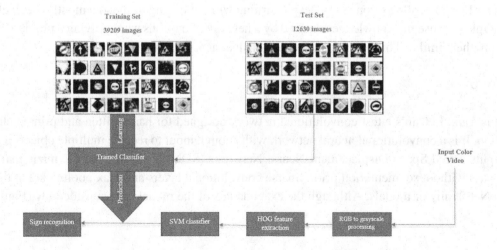

In the detection step, we have performed a histogram of oriented gradients (HOG) feature extraction on a labeled training set of images. Then, we trained a classifier with the set of sign and non-sign images. Finally, we used the trained classifier to detect signs. In this part linear Support Vector Machines (SVM) are used to train a model to classify if an image contains a sign or not. HOG is used as the feature representation.

The idea of HOG is instead of using each individual gradient direction of each individual pixel of an image, we group the pixels into small cells. For each cell, we compute all the gradient directions and group them into several orientation bins. We sum up the gradient magnitude in each sample. So stronger gradients contribute more weight to their bins, and effects of small random orientations due to noise is reduced. This histogram gives us a picture of the dominant orientation of that cell. Doing this for all cells gives us a representation of the structure of the image. The HOG features keep the representation of an object distinct but also allow for some variations in shape.

We can specify the number of orientations, pixels per cell, and cells per block for computing the HOG features of a single channel of an image. The number of orientations is the number of orientation bins that the gradients of the pixels of each cell will be split up in the histogram. The pixels per cells is the number of pixels of each row and column per cell over each gradient the histogram is computed. The cells per block specifies the local area over which the histogram counts in a given cell will be normalized. Having this parameter is said to generally lead to a more robust feature set.

The classifier algorithm we used in this step is called a Linear Support Vector Machine. As a safety measure, we use a scaler to transform the raw features before feeding them to our classifier for training or predicting, reducing the chance of our classifier to behave badly.

In the classification step, we constructed a deep learning pipeline to classify the German traffic Sign dataset (GTSRB). The initial model is a convolutional neural network based on Yann LeCun's LeNet architecture. TensorFlow and the scikit-learn pipeline framework were used with various combinations of transformers and estimators. The scikit-learn pipeline framework is used to manage different pipeline scenarios.

Pipeline can be used to group multiple estimators into one. This is useful because there is often a fixed sequence of steps in data processing, such as feature selection, normalization, and classification. Pipeline serves many purposes here:

- Convenience and encapsulation: Simply call fit and predict once on your data to fit a complete sequence of estimators.
- Selecting Common Parameters: You can search parameters of all pipeline estimators at the same time.
- Safety: Pipelines help prevent statistical leakage from your test data in the model formed during cross-validation, ensuring that the same samples are used to train transformers and predictors.

All but one of the pipeline estimators must be transformers (i.e. they must have a transformation method). The last estimator can be of any type (transformer, classifier, etc.).

A. Training Dataset

The dataset used is the German Traffic Sign Recognition Benchmark (GTSRB) (Stallkamp, et al., 2011). This dataset is composed of 39209 images and 43 classes. The objective is to classify the images of the

Figure 4. example of the predefined classes.

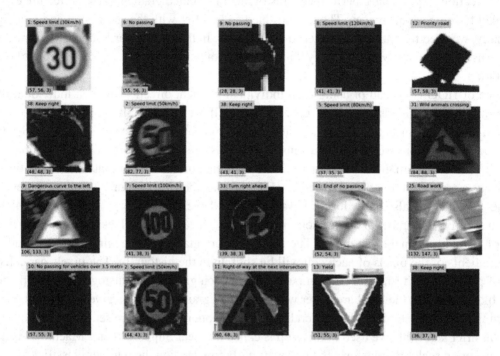

German dataset signs into the predefined classes (Figure 4). The images are of different sizes. The brightness of the image is quite random. Images can be rotated slightly. Images may not be exactly centered.

B. Model Architecture

Our model (Figure 5) is based on LeNet by Yann LeCun (Lecun, et al., 1998). It has 7 layers, including 3 convolutional layers, 2 layers of subsampling (pooling) and 1 fully connected layer, followed by the output layer. The convolutional layers use 5 out of 5 convolutions. The subsampling layers are 2 by 2 average clustering layers. The activation is ReLU except for the output layer that uses Softmax. The output has 43 classes. For this model the network works well. The performance seems to be pretty good. However, it shows a problem of overfitting (due to the lower number of epochs).

Figure 5. Architecture of our model

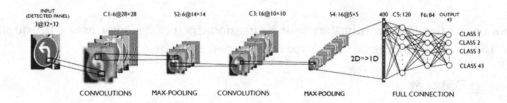

C. Optimization of LeNet Model Parameters

We tried to optimize the basic model (1st model which is LeNet) by modifying some parameters. We tested 3 models presented in Table 1. The modified parameters are convolution layer filters, fully connected layer neurons, epochs, learning rate and adding a dropout layer.

Table 1. The different models obtained after the modification of the 1st model.

	Filters in the 1st convolution layer	Filters in the 2nd convolution layer	Neurons in fully connected layer	Epochs	Learning rate	Adding a dropout layer
Model 1	5x5x6	5x5x16	120	5	$1.0\,e^{-3}$	X
Model 2	5x5x24	5x5x64	480	5	$1.0\,e^{-3}$	X
Model 3	5x5x24	5x5x64	480	20	$0.5\,e^{-3}$	X
Model 4	5x5x24	5x5x64	480	500	$1.0\,e^{-4}$	With a dropout layer

- A convolution layer has a weight, which is its filter, and a bias.
- A fully connected layer is just a regular layer of neurons in a neural network. Each neuron receives the inputs of all the neurons of the previous layer, so closely connected.
- The epoch can be defined as a forward and a backward pass of all learning data.
- The learning rate defines the step size during the gradient descent. This is a parameter chosen by the programmer.
- The dropout layer can be considered as a form of regulation to prevent overfitting. This is a technique of ignoring randomly selected neurons during training.

The following graph (Figure 6) represents the classification rate of each model.

From this simulation, we can deduce that the model 4 is the most efficient compared to other models.

IV. RESULTS AND DISCUSSION

A. Experimental Results:

Our system achieved an overall accuracy of 96.85% in the detection part and an overall accuracy of 96.23% in the classification part using a convolutional neural network model. In Figure 7, we present some results obtained in the detection phase.

In the classification phase, after optimizing our CNN model, we plotted the learning curve and the confusion matrix (Figure 8 and Figure 9). The learning curve is a comparison of the model's performance based on the number of epochs. The convergence of the model is obtained after 500 epochs. The

Figure 6. the curves of the classification rate of the 4 models.

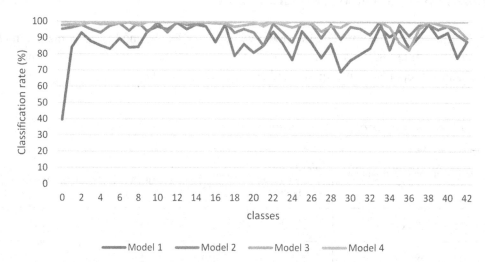

Figure 7. Some results obtained in the detection phase.

confusion matrix allows us to measure the quality of the classification system. We plotted the learning curve and confusion matrix based on the model adopted (see Figure 8 and Figure 9).

In the prediction part, we used the detected signs, in the detection phase, as input to our CNN classifier. As output, we get a percentage of belonging to the five most representative classes. In Figure 10,

Figure 8. The learning curve.

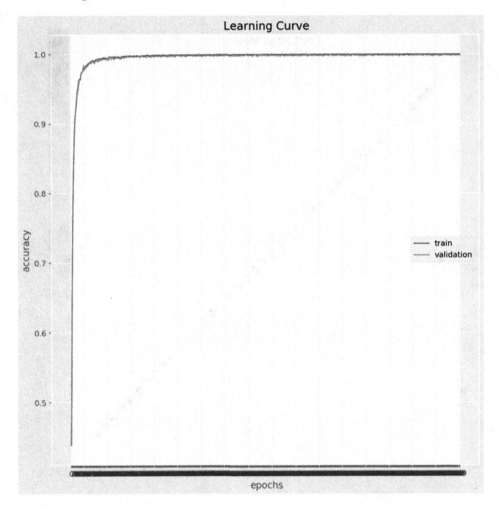

we see some results. We can understand why it did not correctly identify the 40km / h speed limit sign, because we do not have a class of this category (we just have: 20, 30, 50, 60, 70, 80, 100 and 120).

We can already estimate a success rate of up to 100% if the sign is German. This result may deteriorate in the opposite case. It also means that for each country / region, it would be necessary to train the classifier through a learning base of its road signs.

B. Discussion:

In this part, we compare our system with other systems based on the same dataset (GTSRB).

In the paper of Huang et al. (2017), first they filter using the color information parts of the images that does not contain panels. Then, they extract the region where image blocks can be, and then extract the candidate region from the image block. Finally, they use deep learning to verify candidate areas of non-road signs and identify the type of road signs. Their system structure focuses on the HSI color space, and then divides the candidate area into smaller pieces based on the color, texture, size, and similarity of the regions. The HSI color space is used to reduce the impact of changes in light and shadows in the

Figure 9. The confusion matrix.

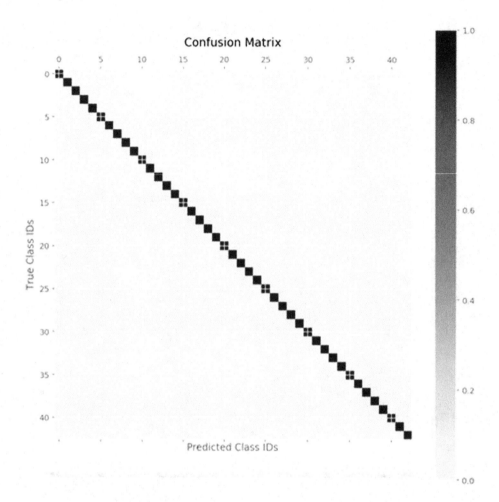

image. Finally, the convolutional neuron network is used to identify the candidate region. Their system is designed for red traffic signs, so they only record red signs as the truth on the ground. The accuracy of the test depends on the selection of the candidate area by the selective search and its correct extraction with a selection frame. The detection system focuses solely on the correct capture of the location of traffic signs. The image region of the selected road signs is integrated into the identification system. In this system, the part of deep learning is based on Caffe. They use the gradient descent method to perform the training. The correct rates for the detection and recognition systems of Huang et al. (2017) are respectively 92.63% and 80.5%, while we obtained 96.85% and 96.23%, which is a very satisfactory result. knowing that our system handles all traffic signs, not just red ones.

In this article (Yi, et al., 2016), they present a real-time signal recognition system consisting of detection and classification modules. In the detection module, they first transform the input color image into probability maps of the panels using a color probability model. The probability map is a gray image, in which the pixels of the traffic signs will have a high intensity and the other pixels a low intensity. Secondly, they extract the proposed road signs by looking for extremely stable extreme regions (MSERs) from probability maps. Third, they filter out false positives and classify the remaining road sign proposals

Figure 10. The results obtained in the prediction part.

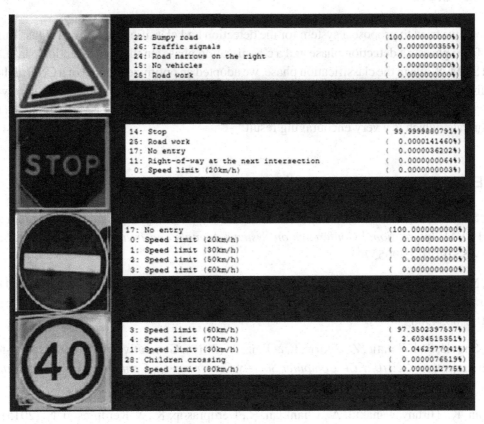

into their super classes using Support Vector Machine (SVM) based on a new HOG color feature. In the detection module, they classified the detected signs into their super classes. However, they still do not know which subclasses they belong to. In addition, there are false alarms in the detected signs. Therefore, they further classify the detected signs in their subclasses or background classes in this module. To this end, they form three CNNs for the three super classes, respectively. In the classification module, they further classify the detected traffic signs in their specific subclasses using a convolutional neural network. Unlike detection, color provides little distinctive information for classification. They only use gray images to reduce the processing time. In addition, they resize all 32 × 32 images because the CNN input should be the same size. This document (Yi, et al., 2016) reach for the detection phase 97.72% and for the classification 97.75%, which is a performance comparable to that of the state-of-the-art methods.

The following table summarizes the success rates found for this works compared to our system.

Table 2. The success rates of some methods based on convolutional neural networks.

Methods	Huang, et al., (2017)	Ours	Yi, et al., (2016)
Detection	92.63	96.85	97.72
Classification	80.5	96.23	97.75

V. CONCLUSION

In this paper, we tried to propose a system for the detection and classification of road signs. Our system consists of two phases: a detection phase and a classification phase. In the sign detection phase, we used HOG and SVM. While in the classification phase, we adopted an optimized model of a CNN architecture. The learning of our classifier was done using the German dataset. In the experimental part, we tested our system on live video scenes and we proved that our system can achieve a very high detection and recognition rate, which is a very encouraging result.

REFERENCES

Ardianto, S., Chen, C.-J., & Hang, H.-M. (2017). Real-time traffic sign recognition using color segmentation and SVM. *International Conference on Systems, Signals and Image Processing (IWSSIP)*, 1-5. 10.1109/IWSSIP.2017.7965570

Bouti, V., Mahraz, M. A., Riffi, J., & Tairi, V. (2017). Robust system for road sign detection and recognition using template matching. *2017 Intelligent Systems and Computer Vision (ISCV)*, 1-4. doi:10.1109/ISACV.2017.8054966

Brkić, K., Šegvić, S., Kalafatić, Z., Sikirić, I., & Pinz, A. (2010). Generative modeling of spatio-temporal traffic sign trajectories. *2010 IEEE Computer Society Conference on Computer Vision and Pattern Recognition - Workshops*, 25-31. 10.1109/CVPRW.2010.5543888

Chaiyakhan, K., Hirunyawanakul, A., Chanklan, R., Kerdprasop, K., & Kerdprasop, N. (2015). Traffic Sign Classification using Support Vector Machine and Image Segmentation. *Proc. Of the 3rd International Conference on Industrial Application Engineering*. 10.12792/iciae2015.013

Chen, T., & Lu, S. (2016). Accurate and efficient traffic sign detection using discriminative adaboost and support vector regression. *IEEE Transactions on Vehicular Technology*, *65*(6), 4006–4015. doi:10.1109/TVT.2015.2500275

Dalal, N., & Triggs, B. (2005). Histograms of oriented gradients for human detection. *2005 IEEE Computer Society Conference on Computer Vision and Pattern Recognition (CVPR'05)*, 886-893. 10.1109/CVPR.2005.177

Drucker, H., Burges, C. J. C., Kaufman, L., Smola, A., & Vapnik, V. (1996). Support vector regression machines. In *Proceedings of the 9th International Conference on Neural Information Processing Systems (NIPS'96)* (pp. 155–161). MIT Press. https://dl.acm.org/doi/10.5555/2998981.2999003

Ellahyani, A., El Ansari, M., & El Jaafari, I. (2016). Traffic sign detection and recognition based on random forests. *Applied Soft Computing*, *46*, 805–815. doi:10.1016/j.asoc.2015.12.041

Habibi, A. H., Jahani, H. E., & Domenec, P. (2016). A practical approach for detection and classification of traffic signs using Convolutional Neural Networks. *Robotics and Autonomous Systems*, *84*, 97–112.

Hong, W., Li, M., Geng, J., & Zhang, Y. (2019). Novel chaotic bat algorithm for forecasting complex motion of floating platforms. *Applied Mathematical Modelling*, *72*, 425–443. doi:10.1016/j.apm.2019.03.031

Huang, S., Lin, H., & Chang, C. (2017). An in-car camera system for traffic sign detection and recognition. *2017 Joint 17th World Congress of International Fuzzy Systems Association and 9th International Conference on Soft Computing and Intelligent Systems (IFSA-SCIS)*, 1-6. doi: 10.1109/IFSA-SCIS.2017.8023239

Kaplan, B. S., Huseyin, G., Ozgur, O., & Cuneyt, A. (2016). On circular traffic sign detection and recognition. *Expert Systems with Applications*, *48*, 67–75. doi:10.1016/j.eswa.2015.11.018

Lecun, Y., Bottou, L., Bengio, Y., & Haffner, P. (1998). Gradient-based learning applied to document recognition. *Proceedings of the IEEE*, *86*(11), 2278–2324. doi:10.1109/5.726791

Lillo-Castellano, J. M., Mora-Jiménez, I., Figuera-Pozuelo, C., & Rojo-Álvarez, J. L. (2015). Traffic sign segmentation and classification using statistical learning methods. *Neurocomputing*, *153*, 286–299. doi:10.1016/j.neucom.2014.11.026

Ma, Y., & Huang, L. (2015). Hierarchical traffic sign recognition based on multi-feature and multi-classifier fusion, *Proc. of the First International Conference on Information Science and Electronic Technology (ISET)*. 10.2991/iset-15.2015.15

Stallkamp, J., Schlipsing, M., Salmen, J., & Igel, C. (2011). The German Traffic Sign Recognition Benchmark: A multi-class classification competition. *The 2011 International Joint Conference on Neural Networks*, 1453-1460. doi: 10.1109/IJCNN.2011.6033395

Yang, T., Long, X., Sangaiah, A. K., Zheng, Z., & Tong, C. (2018). Deep detection network for real-life traffic sign in vehicular networks. *Computer Networks*, *136*, 95–104. doi:10.1016/j.comnet.2018.02.026

Yi, Y., Hengliang, L., Huarong, X., & Fuchao, W. (2016). Towards Real-Time Traffic Sign Detection and Classification. *IEEE Transactions on Intelligent Transportation Systems*, *17*(7), 2022–2031. doi:10.1109/TITS.2015.2482461

Zaklouta, F., & Stanciulescu, B. (2014). Real-time traffic sign recognition in three stages. *Robotics and Autonomous Systems*, *62*(1), 16–24. doi:10.1016/j.robot.2012.07.019

Zaklouta, F., Stanciulescu, B., & Hamdoun, V. (2011). Traffic sign classification using K-d trees and Random Forests. *The 2011 International Joint Conference on Neural Networks*, 2151-2155. doi: 10.1109/IJCNN.2011.6033494

Chapter 5
Virtual Try–On With Generative Adversarial Networks:
A Taxonomical Survey

Andrew Jong
https://orcid.org/0000-0001-8457-8288
San Jose State University, USA

Melody Moh
https://orcid.org/0000-0002-8313-6645
San Jose State University, USA

Teng-Sheng Moh
https://orcid.org/0000-0002-2726-102X
San Jose State University, USA

ABSTRACT

This chapter elaborates on using generative adversarial networks (GAN) for virtual try-on applications. It presents the first comprehensive survey on this topic. Virtual try-on represents a practical application of GANs and pixel translation, which improves on the techniques of virtual try-on prior to these new discoveries. This survey details the importance of virtual try-on systems and the history of virtual try-on; shows how GANs, pixel translation, and perceptual losses have influenced the field; and summarizes the latest research in creating virtual try-on systems. Additionally, the authors present the future directions of research to improve virtual try-on systems by making them usable, faster, more effective. By walking through the steps of virtual try-on from start to finish, the chapter aims to expose readers to key concepts shared by many GAN applications and to give readers a solid foundation to pursue further topics in GANs.

DOI: 10.4018/978-1-7998-4444-0.ch005

INTRODUCTION

In the past five years, Generative Adversarial Networks (GANs) have become a widely researched machine learning topic, especially for computer vision. *Google Scholar* returns over 12,000 results for "generative adversarial networks" when filtered between 2014, the year GANs gained traction, and 2019, the time of this chapter's writing. This significant attention arose from research showing that GANs are capable of generating highly realistic output that closely approximates the original training distribution, to the point that the generated result may be indistinguishable to the human eye. One infamous example of this is *DeepFake*, the application that allows one to puppet a video of another person, to make it appear as if the other person were saying words contrary to what was originally said. In the era of Fake News, this is can be especially worrisome.

Yet GANs also have potentially beneficial applications. For instance, *DeepFake* has been used in the art installation *Dalí Lives* to reanimate the 20th-century painter Salvador Dalí for museum goers; other applications of GANs may help people visualize the future effects of climate change in their neighborhood and inform better understanding for the average citizen. The capability of GANs to generate high quality images on the fly has, consequently, opened new avenues of research in computer graphics as well as virtual, augmented, and mixed reality applications. From the perspective of artificial intelligence, the authors view GAN computer vision applications as most akin to visual imagination in humans, and thus are a worthy research pursuit.

Out of this vast range of applications, this chapter will focus on the application of GANs for Virtual Try-on, i.e. to allow users to virtually try-on digital clothing items at will. Though the chapter presents a narrow focus, virtual try-on shares core components with many GAN applications from photo editing to accelerated graphics rendering. By walking through the steps of virtual try-on from start to finish, the authors aim to expose the reader to key concepts shared by many GAN applications, and give the reader a solid foundation to pursue further topics in GANs in the future.

First, this chapter gives background to introduce virtual try-on and early approaches, but quickly moves on to explain GAN fundamentals, its core modifications, and other related work that set the stage for their application in virtual try-on. Next, the chapter details the evolution of select works from the first virtual try-on GAN to the most recent state-of-art that achieves try-on for video. This section shows the reader how the various components of complex GAN systems are managed together to achieve the feat of virtual try-on. Finally, the chapter concludes with an analysis of current issues and future research directions.

BACKGROUND

Motivation for Virtual Try-on

Worldwide, e-commerce accounts for one-third of clothing sales. Yet, simply because shoppers cannot tell how an article of clothing will look on them until it is tried on in person, e-commerce creates an immense source of waste. Nearly half of online shoppers return clothing due to unmet expectations, and every return adds a severe environmental impact from manufacturing, packaging, and transport. Even more drastically, companies often trash returns as a cheaper option than restocking items.

What if users could virtually try-on digital clothing before purchase? Beyond reducing the carbon footprint, Merle et al. (2012) suggests virtual try-on may improve the overall shopping experience by boosting a shopper's self esteem and positively influencing purchase intentions. The authors hope that mapping the progress in virtual try-on will stimulate further research towards achieving these goals.

Early Virtual Try-on History

The earliest literature to use the term "virtual try-on" dates to 2001. Over the first decade of this century, virtual try-on focused on traditional computer graphics. The first virtual try-on methods either hand-modeled or 3D-scanned the user and clothes into 3D graphics for traditional rendering. While traditional 3D graphics may benefit from detailed cloth simulation, this technology was limited by the time it took to create 3D models.

However, one early work, Zeng et al. (2004), sought to algorithmically implement real-time try-on using only 2D images of a person and garment. Zeng's approach uses a static (hand-designed and non-learnable) algorithm. The static algorithm circumvents the labor of 3D modeling or scanning by warping the garments to match the pose of the user. The user's pose is detected using keypoints that inform the warping of the garments. The warped garment is then merged with the user's image to produce the final result. Though Zeng's approach deviated from traditional computer graphics methods at the time, it is the most similar to the modern approach used by GAN-based virtual try-on. The usage of keypoints and warping algorithm applied to 2D images is shared by today's learnable GAN-based approaches.

Generative Adversarial Networks

Generative Adversarial Networks (GANs) are a family of *generative* machine learning models, meaning they produce an observable X given a target class y: $P(X \mid Y=y)$. To take a computer vision example, suppose the target class y is "dog", then the GAN would generate an image X to closely resemble a dog. GANs achieve this task using artificial neural networks. In particular, GANs use a system of two

Figure 1. This diagram of the Generative Adversarial Network shows its two-component system; the generator generates a fake image, while the discriminator distinguishes between real and fake

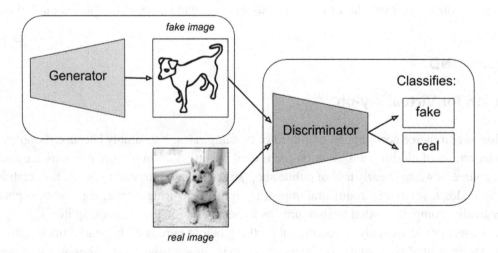

neural networks: a generator (G) learns to produce fake images, in order to fool a discriminator (D) into believing that the fakes are real (Figure 1).

This two-component system gives rise to the 'adversarial' part of the name; in training, the error signal from the generator and discriminator inform the direction of the other's optimization step, formally shown below. The Adversarial GAN loss was proposed by Goodfellow et al. (2014). The generator G aims to minimize the function, while the discriminator D aims to maximize it. These opposite goals form the adversarial nature of the GAN system. The distribution p_{data} is of the training data, while p_z is the generated distribution. Each network tries to outwit the other, leading to the production of high quality results.

$$\min_G \max_D V(D, X) = E_{x \sim p_{data}(x)}[\log D(x)] + E_{z \sim p_z(z)}[\log(1 - D(G(z)))]$$

Conditional GANs come hand-in-hand with the original formulation to allow controlling the generator and discriminator with an input condition. The Conditional GAN equation was proposed by Mirza et al. (2014). Both domains are now conditional probabilities conditioned on y. For example, if generating images of dogs, the input condition could be a dog breed. Adjusting the breed condition would change the breed of the generated image.

$$\min_G \max_D V(D, G) = E_{x \sim p_{data}(x)}[\log D(x|y)] + E_{z \sim p_z(z)}[\log(1 - D(G(z|y)))]$$

On its own, the vanilla GAN, conditional or not, is insufficient to produce high quality results. Below, we detail important modifications that make GANs a feasible approach for virtual try-on. For further reading, a deeper explanation of GANs and their applications may be found in Pan et al. (2019). A detailed survey of notable, fundamental GAN advancements in computer vision may be found in Wang et al. (2019).

GANs for Pixel Translation (Pix2Pix)

A fundamentally important modification to the GAN was proposed by Isola et al. (2017). Image-to-Image translation, also known as 'Pix2Pix', is best described in the words of the original work:

In analogy to automatic language translation, we define automatic image-to-image translation as the task of translating one possible representation of a scene into another, given sufficient training data (Isola, 2014).

Pix2Pix builds upon the conditional GAN framework: it takes a conditional input image, such as a sketch, and translates it into another representation, such as a fully textured handbag. This framework lays the foundation for a vast scope of research applications in deep generative graphics, such as street maps to satellite images, black-and-white to color photos, 3D meshes to full renderings, and more. As it relates to this chapter, Pix2Pix is used in GAN-based virtual try-on, in which the input conditions are the user and garments, and the generated output is the user wearing the garment.

Two fundamentals of Pix2Pix are widely used in virtual try-on and other research applications. The fundamentals are: the addition of the L1 loss term and the usage of the U-Net architecture.

L1 Loss

The L1 loss essentially takes the absolute value difference between predicted and target values:

$$\mathcal{L}_{L1}(G) = E_{x, y, z}[||y - G(x, z)||_1]$$

Recall the conditional GAN equation. Let this equation be represented with L_{cGAN}. Then the combined objective for the generator in Pix2Pix is:

$$G^* = \arg \min_G \max_D \varsigma_{cGAN}(G, D) + \lambda \varsigma_{L1}(G)$$

where λ is a hyperparameter to adjust the strength of the L1 contribution.

Adding the L1 loss to the generator forces the generated output to align with the overall structure and position of the ground truth target. If the output were not constrained, the task would deviate from translating to the true target. As an example with the handbags in Isola's work, without L1 loss to maintain structure, the generated images may be incorrectly scaled, rotated, or moved, and not achieve the desired direct image-to-image translation. In virtual try-on, L1 loss is used to preserve the shape of the user's pose in the generated image.

U-Net Architecture

The second fundamental component of Pix2Pix is the use of the U-Net architecture for the generator. U-Net, a fully convolutional neural network (F-CNN), was first introduced by Ronnenburg et al. (2015) for instance segmentation of cells in biomedical images.

Compared to previous bottleneck encoder-decoder F-CNNs, U-Net adds skip connections between corresponding encoder and decoder layers by concatenating their respective outputs. These skip connections function similarly to the skip connections from ResNet, a fundamental work from computer vision. As with ResNet, the presence of skip connections allows information from early layers to efficiently reach later layers. This also allows gradients from the loss function to backpropagate efficiently to avoid the vanishing gradient problem.

Furthermore, the larger convolutions of early encoder layers produce more information about low-level structure. Since low-level structure should be maintained in image-to-image translation, it is useful to pass this information forward to wield greater influence on the final result.

The Pix2Pix authors found that L1 loss and U-Net are essential to achieve image translation, and is the reason that many modern virtual try-on methods use these core components. The results of ablation studies are shown in Isola et al. 2017. The highest quality is achieved by combining all techniques.

Perceptual Loss Transfers Fine Detail

While Pix2Pix added the L1 loss to transfer low-level structures, this does not transfer high-level structures. The fine detail generated by Pix2Pix is entirely hallucinated by the GAN, not transferred from the input condition. However, realistic virtual try-on requires transferring of high-level structures such as cloth pattern, design, text, and texture. Perceptual losses are an important component to address this issue.

Gatys et al. (2016) introduced Style Loss to achieve detail preservation for style transfer, an application that transfers the style from paintings to photos (or vice versa). Johnson et al. (2016) further expanded on Style Loss by introducing Feature Loss, then categorized both as types of Perceptual Losses. The GAN virtual try-on literature often includes these perceptual losses in their generator's objective. We detail both types below.

Style Loss

Style loss calculates a single scalar that measures the similarity of style between two images. For GANs, the two images are generated and ground truth images. The style of each image is captured by an $n_c \times n_c$ Gram matrix; then, a single scalar for the style loss is then calculated via the L2 distance between the matrices. See Figure 2 for a detailed example. The style loss function is:

$$\ell^{\phi,j}_{style}(\hat{y},y) = \left\| G^{\phi}_j(\hat{y}) - G^{\phi}_j(y) \right\|^2_F$$

Figure 2. This diagram explains the calculation of style loss. The Gram 'style' matrices, G(y) and G(ŷ), are calculated for the real and fake images respectively. Each cell value in the Gram matrix represents an inter-channel relationship within the image. The entire matrix represents the image style. In the example below, the Red-Green relationship is calculated; each dotted arrow represents one channel-wise product (for that coordinate). These products are summed to obtain the value 3 (purple). Due to the commutative property, the Gram matrix is symmetric (G = G^T). These two obtained matrices are compared using L2 loss to produce a single scalar that represents style loss.

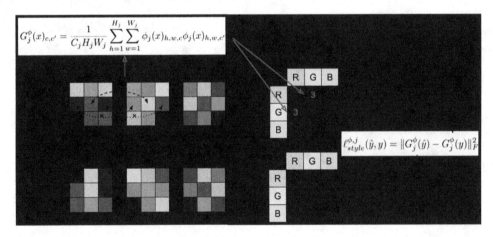

$$G^{\phi}_j(x)_{c,c'} = \frac{1}{C_j H_j W_j} \sum_{h=1}^{H_j} \sum_{w=1}^{W_j} \phi_j(x)_{h,w,c} \phi_j(x)_{h,w,c'}$$

Feature Loss

Feature loss was used in Johnson et al. (2016) as another way to capture detail, specifically for the *content* of the image (for this reason, *feature loss* is sometimes called *content loss*). The intuition is that different convolutional layers activate to detect certain features in an image. Comparing these activations over a predetermined choice of layers with would measure the difference in content. Which layers to choose depends on the architecture and is a hyperparameter; in Johnson et al., the layers chosen from VGG19 were relu2_2, relu3_3, relu4_3, relu5_1, and relu5_3. Feature loss is formally defined as:

$$\ell^{\phi,j}_{feat}(\hat{y},y) = \frac{1}{C_j H_j W_j} \left\| \phi_j(\hat{y}) - \phi_j(y) \right\|^2_2$$

In practice, both style loss and feature loss may be added to the generator's objective function with individually tunable weights.

VIRTUAL TRY-ON WITH GANS

With the astounding discoveries of GANs and pixel translation, the task of virtual try-on has increasingly been linked with GANs in recent years, as shown in Figure 3. Additionally, we note that there has been an academic movement to create fashion datasets of unprecedented size and quality. Human parsing tasks have shown to be more effective and can be used in conjunction to improve the quality of information that we can extract from the human body structure. Many models and networks, which are detailed below, have been created that have combined these works to create virtual try-on systems to transfer clothing.

Figure 3. Rise in results on Google Scholar for papers that include both "virtual try-on" and "GAN" together. Results were manually filtered by relevance and to remove duplicates.

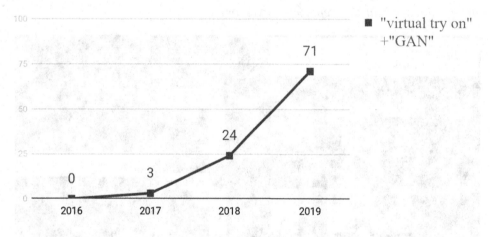

Datasets

There has been a large proliferation of publically available datasets, such as the MVC, LIP, DeepFashion, and DeepFashion2 datasets, that have pushed forward the many component tasks of try-on mechanics. These datasets are of great importance to advance tasks, such as human parsing and pose estimation. Kuan-Hsien Liu, et al. (2016) created the MVC dataset, which contains more than 161K images of 37,499 clothing items. This dataset provides at least 4 different views for most clothing items in the dataset. This dataset also introduced a three-layer hierarchical attribute structure, which starts from gender, clothing category, and specific clothing attributes, such as color or pattern. Ke Gong, et al. (2017) introduced the LIP dataset, a group of 50,642 images which are annotated with 20 categories of human body parts and 16 different body joints. In addition, the LIP dataset contains images of humans from many different complex human poses, including occlusions, back-view, etc. Xiaodan Liang, et al. (2018) built upon the LIP dataset to include a combination of human parsing and pose annotations. These annotations led to more robust human parsing models, such as SSL and JPPNet.

Ziwei Liu, et al. (2016) created the DeepFashion dataset contains 800K images collected from retail websites and Google. Each image is annotated from 50 clothing categories, with an additional 1,000 possible descriptive attributes. The images also have annotated landmarks, to effectively deal with deformation and pose variability of the clothing. The DeepFashion dataset also has 300K cross-pose or cross-domain image pairs, which adds to the robustness of the model. Yuying Ge, et al. (2019) created the DeepFashion2 dataset, which contains 801K images. 43.8K clothing identities are represented in 491K images, which averages out to almost 13 images per clothing type. DeepFashion2 is the only fashion database that has multiple pieces of clothing per image, and has up to 13 definitions of pose and landmarks. This allows there to be a large control of scale, occlusion, and perspective to create a very diverse dataset. The largest fashion database to date, DeepFashion2 supports the following tasks: clothes detection and classification, dense landmark and pose estimation, and cross-domain instance-level clothes retrieval.

Human Parsing

Clothing segmentation is a crucial task for virtual try-on. In order to execute a clothing from image A to image B, image A must undergo clothing segmentation, where each cloth in image A is identified. Then, one can impose each segment onto image B, based on the body segmentation of image B.

Cloth Segmentation

There have been quite a few proposed network architectures to accomplish cloth segmentation. The following describes the architecture details and loss functions of recent research on this topic.

FashionNet, proposed by Ziwei Liu, et al. (2016), is a deep model that takes up a network structure similar to that of VGG-16. The final layer of the VGG-16 model is replaced by three branches. The first branch captures the global features of the clothing image input. The second branch extracts local features over the estimated clothing landmarks. The third branch predicts these landmarks as well as visibility values. Every forward pass has three stages. In the first stage, the third branch is executed to predict landmarks in the input clothing image. Then, the second branch employs pool features to create local features that are invariant to deformations and occlusions in the input image. At the end of every forward pass, the outputs of the first and second branches are concatenated together in "fc7 fusion" to predict clothing category, attributes and model clothes pairs.

The backward pass defines four loss functions, for landmarks, visibility, category and attributes. After calculating these four loss values, the backward pass focuses on the blue branch as its main task. In doing so, it assigns higher weights to the landmark and visibility losses, while assigning lower weights to the attribute and category loss. It has been shown that this joint optimization leads to quicker convergence of the model. The second stage of the backward pass is to learn pairwise relations between clothing images as well as predict clothing categories and attributes.

Match R-CNN was proposed by Yuying Ge, et al. (2019). The network architecture has three main components: the Feature Network, Perception Network, and Matching Network. The Feature Network does feature extraction. ResNet-50 is a part of the Feature Network and it is responsible for the feature extraction, and the FPN uses a top-down architecture to create a pyramid of feature maps. RoI modules are responsible for extracting features from different levels of the pyramid feature map. The Perception Network has three goals: landmark estimation, clothes detection, and mask prediction. The landmark estimation uses 8 convolution and 2 deconvolution layers to predict landmarks. The clothes detection uses one fully connected layer for classification and one fully connected layer for bounding box regression. The mask prediction uses 4 convolution layers, 1 deconvolution layer, and 1 convolution layer. Lastly, the Matching Network contains a feature extractor and a similarity learning network, which estimates the probability of two clothing items matching.

Pose Estimation and Body Segmentation

In analyzing existing approaches to human parsing, Ke Gong, et al. (2017) found that performance of human parsing at the time struggled with the back-view and occluded images. In contrast, parsing the upper-body is much more trivial because there are fewer semantic parts, which take up larger regions. Seeing how the head was a very important cue for human parsing tasks, Ke Gong, et al. (2017) and Xiaodan Liang, et al. (2018) proposed the self-supervised structure-sensitive learning (SSL) and JPPNet to create a more robust analysis of human images.

SSL incorporates joint structure identification into the human parsing loss. This allows the model to incorporate high-level information about human joint-structure, in tandem with the human parsing model. To enforce such knowledge, the joint structure loss weights the human parsing loss, to create a structure-sensitive loss. JPPNet is a joint human parsing a pose estimation network, which synthesizes local refinement and feature extraction connections to enable human parsing and pose estimation tasks in a way that is beneficial to each other. The parsing subnet, pose subnet and refinement network combine to unify the intrinsic connection between the two tasks.

Generating People in Clothing

Lassner et al. (2017) proposed to render clothed-humans with GANs from sampled from latent space, conditionable upon an arbitrary pose. Though not a virtual try-on technique per se, the concept to warp existing clothed humans to other poses is often used in person-to-person clothing try-on.

Lassner et al. makes two key contributions related to virtual try-on work. First is to introduce the concept of pose representation to conditionally generate cloth segmentations. Second is to use an image-to-image translation network to transform cloth segmentations into fully colored images.

The First GAN Try-on: Conditional Analogy GAN

To the authors' best knowledge, Jetchev et al. (2017) was the first to publish results for virtual clothing try-on using GANs. For this task, they aimed to exchange the existing clothes y_i, worn by a person x_i, with new clothes y_j. Supervised learning with a predetermined loss function would require thousands of examples of the same person wearing different clothes in the exact same pose; this dataset would be difficult to obtain as humans are not static objects and naturally move about. Thus, Jetchev et al. decided to use GANs for the discriminator's ability to learn a loss function and judge results in a self-supervised manner, as proven to work by Pix2Pix. They call their specific implementation the conditional analogy GAN (CAGAN).

The proposed method effectively paints over the clothes of the original person. Given a person x_i and a target of garment y_j, the generator produces both an image of the person wearing new clothes and an alpha mask. The alpha mask is then used to composite the original and generated images. Using a mask ensures the person's original identity (such as facial features) is maintained, and that only the target garment is transferred without unduly affecting anything else.

The generator's loss function for this training scheme is:

$$\min_G \max_D \varsigma_{cGAN}(G, D) + \gamma_i \varsigma_{id}(G) + \gamma_c \varsigma_{cyc}(G)$$

where L_{id} is a regularization term on the mask transparency, computed via the L1 norm of the mask (sum of absolute values). L_{id} is designed to limit the mask's transparency and retain the original person's features as closely as possible. However, this results in some undesirable blending of original and transferred textures. L_{cyc} is an additional cycle-consistency loss inspired by Zhu et al. (2017). Once the output of the person wearing new clothes is generated, that output is sent back to CAGAN to rewear the original clothes. The generated output should closely match the original image. The intuition of cycle consistency is to promote stability of the generated output.

VIrtual Try-On Network (VITON)

Han et al. (2018) also approached GAN-based virtual try-on, becoming the second significant literature work to do so. They proposed three criteria:

(1) body parts and pose of the person are the same as in the original image;
(2) the clothing item in the product image deforms naturally, conditioned on the pose and body shape of the person;
(3) detailed visual patterns of the desired product are clearly visible, which include not only low-level features like color and texture but also complicated graphics like em- broidery, logo, etc. (Han, 2018).

CAGAN achieved criteria one with its alpha masking technique, but struggled to achieve criteria two and three. CAGAN's weaknesses can be especially seen in comparisons of VITON and CAGAN results. Han et al. proposed VITON to address these issues. The authors of this chapter dedicate more attention to VITON as it became the baseline for many recent works.

Architecture

To address the clothing deformation criteria, VITON sought to explicitly warp the cloth, unlike CAGAN which had no dedicated process to do so. Thus VITON uses a two-stage system. The first stage is the Encoder-decoder Generator, which performs image-to-image translation with a person representation and target clothing as input conditions, and a course result and clothing mask as the output. The clothing mask is then used to warp the product image using a static shape-context matching algorithm (Belongie, 2002). The course result and warped cloth is then passed to a fully convolutional Refinement network to produce an alpha mask. The final image is obtained using the alpha mask to composite the warped cloth product and coarse person image, upon which a perceptual loss is calculated against the reference image.

Data Representation

A key difference proposed by VITON is to preprocess and include auxiliary information about the person's attributes, rather than to just use the original image. The person representation in VITON is composed of a pose map (detected using an existing keypoint detection network, body shape, and face-and-hair. The auxiliary information is then stacked along the channel dimension. This preprocessing offloads the work required by the image-to-image translation network to result in easier learning, but at the tradeoff of required computation for each input.

Perceptual Loss Function

Han et al. (2018) was the first to demonstrate that perceptual loss could be used in clothing try-on to encourage the transfer of texture detail. The loss function used was the feature loss (described in detail in Feature Loss subsection above). Comparatively, CAGAN relied only on a modified adversarial loss L_{cGAN} to generate detail. Including perceptual loss was instrumental to VITON's ability to transfer textured results, as can be seen in diagrams provided in the VITON work.

Results

A comparison diagram of VITON vs. CAGAN results may be found in Han et al. (2018), not shown here due to usage rights restrictions. Due to CAGAN's alpha masking, results for CAGAN often result in unrealistic blends of the original and target garment. CAGAN also sometimes struggles to place clothing on poses, instead misplacing the garments off-centered from the user. On the contrary, VITON addresses this issue with a static warping algorithm and refinement neural network. VITON results in consistent placement of the target garment on the user, as well as the transfer of patterns that span across the entire garment.

Characteristic Preserving Virtual Try-on

Wang et al. (2018) aimed to extend VITON by further improving the texture detail transfer, especially for complex and isolated pattern designs, logos, and text. While VITON transfers overall patterns, it struggles with detailed designs. To address this, Wang et al. propose a dedicated Geometric Matching Module, i.e. a neural network that learns to warp the clothes via supervised learning, rather than using the static shape-context algorithm used in VITON. The output of the Geometric Matching Module is then passed to a network similar to the Refinement network in VITON. The combined two-network system is named CP-VTON. Finding where to incorporate learning led to CP-VTONs higher quality results. For example, in VITON, logos and images would transfer blurred results. CP-VTON would better preserve these details and keep the text legible with the same visual characteristics such as color and shape. A visual comparison between these works can be found in Wang et al. (2018).

Multi-pose Guided Virtual Try-on

Dong et al. (2019a) sought to improve CP-VTON by improving large pose deformations, such as when the reference image is facing the opposite direction of the target clothes. These cases are tricky as the network must learn a sense of person orientation with only a 2D image. To achieve this, Dong et al. introduce a third stage, the Warp-GAN, that fits between the Geometric Matching Module and the Refinement network, and name the entire 3-stage system MG-VTON. This third stage learns to perform larger transformations than the Geometric Matching Module. When combined in this manner, MG-VTON learns to pose references better than prior work (see comparison figures in Dong et al. 2019a). MG-VTON is able to warp the reference image to the user's pose while preserving the texture of the target clothes, even when the reference image pose is faced in the opposite direction.

SwapNet

Raj, A. et al. (2018) proposed the SwapNet, which is two-stage generative network that operates to transfer garment information from one image to another, while retaining clothing, body poses and shapes. The goal of this transfer is as follows:

Given an image A containing a person wearing desired clothing and an image B portraying another person in the target body shape and pose, we generate an image B composed of the same person as in B wearing the desired clothing in A. (Raj, 2018).

The first stage of the network method is the Warping module, which is similar to the Geometric Matching Module from CP-VTON. The warping module operates on the clothing segmentation of A and body segmentation of B to generate a segmentation of B that is consistent with the labels of B. This module goes through a dual path network. There is one encoder for the body segmentation, one encoder for the clothing segmentation and one decoder that combines the condoded representations. The loss values in the warping module as calculated below.

$$\varsigma_{CE} = -\sum_{c=1}^{18} 1\Big(A_{cs}(i,j) = c\Big)\Big(\log(z_{cs}(i,j))\Big)$$

$$\varsigma_{adv} = E_{x\sim p(A_{cs})}\Big[D(x)\Big] + E_{z\sim p(f1_{enc}(A_{cs},B_{bs}))}\Big[1 - D(f1_{dec}(z))\Big]$$

$$\varsigma_{warp} = \varsigma_{CE} + \lambda_{adv}\varsigma_{adv}$$

The Texturing module takes on a U-Net architecture and the goal of this module is to obtain an embedding the desired clothing by ROI pooling on the 6 main body parts: torso, left/right arm, left/right leg, face. Then, this module generates and upsamples feature maps of original image, which are fed into the U-Net. This module uses clothing segmentation to control high-level structure and shape and clothing embedding to guide hallucination of low-level color and details. The loss values in the texturing module are calculated as below.

$$\varsigma_{L1} = \left\| f2(z'_{cs}, A) - A \right\|_1$$

$$\varsigma_{feat} = \sum_l \lambda_l \left\| \phi_l(f2(z'_{cs}, A)) - \phi_l(A) \right\|_2$$

$$\varsigma_{adv} = E_{x \sim p(A)} \left[D(x) \right] + E_{z \sim p(f2_{cnc})} \left[1 - D(f2_{dec}(z)) \right]$$

SwapGAN

The SwapGAN, as proposed by Yu Liu, et al. (2019) proposed a multistage GAN model, consisting of three generators and one discriminator. The conditional image is the image with the model whose clothes we are trying to embed onto the person in the reference image. Four feature maps are extracted from the conditional image and reference image. Specifically, each image generates a pose feature map, a segmentation feature map, mask feature map, and head feature map. These feature maps are used as conditional inputs or as ground truth values to calculate loss values.

The first generator takes in an input of conditional image and the reference pose feature map and is used to manipulate the person in the conditional image to match pose and body shape of the reference image. This new generated image is the target image where the reference person wears the clothes in the conditional image, while preserving original pose and body shape. Mathematically, the equation for first generator is

XG1 = G1(Xc1Pr)

and its corresponding loss is

$$\varsigma_{G1} = E_{Xc \sim p_{data}(X_c), p_{data}(P_r)} [(D(X_{G_1}, X_c) - 1)^2]$$

The second generator is built on top of the first generator, and takes the output of the first generator as an input. The second generator also takes in the segmentation map of the conditional image as an input. This is used to make sure that the generated image is consistent with the original conditional image. The output of the second generator is a generated image that is consistent with the original conditional image. The main contribution of the second generator is that it considers the style of the clothes in the conditional image when transferring to the target image. Mathematically, the equation for first generator is

$$X_{G11} = G_{11}(X_{G1}, S_c) = G_{11}(G_1(X_c, P_r), S_c)$$

and its corresponding loss is

$$\varsigma_{G11} = E_{Xr \sim Pdata(Xr), Sc \sim Pdata(Sc)} \left[\left(D(X_r, X_{G11}) - 1 \right)^2 \right]$$

The third generator is used to constrain the body shape of the generated images from the first and second generator. The loss is calculated by comparing the mask from the first and second generator with the mask feature map of the conditional image. The loss value is calculated through

$$
\varsigma_{G111} = E_{Mr \sim Pdata(Mr)} \left[\left\| M_{G111(X_{G_I})} - M_r \right\|_1 \right]
$$
$$
+ E_{Mc \sim Pdata(Mc)} \left[\left\| M_{G111(X_{G_{II}})} - M_c \right\|_1 \right]
$$

The total generation loss is calculated

$$
\varsigma_G = \varsigma_{G1} + \varsigma_{G11} + \lambda \varsigma_{G111}
$$

and the discriminator is trained to distinguish fake image pairs from real image pairs, as shown.

$$
\varsigma_D = E_{Xr \sim Pdata(X_r), X_c \sim Pdata(Xc)} \left[\left(D(X_r, X_c) - 1 \right)^2 \right]
$$
$$
+ E_{Xc \sim Pdata(X_c), P_r \sim Pdata(P_r)} \left[D\left(X_{G1}, X_c \right)^2 \right]
$$
$$
+ E_{Xr \sim Pdata(X_r), S_c \sim Pdata(S_c)} \left[D\left(X_r, X_{G11} \right)^2 \right]
$$

An interesting note is that there is a post-processing step of embedding the head feature map from the reference image to the new generated image.

SwapGAN better handles pose deformations from the reference image. However, there has yet to be a published comparison between the MG-VTON and SwapGAN.

Fashion Model to Everyone: M2E-Try On Net

M2E-TON is a virtual try-on system proposed by Zhonghua Wu, et al. (2019). The M2E-TON has three sub-networks, the Pose Alignment Network (PAN), Texture Refinement Network (TRN), and Fitting Network (FTN). The goal of the PAN is to align the pose of the model image M with the target person P. The inputs into the PAN are the model image M, M_d, P_d, the dense pose estimations of the M and P, and M'_w, the model warped image. This conditional generative model generates M'_A, from M, with conditions on M, M_d, P_d, and M'_w. M_d and P_d are used to trasnger poses from model M to target pose and the M'_w provides an effectively strong condition to generate clothing textures.

Before jumping into the TRN, we generate a merged image used the following equation:

$$
\hat{M} = M'_W \odot R + M'_A \odot (1 - R)
$$

The merged image will then be used in the TRN, which will help smooth the merged image, while preserving textual details of garments and produce a refined image M'_R. The FTN, then merges the transferred image M'$_R$ onto the person P, by obtaining regions of interest on person P to create a mask, based on dense pose estimation. This mask is applied on the texture-refine image, M'$_R$ and P to generate the final image, P'. The M2E-TON uses something called unpaired-paired joint training. To ideally train these networks, we need pair images of M, P, P'. Due to the difficulty of acquiring this data, Zhonghua Wu, et al. (2019) proposes two training methods that need to be collaboratively used to train the network. First, the network should be trained on unpaired images, so that the discriminator learns to distinguish between real images and fake images. Then, use paired images of the same identity to train, to add structural correspondence between the input and output images.

Video Virtual Try-on

Given the significant development for virtual try-on with images, the next natural step is to investigate virtual try-on for video. Video try-on would allow a user to easily examine the clothing's appearance on their body at multiple angles, instead of needing to process individual images. However, video try-on adds new challenges, such as how to handle temporal consistency between video frames. By default, the image GAN has no relation between subsequent frames of a video, resulting in frame jumping and unrealistic distortions.

Video Frames for Augmentation

One work proposed by Jong et al. (2019) sought to investigate how the greater information provided in video data could augment the virtual try-on networks. Jong et al. expanded on the warp stage from

Figure 4. Jong et al. proposed that the cloth input condition be chosen at frame x, and a cloth target and corresponding body input condition be selected at frame x + t. This results in using the full video for learning cloth deformations.
Source: Jong, 2019

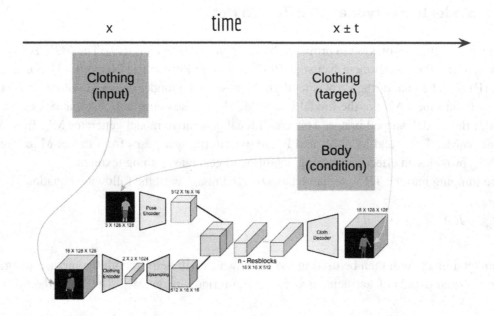

Raj et al. (2018), and found that instead of relying on disjoint images of target outfits, using video to add slightly more data per clothing reference provides a stronger signal to learn cloth transformations (Figure 4), and significantly reduces the required amount of data overall for the warp stage. However, this preliminary work had yet to achieve full virtual try-on.

Complete Video Try-on

Dong et al. (2019b) was the first to achieve video clothing try-on for the entire try-on processing, including warp and texturing stages. The network is named Flow-Warping GAN (FW-GAN), for its incorporation of optical flow to address temporal consistency issues, and the warping of desired clothes and user to the video pose.

FW-GAN requires a video of a reference person wearing the desired clothes. This was collected in a new dataset, VVT, which was obtained from scraping fashion walk videos on fashion websites. The image of the user is then warped to match the pose of the reference, and the desired clothes from the reference are composited with the warped user.

The loss for the generator is as follows:

$$\varsigma_{syn} = \alpha_1 \varsigma_{gan} + \alpha_2 \varsigma_{perceptual} + \alpha_3 \varsigma_{pcl} + \alpha_4 \varsigma_{flow} + \alpha_5 \varsigma_{grid}$$

where L_{gan} is the conditional adversarial loss, $L_{perceptual}$ is the perceptual feature loss for texture transfer, L_{pcl} is a parsing constraint loss that ensures the human part parsing at each generated frame is consistent, L_{flow} is an optical flow loss that analyzes the last k frames to ensure temporal consistency, and L_{grid} is a loss that functions similarly to the Geometric Matching Module from CP-VTON to ensure high quality cloth warping. Due to the video information present, FW-GAN is capable of synthesizing higher quality warping of clothes than previous still-image works such as VITON and CP-VTON.

REPLICATION CASE STUDY

This section details the experiments of this chapter's authors to replicate the texture stage from one of the virtual try-on works, SwapNet, described above. GANs, unlike other methods, can be especially tricky to achieve convergence and high quality results. Unlike in simpler tasks such as classification, the adversarial setup with the generator and discriminator produces a constantly changing loss landscape, making it difficult to achieve convergence. The purpose of this section is to show the reader how to employ critical thinking to conduct experiments for deep learning with generative adversarial networks. By reading through the process of these experiments, future readers can inform their own GAN training to overcome obstacles.

This section details the experiments to achieve cloth transfer results in the Texture Stage of SwapNet. The Texture Stage is the second neural network in the overall system. This stage aims to translate pre-warped clothing segmentations into textured images of the target clothes. After replicating the U-Net architecture of the texture stage, the authors first arrived at the results shown in Figure 5.

The first step to ascertain the root cause of failed convergence is to try and overfit one batch. A neural network should easily be able to overfit one batch of data; if it does not work, this implies something is

Figure 5. Initial results of texture stage in SwapNet replication. The top row shows the clothing segmentation The middle row shows the target image to replicate the textures. The bottom row shows the generated output, which currently shows no discernible output.

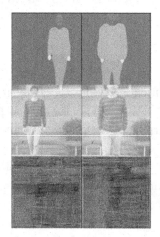  

oth epoch; 0 steps   5th epoch; 13,500 steps   11th epoch; 28,500 steps

wrong with the underlying pipeline. This is shown in Figure 6. As can be seen in the figure, even one batch did not converge properly, implying an error in underlying reimplementation attempt.

Figure 6. Overfit 1 batch experiment. The left chart shows the generator loss diverging, while the discriminator loss has quickly settled at zero. While a zero-value loss is desirable in supervised training, having a zero loss in the discriminator for adversarial training disallows the generator from learning any further, resulting in divergence from the task.

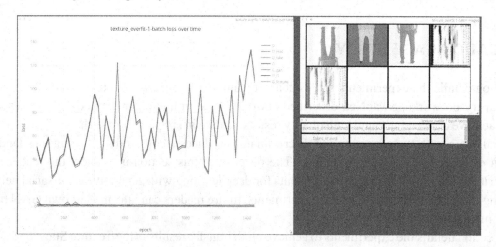

Because overfitting one batch did not work, the next step was to perform component testing of individual pipeline pieces. The input to the SwapNet's texture stage generator consists of the (1) clothing segmentation, and (2) ROI pool values. To check that the issue was not caused by ROI pooling, the authors set the ROI pool input to zero-values. As can be seen in Figure 7, this still resulted in non-convergence and non-sensible output.

Figure 7. Results after ROI pool input is artificially set to zero

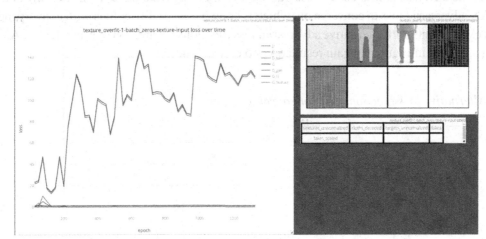

Recall that the texture stage is based on image-to-image translation from Isola et al. (2017), which uses a conditional generator to translate from one domain to another of a picture representation. To simplify the problem even further, the authors attempted to remove the conditional part of the GAN, and simply use a vanilla GAN setup to test convergence. The vanilla GAN takes as input noise and produces realistic images using the adversarial loss. While the images would not be conditioned on the clothes, observing this to work would inform experimental directions. As can be seen in Figure 8, this still resulted in no convergence. However, this was actually a flawed experiment, as setting the input to noise is not the only change needed to revert to a vanilla GAN. Recall that image-to-image translation uses auxiliary losses, such as the L1-loss, to encourage the output to converge towards desired target. This target is meant to

Figure 8. Attempt at vanilla GAN setup by setting input to only noise

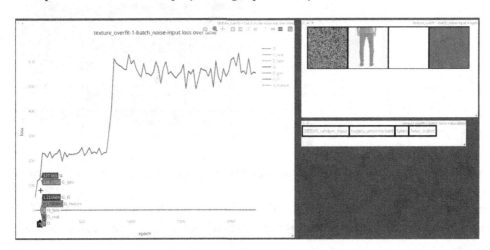

be conditioned on the input. If the input is constantly changing, i.e. noise, then the network attempts to map random input to a particular output, without conditional context as to how to generate that output. This of course leads to no convergence. However, the authors did not realize this at the time.

After even the vanilla GAN setup did not work, the authors hypothesized that the problem could be rooted in the adversarial loss used in the vanilla GAN. Perhaps the dataset was too difficult for the vanilla GAN adversarial loss to converge on, which is known to have difficulties with convergence. This resulted in experiments with alternative adversarial loss functions, such as WGAN and DRAGAN. These experiments, shown in Figure 9, again resulted in no convergence.

Figure 9. Alternative loss functions did not converge either

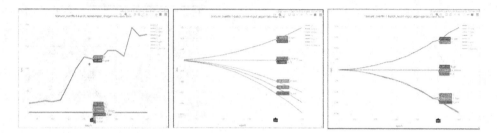

Next, the authors attempted to experiment with hyperparameters of the auxiliary losses. In one experiment, the authors changed the L1 loss weight from 1 to 100. Suddenly, this resulted in discernible output with human body shapes, as can be seen in Figure 10. As another experiment, the authors set the

Figure 10. Experiment where L1 loss was set to 100

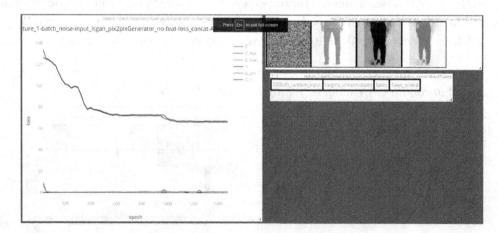

feature loss to zero. This again resulted in higher quality generated output as seen in Figure 11. Further results can be seen in Figure 12.

The results from the experiments imply that the underlying problem was in fact from a faulty implementation of the feature loss. When feature loss was set to 0, realistic shapes appeared quickly. However, as explained in earlier sections, feature loss is necessary for generating high quality detail. As can be seen in Figure 12, though rough shapes are achieved, details such as the face and garment details are missed. This is as far as the authors were able to achieve for the time being without public access to the code nor hyperparameters of SwapNet, delaying full reproduction of the work. This underscores the importance of releasing public code for reproducibility in deep learning.

Figure 11. Training with high L1 loss and no feature loss resulted in distinct body shapes

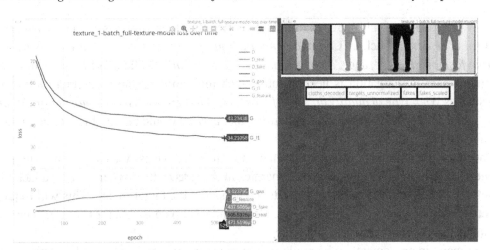

Figure 12. Results from training over a dozen epochs with high L1 loss and no feature loss.

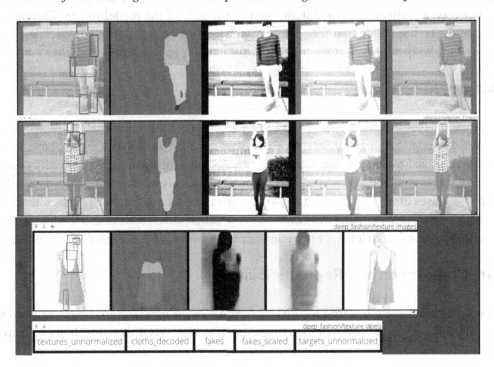

FUTURE RESEARCH DIRECTIONS

Despite the growing number of works related to virtual try-on, there is still much work to be done that has yet to be addressed by existing work. We detail these directions below.

Usability

The usability of virtual try-on is under examined. Specifically, all existing research seeks to answer the question *Can it be done?*, such as *Can one generate high quality textures?*, *Can clothes be extracted directly from fashion models?*, and *Can one generate video try-on?*. While these fundamental questions are important, more investigation is needed into which directions promote practical usability. More questions such as *What type of quality do users focus on?*, *What gives a user the most information about clothing fit?*, and *How do these techniques generalize in the wild?* would be suitable for human-computer interaction research.

There need to be studies on how users will interact with such devices. Virtual try-on systems that use video input need to represent realistic cloth dynamics in the target video. There is also a lack of notion of how well the clothing in the model image fits the person in the target image. This will require more transfer between different-sized body types. We also wonder if it is possible for the target person to feel the material of the clothing in the model image.

There are many improvements to be made in improving resolution quality and effective transfer of clothes without facial or skin pigment distortion between model and target images. Additionally, the many approaches analyzed transfer the entire outfit from the model image, whereas a user would likely only wish to try on a particular clothing item, such as the shirt of the model image. Current research has made progress on improving transfer quality, even with high pose variance between the model and target images, but this quality needs to be further improved for practical application.

Inference Speed

The first virtual try-on GAN used a single end-to-end learning architecture that made inference quite fast. However, because the single architecture was weak quality, subsequent works have introduced preprocessing steps and multi-stage systems. Unfortunately, this prohibits any possibility of real-time try-on as every single input must be preprocessed, and separate networks must be loaded and offloaded from the GPU. If the field aims to achieve a real-time mirror interface, solutions must be found to bypass these drawbacks. Some possible solutions could be to use progressive growing and learning GAN architectures. Furthermore, research into more efficient architectures such as EfficientNet would have merit.

Adequate Comparison and Reproducibility

Despite the numerous papers released for virtual try-on, not all have released code to support their work. This limits the ability of research to compare existing methods effectively. Indeed, many works encountered exclude comparison to a related literature simply because the code is not available. This is also a problem in machine learning as a whole that must be addressed.

Qualitative and quantitative comparison is also under developed. Current comparisons rely on the authors' opinion comparing images at low resolution (128x128), which is roughly one-tenth of high definition resolutions that people are accustomed to today. It is suspect how well texture quality can be compared at such low resolution. Quantitative metrics often involve crowd sourced user-preference studies, which are subject to anchor bias of the provided results, and do not offer much more evaluation than "one looks better than the other". More work is needed to develop metrics that evaluate specific types of quality, such as preservation of the user's identity, realism of cloth placement, detail, consistency across different users, etc.

CONCLUSION

Virtual try-on systems have existed since 2001. The early systems were heavily limited in their scalability and the intensive processing required for graphics. Since then, the discovery of GANs and pixel translation has shown to improve the quality of garment transfer. The chapter presented a focus virtual try-on by walking through the steps of from start to finish. The chapter explained key concepts shared by many GAN applications, and gave readers a solid foundation to pursue further topics in GANs. The chapter has successfully illustrated that, in combination with perceptual and style loss, building systems that are optimized to transfer clothes in high-quality style and perception has become possible.

Additionally, human-parsing tasks have become more robust, and have supplemented research towards more effective transfer techniques. Since then, there has been a large amount of research done on how to create different systems to learn how to warp the clothing from the model image to fit the body type in the target image. Then, there have been different intelligent networks developed to learn how to retain texture of the clothing that is warped onto the target image. These two modules appear in many different forms in the systems detailed above.

The chapter detailed the evolution of select works from the first virtual try-on GAN to the most recent state-of-the-arts that achieves try-on for videos. Virtual try-on systems are on the horizon, but there are many exciting problems that block these systems from being used everywhere. The quality of transfer needs to be improved, clothing transfer needs to give information about the fit of the item, improvements in speed of transfer to create real-time transfer are highly desired, and there needs to be more open-source code of released models and research.

REFERENCES

Divivier, A., Trieb, R., Ebert, A., Hagen, H., Gross, C., Fuhrmann, A., & Luckas, V. (2004). *Virtual try-on topics in realistic, individualized dressing in virtual reality*. Academic Press.

Dong, H., Liang, X., Shen, X., Wang, B., Lai, H., Zhu, J., ... Yin, J. (2019). Towards multi-pose guided virtual try-on network. In *Proceedings of the IEEE International Conference on Computer Vision* (pp. 9026-9035). IEEE.

Dong, H., Liang, X., Shen, X., Wu, B., Chen, B. C., & Yin, J. (2019). FW-GAN: Flow-navigated Warping GAN for Video Virtual Try-on. In *Proceedings of the IEEE International Conference on Computer Vision* (pp. 1161-1170). 10.1109/ICCV.2019.00125

Gatys, L. A., Ecker, A. S., & Bethge, M. (2016). Image style transfer using convolutional neural networks. In *Proceedings of the IEEE Conference on Computer Vision and Pattern Recognition* (pp. 2414-2423). 10.1109/CVPR.2016.265

Ge, Y., Zhang, R., Wang, X., Tang, X., & Luo, P. (2019). DeepFashion2: A Versatile Benchmark for Detection, Pose Estimation, Segmentation and Re-Identification of Clothing Images. In *Proceedings of the IEEE Conference on Computer Vision and Pattern Recognition* (pp. 5337-5345). 10.1109/CVPR.2019.00548

Gong, K., Liang, X., Zhang, D., Shen, X., & Lin, L. (2017). Look into Person: Self-Supervised Structure-Sensitive Learning and a New Benchmark for Human Parsing. *2017 IEEE Conference on Computer Vision and Pattern Recognition (CVPR)*. 10.1109/CVPR.2017.715

Goodfellow, I., Pouget-Abadie, J., Mirza, M., Xu, B., Warde-Farley, D., Ozair, S., Courville, A., & Bengio, Y. (2014). Generative adversarial nets. In Advances in neural information processing systems (pp. 2672-2680). Academic Press.

Han, X., Wu, Z., Wu, Z., Yu, R., & Davis, L. S. (2018). Viton: An image-based virtual try-on network. In *Proceedings of the IEEE Conference on Computer Vision and Pattern Recognition* (pp. 7543-7552). IEEE.

Isola, P., Zhu, J. Y., Zhou, T., & Efros, A. A. (2017). Image-to-image translation with conditional adversarial networks. In *Proceedings of the IEEE conference on computer vision and pattern recognition* (pp. 1125-1134). IEEE.

Jetchev, N., & Bergmann, U. (2017). The conditional analogy gan: Swapping fashion articles on people images. In *Proceedings of the IEEE International Conference on Computer Vision* (pp. 2287-2292). 10.1109/ICCVW.2017.269

Johnson, J., Alahi, A., & Fei-Fei, L. (2016, October). Perceptual losses for real-time style transfer and super-resolution. In *Proceedings of the European Conference on Computer Vision (ECCV)* (pp. 694-711). Springer. 10.1007/978-3-319-46475-6_43

Jong, A., & Moh, T. S. (2019). Short video datasets show potential for outfits in virtual reality. *Proceedings of the IEEE International Conference on High Performance Computing & Simulation (HPCS)*.

Liang, X., Gong, K., Shen, X., & Lin, L. (2019). Look into Person: Joint Body Parsing & Pose Estimation Network and a New Benchmark. *IEEE Transactions on Pattern Analysis and Machine Intelligence*, *41*(4), 871–885. doi:10.1109/TPAMI.2018.2820063 PMID:29994083

Liu, K., Chen, T., & Chen, C. (2016). MVC: A Dataset for View-Invariant Clothing Retrieval and Attribute Prediction. *ICMR '16*.

Liu, Y., Chen, W., Liu, L., & Lew, M. S. (2019). SwapGAN: A Multistage Generative Approach for Person-to-Person Fashion Style Transfer. *IEEE Transactions on Multimedia*, *21*(9), 2209–2222. doi:10.1109/TMM.2019.2897897

Liu, Z., Luo, P., Qiu, S., Wang, X., & Tang, X. (2016). Deepfashion: Powering robust clothes recognition and retrieval with rich annotations. In *Proceedings of the IEEE conference on computer vision and pattern recognition* (pp. 1096-1104). 10.1109/CVPR.2016.124

Mirza, M., & Osindero, S. (2014). *Conditional generative adversarial nets.* arXiv preprint arXiv:1411.1784

Raj, A., Sangkloy, P., Chang, H., Lu, J., Ceylan, D., & Hays, J. (2018). Swapnet: Garment transfer in single view images. In *Proceedings of the European Conference on Computer Vision (ECCV)* (pp. 666-682). Academic Press.

Wang, B., Zheng, H., Liang, X., Chen, Y., Lin, L., & Yang, M. (2018). Toward characteristic-preserving image-based virtual try-on network. In *Proceedings of the European Conference on Computer Vision (ECCV)* (pp. 589-604). Academic Press.

Wu, Z., Lin, G., Tao, Q., & Cai, J. (2019, October). M2e-try on net: Fashion from model to everyone. In *Proceedings of the 27th ACM International Conference on Multimedia* (pp. 293-301). ACM. 10.1145/3343031.3351083

Zeng, X., Ding, Y., & Shao, S. (2009, December). Applying image warping technique to implement real-time virtual try-on based on person's 2D image. In *2009 Second International Symposium on Information Science and Engineering* (pp. 383-387). IEEE. 10.1109/ISISE.2009.9

ADDITIONAL READING

Merle, A., Senecal, S., & St-Onge, A. (2012). Whether and how virtual try-on influences consumer responses to an apparel web site. *International Journal of Electronic Commerce, 16*(3), 41–64. doi:10.2753/JEC1086-4415160302

Pan, Z., Yu, W., Yi, X., Khan, A., Yuan, F., & Zheng, Y. (2019). Recent progress on generative adversarial networks (GANs): A survey. *IEEE Access: Practical Innovations, Open Solutions, 7*, 36322–36333. doi:10.1109/ACCESS.2019.2905015

Ronneberger, O., Fischer, P., & Brox, T. (2015, October). U-net: Convolutional networks for biomedical image segmentation. In *International Conference on Medical image computing and computer-assisted intervention* (pp. 234-241). Springer. 10.1007/978-3-319-24574-4_28

Wang, Z., She, Q., & Ward, T. E. (2019). Generative adversarial networks: A survey and taxonomy. arXiv preprint arXiv:1906.01529.

Zhu, J. Y., Park, T., Isola, P., & Efros, A. A. (2017). Unpaired image-to-image translation using cycle-consistent adversarial networks. In *Proceedings of the IEEE international conference on computer vision* (pp. 2223-2232). 10.1109/ICCV.2017.244

KEY TERMS AND DEFINITIONS

Backpropagation: Neural networks use this technique to propagate the error signal to each of its neurons and evaluate the individual contribution of each neuron to that error.

Generative Adversarial Network: A family of generative models.

Human Parsing: A general task to parse understanding about humans, such to segment various parts of a human body. This includes Body Part Parsing (legs, torso, arms, etc.) and Clothing Part Parsing (hat, shirt, pants, etc.).

Loss Function: A function used to calculate the error of a neural network.

Neural Network: A class of machine learning technique vaguely inspired from biological neurons. Mostly synonymous with 'deep learning'.

U-Net: A specific fully convolutional neural network architecture that employs skip connections between corresponding encoder and decoder layers after the bottleneck. Commonly used in generative adversarial network architectures.

Virtual Reality: A simulated experience that could either be realistic or different from the real world. Virtual reality differs from video games or movies in that virtual reality aims to be immersive.

Virtual Try-On: Using computers to allow users to virtually try-on digital clothing (or other items).

Warp Network: An auxiliary neural network used in virtual try-on GAN architectures that warp a cloth item to the user's pose.

Chapter 6
Visual Classification of Formula One Races by Events, Drivers, and Time Periods

Tobias Lampprecht
University of Reutlingen, Germany

David Salb
University of Reutlingen, Germany

Marek Mauser
University of Reutlingen, Germany

Huub van de Wetering
Technische Universiteit Eindhoven, The Netherlands

Michael Burch
ⓘ https://orcid.org/0000-0003-4756-5335
Technische Universiteit Eindhoven, The Netherlands

Uwe Kloos
University of Reutlingen, Germany

ABSTRACT

Formula One races provide a wealth of data worth investigating. Although the time-varying data has a clear structure, it is pretty challenging to analyze it for further properties. Here the focus is on a visual classification for events, drivers, as well as time periods. As a first step, the Formula One data is visually encoded based on a line plot visual metaphor reflecting the dynamic lap times, and finally, a classification of the races based on the visual outcomes gained from these line plots is presented. The visualization tool is web-based and provides several interactively linked views on the data; however, it starts with a calendar-based overview representation. To illustrate the usefulness of the approach, the provided Formula One data from several years is visually explored while the races took place in different locations. The chapter discusses algorithmic, visual, and perceptual limitations that might occur during the visual classification of time-series data such as Formula One races.

DOI: 10.4018/978-1-7998-4444-0.ch006

1 INTRODUCTION

Formula One data has a dynamic nature (Aigner, et al., 2011), it also consists of event-based data and it shows various differences when observing it from the drivers' perspectives. Moreover, inspecting the data between different time intervals might lead to the detection of several temporal stages in a race, for example, lap by lap, but also between arbitrarily identified race phases. Lots of outside distractions play a crucial role for the identified dynamic race patterns, being it weather conditions, accidents, bad performing cars, or drivers that behave not equally well supposed the race conditions change from time to time.

In this book chapter a look is taken at real-world Formula One data that is acquired on a lap basis for all participating drivers. Getting an overview about such data on a temporally aligned comparable ground truth is important, however, a calendar-based visualization (van Wijk and van Selow, 1999) for overview purposes about all races having taken place so far (see Figure 1) is also required to guide the data exploration process as well as to select certain races, normal as well as abnormal ones. Apart from just inspecting a static line plot for the temporal lap time, driver-by-driver, plenty of interaction techniques (Yi, et al., 2007) are supported to stepwisely analyze the data on the provided data dimensions.

First the structure and the types of data accessible from a Formula One database are taken into account. As a second step simple, well-known, and easy-to-understand visualization techniques designed for the non-experts in information visualization are designed and presented, and finally, a visual classification of the found properties based on events, drivers, and time periods is described. This work is an extended version from an already published paper (Lampprecht, et al., 2019) in which the focus was more on the visual classification of the time-dependent Formula One data. Here, the following visual classification aspects were added to further strengthen the original work:

- Events: These might be caused by special aspects concerning weather conditions, car problems, safety car phases, pit stops, and many more. Such events typically have a large impact on the dynamic visual patterns.
- Drivers: Those can be classified in several ways, for example, bad, good, or excellent drivers, either on previous race results or warm-up races before the actual race takes place. Moreover, drivers might have health issues, they might be in special environments, or general conditions apply that might also change during a race.
- Time Periods: There are several time-based classifications, for example, classified into begin, middle, or towards the end of a race. Moreover, they might be classified into slow, medium, or fast time periods. Finally, the dynamic visual patterns might be used to identify time periods during Formula One races, for example, caused by safety car phases.

To further extend the original work, a more thorough and more detailed application example than in the original work, now taking the visual classification into account, is described. The focus is on all available Formula One races available in the provided database, also the new ones that have not been considered in the original work. To reach the classification goal, a dynamic race position diagram and a lap times line plot is used to show the varying positions during the race with lap time information. Finally, scalability issues and limitations of the web-based visualization tool are discussed.

Figure 1. As an overview all races from 2004 to 2018 are presented in a green color coding. The color indicates the fastest lap of each race in milliseconds (darker green visually encodes faster laps).

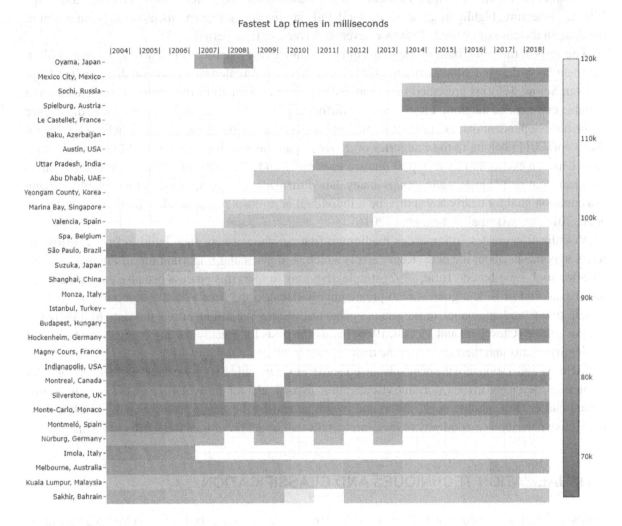

2 RELATED WORK

The visualization of sports data (Perin, et al., 2018) has been in focus for a long time already and is still under investigation in fields like information visualization (Perin, et al., 2018; Ware, 2008), visual analytics (Keim, 2012), and data science (van der Aalst, 2016). Finding insights in the oftentimes time-varying data (Aigner, et al., 2011) is an important task for spectators, reporters, the mass media, but also for the sportsmen themselves. If the visual representation is done in an efficient and understandable way (Shneiderman, 1996), it can have a great impact on the sports analysis tasks. For this reason, mostly simple charts and diagrams (Tufte, 1992) are used for visually encoding the data making it useful for the non-experts in information visualization (Healey and Enns, 2012), i.e. probably the largest group of users in this field.

An important task in a Formula One race might be to identify the dynamics of certain racers, but not as a global behavior, more in intermediate time periods (Aigner, et al., 2011). Such insights can help to detect certain problems during the race maybe caused by driver or car issues, but also by special events like weather conditions. To support a user of such a visualization tool, interactions (Yi, et al., 2007) like filtering, selecting, highlighting, or asking for details are important that can focus on any dimension in the data, in the case of Formula One races events, drivers, or time periods.

The basis of the tool is built by the visual information seeking mantra: overview first, zoom and filter, then details-on-demand (Shneiderman, 1996). To reach this goal a calendar-based visualization (van Wijk and van Selow, 1999) is presented first as an entry point in which all of the races can be detected in a scalable color coded diagram. From this point further exploration processes can be started to dig deeper in the time-dependent data. For example, finding trends, countertrends, but also anomalies (Burch and Weiskopf, 2011) belong to the categories of dynamic patterns worth investigating. Moreover, correlations between events and their impact on race conditions and outcomes might be important as well as the identification of clusters and groups in any data dimension. Exploring the data for such phenomena is a common goal for nearly any sports, be it individual or multi-player sports like football (Andrienko, et al., 2018) or basketball (Chen, et al., 2016).

Visualization creates an important medium to first get an overview, then build, refine, confirm, or reject hypotheses about the data (Keim, 2012) which is in particular important for an interactive visualization tool. Line-based (Tufte, 1992) simple diagrams support this process because they are easy to understand and provide a good way to preattentively (Healey and Enns, 2012) get a quick idea about certain trends and anomalies in the time-dependent dataset. The alignment of the data to a common temporal scale (Cleveland and McGill, 1986) builds the basis for quickly solving comparison tasks and to identify events and their impact in the data.

In this visualization tool the principle introduced by Ogawa and Ma (Ogawa and Ma, 2010) is taken as inspiration, described in their storyline visualization, in particular for the dynamic race position diagrams. Visual clutter (Rosenholtz, et al., 2005) and overdraw can be the major problems here, but however, interactive filtering is a good way to look into details and to get rid of the clutter effect to some extent.

3 VISUALIZATION TECHNIQUES AND CLASSIFICATION

In this section the visualization techniques are described supported by the Formula One race visualization tool. To this end line-based depictions of the time-varying data like dynamic race position diagrams as well as lap times plots are designed and implemented. Those will be explained in detail, i.e. which visual variables are used to encode the data dimensions and data variables. Moreover, a discussion about visual classifications is given, typically based on events, drivers, and time periods. Finally, the integrated interaction techniques to filter, navigate, and browse in the data are presented.

The data source is provided from a web page (https://ergast.com/mrd/) and the data can be accessed via an API, but the data had to be preprocessed first and brought into the appropriate data format for the visualization tool. Several inaccurate data elements were found and gaps had to be closed, for example, by interpolation. The preprocessing resulted in time-series data with extras, describing information about driver names, race locations, lap times, driver positions during the race and many more. JSON objects were used in a NodeJS application using the BlueMix (IBM Cloud) while the programming was based on the JavaScript D3.js library combined with Plotly.

3.1 Line Graphs

Two major line-based views on the time-dependent Formula One race data are supported, always starting with an overview-based calendar-like visualization to select races from for further investigations or comparisons for driver, event, or time period patterns worth building hypotheses about. The goal of this work is to identify visual patterns first and then compare those patterns to confirm, reject, or refine the formerly built hypotheses about Formula One races, i.e by finding a visual category based on the classification scheme.

3.1.1 Dynamic Race Position Diagram

For exploring the order of the drivers in a certain race a view on the start positions is provided from which the order of the positions over time can be visually derived. Until the end of a race is reached a driver might change the positions frequently or stay at a constant position, or a driver might even leave the race due to unforeseen circumstances. Although such a diagram produces a lot of visual clutter (Rosenholtz, et al., 2005) it is still useful since the number of drivers is not that large and race position changes (Munroe, 2019; Ogawa and Ma, 2010; Perin, et al., 2016) do not occur that often (Gronemann, et al., 2016). This means the number of line intersections is acceptable in this special application scenario.

To further strengthen the interpretation of the line-based diagrams color coding is used indicating the start or end position of each driver in the race. This gives a hint about how the fast, average, and slow drivers behave over any time period of a race. Figure 2 shows an example of such a dynamic race position diagram.

3.1.2 Lap Times Plot

For comparing the lap times between the drivers in each race the lap times plot was designed and implemented. This timeline visualization can indicate if certain laps have been driven slower compared to others and hence, provide a way to visually detect or hypothesize about certain events that caused a delay or a longer lap time.

The plot is based on line graphs while the color coding indicates the final position of the driver in the race to visually separate good from bad performing drivers. The time axis is encoded from left to right while the older time points are located to the left hand side. The vertical axis is used for indicating the lap times. The combination of the visual features supports the observation of driving behavior, for example if a strange pattern only happens for one driver or if a whole group of drivers is affected by an event (for example a safety car phase). Figure 3 illustrates a lap times plot for some drivers in the first 50 laps of a Formula One race.

Apart from the static diagram interactions are supported to filter the data for time periods, drivers, and lap times. Moreover, details-on-demand can be provided, for example, a drivers' name and the positions in the race lap-by-lap are shown on demand.

3.2 Visual Classification

In this book chapter the major focus is on providing a visual way to classify certain patterns in the Formula One dataset. On the coarsest level they can be described as patterns concerning the events in races,

Figure 2. Intertwined color coded lines show the dynamic race positions of the drivers in a Formula One race. The time axis (lap number) is starting on top and points towards the bottom.

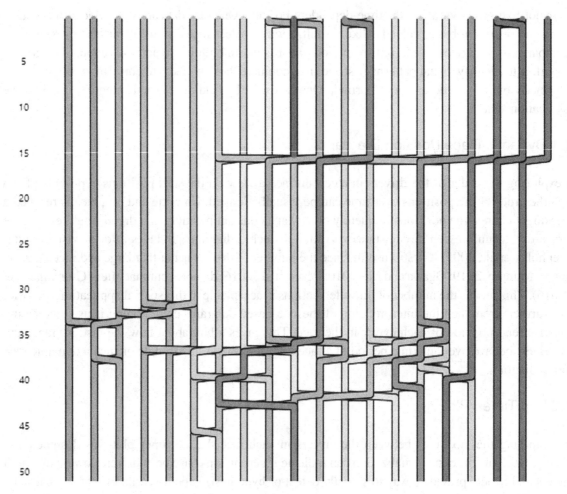

the drivers or driver behavior, as well as the subdivision into time periods. All of the identified visual patterns might be mapped to data patterns to hypothesize about certain data features.

3.2.1 Event-Based

Typical events in a Formula One race worth investigating are:

- **Weather conditions:** Changing weather conditions like wind or heavy rain typically cause the drivers to slow down, not only one but all of them.
- **Car events:** Broken cars or accidents lead to interruptions of a race and can have an impact on a group of cars, but also on all of them.
- **Car conditions:** During a race a car might need to be refueled or tires might be changed causing a pitstop and consequently, a delay and longer lap times.

Figure 3. Showing the lap times for every driver in a race gives insights in the dynamic behavior over time during the race. Color coding is used to show the final positions of the drivers to easily see how the good ones behaved compared to the bad ones. There are several interactions included for temporal filtering, temporal zooming, and details-on-demand, for example.

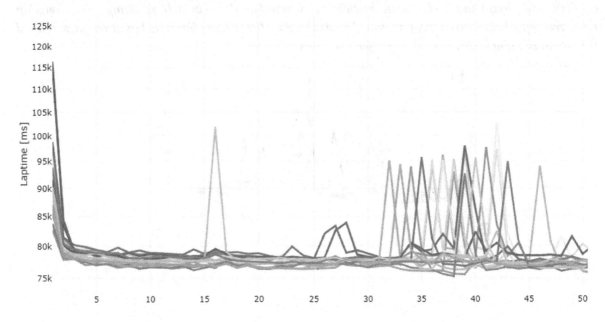

- **Outside distractions:** Any kind of extra unforeseen events can cause a safety car phase, meaning a slow-down for all cars and no overtaking is possible anymore, i.e. no race position changes will occur in this time period.

3.2.2 Driver-Based

From a driver's perspective several patterns could be detected:

- **Constancy:** A driver might stay at the same position in the race all the time which sometimes happens for the leading driver. This could be a very boring race.
- **Stop:** Drivers could break up the race for any kind of reason. This typically causes a position change for all the following drivers.
- **Position change:** Drivers might start at a different position than the one they will have when the race has ended.
- **Alternation:** Drivers might change their race position all the time, even in some kind of alternating behavior, for example after several pit stops.

3.2.3 Time Period-Based

Looking at certain time periods in a race can be useful to separate the race into different temporal phases:

Figure 4. Several events can have an impact on the driver's and car behavior resulting in identifiable visual patterns: (a) The race in Silverstone in 2008 shows many peak patterns for all the cars which are caused by the bad weather at that time. (b) Jules Bianchi had an accident in lap 43 in the race of Suzuka in Japan in 2014. The race was stopped and Lewis Hamilton was declared the winning driver. (c) Fernando Alonso had to change tires twice in a race in Sao Paolo in 2016 resulting in two long lap times recognizable as two outstanding peaks. (d) Outside distractions happened as stray dogs entered the circuit in India in 2011 causing a safety car phase.

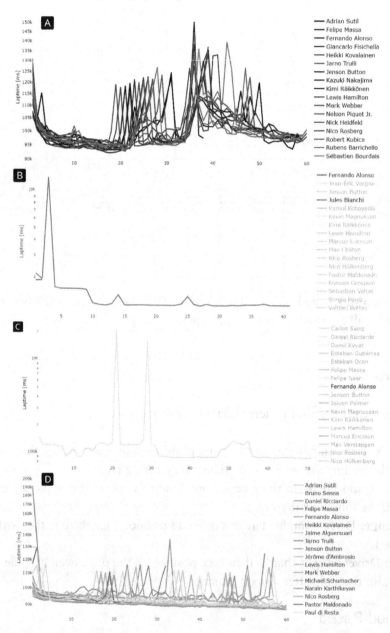

Figure 5. The car drivers may be classified into different patterns based on the positions over time: (a) In Hungary in 2018 the drivers did not change their positions a lot over the race clearly identifiable by only a few line crossings. (b) From the 24 drivers starting in the race only 12 made it to the end in Silverstone in 2011. (c) Lots of position changes happened in a race in Singapore in 2012. (d) In Silverstone in 2018 a frequent position changing occurs all over the race in which cars also alternate between positions.

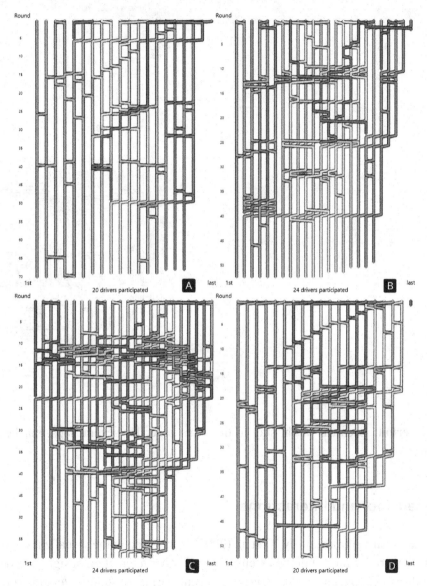

- **Slow speed:** In certain time periods the cars might move slower than in others, maybe caused by bad weather conditions.
- **Fast speed:** Fast time periods typically happen if there are no accidents or bad weather conditions for a number of laps.
- **Change period:** After several pitstops it might happen that a lot of cars change the positions. This typically happens in the beginning of a race.

Figure 6. Each race can be split into several time periods in which certain visual patterns occur: (a) The race of Baku in 2018 shows fast periods (b) but also slower periods (c). The race in Baku in 2016 (d) indicates that in the beginning of the race there were a lot of position changes (e) while towards the end a more stable or constant race position can be observed (f).

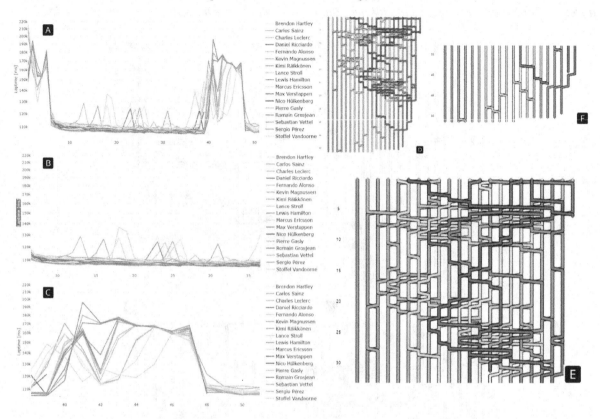

- **Constant period:** Each car might stay in the same order for several laps, maybe because of a safety car phase.

3.3 Web-Based Tool and Interactions

The interaction taxonomy introduced by Yi et al. (2007) is followed in the visualization tool. It consists of seven major categories with additional extensions for further interaction design. The described techniques fall in either selecting, encoding, exploring, reconfiguring, abstracting/elaborating, filtering, or connecting.

The visualization tool is web-based which has several benefits compared to a stand-alone tool, a programming strategy that many information visualization tools follow:

- **Browser tool:** No extra libraries or installations are needed making it more or less independent from the operating system or environment.

- **Non-experts:** Web-based tools can be used by non-experts in computer science because just typing a URL is required and the tool starts immediately.
- **Mobile phone:** The visualization tool can even be used on a mobile phone, for example, by a supporter or a reporter to get quickly informed about the data.
- **Data and insights sharing:** Apart from just consuming the data it could be possible to share the data with other users or to annotate findings and insights as a way to collaboratively interact.
- **Extensions by users:** Web-based tools allow an easy extension by adding functionality, for example, by plugins. Moreover, improvements or extras might be requested online and the designer can decide to modify the tool.

4 APPLICATION EXAMPLE

There are various findings that can be made when inspecting the Formula One dataset by applying the visualization tool to it. Most of the found patterns can be classified into event-, driver-, or time period-based patterns. In the following illustrative examples are provided to show the usefulness of the tool for identifying a list of interesting insights and to make use of the visual pattern classification scheme.

- **Events:** Figure 4 shows several events that have an impact on the visual patterns that are identifiable and hence, can lead to conclusions or hypotheses about what happened there. In (a) the race in Silverstone in 2008 shows various line peaks indicating that obviously there was bad weather at that time. In (b) the horrible accident of Jules Bianchi can be detected in lap 43 in the race of Suzuka in Japan in 2014. The race was stopped and Lewis Hamilton was declared the winning driver. In the scenario (c) a driver namely Fernando Alonso had to change tires twice in a race in Sao Paolo in 2016 resulting in two long lap times recognizable as two outstanding peaks. Finally, in (d) stray dogs entered the circuit causing a safety car phase in a race in India in 2011.
- **Drivers:** Also the car drivers can be classified into certain patterns by inspecting the race positions over time. Figure 5 (a) shows the race in Hungary in 2018 where the drivers did not change their positions a lot over the race which is clearly identifiable by only a few line crossings present in the race position diagram. In (b) it appears that from the 24 drivers starting in the race only 12 made it to the end in Silverstone in 2011. In (c) lots of position changes happened in a race in Singapore in 2012 while in (d), again in Silverstone but now in the year 2018 a frequent position changing pattern occurs all over the race in which cars also alternate between positions.
- **Time periods:** Figure 6 shows how a race can be split into several phases. In (a) the race of Baku in 2018 shows time periods in which the cars are pretty fast all the time (b). However, in (c) there are time periods in which the cars become slower, in this race in the beginning and in the end. The race in Baku in 2016 (d) indicates that in the beginning there were a lot of position changes detectable by many crossing lines (e) while towards the end a more stable or constant race position can be observed, i.e. only a few line crossings can be seen (f).

It may be noted that there are many more insights detectable from the interactive visualizations. In this chapter a small repertoire of the patterns is represented and the visual classification tries to structure those patterns.

5 LIMITATIONS AND SCALABILITY

There are various limitations in such a visualization tool. Those come in the form of data, algorithmic, visual, and perceptual issues worth discussing.

5.1 Data

Although the best to preprocess the data is tried, not all of it is available, as can be seen in the calendar-based overview visualization, for example. However, the missing race data is indicated in the overview, meaning the user can immediately see if it is worth inspecting the race data or not.

To fix this problem of missing race data another data source might be acquired. However, fixing missing data values in one race might be solved by interpolating between two or more data points or by sampling the missing data point from another similarly looking pattern, but there is no guarantee that the computed data is the correct one.

5.2 Algorithmic

Algorithmically, the race data can be preprocessed easily, however, if an increase in the number of races occurs in the future it might result in slower runtimes for the data preprocessing algorithms. Moreover, if clustering or data mining algorithms will be introduced in the future, algorithmic scalability might become a problem, in particular, if the race data has to be processed on a much finer temporal scale.

To mitigate this problem, preprocessing the data over night can be a solution and then, always using the prepared data for the interactive visualization can accelerate the visual output. This keeps away the burden of data handling each time the tool gets started.

5.3 Visual

If too many drivers take part in a race and/or the races consist of many laps, the line-based diagrams could contain a lot of visual clutter caused by line crossings. However, since the number of position changes is rather low this does not become a real problem for the race position diagram. However, for the lap times plot many overlaps and occlusions by the lines of other drivers having similar lap times might occur.

Interaction techniques should be used to circumvent this problem, for example by filtering for a certain number of drivers or zoom in the diagram to explore the details in case there is much overlap between the lines.

5.4 Perceptual

Color coding plays a crucial role in the visualizations. It is useful to indicate the positions of the cars in the end to support the user when observing and comparing the dynamic driver behavior. However, color coding can be a problem if too many drivers have to be plotted and if the lines intersect and overlap each other. This could cause ambiguities, i.e. taking one line for the other, because it has a similar color.

Perceptually, the color coding is always a problem, but it might be helpful to switch between several color scales to detect the right one for the task at hand. Moreover, also interaction techniques are useful, for example, by highlighting a line to understand and track it over the entire time span.

6 CONCLUSION AND FUTURE WORK

In this chapter an interactive web-based visualization tool for Formula One data is described. To reach this goal, three visualizations are designed and implemented: a calendar-based overview, a race position diagram, and a lap times plot. The visualizations are useful to show typical race patterns focusing on events, drivers, but also on certain time periods. A visual classification of such patterns was explained and some of the findings were illustrated in an application example. Finally, limitations and scalability issues were discussed focusing on the data but also on algorithmic, visual, and perceptual challenges. For future work a user evaluation is planned to explore the usefulness of the visualization tool. Furthermore, adding other data sources to the tool as an extension would have benefits for the visualizations, for example, weather events or temperatures and the like. Also more algorithmic solutions to the pattern identification process might be a possible way to enhance and augment the tool.

REFERENCES

Aigner, W., Miksch, S., Schumann, H., & Tominski, C. (2011). *Visualization of Time-Oriented Data.* Springer. doi:10.1007/978-0-85729-079-3

Andrienko, G. L., Andrienko, N. V., Budziak, G., von Landesberger, T., & Weber, H. (2018). Exploring pressure in football. *Proceedings of the 2018 International Conference on Advanced Visual Interfaces, AVI,* 54:1–54:3.

Burch, M., & Weiskopf, D. (2011). Visualizing dynamic quantitative data in hierarchies - TimeEdgeTrees: Attaching dynamic weights to tree edges. *IMAGAPP & IVAPP 2011 - Proceedings of the International Conference on Imaging Theory and Applications and International Conference on Information Visualization Theory and Applications,* 177–186.

Chen, W., Lao, T., Xia, J., Huang, X., Zhu, B., Hu, W., & Guan, H. (2016). Gameflow: Narrative visualization of NBA basketball games. *IEEE Transactions on Multimedia, 18*(11), 2247–2256. doi:10.1109/TMM.2016.2614221

Cleveland, W. S., & McGill, R. (1986). An experiment in graphical perception. *International Journal of Man-Machine Studies, 25*(5), 491–501. doi:10.1016/S0020-7373(86)80019-0

Gronemann, M., Jünger, M., Liers, F., & Mambelli, F. (2016). Crossing minimization in storyline visualization. *Proceedings of 24th International Symposium of Graph Drawing and Network Visualization,* 367–381. 10.1007/978-3-319-50106-2_29

Healey, C. G., & Enns, J. T. (2012). Attention and visual memory in visualization and computer graphics. *IEEE Transactions on Visualization and Computer Graphics, 18*(7), 1170–1188. doi:10.1109/TVCG.2011.127 PMID:21788672

Keim, D. A. (2012). Solving problems with visual analytics: Challenges and applications. *Proceedings of Machine Learning and Knowledge Discovery in Databases - European Conference,* 5–6.

Lampprecht, T., Salb, D., Mauser, M., van de Wetering, H., Burch, M., & Kloos, U. (2019). Information Visualization - Biomedical Visualization and Geometric Modelling and Imaging, IV 2019. Piscataway: Institute of Electrical and Electronics Engineers.

Munroe, R. (2019). *XKCD number 657: Movie narrative charts*. https://xkcd.com/657

Ogawa, M., & Ma, K. (2010). Software evolution storylines. *Proceedings of the ACM Symposium on Software Visualization*, 35–42.

Perin, C., Boy, J., & Vernier, F. (2016). Using gap charts to visualize the temporal evolution of ranks and scores. *IEEE Computer Graphics and Applications*, *36*(5), 38–49. doi:10.1109/MCG.2016.100 PMID:28113147

Perin, C., Vuillemot, R., Stolper, C. D., Stasko, J. T., Wood, J., & Carpendale, S. (2018). State of the art of sports data visualization. *Computer Graphics Forum*, *37*(3), 663–686. doi:10.1111/cgf.13447

Rosenholtz, R., Li, Y., Mansfield, J., & Jin, Z. (2005). Feature congestion: A measure of display clutter. In *Proceedings of the SIGCHI Conference on Human Factors in Computing Systems*, (pp. 761–770). ACM. 10.1145/1054972.1055078

Shneiderman, B. (1996). The eyes have it: A task by data type taxonomy for information visualizations. *Proceedings of the IEEE Symposium on Visual Languages*, 336–343. 10.1109/VL.1996.545307

Tufte, E. R. (1992). *The Visual Display of Quantitative Information*. Graphics Press.

van der Aalst, W. M. P. (2016). *Process Mining - Data Science in Action* (2nd ed.). Springer. doi:10.1007/978-3-662-49851-4

van Wijk, J. J., & van Selow, E. R. (1999). Cluster and calendar based visualization of time series data. *Proceedings of IEEE Symposium on Information Visualization*, 4–9. 10.1109/INFVIS.1999.801851

Ware, C. (2004). *Information Visualization: Perception for Design*. Morgan Kaufmann.

Ware, C. (2008). *Visual Thinking: for Design*. Morgan Kaufmann Series in Interactive Technologies, Paperback.

Yi, J. S., Kang, Y., Stasko, J., & Jacko, J. A. (2007). Toward a deeper understanding of the role of interaction in information visualization. *IEEE Transactions on Visualization and Computer Graphics*, *13*(6), 1224–1231. doi:10.1109/TVCG.2007.70515 PMID:17968068

Chapter 7
An Overview of Feature–Based Shadow Detection Methods

Suhaib Musleh
Kuwait University, Kuwait

Muhammad Sarfraz
 https://orcid.org/0000-0003-3196-9132
Kuwait University, Kuwait

Hazem Raafat
 https://orcid.org/0000-0001-7356-5078
Kuwait University, Kuwait

ABSTRACT

Shadows occur very frequently in digital images while considering them for various important applications. Shadow is considered as a source of noise and can cause false image colors, loss of information, and false image segmentation. Thus, it is required to detect and remove shadows from images. This chapter addresses the problem of shadow detection in high-resolution aerial images. It presents the required main concepts to introduce for the subject. These concepts are the main knowledge units that provide for the reader a better understanding of the subject of shadow detection and furthering the research. Additionally, an overview of various shadow detection methods is provided together with a detailed comparative study. The results of these methods are also discussed extensively by investigating their main features used in the process to detect the shadows accurately.

INTRODUCTION

Shadow is a phenomenon that occurs when light is occluded by a solid object. Shadow presence in digital images is useful for some computer applications to estimate buildings height for example, but shadow-free images are of high demand for many other computer applications to complete their tasks successfully, such as image segmenting and object tracking. Shadow detection in digital aerial images

DOI: 10.4018/978-1-7998-4444-0.ch007

is an important and challenging field. The detection and removal processes play a significant role in improving the accuracy of many applications because these processes recover many distorted information in the target image. The recovered information is an essential part of the image, which is considered as input for many applications, such as object recognition application.

Shadow detection in videos depends on the motion of the images-sequence. The detection process uses the shaded areas in each image of the video sequence, which makes the process easier. In static image, like in digital aerial images, it is difficult to detect shadow because there is no reference of images-sequence like in video, which means less information available to be exploited in the detection process. Many challenges appear in the process of shadow detection, mainly the misdetection of dark objects and shadow boundaries. As a fact, shadow detection is the first step before shadow removal. Hence, shadow removal accuracy depends on the accuracy of the shadow detection process itself. We consider in our research only the process of shadow detection. The existing shadow detection methods that are presented in this research depend on different features to detect the shadows.

Shadow Detection methods depend on different features to detect the shadows in the image. Some methods exploit the geometrical properties of image objects that occlude the light and cause the shadow, and some methods exploit the illumination direction of light source in the scene. Other methods exploit the image pixels intensity values and chromaticity (Horprasert, Harwood, & Davis, 1999) using invariant color models. Chromaticity is a helpful feature for many methods, because chromaticity is not changed when the illumination changes. By using chromaticity feature, shadow can be detected in an image by finding the area that is darker than its neighboring area but both are having the same chromaticity information. Method selection depends on the image that is infected with shadows, static or dynamic image, and on the prior information availability about that image.

This chapter addresses the problem of shadow detection in high-resolution aerial images. It presents the required main concepts to introduce for the research subject. These concepts are the main knowledge units that provide for the reader a better understanding of the subject of Shadow detection and furthering the research. Additionally, an overview of various shadow detection methods is provided together with a detailed comparative study. The results of these methods are also discussed extensively by investigating their main features used in the process to detect the shadows accurately. The chapter has been organized as follows. Next section provides a background material on the shadow detection methods in the literature. The section after highlights main concepts to introduce for the research subject in the next section. After that, an overview of various shadow detection methods is provided together with a detailed comparative study in the second last section. The results of these methods are also discussed extensively by investigating their main features used in the process to detect the shadows accurately. Final section concludes the chapter.

BACKGROUND

Various authors have worked in the area of shadow detection. For the methods that depend on image pixels intensity values and color information, Polidorio et al., in (Polidorio, Flores, Imai, Tommaselli, & Franco, 2003), exploited two properties of shadows, high blue/violet wavelength and low brightness to detect shadow in images. In the beginning, the *RGB* image was converted to *HSI* model using the appropriate equations. Then a partition process was applied on the saturation and intensity components to detect the shadows.

In (Tsai, 2006), another shadow detection method was presented by Tsai to detect shadows in aerial images. First, the *RGB* color image was converted into many invariant color systems, such as *HSI*. Second, Tsai used an appropriate equation to calculate the ratio images of hue over intensity equivalent components for the used invariant color systems. As a result, ratio images were generated from the previous process. Finally, different thresholds were applied on the different ratio images to detect the shadows in each image. In comparison among Tsai algorithm and the existing methods of (Huang, Xie, & Tang, 2004) and (Polidorio et al., 2003), Tsai method demonstrated better results.

Chung et al. (Chung, Lin, & Huang, 2009b) presented a successive thresholding scheme to improve the presented work of Tsai. They made some modification in the ratio image of Tsai by applying an exponential function to Tsai ratio image to improve it. After that, a global threshold was applied on the modified ratio image to partition the pixels into candidate shaded regions and non-shaded regions. Finally, a local threshold was applied on the candidate shaded regions iteratively to catch the true shaded pixels.

In (Mostafa, & Abdelhafiz, 2017), a new technique was proposed. Shadow detector index (*SDI*) was used for shadow detecting in satellite images. In (Mostafa et al., 2017), authors worked on a new image index method that used the intensity of pixels for the *RGB* color channels based on the shaded pixels properties. After that, the shaded pixels were separated by applying an automatic threshold scheme on an indexed histogram.

An automatic technique to detect and remove soft shadow from satellite images was proposed by (Su, Zhang, Tian, Yan, & Miao, 2016). The technique exploited the image matting and classification of the Bimodal Histogram (*BH*). The *BH* depended on values of the shadow pixels. The classification operation was accomplished by picking up a threshold that was the mean of the two tops in the related *BH*.

Mo et al. (Mo, Zhu, Yan, & Zhao, 2018) presented an automatic shadow detection method in digital aerial images. The method was proposed to overcome the manual processes that were used in the existing methods. The method of (Mo et. al., 2018) works on pixel level, it used Gaussian Mixture representation to imitate the gray distribution and refine the shadow in the image. That was joined with image segmentation to find shadow areas accurately with whole object shape.

Yarlagadda and Zhu (Yarlagadda, & Zhu, 2018) proposed a shadow detection method for digital single image. The proposed method exploited the reflectance feature in the shadow detection process. First, the digital image is segmented. Then, based on reflectance, the segmented pairs of regions are classified as shadow and shadow-free regions.

Shadow detection methods based on pixels properties may produce some errors in detecting the shadow around object edges. To overcome this misclassifying, Kang et al. (Kang, Huang, Li, Lin, & Benediktsson, 2018) proposed a method based on Extended Random Walker (*ERW*) approach which combines the spatial relations and shadow characteristics between neighboring pixels. First and by using Otsu global thresholding method (Otsu, 1979), training sets were generated. Then, the support vector machine was used to produce a coarse shadow image, which classified pixels into shadow and nonshadow. Finally, the coarse image was further processed using the *ERW* approach, which increased the accuracy of the shadow detection process.

The method of (Nair, Ram, & Sundararaman, 2019) presented a developed machine-learning algorithm. The *RGB* digital image was converted to *HSV* and 26 attributes were identified. The algorithm was trained using selected images as sample dataset to classify image pixels into shadow and nonshadow. Finally, the trained algorithm was used to distinguish shadow and nonshadow pixels in the new input images.

A novel method for shadow detection and removal was proposed in (Song, Huang, & Zhang, 2014). First, a shadow mask was generated by using a threshold to find shaded regions. Noise and incorrect detected shadow were extracted by the morphological filtering process. After that, (Song et al., 2014) used the example based learning approach to remove shadow. The shaded and corresponding nonshaded areas were first manually identified from the image as samplings to accomplish shadow and nonshadow libraries, and this correlated with Markov Random Field (*MRF*). In the reparation operation, infected pixels with shadow were repaired using the related shaded pixels by exploiting the Bayesian belief propagation method to solve the *MRF*.

There are various methods that exploit the geometrical properties of objects in the image to detect shadows (Hsieh, Hu, Chang, & Chen, 2003; Yoneyama, Yeh, & Kuo, 2003; Nicolas, & Pinel, 2006; Fang, Qiong, & Sheng, 2008; Chen, & Aggarwal, 2010). A method for shadow detection of single and multiple objects in a static background images was proposed in (Vakhare, 2015). First, the edges between objects and their shadows were determined. After that, Vakhare ruled out the background and work on the objects and their shadows. Finally, the objects geometrical properties and shadows orientation were exploited to detect the shadows.

An object oriented shadow detection and removal technique was presented in (Zhang, Sun, & Li, 2014). The candidate shadow regions were determined by first segmenting the image. Then, shadow regions were found by applying a threshold on the segmented image. Finally, object geometrical properties were exploited with spatial relationship to extract misclassified dark objects to increase the accuracy.

For the methods that exploit the illumination direction of light source in the image to detect shadows, a shadow detection method based on the illumination direction property was presented in (Russell, Zou, & Fang, 2003). First, authors found the illumination direction of light source. Second, they calculated the pixels intensity values of scanned image-lines for the object and its shadow. These calculations were completed in the opposite direction of illumination source looking for decreasing function intervals to determine the shadow.

SOME IMPORTANT CONCEPTS & REQUIREMENTS

This section highlights some important and necessary concepts and requirements, as methods and tools, needed to reach the results of shadow detection. It includes some basics on Digital Image, Human Vision Mechanism, Color Perception, *RGB* and Alternative Color Models, Shadow Formation, Shadow Detection in Digital Image, and Digital Image Enhancement. Further details are provided in the following subsections.

Digital Image

We represent an image as a two-dimensional array $A(x \times y)$, see Figure 1, where x and y represent the number of columns and rows respectively in that array. Let $i \in \{0, 1, 2,..., x - 1\}$ and $j \in \{0, 1, 2,..., y - 1\}$, a value of $A(i,j)$ is the intensity of the element called pixel in the coordinate position (i,j) of the two dimensional array "image". Pixels are the smallest units that form the image on the display screens. Pixels intensity values represent the brightness strength of these pixels when a digital image is displayed on a display screen. Positions and intensity values of pixels play a magnificent role in the image formation and clearness according to many criteria. When intensity values $A(i,j)$ of pixels have discrete quantities, we call the image as a digital image with dimensions of width (x) and height (y). Resolution of a digital image is the total number of pixels in that image, which can be represented by $x \times y$ pixels. More pixels in the digital image means higher resolution and clearness. Different value functions can be applied on the image pixels to change their values for image enhancement purposes. We can choose the required function to be applied on the digital image according to the desired purpose using image-processing applications.

Figure 1. Digital image as 2-dimensional array x×y pixels.

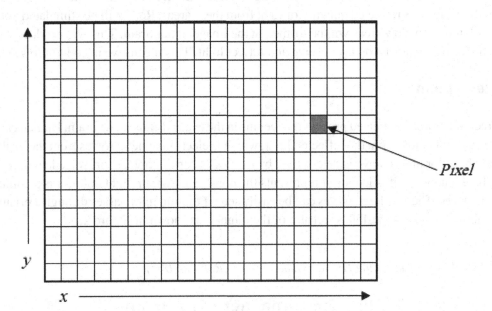

Human Vision Mechanism

Images play a significant role in our daily life, they present a huge source of information that human perceives. It is very important to understand how our vision system works to know how we realize image colors. Understanding the work mechanism of human eye and how it helps the brain in the process of image colors formation, is the key to develop many image processing applications using the suitable color model to represent an image. True image colors is important for image clearness, and color clearness is affected by the illumination quantity in the scene.

Illumination affects image colors formation and clearness in human brain. Human eye is the responsible organ for the vision process. The eye receives the reflected prospective light waves from the scene and passes signals to the brain to form the image and realize scene colors. The image clearness is important to provide us with the information we need to interact with things around us. When we look to any object, we allow light to be reflected from that object to our eye. The eye works as a tiny window that allows the reflected light to be focused on a place called Retina inside the eye. The focused light is received then by receptors.

Two main receptors are distributed on Retina surface, Cones and Rods. The Cones receptors are sensitive to color which always need high light quantity to be stimulated. Rods responsibility is to give a general picture of the scene without colors. Rods are not sensitive to colors and they are stimulated by low light quantity. This can answer the question of why objects around us look colored in daytime, while they look colorless in moonlight? The answer is because Rods receptors are stimulated not the Cones when the eye receives low light like in moonlight, only the Cones are responsible for receiving high quantity of light which is required to perceive colors. Hence, we see objects with colors in daytime while we see objects without colors in moonlight. This leads to another question, if we look to a scene that has two groups of areas, first group reflects high quantity of light while the second group reflects less quantity of light because some solid objects occlude the light. How will areas that reflect less or no light look? Our eye will receive less reflected quantity of light from these areas, Rods will be stimulated not Cones, then less colored or shadow areas will be formed in the image in our brain. This will produce color loss in the scene for the areas that do not receive and reflect light. This means we need light to see colors.

Color Perception

Color perception is a sophisticated process that begins in the eye and ends in the brain. Human can distinguish thousands of colors from the reflected light, which is electromagnetic waves from the visible light spectrum. The color of any wave is determined by its length, for example, short wave length represents the color blue, and when it is longer, it represents the color red. For sun light color, it is a combination of different waves. These colored waves can be easily seen if the sun light passes through a prism, it will form a rainbow colors. The visible spectrum of the rainbow is shown in Figure 2.

Figure 2. Visible spectrum to the Human visual system (Ronan, 2007).

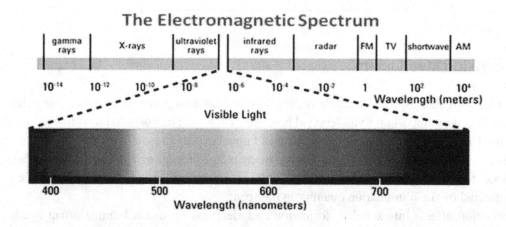

As mentioned in previous section, receptors Cones inside the eye are sensitive to the light. Depending on the quantity of light and wavelengths that are received by the eye, different number and types of Cones are stimulated. The stimulated Cones send three main colors Red, Green, and blue as signals to the brain. The combination of these colors and their quantity determine the final color that is perceived by the brain. As a conclusion, all colors can be represented from the basic Red, Green, and blue colors (*RGB*). This is the reason behind using the *RGB* color model in computer display screens and other devices.

RGB **Color Model and Alternative Models**

Simply, color is the reflected light from things around us. There are many models are used to represent color. The color model is the system that generates the range of all secondary colors depending on a specific small number of main colors, such as *RGB* color model. *RGB* model uses only three main color components: Red, Green, and Blue to represent all ranges of colors. Color models are classified into two main categories:

1- Additive, which uses light to represent colors. Such as *RGB* model.
2- Subtractive, which uses printing ink to represent colors. Such as CMYK model.

In our research, we work with the additive color model *RGB* and its alternative representation models, such as Hue, Saturation, and Intensity (*HSI*) model. The *HSI* color model is one of many invariant color models that separate the luminance and color information "chromaticity" components from each other when representing a color. Although there are many invariant color models, we focus on two well-known models, *HSI* and Hue, Saturation, Value (*HSV*). The transformation from *RGB* to any invariant color model can be performed using different mathematical equations based on the desired destination color model.

The color components of different invariant color models are equivalent to each other since they use the same principle for representing colors. For example *H* and *I* components in *HSI* model, which hold the "color information" and pixel intensity value respectively, are equivalents to *H* and *V* components in *HSV* model, because the invariant color model *HSV* use the same principle to represent colors. *H* component holds the "color information" and *V* component holds the pixel intensity value. Invariant color models play a significant role in the shadow detection applications.

Shadow Formation

Shadow is formed when the light is blocked from reaching an area by a non-transparent object (Bertalmio, Caselles, & Provenzi, 2009; Li, Zhang, & Shen, 2012). When a non-transparent object blocks the light, a cast shadow appears in front of that object in the same direction of light source. Illumination decreases in shadow areas, which makes the shadow areas darker than neighboring nonshshadow areas. Darkness level of the shadow areas depends on the quantity of the light is occluded from the direct light source and on the quantity of the light that may be received indirectly from neighboring nonshadow areas in the scene.

Shadow is classified into two categories: Umbra and Penumbra. Umbra shadow is the darker area in cast shadow or "inner shadow area", see Figure 3. Light reflection is very low in umbra area, which is located closer to the object that blocks the light. Penumbra shadow or "outer shadow area" is less dark i.e. brighter that Umbra because it is far away from the object that blocks the light and it gets some light quantity from surrounded nonshadow areas. It is clear from Figure 3 that when moving away from Umbra "inner area" to Penumbra "outer area", the shadowed area becomes brighter. This is because outer area can receive and reflect little quantity of light from light source and indirect light that comes from neighboring nonshadow areas.

Figure 3. Principle of shadow formation (Su et al., 2016).

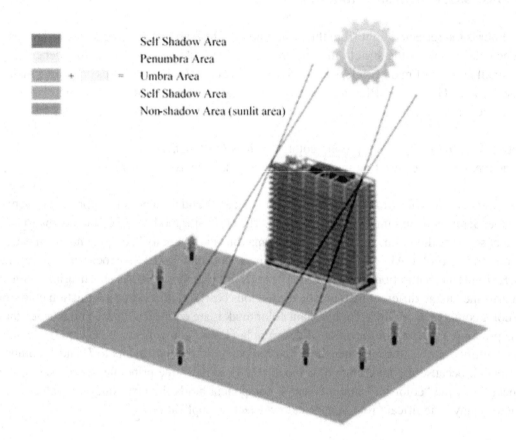

Shadow Detection in Digital Image

In the image-processing field, shadow detection in digital image is useful for various real applications (Leone, & Distante, 2007; Huang, & Chen, 2009; Tian, Lu, & Hampapur, 2005; Zhang, Fang, & Xu, 2006; Chen, Chi, Chen, & Hsu, 2003; Matthew, Felde, Golden, Gardner, & Anderson, 2000). Shadow presence in images, like in aerial images, makes the infected areas colorless. These shadow areas become darker, which means loss of important information. There are two types of shadows to be detected:

1- Static shadows that appear in still images taken by a camera, i.e. single image.
2- Dynamic shadows that appear in frames sequence, i.e. video.

Shadow detection in digital images is the process of finding the suitable feature that can be exploited in detecting the shadowed pixels. After detecting the shadow, the shadow removal process can be applied to compensate the pixels with their true color values. Depending on many factors, the shadow in the infected digital image can be detected using specific method that exploits a determined feature for the detection process. We work in our research on the static shadow detection in digital aerial images based on image pixels intensity values.

Digital Image Enhancement

Enhancement of a digital image is the process where the resultant image parts are more acceptable by the viewer or more suitable to be used as input for a specific application. Many applications that work with digital images need to enhance the input image in a desired way before start working on it. The enhancement process is very important and interesting because viewer can notice the explicit difference in the resultant image according to the desired enhancement process.

Image enhancement methods can be categorized into two groups: spatial and frequency methods. The spatial methods work on the image plane and deal with image pixels directly to perform any enhancement process. The frequency methods work on image after modifying it to Fourier transformation (Gonzalez, & Woods, 2002). Different mathematical equations and calculations are used according to the desired enhancement process. Enhancement in the gray level images is the simplest process among all image enhancement processes. It deals with 8 bit-image representation that gives a value between [0-255] for each pixel, 0 for "Black" and 255 for "White". There are three main useful functions are used for gray image enhancement:

Negative Transformation Function

The negative function reverses all pixels intensities from the range [0,255] to [255,0]. For each pixel intensity value in the input image, it is subtracted from 255 to produce the negative output image. For example, black pixels of "0" intensity value become white of "255" intensity value and white pixels of "255" intensity value become black of "0" intensity value. In general, in the negative transformation process, darker pixels become bright and brighter pixels become dark, see Figure 4 for a medical image. Figure 4(a) is an original 8-bit image of breast tissue and Figure 4(b) is its negative transformation.

Figure 4. Negative transformation for an 8-bit image (Gonzalez & Woods, 2002).

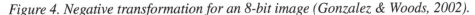

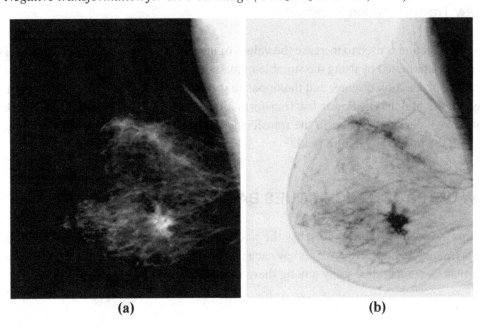

(a)   (b)

Log Transformation Function

The log function expands intensity values of dark pixels and compresses bright intensity values, see Figure 5, an original 8-bit image Figure 5(a) and its log transformation Figure 5(b). Many dark pixels in the original image, which some of them are not easy to be distinguished by naked eye, became brighter after applying the log transformation function. It has expanded the intensity values of those darker pixels to become bright and compressed the intensity values of the brighter pixels.

Figure 5. Log transformation for an 8-bit image (Gonzalez & Woods, 2002).

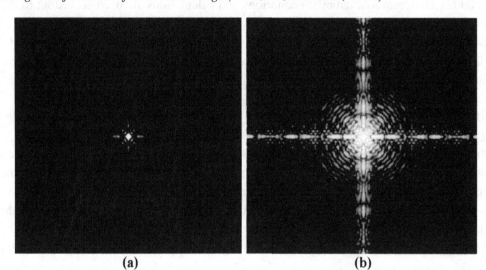

(a)   (b)

Power-Law Transformation Function

The power-law function is used to increase the values of narrow range of pixels dramatically. This range of pixels can be determined by using the suitable mathematical formula. Increasing the values of pixels will make these pixels look brighter and the opposite is true. As we can see from Figure 6, an original 8-bit image Figure 6(a) and its Power-law transformation Figure 6(b). Some determined dark pixels in the original image became brighter in the transformed image. Power-law function is useful for many applications in the image-processing field.

SHADOW DETECTION TECHNIQUES BASED ON FEATURES

In this section, we demonstrate and discuss the main features used in the literature to detect shadows (Musleh, Sarfraz, & Niepel, 2018). We review each method, present the features used by each algorithm, and finally make a comparative study among these algorithms according to their results.

Figure 6. Power-law transformation for an 8-bit image (Gonzalez & Woods, 2002).

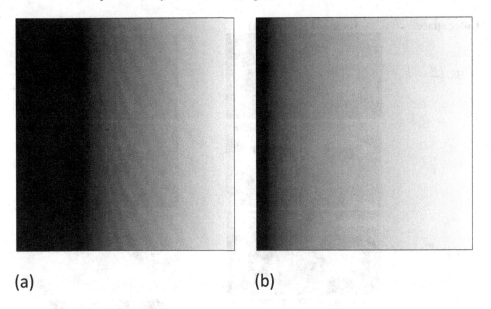

(a)   (b)

Pixel Intensity Based Methods

Here we highlight the shadow detection methods which are pixel intensity based.

Tsai Method

In (Tsai, 2006), a method that exploited the chromaticity and brightness of the shaded regions was presented by Tsai. The method was implemented using the following five invariant color models:

1. (YC_bC_r): luma, blue-difference chroma, and red-difference chroma (Gonzalez, & Woods, 2002).
2. (YIQ): luma, inphase, and quadrature (Pratt, 1991; Gonzalez, & Woods, 2002; Bingley, 1957).
3. *HSI*.
4. *HSV*.
5. (HCV): hue, chroma, and value (Smith, 1992).

First, the input *RGB* aerial image was converted into the five invariant color models, *YIQ*, YC_bC_r, *HSV*, *HCV*, and *HSI*. Then a ratio image (R), which is known as the mathematical division of Hue over Intensity equivalent components, was calculated for all images pixels. Figure 7 demonstrates the ratio images for the used five invariant color models. Numerator represents the equivalent Hue component and denominator represents the equivalent Intensity component for all the five invariant color models components. *R* was exploited to find a threshold using Otsu method (Otsu, 1979) to classify its pixels into two groups, candidate shadow and shadow-free groups depending on the threshold value. See Figure 7, candidate shadow areas are the brighter areas.

Figure 10 shows resultant shadow masks of *R* for the five color models using image Figure 8(a), all shadows appear in white color in the masks. Image of Figure 10(a) based on *HSI* color model (Threshold

Figure 7. The ratio images of five invariant color models (Tsai, 2006).

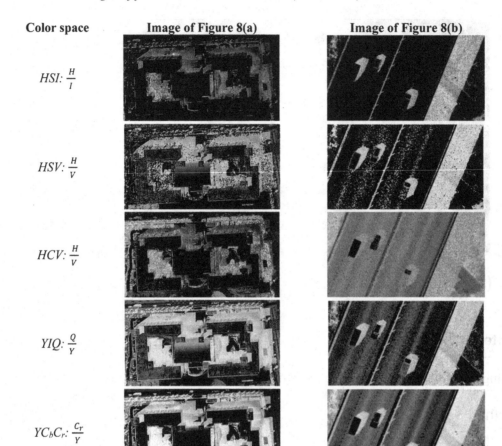

Color space	Image of Figure 8(a)	Image of Figure 8(b)
$HSI: \frac{H}{I}$		
$HSV: \frac{H}{V}$		
$HCV: \frac{H}{V}$		
$YIQ: \frac{Q}{Y}$		
$YC_bC_r: \frac{C_r}{Y}$		

= 66 for R). Figure 10(b) based on *HSV* color model (Threshold = 107 for R). Figure 10(c) based on *HCV* color model (Threshold = 86 for R). Figure 10(d) based on *YIQ* color model (Threshold = 134 for R). Figure 10(e) based on YC_bC_r color model (Threshold = 118 for R).

Objects shape preservation for casting shadow was presented in Tsai algorithm as a main part of his method, and he completed the process of reconstruction for shadow compensation. The compensation process for shadows is an important part after the detection process, but since our research concentrates on the process of shadow detecting, image reconstruction process is not presented in the review of Tsai algorithm.

Chung Method

A successive thresholding scheme (*STS*) was presented in (Chung et al., 2009b) to improve the shadow detection of Tsai method (Tsai, 2006). The presented *STS* improved the accuracy of Tsai method especially when the image contains low brightness regions. After transforming the *RGB* color image to *HSI* color model image, Chung et al. modified Tsai's R by applying an exponential function to it and generated a

Figure 8. RGB testing images used by Tsai method (Tsai, 2006).

(a)   (b)

Figure 9. Manually shadow detection as ground truth for image Figure 8(a) (Tsai, 2006).

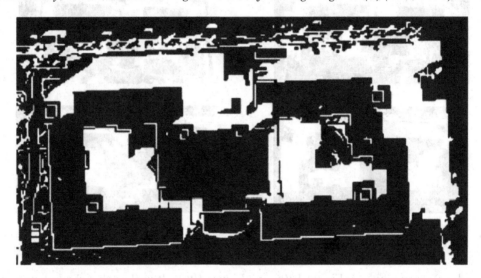

modified ratio image (R'). This helped for a better classifying when applying a threshold to R'. After that, a global threshold was obtained based on Otsu thresholding method (Otsu, 1979). The threshold was applied to R' to generate raw shadow image. The raw shadow image consists of two regions, candidate shadow and shadow-free regions.

Figure 11 shows a comparison between R of Tsai and R' of Chung. Figure 11(a) is the original image, Figure 11(b) is Tsai's R of Figure 11(a), Figure 11(c) is Chung's R' of Figure 11(a), Figure 11(d) is shadow detecting for Figure 11(b), Figure 11(e) is shadow detecting for Figure 11(c), shadows are in white for Figure 11(d) and Figure 11(e). Although the modified ratio helped in distinguishing shadowed areas more accurately and making the classification process for shadow and shadow-free pixels easier, a misclassification happened for some regions. To improve the detection process, a connected component (Gonzalez, & Woods, 2002) was applied to group all candidate shaded pixels as candidate shadow regions. Then a local threshold was generated to detect true shadow in the group of candidate shadow regions in a process known as *STS*. The *STS* improved the results of shadow detection.

Figure 12 shows a comparison between using *STS* and the global threshold. Figure 12(a) is the original image, Figure 12(b) is R' of Figure 12(a), Figure 12(c) is the shadow detecting for Figure 12(a) using global threshold, Figure 12(d) is the shadow detecting for Figure 12(a) using the successive thresholding

Figure 10. Resultant shadow masks of the five color models for the ratio images of Figure 8(a) using Tsai method (Tsai, 2006).

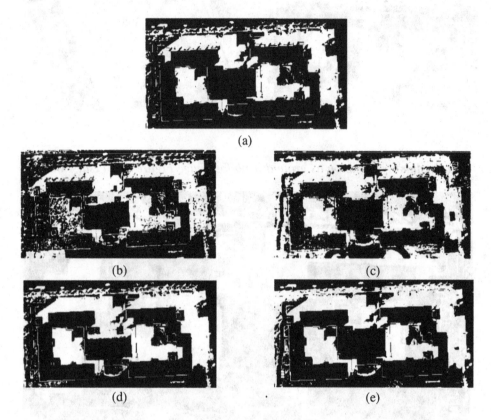

(a)

(b)   (c)

(d)   (e)

scheme, shadows are in white for Figure 12(c) and Figure 12(d). It is clear that shadow in Figure 12(d) was better detected than in Figure 12(c) comparing with the ideal detection in Figure 13(a). For any remaining candidate shadow regions, a fine-shadow determination technique was used to distinguish true shadow regions from nonshadow regions.

Figure 13 shows comparison among Huang (Huang et al., 2004), Tsai, and Chung algorithms using image Figure 12(a). Image of Figure 13(a) shows the result of ideal shadow detection, Figure 13(b) shows the result of shadow detection using Huang algorithm, Figure 13(c) shows the result of shadow detection using Tsai algorithm, Figure 13(d) shows the result of shadow detection using Chung algorithm, Shadows are in white color. As seen, Chung algorithm demonstrated the best results.

Illumination Direction of Light Source Based Method

Here we highlight the shadow detection methods which are based on illumination direction of light source. In (Russell et al., 2003), a method for detecting moving shadows of vehicles was proposed. The traditional shadow detection methods work on pixel or area level, but the proposed method of Russell works on image lines analysis. Russell method reduced the number of misclassified shadow pixels when edges between objects and their shadows are ambiguous. The method exploited the illumination direction and pixels intensity features to detect shadow pixels in the scanned image-lines pixels. In the

Figure 11. Comparison between Tsai ratio image and Chung modified ratio image (Chung et al., 2009b).

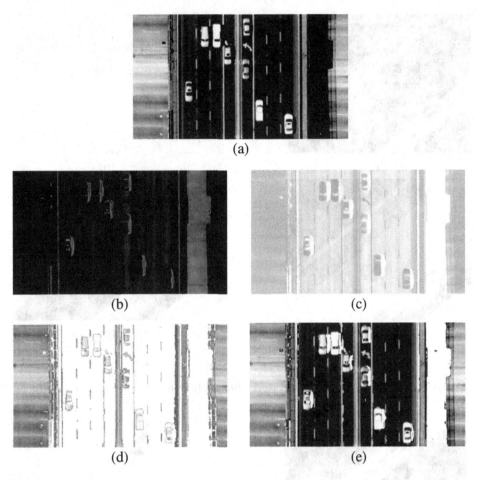

beginning, it was supposed that background frame and foreground of the vehicle and its shadow are available, like in Figure 14. After Russell has determined the direction of illumination of light source in the image based on (Wang, Chung, & Chen, 2004) technique, the method detected shadow by searching for decreasing intervals for the pixels lied on the scanned image-lines of the foreground image (vehicle and its shadow) in the opposite direction of the light source. The method classified the decreasing values of the pixels on the image-line as shadow until finished when facing a sudden bigger value for a pixel, which means that the searching process exceeded the object that occluded the light and the light started to reach again to the regions. This is because it was observed that the intensity values of shadow pixels p become smaller "darker" when moving in the direction from the shadow of an object to the object itself until reaching that object.

See Figure 3, when moving from penumbra area in direction to the building, shadow pixels become darker. This occurs because pixels receive less light when moving from penumbra shadow to the object itself (Russell, & Zou, 2012). When exceeding the object in the opposite direction of the light, pixels become nonshadow and their values become bigger "brighter" because they start to receive light again. See Figure 15 of a car to the right side and its shadow to the left side, a decreasing interval starts from point A and finishes in B where pixels values after the shadow of the car start to become bigger in direc-

Figure 12. Comparison between using the global threshold and STS (Chung et al., 2009b).

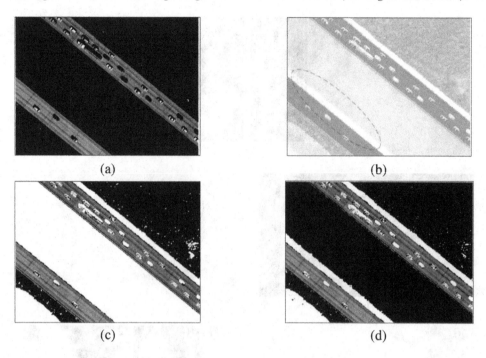

(a)   (b)

(c)   (d)

Figure 13. Comparison among Huang, Tsai, and Chung algorithms using image Figure 12(a) (Chung et al., 2009b).

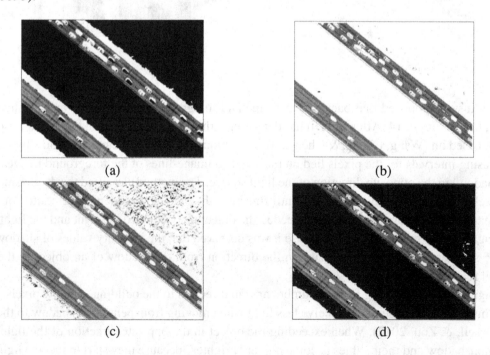

(a)   (b)

(c)   (d)

Figure 14. Determination of illumination direction (Wang et al., 2004).

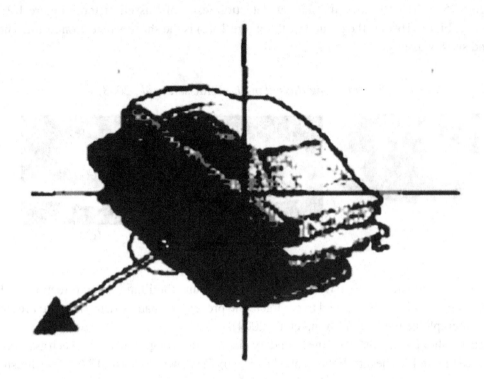

tion to point C because pixels start to receive light and become nonshadow. In Figure 15, the direction of light is from right to left. The figure shows the intensity values for scanned image-line along x-axis, see Equation (1).

From Figure 15, we can conclude:

$$I(po) > I(pi) > I(pu) \tag{1}$$

Figure 15. Intensity values for scanned image-line pixels along x-axis (Russell et al., 2003, p. 1).

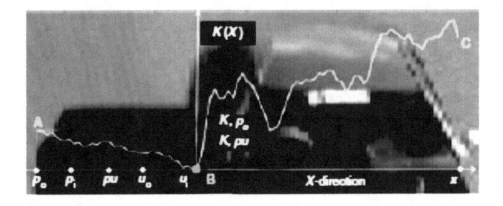

where $I(p_o)$, $I(p_i)$, and $I(p_u)$ are the Intensity values of the pixels (p_o), (p_i), and (p_u) that lie on the *x*-axis of Figure 15. Figure 16 shows the shadow detection result of Russell method. Figure 16(a) is the original image, Figure 16(b) is the ground truth, Figure 16(c) is the shadow detection result. The object is in red and shadow is in green.

Figure 16. Shadow detection result using Russell method (Russell et al., 2003).

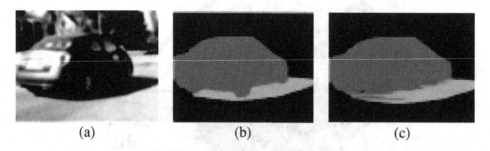

(a)   (b)   (c)

As mentioned, Russell has used Wang method to determine the illumination direction of the light source in the scene, which was required to complete the process of shadow detecting. We present in the following paragraph the method of (Wang et al., 2004).

At first, a threshold is calculated for the boundary pixels of the foreground figure, such as a vehicle and its shadow, see Figure 14. The threshold is calculated using Otsu method (Otsu, 1979). The threshold task is to separate the figure into two groups: dark and bright areas. After the separation process is completed, the figure is partitioned into four overlapping sections: up, down, right, and left (*Us*, *Ds*, *Rs*, *Ls*). Each *Us*, *Ds*, *Rs* and *Ls* section denotes the total number of dark pixels locate within it. *x* and *y* are the biggest numbers in the set (*Us*, *Ds*, *Rs*, *Ls*). Afterwards, a set of eight numbers denotes eight defined directions {0,1,2,3,4,5,6,7} as shown in Figure 17. The eight numbers are referred to as illumination directions.

After that, the following Equations (2) to (4) ar calculated to get the direction of illumination source:

Let N = (Us + Ds + Rs + Ls) / 4   (2)

And let *a* and *b* are the numbers of directions related to *x* and *y*.

Then A = (a+b)/2 and B = |a −b | (3)

The direction of illumination *DI*, is calculated as the following:

Figure 17. Eight directions of illumination.

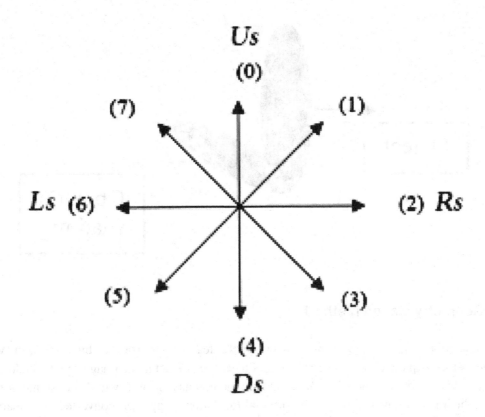

$$DI = \begin{cases} -1, & If\ (x,y < N)\ or\ (B = 4) \\ a, & If\ (x \geq N,\ y < N) \\ b, & If\ (x < N,\ y \geq N) \\ B+1, & If\ (B = 6) \\ A, & Else \end{cases}$$

(4)

$DI = -1$, i.e. the direction of illumination is not defined.

Back to Figure 14, the biggest two numbers of dark pixels in the figure are Ls and Ds, and $x = Ls$ & $y = Ds$. As known from Figure 17, numbers of directions related to Ls and Ds are 6 and 4 respectively, i.e., $a = 6$ and $b = 4$. Hence, $A = (a + b)/2 = 5$ and $B = |a - b| = 2$. Back to the defined Equations (2) to (4), the number of direction will be 5, which is the light direction in the Figure 14. Arrow is to the left lower direction.

Figure 18. An object and its shadow.

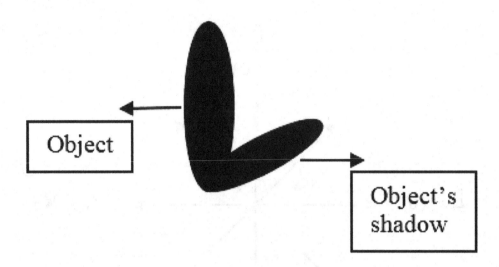

Object Geometry Based Method

A shadow detection method based on the object geometry feature was proposed by Vakhare in (Vakhare, 2015). The method exploited the geometrical relation between object in the image and its shadow. Figure 18 shows an object and its shadow in black. Vakhare method has the ability to detect single or multiple shadows in the image. In the beginning, the original *RGB* input image was converted to a binary image (2 bit-image: black and white) for improving purposes. After that, a region labeling process was performed using the binary image to generate an image of black color background "pixels of values 0" and remaining foreground of object and its shadow of white color "pixels of values 1", see Figure 19. Figure 19(a) is the original *RGB* image and Figure 19(b) is the converted binary image of white foreground and black background.

Finally, the following calculations are applied on the foreground (object and its shadow) of the binary image Figure 19(b) which consists of white foreground and black background:

Figure 19. Converting RGB image to binary image of white foreground and black background (Vakhare, 2015, p. 418).

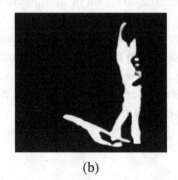

(a)   (b)

1. X_m is the mode of X.
2. Y_{max} is the absolute maximum value between two points vertically in the foreground object. A line is drawn horizontally at this point. (Line 1).
3. Calculate the Absolute value ($X_{maximum}$ - X_m) and the Absolute value ($X_{minimum}$ - X_m).
4. If value ($X_{minimum}$ - X_m) < value ($X_{maximum}$ - X_m):
    Distance = the absolute value ($X_{minimum}$ - X_m). At this point $X_{minimum}$, a line is drawn vertically. (Line 2),
    Else Distance = the absolute value ($X_{maximum}$ - X_m). At this point $X_{maximum}$, a line is drawn vertically. (Line 2).
5. Find the direction of the object by:
    $\alpha = 1/2 \, Tan^{-1}(2\mu 1.1/\mu 2.0 - \mu 0.2)$ using method of (Chang, Hu, Hsieh, & Chen, 2002).
6. In the crossing point between line 2 and line 1, line 3 is drawn in direction of α. Pixels along line 3, with length of $4 \times$ Distance, are made of black color "0", i.e. the same color of the background.
7. Region labeling is applied again to the binary image and object is made of black color "0" i.e. the same color of background

The result of the above calculations is a 2-bit image that consists of the detected shadow in white color "value 1 for shadow pixels" and the remaining black background "value 0 for background pixels". This resultant binary image is used as a mask to detect shadow from the original input image.

For simplicity, all the above calculations of Vakhare method are summarized below using Figure 20 to trace shadow detecting for a foreground (object and its shadow). The calculations can be traced step by step for better understanding. Shadow detection result is shown in Figure 21. Figure 21(a) is the original *RGB* input image, Figure 21(b) is the resultant shadow mask. Shadow appears in white color.

Let we have the above standing object and its shadow, then the following calculations are performed according to the Vakhare calculations to detect the shadow:

Figure 20. Geometrical calculations tracing of Vakhare method for an object and its shadow.

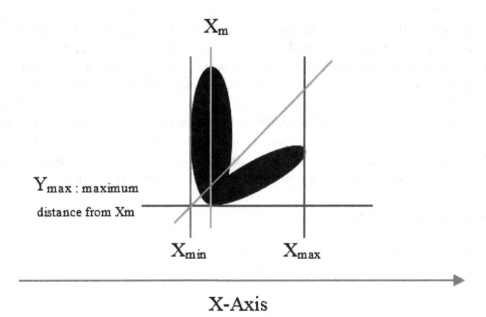

Figure 21. Resultant shadow mask for an input RGB image using Vakhare method (Vakhare, 2015).

(a)

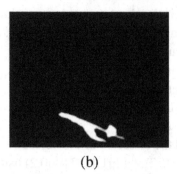

(b)

- $X_{minimum}$ is represented in the blue line (which is line 2 in the above calculations).
- $X_{maximum}$ is represented in the red line.
- $X_m X_{mode}$ represents point X on X-axis which its image f(X) is the farthest point on the top of the object from X-axis.
- $Y_{maximum}$ is represented in the purple line (which is line 1 in the above calculations). The purple line is the farthest Y point from the top point in the standing object.
- Direction line (which is line 3 in the above calculations) is the directed green line starting from the cross point between line 1 and 2 in direction of α.

Explanation: Back to Vakhare geometrical calculations, the object and its shadow are made in white color and black background respectively, but object and its shadow in Figure 20 are made in black and white background respectively only for better presentation purpose.

COMPARATIVE STUDY

We present in this section the results for the above-investigated existing methods based on the feature used by each method to detect the shadow. The accuracy results are presented in tables for the mentioned methods. Accordingly, a comparative study was conducted among the mentioned methods to evaluate their performance and find out the advantages and disadvantages for using each method.

In (Tsai, 2006), Tsai implemented his algorithm in personal computer under Microsoft Windows XP environment using MATLAB. He used ground truth masks for shadow areas to compare them with his resultant images of shadow detection. For accuracy assessment, Tsai followed the terminology in (Prati, Mikic, Trivedi, & Cucchiara, 2003; Yao, & Zhang, 2004) and error matrix of (Lillesand, & Kiefer, 2000; Philipson, 1997). He used three accuracy measurements at the pixel level as follows:

1) Producer's accuracy for shadow areas (PS):

$$PS = \frac{TP}{TP+FN} \tag{5}$$

2) Producer's accuracy for shadow-free areas (Pf):

$$Pf=\frac{TN}{TN+FP} \qquad (6)$$

3) User's accuracy for shadow areas (Us):

$$Us=\frac{TP}{TP+FP} \qquad (7)$$

4) User's accuracy for shadow-free areas (Uf):

$$Uf=\frac{TN}{TN+FN} \qquad (8)$$

5) Overall accuracy (OA):

$$OA=\frac{TP+TN}{IP}, \qquad (9)$$

where TP is number of shaded pixels have been detected correctly, FN is number of shaded pixels have been identified as nonshaded pixels, FP is number of nonshaded pixels have been identified as shaded pixels, TN is number of nonshaded pixels have been detected correctly, and IP is total number of image pixels. Accuracy of Tsai method is presented in Table 1, using the Equations (5) to (9).

Table 1. Tsai method accuracy using image Figure 8(a).

Algorithm	Used Color Model	Producer Accuracy		User Accuracy		OA (%)
		P_s(%)	P_f(%)	U_s(%)	U_f(%)	
Tsai	YC_bC_r	97.5	93.2	88.7	98.6	94.7
	HSV	79.6	86.6	76.5	88.6	84.1
	HSI	89.9	99.0	97.9	94.7	95.7
	YIQ	95.6	94.4	90.3	97.5	94.8
	HCV	88.8	78.3	69.1	92.7	82.0

In (Chung et al., 2009b), the algorithm was implemented in IBM Pentium IV, 3.2 GHz microprocessor and 1-GB RAM under Microsoft Windows XP environment. The development environment of Chung program was Borland C++. The developed program has been uploaded by the authors, and it can be retrieved via (Chung, Lin, and Huang, 2009a). The results of Chung algorithm were compared with the results of Tsai and (Huang et al., 2004) using six testing images. In the first three images, Tsai and Chung methods had better detection performance than Huang method. In the other three images that contained low brightness objects, Chung method had better shadow detection performance in comparison with the previous two methods. See the accuracy for the three methods as shown in Table 2 using the Equations (5) to (9).

Table 2. Accuracy of three methods using image Figure 12(a).

No.	Algorithm	Producer Accuracy		User Accuracy		OA (%)
		$P_s(\%)$	$P_j(\%)$	$U_s(\%)$	$U_j(\%)$	
1	Huang	99.5	22.4	14.7	99.7	31.5
2	Tsai	99.6	27.0	15.5	99.8	35.6
3	Chung	93.3	98.9	92.2	99.1	98.2

In Russell method, the algorithm was implemented in PC of 3.6 GHz Processor with 16 GB RAM using MATLAB. The algorithm was evaluated by finding the detection rates and discrimination. Shadow detection rate (D_r) is the percentage of shaded pixels (TP_S and FN_S) are correctly detected as shaded (TP_S), while shadow discrimination rate (S_d) is the percentage of object pixels (TP_F and FN_F) are correctly detected as object (TP_F). Resultant accuracy of Russell method using three testing images are presented in Table 3. Results were calculated using Equations (10) and (11). The calculations of the discrimination and detection rates are presented in the following equations:

$$Dr = \frac{TPS}{TPS+FNS} \qquad (10)$$

$$Sd = \frac{TPF}{TPF+FNF} \qquad (11)$$

In Vakhare method implementation, four different testing images were used. Two images contained one object and its shadow, while the other two images contained multiple objects and their shadows. Vakhare used the Equations (5) to (9) to evaluate the method. The results are shown in Table 4.

After reviewing the mentioned existing methods and showing their experimental results according to the stated researches, we evaluate the methods as follows. It is clear from the low producer's accuracy of images Table 4(b) and Table 4(d) that Vakhare method performance decreased when the shadow and background are not contrasted in the image. Vakhare method depends on the prior information of the objects in the image. Finding the direction of the object in Vakhare algorithm reduced the detection errors when the object and shadow are not perpendicular. The advantages and disadvantages of Vakhare method are presented in Table 7 and Table 8.

Russell method was proposed for dynamic shadows detection, such as moving vehicles shadows in the traffic video frames. Finding the decreasing pixels values intervals in the image lines solved the issue

Table 3. Accuracy of Russell method (Russell et al., 2003).

Frames	Number of used ground truth images	Russell Algorithm	
		D_r (%)	S_d (%)
(a)	182	93.2	89.2
(b)	85	93.8	93.8
(c)	142	90.0	93.1

of ambiguity between shadow and foreground. Because Russell method works on moving shadows of the video frames sequence, Russell supposed the availability of the background frame. Russell method advantages and disadvantages are shown in Table 7 and Table 8.

From Table 1, we can see that using the *HSI* color model showed the best result for Tsai algorithm in comparison with the other invariant color models. This is clear from shadow detection result of Figure 10(a) that almost matched the ground truth image of Figure 9. Tsai and Chung methods share the same idea of finding the ratio image to detect shadow but applying the exponential function to Tsai ratio image and using the *STS* by Chung have enhanced the accuracy of Tsai algorithm. This can be seen from results of Table 2 of implementing three methods using image Figure 12(a) that has low brightness regions. Among all mentioned existing methods, Chung and Tsai methods do not need any prior information of the scene and they are suitable for shadow detecting in static aerial images.

Comparisons among the four methods are presented in Table 5 according to three factors: the used feature, algorithm working level, and shadow type that is supposed to be detected. Accuracy average of each algorithm is presented in Table 6. The averages cannot be comparative because each algorithm works on specific type of images. Accordingly, different type of testing images were used with the methods.

Table 4 Accuracy of Vakhare method (Vakhare, 2015).

Images	Producer Accuracy		User Accuracy		OA (%)
	P_s (%)	P_f (%)	U_s (%)	U_f (%)	
(a)	88.4	1.3	96.6	99.8	96.5
(b)	30.7	1.4	77.8	99.8	96.5
(c)	86.9	2.9	96.9	99.5	99.4
(d)	48.0	2.3	71.9	97.4	96.6

CONCLUSION

The chapter has presented a comprehensive understanding of the concepts and techniques used in shadow detection. It introduced the basic concepts of digital images, color models, shadow formation, and image enhancement. It has also presented the relevant existing research and provided a deep study on the existing shadow detection methods based on their used features. It has presented various existing shadow detection methods from the literature. It focused on the shadow detection techniques based

Table 5. Comparison among four methods.

No.	Algorithm	Method Based Feature	Working Level	Shadow Type
1	Chung	Pixels intensity	Pixel	Static
2	Vakhare	Object geometry	Area	Static
3	Russell	Illumination direction and pixels intensity	Image line	Dynamic
4	Tsai	Pixels intensity	Pixel	Static

Table 6. Accuracy averages of four methods.

No.	Algorithm	Input Image	OA (%)		OA Averages	
1	Tsai using *HSI* model	Figure 8(a)	95.7		96.1	
		Figure 8(b)	96.6			
2	Chung	Figure 22(a)	97.1		95.1	
		Figure 22(b)	96.8			
		Figure 22(c)	90.6			
		Figure 22(d)	96.3			
		Figure 12(a)	98.2			
		Figure 22 (e)	91.4			
3	Vakhare	Table 4(a)	96.5		97.2	
		Table 4(b)	96.5			
		Table 4(c)	99.4			
		Table 4(d)	96.6			
		Testing Image Frames	$D_r(\%)$	$S_d(\%)$	**Average of $D_r(\%)$**	**Average of $S_d(\%)$**
4	Russell	Table 3(a)	93.2	89.2	92.4	92.0
		Table 3(b)	93.8	93.8		
		Table 3(c)	90.0	93.1		

on their main features. It has concentrated specifically on four methods namely Tsai, Chung, Russell, and Vakhare. An extensive investigation of these methods was conducted and a comparative study was accomplished depending on main three features: image pixels intensity, illumination direction in the scene, and objects geometry in the image. This chapter also presented the advantages of the existing mentioned methods, which will help in decision making as to which technique to be used for shadow detection according to the image and shadow type. As a future study, the authors are working to devise new improved method(s) competing with existing efficient ones.

Figure 22. The original RGB testing images used by Chung (Chung et al., 2009b).

Table 7. Methods advantages.

No.	Algorithm	Advantages
1	Vakhare	In shadow detection phase, the method calculations conducted only on foreground (objects and their shadows) not on the whole image.
2	Chung	The method detects shadow more accurately than Tsai especially when the input image has low brightness regions.
3	Tsai	No need for any prior knowledge of the scene, such as light direction or object geometry.
4	Russell	Finding the decreasing intervals for the pixels on the scanned lines of the image to detect the shadow, solve the problem of camouflage between foreground object and shadow.

Table 8. Methods disadvantages.

No.	Algorithm	Disadvantages
1	Vakhare	The method does not work properly if the background and shadow are not well contrasted.
2	Chung	In comparison with Huang and Tsai algorithms, Chung algorithm is time consuming due to the huge number of operations it has to conduct.
3	Tsai	Method performance decreases when it is used with images that have low brightness regions.
4	Russell	At the beginning, the method supposes that the foreground (object and its shadow) are extracted from the background, so accuracy depends on how correctly the extraction process has been performed.

REFERENCES

Bertalmio, M., Caselles, V., & Provenzi, E. (2009). Issues about retinex theory and contrast enhancement. *International Journal of Computer Vision, 83*(01), 101–119. doi:10.100711263-009-0221-5

Bingley, F. (1957). *Color vision and colorimetry*. McGraw Hill.

Chang, C., Hu, W., Hsieh, J., & Chen, Y. (2002). Shadow Elimination for Effective Moving Object Detection with Gaussian Models. *IEEE Conference on Pattern Recognition*, 540-543. 10.1109/ICPR.2002.1048359

Chen, C., & Aggarwal, J. (2010). Human shadow removal with unknown light source. *International Conference on Pattern Recognition*, 2407-2410. 10.1109/ICPR.2010.589

Chen, J., Chi, M., Chen, M., & Hsu, C. (2003). ROI video coding based on H2.63+ with robust skin-color detection technique. *IEEE Transactions on Consumer Electronics, 49*(03), 724–730. doi:10.1109/TCE.2003.1233810

Chung, K., Lin, Y., & Huang, Y. (2009a). *The Algorithm program*. Retrieved from http://140.118.175.164/Huang/STS-BasedAlgorithm.zip

Chung, K., Lin, Y., & Huang, Y. (2009b). Efficient Shadow Detection of Color Aerial Images Based on Successive Thresholding Scheme. *IEEE Transactions on Geoscience and Remote Sensing, 47*(02), 671–682. doi:10.1109/TGRS.2008.2004629

Fang, L., Qiong, W., & Sheng, Y. (2008). A method to segment moving vehicle cast shadow based on wavelet transform. *Pattern Recognition Letters, 29*(16), 2182–2188. doi:10.1016/j.patrec.2008.08.009

Gonzalez, R., & Woods, R. (2002). *Digital Image Processing* (2nd ed.). Prentice Hall.

Horprasert, T., Harwood, D., & Davis, L. (1999). A statistical approach for real-time robust background subtraction and shadow detection. In *IEEE ICCV'99 Frame-Rate Workshop*. University of Maryland.

Hsieh, J., Hu, W., Chang, C., & Chen, Y. (2003). Shadow elimination for effective moving object detection by Gaussian shadow modeling. *Image and Vision Computing, 21*(06), 505–516. doi:10.1016/S0262-8856(03)00030-1

Huang, J., & Chen, C. (2009). Moving cast shadow detection using physics-based features. *IEEE Conference on Computer Vision and Pattern Recognition*, 2310-2317. 10.1109/CVPR.2009.5206629

Huang, J., Xie, W., & Tang, L. (2004). Detection and compensation for shadows in colored urban aerial images. *5th World Congr. Intell. Control Autom*, 3098-3100. 10.1109/WCICA.2004.1343090

Kang, X., Huang, Y., Li, S., Lin, H., & Benediktsson, J. (2018). Extended Random Walker for Shadow Detection in Very High Resolution Remote Sensing Images. *IEEE Transactions on Geoscience and Remote Sensing, 56*(02), 867–876. doi:10.1109/TGRS.2017.2755773

Leone, A., & Distante, C. (2007). Shadow detection for moving objects based on texture analysis. *Pattern Recognition, 40*(04), 1222–1233. doi:10.1016/j.patcog.2006.09.017

Li, H., Zhang, L., & Shen, H. (2012). A perceptually inspired variational method for the uneven intensity correction of remote sensing images. *IEEE Transactions on Geoscience and Remote Sensing, 50*(08), 3053–3065. doi:10.1109/TGRS.2011.2178075

Lillesand, T., & Kiefer, R. (2000). *Remote Sensing and Image Interpretation* (4th ed.). Wiley.

Matthew, M., Felde, G., Golden, S., Gardner, J., & Anderson, G. (2000). An algorithm for de-shadowing spectral imagery. *Proceedings of SPIE - The International Society for Optical Engineering, 4816*(10), 203-210.

Mo, N., Zhu, R., Yan, L., & Zhao, Z. (2018). Deshadowing of Urban Airborne Imagery Based on Object-Oriented Automatic Shadow Detection and Regional Matching Compensation. *IEEE Journal of Selected Topics in Applied Earth Observations and Remote Sensing, 11*(02), 585–605. doi:10.1109/JSTARS.2017.2787116

Mostafa, Y., & Abdelhafiz, A. (2017). Accurate Shadow Detection from High-Resolution Satellite Images. *IEEE Trans. on Geoscience and Remote Sensing Letters, 14*(4), 494-498.

Musleh, S., Sarfraz, M., & Niepel, L. (2018). A Comparative Study on Shadow Detection Methods Based on Features. *IEEE International Conference on Computing Sciences and Engineering (ICCSE).* 10.1109/ICCSE1.2018.8373992

Nair, V., Ram, P., & Sundararaman, S. (2019). Shadow detection and removal from images using machine learning and morphological operations. *ITE The Journal of Engineering, 2019*(01), 11–18. doi:10.1049/joe.2018.5241

Nicolas, H., & Pinel, J. (2006). Joint moving cast shadows segmentation and light source detection in video sequences. *Signal Processing Image Communication, 21*(1), 22–43. doi:10.1016/j.image.2005.06.001

Otsu, N. (1979). A threshold selection method from gray level histograms. *IEEE Transactions on Systems, Man, and Cybernetics, 9*(01), 62–69. doi:10.1109/TSMC.1979.4310076

Philipson, W. (1997). Manual of Photographic Interpretation (2nd ed.). Bethesda, MD: American Society Photogrammetry and Remote Sensing (ASPRS).

Polidorio, A., Flores, F., Imai, N., Tommaselli, A., & Franco, C. (2003). Automatic shadow segmentation in aerial color images. *XVI Brazilian Symp. Comput. Graph. Image Process*, 270-277. 10.1109/SIBGRA.2003.1241019

Prati, A., Mikic, I., Trivedi, M., & Cucchiara, R. (2003). Detecting moving shadows: Algorithms and evaluations. *IEEE Transactions on Pattern Analysis and Machine Intelligence, 25*(07), 918–923. doi:10.1109/TPAMI.2003.1206520

Pratt, W. (1991). *Digital Image Processing* (2nd ed.). Wiley.

Ronan, P. (2007). *Electromagnetic Spectrum*. Retrieved from http://www.kiwiwise.co.nz/photo/fantail-vector

Russell, A., & Zou, J. (2012). Vehicle detection based on color analysis. *IEEE Conf. on Communications and Information Technologies (ISCIT)*, 620-625.

Russell, M., Zou, J., & Fang, G. (2003). Real-time vehicle shadow detection. *IEEE Electronics Letters*, *51*(16), 1253–1255. doi:10.1049/el.2015.1841

Smith, H. (1992). Putting colors in order. *Dr. Dobb's Journal*, *1993*(01), 40.

Song, H., Huang, B., & Zhang, K. (2014). Shadow Detection and Reconstruction in High-Resolution Satellite Images via Morphological Filtering and Example-Based Learning. *IEEE Transactions on Geoscience and Remote Sensing, 52*(05), 2545–2554. doi:10.1109/TGRS.2013.2262722

Su, N., Zhang, Y., Tian, S., Yan, Y., & Miao, X. (2016). Shadow Detection and Removal for Occluded Object Information Recovery in Urban High-Resolution Panchromatic Satellite Images. *IEEE Journal on Geoscience and Remote Sensing, 9*(6), 2568-2582.

Tian, Y., Lu, M., & Hampapur, A. (2005). Robust and efficient foreground analysis for real-time video surveillance. *IEEE Conference on Computer Vision and Pattern Recognition*, 1182-1187.

Tsai, V. (2006). A comparative study on shadow compensation of color aerial images in invariant color models. *IEEE Transactions on Geoscience and Remote Sensing, 44*(06), 1661–1671. doi:10.1109/TGRS.2006.869980

Vakhare, P. (2015). Shadow detection and elimination using geometric approach for static images. *IEEE Conference on Applied and Theoretical Computing and Communication Technology (iCATccT)*, 415-419. 10.1109/ICATCCT.2015.7456919

Wang, J., Chung, Y., & Chen, S. (2004). Shadow detection and removal for traffic images. *IEEE Int. Conf. on Networking, Sensing and Control*, 649-654. 10.1109/ICNSC.2004.1297516

Yao, J., & Zhang, Z. (2004). Systematic static shadow detection. *Proc. 17th Int. Conf. Pattern Recognition*, 76-79.

Yarlagadda, S., & Zhu, F. (2018). A Reflectance Based Method For Shadow Detection and Removal. *IEEE Southwest Symposium Conference on Image Analysis and Interpretation (SSIAI)*, 9-12. 10.1109/SSIAI.2018.8470343

Yoneyama, A., Yeh, C., & Kuo, C. (2003). Moving cast shadow elimination for robust vehicle extraction based on 2d joint vehicle/shadow models. *IEEE Conference on Advanced Video and Signal Based Surveillance*, 229–236. 10.1109/AVSS.2003.1217926

Zhang, H., Sun, K., & Li, W. (2014). Object-Oriented Shadow Detection and Removal from Urban High-Resolution Remote Sensing Images. *IEEE Transactions on Geoscience and Remote Sensing, 52*(11), 6972–6982. doi:10.1109/TGRS.2014.2306233

Zhang, W., Fang, X., & Xu, Y. (2006). Detection of moving cast shadows using image orthogonal transform. *International Conference on Pattern Recognition*, 626-629. 10.1109/ICPR.2006.441

Chapter 8
Medical Image Zooming by Using Rational Bicubic Ball Function

Samsul Ariffin Abdul Karim
Universiti Teknologi PETRONAS, Malaysia

Nur Atiqah Binti Zulkifli
Universiti Teknologi PETRONAS, Malaysia

A'fza Binti Shafie
Universiti Teknologi PETRONAS, Malaysia

Muhammad Sarfraz
https://orcid.org/0000-0003-3196-9132
Kuwait University, Kuwait

Abdul Ghaffar
https://orcid.org/0000-0002-5994-8440
Ton Duc Thang University, Vietnam

Kottakkaran Sooppy Nisar
Prince Sattam bin Abdulaziz University, Saudi Arabia

ABSTRACT

This chapter deals with image processing in the specific area of image zooming via interpolation. The authors employ bivariate rational cubic ball function defined on rectangular meshes. These bivariate spline have six free parameters that can be used to alter the shape of the surface without needed to change the data. It also can be used to refine the resolution of the image. In order to cater the image zomming, they propose an efficient algorithm by including image downscaling and upscaling procedures.

DOI: 10.4018/978-1-7998-4444-0.ch008

To measure the effectiveness of the proposed scheme, they compare the performance based on the value of peak signal-to-noise ratio (PSNR) and root mean square error (RMSE). Comparison with existing schemes such as nearest neighbour (NN), bilinear (BL), bicubic (BC), bicubic Hermite (BH), and existing scheme Karim and Saaban (KS) have been made in detail. From all numerical results, the proposed scheme gave higher PSNR value and smaller RMSE value for all tested images.

1. INTRODUCTION

The technology of image processing in medical field is vigorously grow in the industry as the demand increases from time to time. Foremost among them have been explored the digital medical imaging modalities for past two decades. For instance, the technology in film scanners, ultrasound, Magnetic Resonance Imaging (MRI), Computed Tomography (CT), Positron Emission Tomography (PET), Single Positron Emission Computed Tomography (SPECT), Digital Subtraction Angiography (DSA), and Magnetic Source Imaging (MSI) etc. These modalities constitute about 30% of the radiologic imaging examinations and 70% of examinations on skull, chest, breast, abdomen and bone which has been done in conventional x-rays and digital luminescent radiography (Wong, 2012). The image within the patient's body have different kind of film digitizers such as, laser scanner, solid-state camera, drumscanner, and video camera that capable to convert X-ray films into digital format for image processing. Therefore, image zooming on the selected parts are important especially when the expert want to detect any anomalies at the body paertss. Usually in imaze zooming, a two-dimensional (2-D) specifically grayscale medical image such as X-ray film with a size of 256 x 256 bits are employed as a tested image.

Image zooming is one of application in image interpolation. It is process of magnifying or reducing the size of the image and interpolation activity takes place during the process. Usually medical digital images produced have low resolution images due to the nature of the acquisition. Moreover, when the medical image is zoomed at certain part will cause the reduction of resolution if its done without interpolation. There are numbers of studies proposed a method and solution to improve the visual and objective quality of a medical image such as image upscaling, image zooming and image rotation. From the previous works, spline is the most common method for image interpolation that used to attain high quality of medical images. For example, Gao et al. (2008) proposed trigonometric spline with control parameters for medical image interpolation. Another study, they introduced the bivariate rational spline to interpolate medical image in respective activity such resizing, zooming and enhancement (Gao et al., 2008; Gao et al., 2009; Zhang et al., 2009; Zhang et al., 2012). Meanwhile, in Pal (2016), the authors has studied the zooming operation based on the principle of analog clock and utilizing the combination point and eighbourhood in image processing.

Table 1 summariz some related literature review including our recent study i.e. Zulkifli et al. (2019). Meanwhile Table 1 shows some abbreviations used in this study.

The main objective of the current study is to develop an efficient algorithm to zooming some medical images such as CT scan, MRI and thermal camera. To achieve this, we utilized the rational bicubic Ball with six parameters initiated by Zulkifli et al. (2019). The main different between the present study and

Table 1. Literature review

Scheme	Features
Abbas et al. (2017)	Advantage: The model have free parameters to modify the final resolution of image, easy to understand and implement, and the results are presented in both subjective and objective measurements. Implication: They used Bernstein Bézier cubic trigonometric basis functions with no free parameters in description.
Gao et al. (2008)	Advantage: The model can pass through the known data, simple and explicit expression, and the expression is piecewise with free parameters. Implication: The results only display visually and image of the comparison method is not very noticeable.
Gao et al. (2009)	Advantage: The model can pass through the known data, simple and explicit expression, and the expression is piecewise with free parameters. Implication: Extent work from Gao et al. (2008) in different application.
Zhang et al. (2009)	Advantage: The model can pass through the known data, simple and explicit expression, and the expression is piecewise with free parameters. Implication: The results only display visually and image of the comparison method is not very noticeable.
Zhang et al. (2012)	Advantage: Have free parameters, can preserve high frequency of image on region edge, keep the contour clear. Implication: Have only one parameter.
Pal (2016)	Advantage: Can evaluates many medical image from various sources such as CT- scan, MRI and X-ray. Disadvantage: Using polynomial with bicubic interpolation basis which is not very familiar method and have no free parameter in description.
Zulkifli et al. (2019)	Discussed the application of bivariate Ball spline function in image interpolation with factors 2 and 4. Their scheme is better than some existing scheme.

the one in Zulkifli et al. (2019) is that, is this study we have extend their algorithm i.e. image upscaling for medical image zooming.

The remainder of chapter is organized as follows. Section 2 and 3 in respective discussing the construction of rational bi-cubic Ball initiated by Zulkifli et al. (2019) and Image Quality Assessment (IQA) as measurement of performance evaluation. Section 4 presents an algorithm used for implementation of the proposed scheme. Followed by results and discussion in Section 5 with overall summary of the scheme in conclusion explained in Section 6.

Table 2. List of abbreviation

Abbreviation	Definition
Medical imaging	Technique or process of capturing and observing an activity of the interior of body that concern with interaction of radiation and tissue for the clinical analysis in form of two-dimension or three-dimension signal.
Image zooming	The process by which image pixels get expanded (image magnification) and the interpolation takes place to form a new image pixels.
Free parameter	Variable in the proposed scheme used to refine the image resolution.
IQA	The final quality assessment of interpolating image that cannot be perceived by human eyes.
PSNR	Ratio between the maximal power of the reference image and the noise power of interpolated image.
RMSE	Average pixels error between the two images such as reference image and interpolating image.
X-ray	Type of electromagnetic radiation that able to see under humans' skin, bone and beneath it. It used for imaging test to help medical diagnose the disease.

2. REVIEW ON RATIONAL BICUBIC BALL INTERPOLATION

In this section, we review the construction of rational bi-cubic Ball function initiated in Karim (2015) and Zulkifli et al. (2019).

2.1 Rational Bicubic Ball with Six Parameters

The rational bicubic function over each rectangular patch $[x_i, x_{i+1}] \times [y_j, y_{j+1}]$, where $i = 0, 1, \ldots, n-1$; $j = 0, 1, \ldots, m-1$ is defined as follows:
Let,

$$h_i = x_{i+1} + x_i, \ \hat{h}_j = y_{j+1} + y_j,$$

$$\theta = \frac{x - x_i}{h_i}, \ \varnothing = \frac{y - y_{ij}}{\hat{h}_j} \text{ with } 0 \le \theta \le 1, \ 0 \le \varnothing \le 1 \text{ and}$$

$$\alpha_{i,j}, \ \beta_{i,j}, \ \gamma_{i,j}, \ \hat{\alpha}_{i,j}, \ \hat{\beta}_{i,j}, \ \hat{\gamma}_{i,j} > 0, \ i = 0, \ldots, n, \ j = 0, \ldots, m$$

$$B_{i,j}(x, y) = J(\theta) I_{i,j} J_j(\varnothing)^T \qquad (1)$$

with

$$J_i(\theta) = \begin{bmatrix} a_0(\theta) & a_1(\theta) & a_2(\theta) & a_3(\theta) \end{bmatrix}$$

$$J_j(\varnothing) = \begin{bmatrix} \hat{a}_0(\varnothing) & \hat{a}_1(\varnothing) & \hat{a}_2(\varnothing) & \hat{a}_3(\varnothing) \end{bmatrix}$$

$$\text{where, } a_0(\theta) = \frac{\alpha_{i,j}(1-\theta)^2 + \gamma_{i,j}\theta(1-\theta)^2}{q_i(\theta)}$$

$$\hat{a}_0(\varnothing) = \frac{\hat{\alpha}_{i,j}(1-\varnothing)^2 + \hat{\gamma}_{i,j}\varnothing(1-\varnothing)^2}{q_i(\varnothing)}$$

$$a_1(\theta) = \frac{\beta_{i,j}\theta^2 + \gamma_{i,j}(1-\theta)\theta^2}{q_i(\theta)}$$

$$\hat{a}_1\left(\varnothing\right) = \frac{\hat{\beta}_{i,j}\varnothing^2 + \hat{\gamma}_{i,j}\left(1-\varnothing\right)\varnothing^2}{q_j\left(\varnothing\right)}$$

$$a_2\left(\theta\right) = \frac{\alpha_{i,j}h_i\left(1-\theta\right)^2\theta}{q_i\left(\theta\right)}$$

$$\hat{a}_2\left(\varnothing\right) = \frac{\hat{\alpha}_{i,j}\hat{h}_j\left(1-\varnothing\right)^2\varnothing}{q_i\left(\theta\right)}$$

$$a_3\left(\theta\right) = \frac{-\beta_{i,j}h_i\left(1-\theta\right)\theta^2}{q_i\left(\theta\right)}$$

$$\hat{a}_3\left(\varnothing\right) = \frac{-\hat{\beta}_{i,j}\hat{h}_j\left(1-\varnothing\right)\varnothing^2}{q_j\left(\varnothing\right)}$$

$$q_i\left(\theta\right) = \alpha_{i,j}\left(1-\theta\right)^2 + \gamma_{i,j}\left(1-\theta\right)\theta + \beta_{i,j}\theta^2$$

$$q_j\left(\varnothing\right) = \hat{\alpha}_{i,j}\left(1-\varnothing\right)^2 + \hat{\gamma}_{i,j}\left(1-\varnothing\right)\varnothing + \hat{\beta}_{i,j}\varnothing^2$$

where

$F_{i,j}$: First partial derivative

$F^x_{i,j}$: First partial derivative on x directions

$F^y_{i,j}$: First partial derivative on y directions

$F^{xy}_{i,j}$: Mixed partial derivatives at the interior points

Figure 1 shows the example of the idea on image interpolation with factor 4.

3. IMAGE QUALITY ASSESSMENT

Image Quality Assessment (IQA) can be used to measure the quality of the image. It is also known as objective quality measurements that provide automatic evaluation through quantifying metrics. Meanwhile, the subjective quality measure has to be performed by Human Visual System (HVS) that only understands an image mainly according to its low-level features (Kok and Tam, 2019). In this study, there are two types of IQA that have been used to test the effectiveness of the proposed scheme i.e. Peak

Figure 1. Pixel points of image; (a) 1 by 1 pixel and (b) 4 by 4 pixel

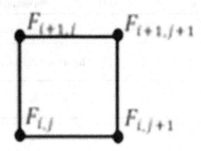

Signal-to-Noise Ratio (PSNR) and Root Mean Square Error (RMSE), defined in Equations (2) and (3), respectively. Both measurements have been used in many studies (Karim and Saaban, 2017).

a)   a) Peak signal-to-noise ratio (PSNR)

$$PSNR = 10\log_{10}\frac{255^2}{MSE} \tag{2}$$

where,

$$MSE = \frac{1}{mn}\sum_{i=0}^{n}\sum_{j=0}^{m}\left|z_{ij} - \overline{z}_{ij}\right|^2$$

b)   b) Root Mean Square Error (RMSE)

$$RMSE = \sqrt{\frac{1}{mn}\sum_{i=0}^{n}\sum_{j=0}^{m}\left|z_{ij} - \overline{z}_{ij}\right|^2} \tag{3}$$

4. METHODOLOGY

This section is devoted to experiment and implementation of the proposed scheme in application image zooming. We have chosen some standard tested images based on X-ray films such as wrist and pelvic fracture. The proposed algorithm is almost the same as our image interpolation algorithm proposed in Zulkifli et al. (2019). The main different here is in the first step. To zoom the images, we do require

Table 3. List of abbreviation of Equation (2) and (3).

Symbol	Definition
m, n	Image pixels
$z_{i,j}$	Input pixel i.e. grayscale intensity
$\bar{z}_{i,j}$	Interpolating input pixels

that, the tested images being crop in the selected region and the image size is 128 x 128 (gray scale). Then, these cropped images are subjected to the standard image interpolation procedures as discussed in details in Zulkifli et al. (2019). We summarize the main algorithm here and is visualized in Figure 2.

Algorithm: Image zooming
Input: Images, stopping criteria, and free parameters
Output: Zooming images, PSNR, RMSE
Step 1:Crop selected region on the image resulting 128 x 128 pixels. Define this as new image. These new image will be used for Step 1 until Step 6.
    Step 2:   Simulate by varying the free parameters and calculate PSNR and RMSE
    Step 3:   Check which parameters gave higher PSNR value
    Step 4:   Calculate RMSE value
    Step 5:   Compare with existing schemes by calculating respective PSNR and RMSE
    Step 6:   Compile all results and displays all zooming images
Repeat for different test images. Figure 2 shows the flowchart of the algorithm.

4.1 Data Collection: Digital Medical Image

The collected medical image is taken using the specific camera with advanced electromagnetic waves technology that used to help medical detect certain desease. For example, the fracture bones can be diagnosed by detection any broken bones. This sub-section will be showing the list of collected image with its zooming part which has been cropped using a built-in tool in MATLAB software in Table 4. All the cropped part of the image is then set with size 256×256 pixels before it being down-sampled to factor 2 resulting a size of 128×128 pixels. The down-sampled image is considered as the original image or reference image Ias input in our algorithm) that will be magnified with factor 2 later using the proposed interpolation method. This is the standard procedure in image zooming. Since most medical images are copyright and we only able to obtain permission for both images.

4.1. Parameter Selection

The proposed scheme consists of six free parameter that can be used to modify the end result of image resolution. In order to find the suitable parameter value for each medical tested image, we employed an algorithm as shown in Figure 2 to investigate the behavior of parameter towards PSNR. Based on Equation (1), the rational bi-cubic Ball function is reduced to the standard bicubic Hermite when $\alpha_{i,j} = 1$,

Figure 2. Flowchart steps of image zooming

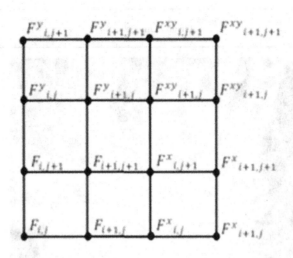

$\beta_{i,j} = 1$, $\gamma_{i,j} = 2$, $\hat{\alpha}_{i,j} = 1$, $\hat{\beta}_{i,j} = 1$, $\hat{\gamma}_{i,j} = 2$. The varying parameter values for all medical tested images and its impact towards PSNR are shown in Table 5. Meanwhile the optimum value of parameter for all images that have been obtained via extensive simulation shown in Table 6.

5. RESULTS AND DISCUSSION

As mentioned in the previous section, there are two tested medical images as listed in sub-section 4.1. These medical images are standard tested images for image zooming. The algorithm is implemented by using MATLAB software version 2018 equipped with Intel® Core ™ i5-8250U 1.60GHz. The stopping criteria used in this study is PSNR value. Since the higher PSNR value, the better interpolation image Zulkifli et al. (2019). Every simulation were done three times for each parameter values and images. The final PSNR and RMSE values are obtained by taking average between three simulations (for each parameters value and images). This to ensure that, we will obtain a more accurate image zooming as well as a better results.

The performance of interpolated image between the proposed scheme will be compared in terms of PSNR and RMSE with some existing scheme such as nearest neghbour, bilinear, bicubic spline, bicubic Hermite and Karim and Saaban (2017). Besides the IQA as the objective quality measurement, the visually comparison between the proposed scheme against all existing schems are also presented in Figure 3 to Figure 4. From Figures 3-4, it is very difficult the measure which scheme is better to zoom the images. Therefore, we calculate the value of PSNR and RMSE for all schemes. These value is shown in Table 7 and 8 (and Figures 5-6), respectively. Based on Tables 7 and 8, for all tested images, the proposed scheme gave higher PSNR value and smaller RMSE value compared with all existing.

Based on numerical and graphical results presented in this section, we conclude that, overall, the proposed scheme is better than existing schemes. If the user require to zoom the images with higher PSNR value, then the proposed rational bi-cubic Ball function is a good alternative than Karim and

Table 4. List of medical image.

Image	Original image	Cropped part (256 × 256 pixels)
Wrist from Singh and Singh (2019)		
Pelvic fracture from Lukies (2019)		

Table 5. PSNR of various parameter values.

Parameter value	Wrist	Pelvic fracture
$\alpha_{i,j} = 0.1$, $\beta_{i,j} = 0.1$, $\gamma_{i,j} = 0.1$, $\hat{\alpha}_{i,j} = 0.1$, $\hat{\beta}_{i,j} = 0.1$, $\hat{\gamma}_{i,j} = 0.1$	59.06	57.92
$\alpha_{i,j} = 1$, $\beta_{i,j} = 0.1$, $\gamma_{i,j} = 0.1$, $\hat{\alpha}_{i,j} = 1$, $\hat{\beta}_{i,j} = 0.1$, $\hat{\gamma}_{i,j} = 0.1$	58.97	57.70
$\alpha_{i,j} = 0.1$, $\beta_{i,j} = 1$, $\gamma_{i,j} = 0.1$, $\hat{\alpha}_{i,j} = 0.1$, $\hat{\beta}_{i,j} = 1$, $\hat{\gamma}_{i,j} = 0.1$	58.82	57.72
$\alpha_{i,j} = 0.1$, $\beta_{i,j} = 0.1$, $\gamma_{i,j} = 1$, $\hat{\alpha}_{i,j} = 0.1$, $\hat{\beta}_{i,j} = 0.1$, $\hat{\gamma}_{i,j} = 1$	58.54	57.20
$\alpha_{i,j} = 1$, $\beta_{i,j} = 1$, $\gamma_{i,j} = 1$, $\hat{\alpha}_{i,j} = 0.1$, $\hat{\beta}_{i,j} = 0.1$, $\hat{\gamma}_{i,j} = 0.1$	59.06	57.92
$\alpha_{i,j} = 0.1$, $\beta_{i,j} = 0.1$, $\gamma_{i,j} = 0.1$, $\hat{\alpha}_{i,j} = 1$, $\hat{\beta}_{i,j} = 1$, $\hat{\gamma}_{i,j} = 1$	59.06	57.92
$\alpha_{i,j} = 1$, $\beta_{i,j} = 0.1$, $\gamma_{i,j} = 0.1$, $\hat{\alpha}_{i,j} = 0.1$, $\hat{\beta}_{i,j} = 0.1$, $\hat{\gamma}_{i,j} = 0.1$	58.85	57.74
$\alpha_{i,j} = 0.1$, $\beta_{i,j} = 1$, $\gamma_{i,j} = 0.1$, $\hat{\alpha}_{i,j} = 0.1$, $\hat{\beta}_{i,j} = 0.1$, $\hat{\gamma}_{i,j} = 0.1$	59.14	57.98
$\alpha_{i,j} = 0.1$, $\beta_{i,j} = 0.1$, $\gamma_{i,j} = 1$, $\hat{\alpha}_{i,j} = 0.1$, $\hat{\beta}_{i,j} = 0.1$, $\hat{\gamma}_{i,j} = 0.1$	58.80	57.62
$\alpha_{i,j} = 0.1$, $\beta_{i,j} = 0.1$, $\gamma_{i,j} = 0.1$, $\hat{\alpha}_{i,j} = 1$, $\hat{\beta}_{i,j} = 0.1$, $\hat{\gamma}_{i,j} = 0.1$	59.18	57.99
$\alpha_{i,j} = 0.1$, $\beta_{i,j} = 0.1$, $\gamma_{i,j} = 0.1$, $\hat{\alpha}_{i,j} = 0.1$, $\hat{\beta}_{i,j} = 1$, $\hat{\gamma}_{i,j} = 0.1$	58.76	57.67

continued on following page

Table 5. Continued

Parameter value	Wrist	Pelvic fracture
$\alpha_{i,j} = 0.1$, $\beta_{i,j} = 0.1$, $\gamma_{i,j} = 0.1$, $\hat{\alpha}_{i,j} = 0.1$, $\hat{\beta}_{i,j} = 0.1$, $\hat{\gamma}_{i,j} = 1$	58.80	57.54
$\alpha_{i,j} = 0.1$, $\beta_{i,j} = 1$, $\gamma_{i,j} = 1$, $\hat{\alpha}_{i,j} = 1$, $\hat{\beta}_{i,j} = 1$, $\hat{\gamma}_{i,j} = 1$	59.04	57.87
$\alpha_{i,j} = 1$, $\beta_{i,j} = 0.1$, $\gamma_{i,j} = 1$, $\hat{\alpha}_{i,j} = 1$, $\hat{\beta}_{i,j} = 1$, $\hat{\gamma}_{i,j} = 1$	58.87	57.72
$\alpha_{i,j} = 1$, $\beta_{i,j} = 1$, $\gamma_{i,j} = 0.1$, $\hat{\alpha}_{i,j} = 1$, $\hat{\beta}_{i,j} = 1$, $\hat{\gamma}_{i,j} = 1$	59.12	58.01
$\alpha_{i,j} = 1$, $\beta_{i,j} = 1$, $\gamma_{i,j} = 1$, $\hat{\alpha}_{i,j} = 0.1$, $\hat{\beta}_{i,j} = 1$, $\hat{\gamma}_{i,j} = 1$	58.81	57.69
$\alpha_{i,j} = 1$, $\beta_{i,j} = 1$, $\gamma_{i,j} = 1$, $\hat{\alpha}_{i,j} = 1$, $\hat{\beta}_{i,j} = 0.1$, $\hat{\gamma}_{i,j} = 1$	59.06	57.82
$\alpha_{i,j} = 1$, $\beta_{i,j} = 1$, $\gamma_{i,j} = 1$, $\hat{\alpha}_{i,j} = 1$, $\hat{\beta}_{i,j} = 1$, $\hat{\gamma}_{i,j} = 0.1$	59.13	58.05
$\alpha_{i,j} = 1$, $\beta_{i,j} = 1$, $\gamma_{i,j} = 1$, $\hat{\alpha}_{i,j} = 1$, $\hat{\beta}_{i,j} = 1$, $\hat{\gamma}_{i,j} = 1$	59.06	57.92
$\alpha_{i,j} = 0.1$, $\beta_{i,j} = 1$, $\gamma_{i,j} = 1$, $\hat{\alpha}_{i,j} = 0.1$, $\hat{\beta}_{i,j} = 1$, $\hat{\gamma}_{i,j} = 1$	58.74	57.53
$\alpha_{i,j} = 1$, $\beta_{i,j} = 0.1$, $\gamma_{i,j} = 1$, $\hat{\alpha}_{i,j} = 1$, $\hat{\beta}_{i,j} = 0.1$, $\hat{\gamma}_{i,j} = 1$	58.86	57.57
$\alpha_{i,j} = 1$, $\beta_{i,j} = 1$, $\gamma_{i,j} = 0.1$, $\hat{\alpha}_{i,j} = 1$, $\hat{\beta}_{i,j} = 1$, $\hat{\gamma}_{i,j} = 0.1$	59.19	58.11

Table 6. Optimum parameter values for each medical tested image.

Image	Parameter					
	$\alpha_{i,j}$	$\beta_{i,j}$	$\gamma_{i,j}$	$\hat{\alpha}_{i,j}$	$\hat{\beta}_{i,j}$	$\hat{\gamma}_{i,j}$
Wrist	1.1	1.1	0.01	1.1	1.1	0.01
Pelvic fracture	1.1	1.1	0.01	1.1	1.1	0.01

Table 7. PSNR analysis.

Image	Nearest neighbour	Bilinear	Bicubic spline	Bicubic Hermite	Karim and Saaban (2017)	The proposed scheme
Wrist	54.57	56.80	58.45	58.94	58.94	**59.19**
Pelvic fracture	52.73	55.35	57.60	57.77	57.77	**58.13**

Table 8. RMSE analysis.

Image	Nearest neighbour	Bilinear	Bicubic spline	Bicubic Hermite	Karim and Saaban (2017)	The proposed scheme
Wrist	0.48	0.37	0.30	0.29	0.29	**0.28**
Pelvic fracture	0.59	0.44	0.34	0.33	0.33	**0.32**

Saaban (2017) scheme. Indeed, for all images, the proposed scheme is better than standard bi-cubic spline interpolation. This finding can be considered as significant in the field of image zooming, since bi-cubic spline is a standard as well as established method used by the image processing communities (Abbas et al., 2017).

6. CONCLUSION

In this study, rational bi-cubic Ball function initiated by Zulkifli et al. (2019) have been used to zomm some medical images. We employ efficient algorithm in order to zoom the images. The free parameters in the description of the rational bi-cubic Ball function are manipulate via numerical simulation. This process is repeated with various values of the parameters. The stopping criteria is PSNR value i.e. the higher PSNR value achieved while simulation are done. Based on all numerical and graphical results presented in this study, we have achieved the main result i.e. to produce higher quality zooming images with higher PSNR value and smaller RMSE value for all tested images. One possible extension to the current study is the find the optimal value for all free parameters via nerural network apparoach such as genetic algorithm (GA) and particle swarm optimization (PSO). Another possible study is to compare the performance between CPU and GPU. This will enables user to deal with high intensity images.

Figure 3. Interpolation image wrist using scheme: (a) nearest neighbor, (b) bilinear, (c) bicubic spline, (d) bicubic Hermite, (e) Karim and Saaban (2017), (f) the proposed scheme.

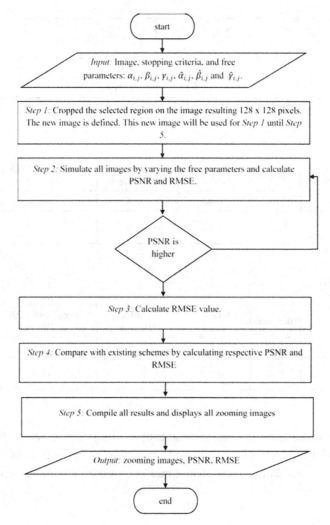

Funding: The authors would like to acknowledge Universiti Teknologi PETRONAS (UTP) and Ministry of Education, Malaysia for the financial support received in the form of a research grant: FRGS/1/2018/STG06/UTP/03/1/015MA0-020 and YUTP:0153AA-H24.

Conflict of Interest: None

Figure 4. Interpolation image pelvic fracture using scheme: (a) nearest neighbor, (b) bilinear, (c) bicubic spline, (d) bicubic Hermite, (e) Karim and Saaban (2017), (f) the proposed scheme.

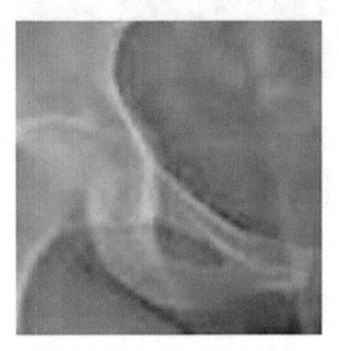

Figure 5. Medical tested image vs PSNR.

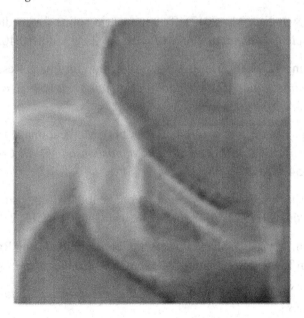

Figure 6. Medical tested image vs RMSE.

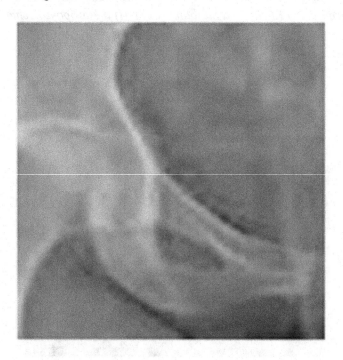

REFERENCES

Abbas, S., Hussain, M., & Irshad, M. (2017). Trigonometric spline for medical image interpolation. *Journal of the National Science Foundation of Sri Lanka*, *45*(1), 33. doi:10.4038/jnsfsr.v45i1.8036

Gao, S., Zhang, C., & Zhang, Y. (2009, May). A New Algorithm for Image Resizing Based on Bivariate Rational Interpolation. In *International Conference on Computational Science* (pp. 770-779). Springer. 10.1007/978-3-642-01973-9_86

Gao, S., Zhang, C., Zhang, Y., & Zhou, Y. (2008, December). Medical image zooming algorithm based on bivariate rational interpolation. In *International Symposium on Visual Computing* (pp. 672-681). Springer. 10.1007/978-3-540-89646-3_66

Karim, S. A. A. (2015). Shape preserving by using rational cubic ball interpolant. *Far East Journal of Mathematical Sciences*, *96*(2), 211–230. doi:10.17654/FJMSJan2015_211_230

Karim, S. A. A., & Saaban, A. (2017). Shape Preserving Interpolation Using Rational Cubic Ball Function and Its Application in Image Interpolation. Mathematical Problems in Engineering.

Kok, C. W., & Tam, W. S. (2019). *Digital Image Interpolation in Matlab*. John Wiley & Sons. doi:10.1002/9781119119623

Lukies, M. (n.d.). *Normal pelvis and both hips: Radiology Case*. Retrieved August 26, 2019, from https://radiopaedia.org/cases/normal-pelvis-and-both-hips

Pal, M. (2016). Investigating Polynomial Interpolation Functions for Zooming Low Resolution Digital Medical Images. *International Journal of Computer and Information Engineering*, *10*(2), 396–402.

Singh, Arun Pal, & Singh. (2019, July 30). *Normal Wrist X-Ray: Bone and Spine*. Retrieved August 26, 2019, from https://boneandspine.com/normal-wrist-x-ray/

Wong, S. T. (Ed.). (2012). *Medical image databases* (Vol. 465). Springer Science & Business Media.

Zhang, C. Q., Zhang, Y. N., & Zhang, C. M. (2012). Surface Constraint of a Rational Interpolation and the Application in Medical Image Processing. *Research Journal of Applied Sciences, Engineering and Technology*, *4*(19), 3697–3703.

Zhang, Y., Gao, S., Zhang, C., & Chi, J. (2009). Application of a bivariate rational interpolation in image zooming. *International Journal of Innovative Computing, Information, & Control*, *5*(11), 4299–4307.

Zulkifli, N. A., Karim, S. A. A., Shafie, A., Sarfraz, M., Gaffar, A., & Nisar, K. S. (2019). Image interpolation using rational bi-cubic Ball. *Mathematics*, *7*(11), 1045. doi:10.3390/math7111045

Chapter 9
Segmentation of Pectoral Muscle in Mammogram Images Using Gaussian Mixture Model– Expectation Maximization

Ichrak Khoulqi

(iD) https://orcid.org/0000-0001-7657-1780

Faculty of Sciences and Technics, Sultan Moulay Slimane University, Morocco

Najlae Idrissi

(iD) https://orcid.org/0000-0003-0038-2988

Faculty of Sciences and Technics, Sultan Moulay Slimane University, Morocco

Muhammad Sarfraz

(iD) https://orcid.org/0000-0003-3196-9132

Kuwait University, Kuwait

ABSTRACT

Breast cancer is one of the significant issues in medical sciences today. Specifically, women are suffering most worldwide. Early diagnosis can result to control the growth of the tumor. However, there is a need of high precision of diagnosis for right treatment. This chapter contributes toward an achievement of a computer-aided diagnosis (CAD) system. It deals with mammographic images and enhances their quality. Then, the enhanced images are segmented for pectoral muscle (PM) in the Medio-Lateral-Oblique (MLO) view of the mammographic images. The segmentation approach uses the tool of Gaussian Mixture Model-Expectation Maximization (GMM-EM). A standard database of Mini-MIAS with 322 images has been utilized for the implementation and experimentation of the proposed technique. The metrics of structural similarity measure and DICE coefficient have been utilized to verify the quality of segmentation based on the ground truth. The proposed technique is quite robust and accurate, it supersedes various existing techniques when compared in the same context.

DOI: 10.4018/978-1-7998-4444-0.ch009

INTRODUCTION

Breast cancer is one of the significant issues in medical sciences today. Specifically, women are suffering most worldwide due to its being common and invasive. It is a kind of malignant tumor (Kwok et al., 2004; Raba et al., 2005; Camilus et al., 2010; Keller et al., 2011; Tzikopoulos et al., 2011; Vaidehi and Subashini, 2013; Oliver et al., 2014; Galdran et al., 2015; Sreedevi and Sherly, 2015; Othman and Ahmad, 2016; Gardezi et al., 2018; Punitha, et al., 2018; Pavan et al., 2019; Khoulqi & Idrissi, 2020). For timely treatment and minimization in mortality rate, the early detections as well as preventions are vital and can be highly helpful (NCI, 2016). Early diagnosis can result to control the growth of the tumor. However, there is a need of high precision of diagnosis for right treatment.

Mammography is a radiography technique of pathology, it specifically deals with the examination women breasts (Khoulqi & Idrissi, 2019; 2020; Rampun, et al. 2019; Punitha, et al., 2018; Molinara, et al., 2013; Zheng, et al., 2010; Ferrari, et al., 2004). It helps and guides to diagnose the signs of breast diseases during the examination process. The symptoms of breast diseases may be like inflammation, skin changes, palpable nodule, discharge, and others. Mammography helps in highlighting abnormalities in the breasts (Cheikhrouhou, 2012) and the mammography images (Mammograms) help to discover the cancer in the breasts.

Mammograms provide a detailed anatomy of the breasts. In a mammogram, one can see the opaque radio zones very clearly. The fibro glandular tissue and calcium which are the essential components of the mammary lesions (Cheikhrouhou, 2012) are visualized due to opaque radio zones. Mammography is normally practiced from various dimensions and directions; each of the mammograms is called an incidence. An incidence would be a good candidate to be used for further processing if maximum of the breast tissue can be visualized by a maximum spread on the X-ray plate. Then, distinct implications can be used depending on the breast part to be examined. The profile, face and the oblique external incidences are very commonly used ones. The face and oblique external incidences are called Craniocaudal (CC) and Medio Lateral Oblique (MLO) respectively.

BACKGROUND

In the context of pectoral muscle (PM) segmentation from breast tissues, several studies have been carried out in the literature. For the automatic segmentation of the PM, Guo, et al (2020) proposed a study which is based on boundary identification and shape prediction. Their work identifies the PM region in MLO view mammograms.

The authors in (Khoulqi & Idrissi, 2019; 2020) believe that computer-aided diagnosis (CAD) systems are beneficial for breast cancer detection as it improves the diagnosis accuracy. They have presented some contribution towards the development of a breast CAD system. This work is based on split and merge methodology. Their algorithm used a technique of voting.

Mammography can be utilized for measuring breast density (BD) which is helpful to diagnose breast cancer. For very commonly clinical routines, the radiologists evaluate images using Breast Imaging Reporting and Data System (BIRADS) (Wikipedia, March 29, 2020) assessment. Since this method has human intervention and hence has some kind of variability. Therefore, to relieve the burden of medical experts like radiologists and to have a first aid opinion, there is a need to find out some robust and automated approach to measure BD and hence to extract PM which is a challenging task.

Using the adaptive gamma corrections, the authors in (Gardezi, et al., 2018) have suggested a method for the segmentation of pectoral muscle. They have presented their method for pectoral suppression in mammograms; it works well in various settings including variety of shapes, tissues density and the pectoral boundary curvature. To segregate the breast parenchyma from the remaining breast region, the method has used the mammograms' morphological information. The proposed approach has been implemented and tested on MIAS dataset using Jaccard similarity index (JSI). An overall detection was found as good as 98.45% for the pectoral regions and JSI of 92.79% with the ground truth.

In (Ojo et al, 2014), the authors used the region description method that measures the properties of image regions such as: surface, perimeter, compactness of shape and polygonal approximation to remove pectoral muscle, noise and artifacts. For the extraction of the region of interest, they used a global thresholding which is set after several experiments to separate the regions adjacent to the pectoral muscles that are different in intensity. After that a polygonal approximation method (division technique) was used to extract the pectoral region from the images.

Ganesan, et al. (2013) have made a detailed review on pectoral muscle segmentation, they have provided a good platform about the current state of the art research in the area. Their work can be considered as a significant and consolidated effort which provides a good basis of further research. It is based on a comprehensive review of research papers for the automated detection of breast cancer.

Gubern-Mérida et al. (2012) proposed an atlas-based segmentation method for pectoral muscle segmentation to detect breast cancer. They studied on the performance of a multi-atlas registration based approach and compared it with a probabilistic model. After applying on a good data, they ultimately conclude that the multi-atlas approach is slightly improved one as compared to the probabilistic approach as far as performance is concerned.

In another study (Boucher and Vicent, 2009), the segmentation of the pectoral muscle on a mammogram is based on the study of images using the active contour algorithm to separate the pectoral muscle from the other parts that form the breast. The pectoral muscle happens to be the denser tissues than those forming the breast and it appears more clearly in the mammogram. The problem is that the boundary between these two regions is irregular because of noise, so the gradient of the image is difficult to analyze. Hence, the utility of using information about the regions to form the energy mining equation, and to do this they have adopted the Glutton algorithm since it has a simple and efficient implementation.

Bora, et al. (2016) have provided a solution for automatic segmentation of pectoral muscle. They have presented an approach which is based on texture gradient. In another work (Pereira et al, 2014), authors used mammographic images using both CC and MLO views, their work proceeds for segmentation and detection of mammograms in three stages. Ganesan, et al. (2013) have made a detailed review on pectoral muscle segmentation. Gubern-Mérida et al. (2012) proposed an atlas-based segmentation method for pectoral muscle segmentation to detect breast cancer. In another study (Boucher and Vicent, 2009), the segmentation of the pectoral muscle on a mammogram is based on the study of images using the active contour algorithm.

There are various other studies on the breast cancer detection based on PM. For the sake of brevity, the reader is referred to Figure 1, it overviews around twenty seven studies from 2004 to 2020. The authors, year of publication and the brief idea of the study are depicted in the figure. The interested reader can dig out further exploration by accessing these contributions.

Figure 1. A survey of pectoral segmentation methods in the current literature.

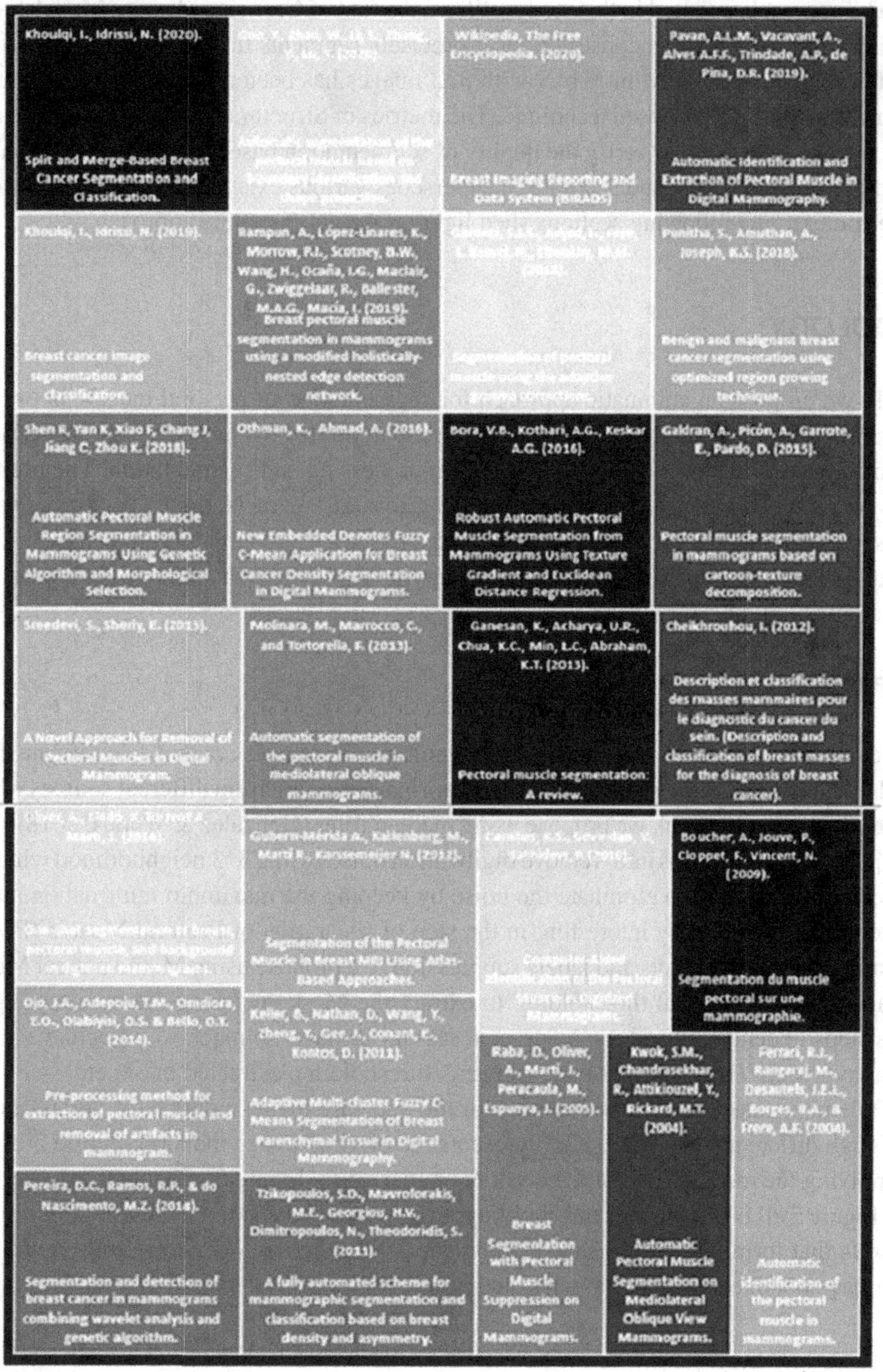

This paper proposes a new and effective methodology to remove PM from MLO views in the mammograms. The approach, adopted in this study, utilizes the tool of Gaussian Mixture Model-Expectation Maximization (GMM-EM) in its construction. It precisely segments the Pectoral Muscle in Mammograms. A standard database of Mini-MIAS with 322 images has been utilized for the implementation and experimentation of the proposed technique. The metrics of Structural Similarity measure and DICE Coefficient have been utilized to verify the quality of segmentation based on the ground truth. The proposed technique is quite robust and accurate; it supersedes various existing techniques when compared in the same context. The following sections shed light on the details of the approach.

METHODOLOGY

In this work, we propose an automatic approach for segmentation of pectoral muscle in order to have a clear mammogram for the following steps of the computer-aided diagnostic system (CAD). Our proposed technique comprises of two major stages of preprocessing and segmentation. The preprocessing stage helps to get clean images for further processing towards segmentation. The segmentation stage allows the separation of pectoral muscle and the breast tissues. The Mammogram Database used in the implementation and testing in this work is taken from the Mini-MIAS database (Suckling, et al., 1994) which contains 322 of the MLO views.

Preprocessing

The preprocessing step is very important as the mammography images contain a significant quantity of noise, labels, artifacts and digitization lines. This is normally coming from different sources when taking x-ray images. For noise removal, we propose using median filter (Gonzalez & Woods, 2018) since it is a nonlinear spatial filter that helps us to remove digitization noises using 3*3 neighborhood windows. This filtering technique allows us to eliminate the noise by keeping the maximum information and without blurring the edges that are very interesting in the step of separation of Pectoral Muscle (PM) and the Breast Tissues. Then, for artifacts and labels suppression, we propose using Mathematical Morphology operators and adaptative global thresholding to extract the Mask enclosing the mammary gland. We use various steps in denoising and removing unnecessary artifacts so much so we achieve a pretreated mammography image. These steps include filtering, thresholding, extracted mask, etc.

Figure 2 demonstrates the obtained results, for the database image mdb006, of preprocessing stage passing through different steps. Figure 2(a) presents the original image mdb006, Figure 2(b) is the image after applying the median filter and the salt & pepper noise, Figure 2(c) is obtained after removing scan lines, Figure 2(d) is obtain after thresholding, Figure 2(e) is the extracted mask after removing the isolated pixels that form the labels using Mathematical Morphology operators, and Figure 2(f) is the pretreated image obtained after multiplying the mask.

Figure 2. Preprocessing stage for the image mdb006: (a) Original image, (b) Filtered image, (c) Removing Scan Lines, (d) Thresholding, (e) Extracted Mask, (f) Pretreated image.

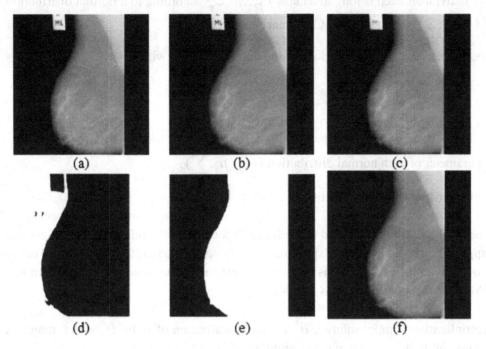

Segmentation

Pectoral muscle is a dense region that may affect the process of segmentation and detection of cancerous regions, this is because of the higher intensity of the PM than the surrounding tissues. The existence of PM gives us the false positive results in the steps that consist of the extraction of suspicious zones, so we are obliged to remove it. This motivates to the idea of segmentation and this paper proposes a methodology approach in this regard which is described in the following sections. This proposed approach of segmentation of PM is based on Gaussian Mixture Model-Expectation Maximization (GMM-EM) (Chatzidimitriou, et al. 2018; Qiao, et al, 2019). The details are explained in the following subsections.

Gaussian Mixture Model-Expectation Maximization (GMM-EM)

The histogram of mammography images can be represented by a Gaussian mixture model (GMM) in which each region composes a type such as: pectoral muscle, breast tissue, background, tumor if present follows a Gaussian distribution. A Gaussian mixture (Balafar, 2011) is a set of k-distrubution probabilities representing k-clusters, it combines several normal distributions where each of them has a mean and a standard deviation. It is a static model expressed according to a mixture density. It is normally used to estimate the distribution of random variables parametrically by modelling them as a sum of several Gaussian distributions.

So, the aim is to determine the variance and the mean of each Gaussian variable which composes it. These parameters are optimized according to a maximum likelihood criterion in order to approach as close as possible to the desired distribution. It goes as follows:

- Suppose that x is a sample of n individuals $(x_1, ..., x_n)$.
- These individuals each belong to a class $C_1, ..., C_g$ according to a normal distribution of mean $\mu_k (k = 1, ..., g)$ and $\sum_k$ the Covariance matrix.
- We note $\pi_1, ..., \pi_g$ the proportions of the different classes with $0 < \pi_k < 1$ and

$$\sum_{k=1}^{g} \pi_k = 1.$$

- The parameter of each normal distribution is $\theta_k (\mu_k, \sum_k)$.
- The global parameter of the mixture is $\varnothing = (\pi_1, ..., \pi_g, \theta_1, ..., \theta_g)$.

In the next sphase, we step forward towards the Expectation Maximization (EM) algorithm. It is an iterative approach, it has two steps: Expectation (E) step and Maximization (M) step. These two steps alternate mutually in the EM iterations for its performance. For our objectives, we determine the steps that the EM algorithm goes through as follows:

Step 1: (initialization): Initial solution θ^0 i.e. the initialization of θ by θ^0 which returns to the initialization of π_k the conditional probabilitiesthat $x_i \in C_k$.

Step 2: From the sample, we calculate the log of likelihood as follows:

$$L(x, \varnothing) = \sum_{i=1}^{n} \log(\sum_{k=1}^{g} \pi_k f(x_i, \theta_k)) \tag{3}$$

Step 3: (Expectation): Calculation of conditional probabilities π_k for the current value of θ is shown in Equation (4).

$$\pi_{k.i}^{(r+1)} = \frac{\pi_k^{(r)} f_k\left(x_i, \theta_k^{(r)}\right)}{\sum_{l=1}^{g} \pi_{l.i}^{(r)} f_l\left(x_i, \theta_l^{(r)}\right)} \tag{4}$$

Step 4: (Maximization): Updating the estimation of θ.

Step 5: We recalculate the log of likelihood if it converges to the same value we stop the calculations, otherwise we go back to Step 3.

Working of the Proposed Approach

After pre-processing the mammography images, we go through the Gaussian mixture model to determine the number of gaussians and then we will maximize the likelihood to obtain a good clustering result that provides us with a more accurate segmentation of the pectoral muscle. Figure 3 demonstrates the result of applying GMM-EM approach on the mammography image mdb006 from the dataset mini-MIAS. Figure 3(a) is the pretreated image and Figure 3(b) produces the image when pectoral muscle is removed using GMM-EM.

Figure 3. Applying GMM-EM on the mammography image mdb006: (a) Pretreated image, (b) Removed pectoral muscle using GMM-EM.

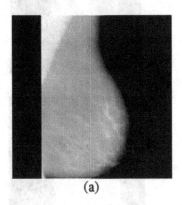 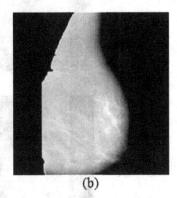

(a)   (b)

EXPERIMENTS AND DISCUSSION

In this section, the proposed approach GMM-EM is applied to mammography images. The method is fully automatic for seed region growing, we set an intial point that is adapted to the different data of Mini-MIAS.

Visual Results

Although, all of Mini-MIAS datatset has been tested and experimeted fully, but fewer images are shown as sample implementation to demonstrate the visual results. In the first experiment, we chose a set of three mammography images mdb005, mdb057 and mdb116 from the database of Mini-MIAS. Figure 4 represents the visual results obtained using the proposed approaches on the three images. The first column (from left) is showing the names of images in Figure 4, the second column represents the pretreated images and the third column represents the images after applying the GMM-EM method, the pectoral muscle is removed in each image.

Let us have another experiment on a different set of images. Figure 5 represents the example for the visual results obtained using the proposed approaches on three different mammography images mdb182, mdb266, and mdb303 from the database of Mini-MIAS. Very similar to Figure 4, middle column is showing the pretreated images. The last column represents the images after applying the GMM-EM method and pectoral muscle is removed in each image.

Numerical Results

In the previous section, we saw the effectiveness of GMM-EM using visual results. To assess the accuracy of the segmentation of the proposed approach, various similarity measures are popular in the current

Figure 4. Implementation on images mdb005, mdb057 and mdb116 using GMM-EM.

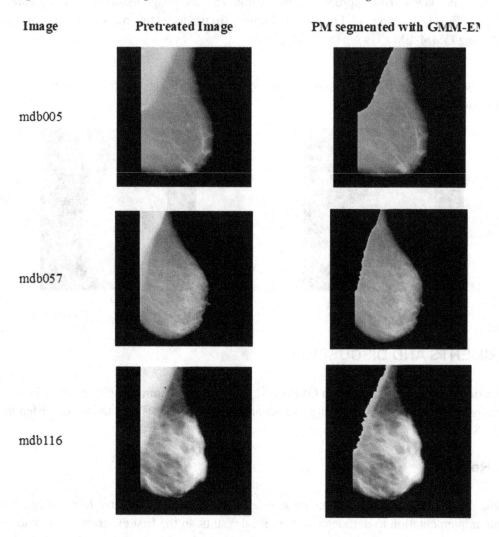

literature. These include DICE coefficient of similarity (Choi, 2010; Csurka et al., 2013; Fernandez-Moral et al., 2018; Idrissi, 2008; Song et al., 2017; Rampun, et al. 2019; Shen, et al., 2018; Wijaya, et al., 2016), Structural Similarity (SSIM) measure (Shen, et al., 2018; Wang, et al., 2004), peak signal-to-noise ratio (PSNR) (Huynh-Thu and Ghanbari 2012), mean squared error (MSE) (Choi, 2010; Wijaya, et al., 2016), Jaccard similarity index (JSI) (Choi, 2010; Rampun, et al. 2019; Wijaya, et al., 2016), Zijdenbos similarity index (Prescott,et al., 2009) and others. For our proposed work, we have chosen DICE and SSIM to find out the goodness of segmentation between the segmented regions and the ground truth. These are popular measures and are used to determine the perceived quality of digital images.

Implementations of DICE and SSIM metrics are done successfully for GMM-EM. If the values of DICE and SSIM are close to 1, it reflects better segmentation accuracy. The Table 1 depicts the results obtained from the metrics of evaluation using the proposed approach of GMM-EM. These results are also demonstrated, for further clarification, in the graphics made in Figure 6 corresponding to Table 1. One can see that the proposed segmentation method, for both of the similarity measures, shows prominent

Figure 5. Implementation on images mdb182, mdb266, and mdb303 using GMM-EM.

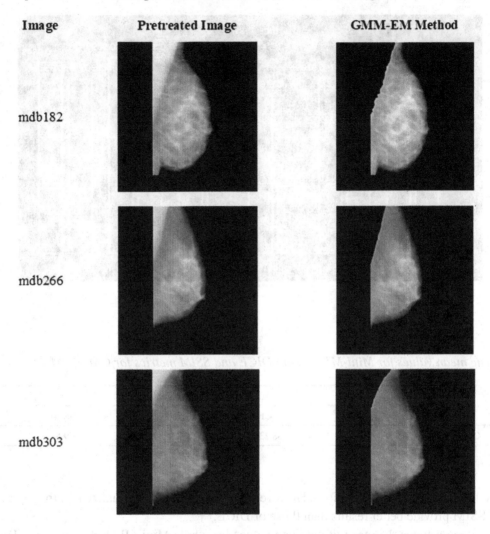

Table 1.The obtained values using DICE and SSIM metrics for the approach GMM-EM.

Experiments	DICE	SSIM
mdb005	0.9069	0.9723
mdb057	0.9244	0.9709
mdb116	0.8782	0.9566
mdb182	0.9177	0.9804
mdb266	0.9555	0.9895
mdb303	0.9705	0.9843

Figure 6. Demonstration of the performance of GMM-EM method using DICE and SSIM metrics.

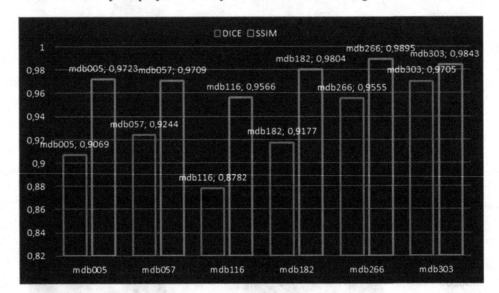

Table 2. The mean values for Mini-MIAS using DICE and SSIM metrics for GMM-EM.

Method	% Evaluation	
	DICE	SSIM
GMM-EM	88.23	89.58

results on the accuracy of segmentations. However, one can very easliy visualize that the segmentation values of SSIM provide better results than those of DICE.

Table 2 demonstrates the mean of obtained values for whole Mini-MIAS dataset using DICE and SSIM metrics for the proposed approach of GMM-EM. Although, all the results obtained are appealing. However, GMM-EM has experienced best results of 89.58% using SSIM. These results have also been demonstrated in Figure 7 to have a visual feeling.

COMPARATIVE STUDY

The proposed technique has been compared with various existing techniques including the ones in (Kwok et al., 2004; Raba et al., 2005; Camilus et al., 2010; Keller et al., 2011; Oliver et al., 2014; Othman and Ahmad, 2016). These referred works, from the existing literature, are in the same context as the proposed work. Table 3 draws up a comparison with the proposed approach in such a way that the first column provides the reference paper, second column briefs about the method, third column mentions about the dataset used, and the fourth column throws light on the level of accuracy achieved in the corresponding technique.

Figure 7. Visualization of the mean values for Mini-MIAS using DICE and SSIM metrics for GMM-EM.

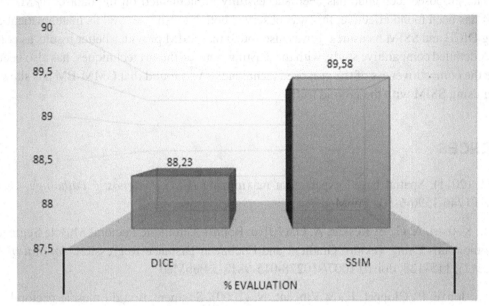

The proposed technique has proven to be impressive by achieving very high accuracy results. GMM-EM (89.58% by SSIM with the ground truth) has shown as best as compared to every reported method in Table 3.

CONCLUSION

A novel technique, namely GMM-EM, has been proposed for the segmentation of pectoral muscle in mammogram images. It is based on the ideas of using the tool of Gaussian Mixture Model-Expectation Maximization. It detects tumor growth with very high precision and provides automated and effective

Table 3. A detailed comparative study with some existing techniques.

Reference	Main Concepts in Technique	Dataset	Accuracy
Kwok et al., 2004	Morphological information, Pectoral edges by straight line and Cliff detection.	322 MIAS	83.9% of accuracy
Raba et al., 2005	The idea of region growing is utilized to fill the pectoral region.	322 MIAS	The method produces 86% of good extraction
Camilus et al., 2010	The pectoral edges are detected by a graph cut and the idea of Bézier curve was then utilized to refine the edges.	84 MIAS	0.64 mean FP against the ground truth.
Keller et al., 2011	Fuzzy c-means and linear discriminant analysis.	100 MIAS	Correlation of 0.83 and an average JSI of 0.62.
Oliver et al., 2014	Information of position, intensity, and texture is used.	149 MIAS	83% by DICE.
Othman and Ahmad, 2016	Fuzzy c-mean and multi-selection of seeds label.	322 MIAS	Used SSIM, but % is not available.
Proposed method GMM-EM	Gaussian Mixture Model-Expectation Maximization	322 MIAS	89.58% by SSIM.

solution. The proposed technique has been successfully implemented on the dataset of Mini-MIAS. GMM-EM has been found effective, this was observed both by visual as well as matehmatical evaluations using DICE and SSIM measures. It was also found that SSIM provides better results as compared to DICE. A detailed comparative study, with the existing state-of-the-art techniques, has also been made to observe the competitiveness of the proposed technique. It was found that GMM-EM has shown to be competing using SSIM with the ground truth.

REFERENCES

Balafar, M. (2011). Spatial based expectation maximizing (EM). *Diagnostic Pathology*, *6*(1), 103. doi:10.1186/1746-1596-6-103 PubMed

Bora, V. B., Kothari, A. G., & Keskar, A. G. (2016). Robust Automatic Pectoral Muscle Segmentation from Mammograms Using Texture Gradient and Euclidean Distance Regression. *Journal of Digital Imaging*, *29*(1), 115–125. doi:10.1007/s10278-015-9813-5 PubMed

Boucher, A., Jouve, P., Cloppet, F., & Vincent, N. (2009). Segmentation du muscle pectoral sur une mammographie. ORASIS'09 - Congrès des jeunes chercheurs en vision par ordinateur, 2009, Trégastel, France. https://hal.inria.fr/inria-00404631/document

Camilus, K. S., Govindan, V., & Sathidevi, P. (2010). Computer-Aided Identification of the Pectoral Muscle in Digitized Mammograms. *Journal of Digital Imaging*, *23*(5), 562–580. doi:10.1007/s10278-009-9240-6 PubMed

Chatzidimitriou, K., Diamantopoulos, T., Papamichail, M., & Symeonidis, A. (2018). Practical Machine Learning in R. https://leanpub.com/practical-machine-learning-r

Cheikhrouhou, I. (2012). Description et classification des masses mammaires pour le diagnostic du cancer du sein [Description and classification of breast masses for the diagnosis of breast cancer] (Doctoral Thesis). University of Évry Val d'Essonne, France. https://dblp.org/rec/phd/hal/Cheikhrouhou12

Choi, S.-S., Cha, S.-H., & Tappert, C. C. (2010). A Survey of Binary Similarity and Distance Measures. *Journal of Systemics, Cybernetics and Informatics*, *8*(1), 43–48.

Csurka, G., Larlus, D., & Perronnin, F. (2013). What is a good evaluation measure for semantic segmentation? The Proceedings of the British Machine Vision Conference (BVMC 2013), 32.1-32.11. doi:10.5244/C.27.32

Fernandez-Moral, E., Martins, R., Wolf, D., & Rives, P. (2018). A New Metric for Evaluating Semantic Segmentation: Leveraging Global and Contour Accuracy. 2018 IEEE Intelligent Vehicles Symposium (IV), 1051-1056. doi:10.1109/IVS.2018.8500497

Ferrari, R. J., Rangaraj, M., Desautels, J. E. L., Borges, R. A., & Frere, A. F. (2004). Automatic identification of the pectoral muscle in mammograms. *IEEE Transactions on Medical Imaging*, *23*(2), 232–245. doi:10.1109/TMI.2003.823062 PubMed

Galdran, A., Picón, A., Garrote, E., & Pardo, D. (2015). Pectoral muscle segmentation in mammograms based on cartoon-texture decomposition. In R. Paredes, J. Cardoso, & X. Pardo (Eds.), Lecture Notes in Computer Science: Vol. 9117. *Pattern Recognition and Image Analysis. IbPRIA 2015* (pp. 587–594). Springer., doi:10.1007/978-3-319-19390-8_66.

Ganesan, K., Acharya, U. R., Chua, K. C., Min, L. C., & Abraham, K. T. (2013). Pectoral muscle segmentation: A review. *Computer Methods and Programs in Biomedicine, 110*(1), 48–57. doi:10.1016/j.cmpb.2012.10.020 PubMed

Gardezi, S. J. S., Adjed, F., Faye, I., Kamel, N., & Eltoukhy, M. M. (2018). Segmentation of pectoral muscle using the adaptive gamma corrections. *Multimedia Tools and Applications, 77*(3), 3919–3940. doi:10.1007/s11042-016-4283-4

Gonzalez, R. C., & Woods, R. E. (2018). *Digital Image Processing* (4th ed.). Pearson.

Gubern-Mérida, A., Kallenberg, M., Martí, R., & Karssemeijer, N. (2012). Segmentation of the Pectoral Muscle in Breast MRI Using Atlas-Based Approaches. In N. Ayache, H. Delingette, P. Golland, & K. Mori (Eds.), Medical Image Computing and Computer-Assisted Intervention: Vol. 7511. MICCAI 2012. MICCAI 2012. Lecture Notes in Computer Science. Springer. doi:10.1007/978-3-642-33418-4_46

Guo, Y., Zhao, W., Li, S., Zhang, Y., & Lu, Y. (2020). Automatic segmentation of the pectoral muscle based on boundary identification and shape prediction. *Physics in Medicine and Biology, 65*(4), 045016. Advance online publication. doi:10.1088/1361-6560/ab652b PubMed

Huynh-Thu, Q., & Ghanbari, M. (2012). The accuracy of PSNR in predicting video quality for different video scenes and frame rates. *Telecommunication Systems, 49*(1), 35–48. doi:10.1007/s11235-010-9351-x

Idrissi, N. (2008). La navigation dans les bases d'images: prise en compte des attributs de texture (Ph.D. Thesis). University Mohamed V and Nantes University.

Keller, B., Nathan, D., Wang, Y., Zheng, Y., Gee, J., Conant, E., & Kontos, D. (2011). Adaptive Multi-cluster Fuzzy C-Means Segmentation of Breast Parenchymal Tissue in Digital Mammography. In G. Fichtinger, A. Martel, & T. Peters (Eds.), Medical Image Computing and Computer-Assisted Intervention: Vol. 6893. MICCAI 2011. MICCAI 2011. Lecture Notes in Computer Science (pp. 562–569). Springer. doi:10.1007/978-3-642-23626-6_69

Khoulqi, I., & Idrissi, N. (2019). Breast cancer image segmentation and classification. *Proceedings of the 4th International Conference on Smart City Applications (SCA '19)*, 1–9. 10.1145/3368756.3369039

Khoulqi, I., & Idrissi, N. (2020). Split and Merge-Based Breast Cancer Segmentation and Classification. In M. Sarfraz (Ed.), *Critical Approaches to Information Retrieval Research* (pp. 225–238). IGI Global., doi:10.4018/978-1-7998-1021-6.ch012.

Kwok, S. M., Chandrasekhar, R., Attikiouzel, Y., & Rickard, M. T. (2004). Automatic Pectoral Muscle Segmentation on Mediolateral Oblique View Mammograms. *IEEE Transactions on Medical Imaging, 23*(9), 1129–1140. doi:10.1109/TMI.2004.830529 PubMed

MacQueen, J. B. (1967). Some methods for classification and analysis of multivariate observations. *Proceedings of the Fifth Berkeley Symposium on Mathematical Statistics and Probability*, 281-297.

Maitra, I. K., Nag, S., & Bandyopadhyay, S. K. (2011). Detection and isolation of pectoral muscle from digital mammogram: An automated approach. *International Journal of Advanced Research in Computer Science*, 2(3), 375–380. http://www.ijarcs.info/index.php/Ijarcs/article/view/555/543

Molinara, M., Marrocco, C., & Tortorella, F. (2013). Automatic segmentation of the pectoral muscle in mediolateral oblique mammograms. Proceedings of the 26th IEEE International Symposium on Computer-Based Medical Systems, 506-509. doi:10.1109/CBMS.2013.6627852

NCI (National Cancer Institute). (2016). Annual Report to the Nation: Cancer Death Rates Continue to Decline; Increase in Liver Cancer Deaths Cause For Concern. https://www.cancer.gov/news-events/press-releases/2016/annual-report-nation-1975-2012

Ojo, J. A., Adepoju, T. M., Omdiora, E. O., Olabiyisi, O. S., & Bello, O. T. (2014). Pre-processing method for extraction of pectoral muscle and removal of artifacts in mammogram. IOSR Journal of Computer Engineering, 16(3), 6–9. doi:10.9790/0661-16350609

Oliver, A., Lladó, X., Torrent, A., & Martí, J. (2014). *One-shot segmentation of breast, pectoral muscle, and background in digitised mammograms. In 2014 IEEE International Conference on Image Processing (ICIP)*. IEEE., doi:10.1109/ICIP.2014.7025183.

Othman, K., & Ahmad, A. (2016). New Embedded Denotes Fuzzy C-Mean Application for Breast Cancer Density Segmentation in Digital Mammograms. IOP Conference Series: Materials Science and Engineering, 160:012105, International Engineering Research and Innovation Symposium (IRIS), Melaka, Malaysia. DOI: 10.1088/1757-899X/160/1/012105

Pavan, A. L. M., Vacavant, A., Alves, A. F. F., Trindade, A. P., & de Pina, D. R. (2019). Automatic Identification and Extraction of Pectoral Muscle in Digital Mammography. *IFMBE Proceedings*, 68(1). doi:10.1007/978-981-10-9035-6_27

Pereira, D. C., Ramos, R. P., & do Nascimento, M. Z. (2014). Segmentation and detection of breast cancer in mammograms combining wavelet analysis and genetic algorithm. *Computer Methods and Programs in Biomedicine*, 114(1), 88–101. doi:10.1016/j.cmpb.2014.01.014 PubMed

Prescott, J. W., Pennell, M., Best, T. M., Swanson, M. S., Haq, F., Jackson, R., & Gurcan, M. N. (2009). An automated method to segment the femur for osteoarthritis research. In *Proceedings of the Annual International Conference of the IEEE Engineering in Medicine and Biology Society*. IEEE., doi:10.1109/IEMBS.2009.5333257.

Punitha, S., Amuthan, A., & Joseph, K. S. (2018). Benign and malignant breast cancer segmentation using optimized region growing technique. Future Computing and Informatics Journal, 3(2), 348–358. doi:10.1016/j.fcij.2018.10.005

Qiao, J., Cai, X., Xiao, Q., Chen, Z., Kulkarni, P., Ferris, C., Kamarthi, S., & Sridhar, S. (2019). Data on MRI brain lesion segmentation using K-means and Gaussian Mixture Model-Expectation Maximization. *Data in Brief*, 27, 104628. Advance online publication. doi:10.1016/j.dib.2019.104628 PubMed

Raba, D., Oliver, A., Martí, J., Peracaula, M., & Espunya, J. (2005). Breast Segmentation with Pectoral Muscle Suppression on Digital Mammograms. In J. S. Marques, N. Pérez de la Blanca, & P. Pina (Eds.), Lecture Notes in Computer Science: Vol. 3523. *Pattern Recognition and Image Analysis. IbPRIA 2005* (pp. 471–478). Springer., doi:10.1007/11492542_58.

Rampun, A., López-Linares, K., Morrow, P. J., Scotney, B. W., Wang, H., Ocaña, I. G., Maclair, G., Zwiggelaar, R., Ballester, M. A. G., & Macía, I. (2019). Breast pectoral muscle segmentation in mammograms using a modified holistically-nested edge detection network. *Medical Image Analysis*, *57*, 1–17. doi:10.1016/j.media.2019.06.007 PubMed

Shen, R., Yan, K., Xiao, F., Chang, J., Jiang, C., & Zhou, K. (2018). Automatic Pectoral Muscle Region Segmentation in Mammograms Using Genetic Algorithm and Morphological Selection. *Journal of Digital Imaging*, *31*(5), 680–691. doi:10.1007/s10278-018-0068-9 PubMed

Song, Y., & Cai, W. (2017). Handling of Feature Space Complexity for Texture Analysis in Medical Images. In A. Depeursinge, O. S. Al-Kadi, & J. R. Mitchell (Eds.), *Biomedical Texture Analysis, Fundamentals, Tools and Challenges* (pp. 163–191). Academic Press., doi:10.1016/B978-0-12-812133-7.00006-5.

Sreedevi, S., & Sherly, E. (2015). A Novel Approach for Removal of Pectoral Muscles in Digital Mammogram. *Procedia Computer Science*, *46*, 1724–1731. doi:10.1016/j.procs.2015.02.117

Strutz, T. (2016). *Data Fitting and Uncertainty: A practical introduction to weighted least squares and beyond* (2nd ed.). Springer., doi:10.1007/978-3-658-11456-5.

Suckling, J., Parker, J., Astley, S., Hutt, I. W., Boggis, C., Ricketts, I. W., Stamatakis, E., Cerneaz, N., Kok, S., Taylor, P., Betal, D., & Savage, J. (1994). The Mammographic Image Analysis Society Digital Mammogram Database. Exerpta Medica. *International Congress Series*, *1069*, 375–378.

Tzikopoulos, S. D., Mavroforakis, M. E., Georgiou, H. V., Dimitropoulos, N., & Theodoridis, S. (2011). A fully automated scheme for mammographic segmentation and classification based on breast density and asymmetry. *Computer Methods and Programs in Biomedicine*, *102*(1), 47–63. doi:10.1016/j.cmpb.2010.11.016 PubMed

Wang, Z., Bovik, A. C., Sheikh, H. R., & Simoncelli, E. P. (2004). Image quality assessment: From error visibility to structural similarity. *IEEE Transactions on Image Processing*, *13*(4), 600–612. doi:10.1109/TIP.2003.819861 PubMed

Wijaya, S. H., Afendi, F. M., Batubara, I., Darusman, L. K., Altaf-Ul-Amin, M., & Kanaya, S. (2016). Finding an appropriateequation to measuresimilaritybetweenbinaryvectors: Case studies on Indonesian and Japaneseherbalmedicines. *BMC Bioinformatics*, *17*(1), 520. doi:10.1186/s12859-016-1392-z PubMed

Wikipedia, The Free Encyclopedia. (2020). BI-RADS. https://en.wikipedia.org/wiki/BI-RADS

Wikipedia, The Free Encyclopedia. (2020). Random Sample Consensus. https://en.wikipedia.org/wiki/Random_sample_consensus#cite_note-1

Yang, D., Gan, J., Wen, B., & Xu, T. (2017). The Algorithm for Extracting Elements of National Costume Based on Region Growing. In Proceedings of the 2017 2nd International Conference on Control, Automation and Artificial Intelligence (CAAI 2017). Atlantis Press, doi:10.2991/caai-17.2017.71

Zheng, J., Fuentes, O., Leung, M. Y., & Jackson, E. (2010). Mammogram Compression Using Super-Resolution. In J. Martí, A. Oliver, J. Freixenet, & R. Martí (Eds.), Lecture Notes in Computer Science: Vol. 6136. *Digital Mammography. IWDM 2010* (pp. 46–53). Springer., doi:10.1007/978-3-642-13666-5_7

Chapter 10
Use of PCA Solution in Hierarchy and Case of Two Classes of Data Sets to Initialize Parameters for Clustering Function:
An Estimation Method for Clustering Function in Classification Application

Peilin Li

University of South Australia, Australia

ABSTRACT

In literature, the initial parameters are critical for K-means function. By seedling randomly or ad hoc approach, the results are not optimal. This chapter details an estimation method using the principal component analysis (PCA) solution based on the connection between PCA solution and membership of clusters from K-means from research. All the mathematical justification is provided. The evaluation has been done empirically with a comparative study. The validation results show the significant feasibility of the proposed method to initialize parameters.

INTRODUCTION

This chapter proposes a systematic way to estimate the initial parameters for K-means function with PCA solution possibly. The method has been developed based on a mathematical connection between PCA solution and the membership of K-means clusters considering the case of two classes of data sets in this approach. The algorithm is started with the original image data without trial of the number of clusters. The PCA solution is firstly applied to each data set to find the principal component with the maximal

DOI: 10.4018/978-1-7998-4444-0.ch010

variance. Then the image data is projected onto the first eigenvector subspace followed by the global threshold to split the data set into two exclusive subsets. In each subset, PCA is applied again to find a new principal component iteratively. Since there is no interrelation between any two of the split data subsets, the eigenvector subspaces of the original image and those sub-images are independent between each other. The procedure is applied on every split data set in hierarchy until a certain criterion is met. At the end, the means of the number of clusters are adopted as the initial parameters for K-means function.

BACKGROUND

The machine vision system is designed as input to identify the targets in the feature-fluent background. However, the identification of the target is nontrivial because the natural image data is normally nonlinear with an unknown density in the color space (Jimenez, Ceres, & Pons, 2000). With reference to the autonomous human vision, the unsupervised machine learning has been investigated and approached in applications (LeCun, Bengio, & Hinton, 2015). In which, the clustering function is one of the classical methods for classification application (Duda, Hart, & Stork, 2000; Jain, 2010). Without any prior knowledge of the cluster information, the clustering has been a challenging problem due to the difficulties of finding a proper design of an objective or a metric for the structure of the data. Among the categories of clustering (Xu & Wunsch, 2005), the partitional clustering incorporates the shape and the number of clusters by using certain metrics and prototypes in a squared error function, for example, K-means function. However, some parameters are required by the function (Du & Swamy, 2006), namely the number of clusters K, the initial value for the clusters, and dissimilarity metric. In the original K-means algorithm, these parameters are chosen randomly (Chen, Tai, Harrison, & Pan, 2005; Pena, Lozano, & Larranaga, 1999). Hence, the seedling of these initial parameters can direct the function to converge into different local optima by the multivariate fact (Xu & Wunsch, 2005).

To address this issue, many different approaches have been proposed, like constructive clustering technique ISODATA (Ball & Hall, 1965), self-creating learning algorithms (Y.-J. Zhang & Liu, 2002), a method with imbalanced spatial distribution with a cluster (T. Zhang, Cheng, & Ma, 2014), etc. On top of these algorithmic methods, the advanced statistical Bayesian information criterion (BIC) has been used in the individual splitting algorithms (Feng & Harmerly, 2007; Ishioka, 2005). The algorithmic variants are also proposed by different means such as the harmonic (B. Zhang, Hsu, & Dayal, 1999) and symmetric measures (M.-C. Su & Chou, 2001). In addition, some researches are conducted using statistical formulae such as gap statistics (Tibshirani, Walther, & Hastie, 2001), silhouette statistics (Dudoit & Fridlyand, 2002), jump methods (Sugar & James, 2003), prediction strength (Tibshirani & Walther, 2005), and the contrast statistics (Lyakh, Gurianov, Gorshkov, & Vihovanets, 2012). These initialization methods are categorized as the resampling methods by dividing the data repeatedly and randomly into non-overlapping subsets based on how the statistics are used (Dudoit & Fridlyand, 2002). Even though the resampling method seems robust to the varying covariance structure of the variables, the hierarchical procedure by running K-means multiple times is costly to achieve the optimal number of the clusters (Chiang & London, 2010). On the other hand, the methods by embedding robust statistics rely on the initialization of the parameters as well in metrics space such as median (Kaufman & Rousseeuw, 1990), midranges (Carroll & Chaturvedi, 1998), and k-modes (Huang & Ng, 2003) respectively. To achieve the proper optima, K-means has also been hybridized with other methods such as Ward's method (Ward & Jr, 1963; Willigan & Sokol, 1980) or with hierarchical density clustering algorithm (Wong, 1982). The similar issue exists for an alternative algorithm, like Expectation-Maximization (EM), although to a lesser extent (Meila & Heckerman, 1998; Steinley, 2006). The random initialization of the parameter for the clustering method normally give poor classification results (Chen, Tai, R.Harrison, & Pan, 2005). An alternative initialization method has been proposed using the mean of the index in the lower and upper area with consecutive Euclidean distance along one attribute (Khan, 2012). However, the features in different coordinate directions may not be constant. Even by using the principal axis with maximum variance for partition (Sujatha & Sona, 2013), the axis direction may not be in alignment of the optimal variance constantly when the clusters are nonlinear. Instead, an spectral clustering algorithm has been proposed by selecting the most relevant eigenvector for analysis in clustering algorithm using PCA (Xiang & Gong, 2008). The estimated weight parameter was sensitive to the dense data in large scale using the affinity matrix. PCA has also been addressed in a hierarchical way by the comparison study (T. Su & Dy, 2007). The projected mean of the selected cluster for splitting the cluster might not give an optimal threshold. Even there is a chance to lose the probability from other terms in which the different data clusters have a high separability, the well-separated cluster can still carry high contrast which can be split further. The initial parameters is also essential to some other methods such as a Min-Max method which has been developed to assign the weights based on the variance in an iterative manner (Tzortzis & Likas, 2014), the local distance and the centrality measure based method (Ji, Pang, Zheng, Wang, Ma, et al., 2015), and the density and the local distance based method for the clustering function (Ji, Pang, Zheng, Wang, & Ma, 2015). On top of that, the initial seedling data have also been located based on the density function and the kd-tree structure (Kumar & Reddy, 2017). As for the agglomerative method, the cutting of the dendrogram is normally difficult without prior knowledge. Also, the dissimilarity or the affinity matrix is sensitive to the size of the data in the cluster. When the methods are using a certain local distance measure to define the dense of the cluster, the distance measure is a deformed variance of the data in the cluster. Hence, the spatial location of the cluster in the coordinate space has been neglected. Even the silhouette index has been proposed to merge the clusters based on the other method such as the Ward framework (Nidheesh, Nazeer, & Ameer, 2018). The merging of the clustering with high silhouette index is still based on the formed local optima. Hence, the outcoming resultant clusters are affected by the local optima even with the kernel for the nonlinear data structure with spatial property.

Whatever the parametric model or multi-model of the sequence of data package, the way to originate the initial parameters for the clustering function is of interest (Douglas, 2003). For example, to deal with the natural nonlinear image data in the color space, the method with the ellipsoids model can be introduced and used to estimate the number of different colors considering the distance between clusters to represent the variance information of different colors. To make the procedure automatic, principal component analysis (PCA) scheme can be adopted using the centered covariance matrix of independent data set. However, the projection of data onto a principal eigenvector from PCA has no guarantee to have sparse properties to keep up to the data (Benezeth, Jodoin, Emile, & Rosenberger, 2010) even with the incremental solution of PCA used for the Eigen-background estimation (Li, Chen, & Zhang, 2006). Note that not all the clusters can be seen directly on one histogram of projection data on the maximum eigenvector immediately when the data is nonlinear (Wang, Jeng, Yang, & Hsieh, 2016; Xiang & Gong, 2008). However, the way to use PCA solution is reasonable mathematically to estimate the hidden clusters closely.

USE OF PCA SOLUTION TO ESTIMATE THE INITIAL PARAMETERS FOR CLUSTERING

Preliminary and Justification of Connection Between PCA Solution and K-means Membership in Case of two Classes of Data Sets

The use of PCA solution is originated by the variance of the data mathematically. Normally, the natural image data are nonlinear represented by the multicolor in color space. Without a prior for the distribution of the data sets, a hyperplane requires the training samples of credit to fix the parameters for the classification. Also, the overlap of the nonlinear clusters can cause the credit for the nonlinear classes of data lowered as the number of clusters is increased. Hence, the projection of data on PCA subspace cannot reveal all the parameters of the overlapped clusters directly. On the other hand, a random seedling can direct the solution to different local optima. Since the clusters can be represented by the variable of the centroid, the idea is to cover the variable with a hyperellipsoid instead of any distribution model. The location of any two hyperellipsoid can be derived based on the variance of the data sets or clusters. Hence, the method is originated based on the contrast of the multicolor in variance by PCA solution. However, the hidden clusters need to be revealed in a certain way other than a decisive hyperplane. This section details how to find the parameters close to the ideal optima. Starting with the preliminary of PCA, the case of two classes of data sets has been justified in the proposed estimation method. Then the estimation method proposed is implemented in some image classification applications.

Preliminary of Connection Between PCA Solution and K-means Membership

The statistical PCA which is known as Karhunen-Loeve transform (KLT) (Rao & Yip, 2001) has a mapping function to extract a certain feature in a low-dimensional space. PCA automatically extracts the eigenvectors based on the maximization of the variance of the projected data using the centered covariance matrix of the data (Jolliffe, 2002). The following defines PCA using the image data.

Definition 2.1 (Jolliffe, 2002). Consider an original image data with p random variables arranged as a column vector, denoted $\mathbf{x}$. The kth PC (principal component), y_k, where $k=1, 2, \ldots, p$, is given by:

$$y_k = \mathbf{w}_k^T \mathbf{x} \tag{1}$$

where $\mathbf{w}_k = [w_1, w_2, \cdots, w_p]^T$ is an eigenvector of the covariance matrix corresponding to its eigenvalue λ_k. The main objective of PCA is to find $\mathbf{w}_k$ providing the maximum variance of the kth PC using the second central moment. The variance can be expressed and expanded into Eq.2:

$$\text{var}\left(\mathbf{w}_k^T \mathbf{x}\right) = E\left[\left(\mathbf{w}_k^T \mathbf{x} - E\left(\mathbf{w}_k^T \mathbf{x}\right)\right)^2\right] = \mathbf{w}_k^T \Sigma \mathbf{w}_k \tag{2}$$

where $E\left(\mathbf{w}_k^T \mathbf{x}\right)$ is the expectation of the kth PC variable, var(.) represents the variance, and Σ is the covariance matrix of the elements of vector $\mathbf{x}$. The result of Eq.2 is the objective function to be maximized to find the largest PC. Since the maximum will not be determined for finite $\mathbf{w}_k$, a normalized constraint $\mathbf{w}_k^T \mathbf{w}_k = 1$ must be imposed. The quadratic objective function can be defined by Eq.3:

Maximize: $\mathbf{w}_k^T \Sigma \mathbf{w}_k$ (3)

Subjective to: $\mathbf{w}_k^T \mathbf{w}_k = 1$

By combining the normalization constraint to the objective function, the standard optimization problem becomes Eq.4 using the Lagrange Multipliers (Jolliffe, 2002):

Maximize: $\mathbf{w}_k^T \Sigma \mathbf{w}_k - \lambda_k \left(\mathbf{w}_k^T \mathbf{w}_k - 1\right)$ (4)

where λ_k is a Lagrange multiplier. Taking a derivation of Eq.4 with respect to the variable $\mathbf{w}_k$ gives the standard characteristic function by Eq.5:

$\Sigma \mathbf{w}_k - \lambda_k \mathbf{w}_k = 0$ (5)

This function can be expressed in another form by $\left(\Sigma - \lambda_k \mathbf{I}_p\right)\mathbf{w}_k = 0$, where $\mathbf{I}_p$ is an $(p \times p)$ identity matrix. Here λ_k is the eigenvalue, and $\mathbf{w}_k$ is the corresponding eigenvector of covariance matrix Σ. Substituting Eq.5 into the objective function, and using the normalization constraint, the solution for the maximum variance of the variable is the eigenvector corresponding to the largest eigenvalue of the covariance matrix Σ by Eq.6:

$\mathbf{w}_k^T \Sigma \mathbf{w}_k = \mathbf{w}_k^T \lambda_k \mathbf{w}_k = \lambda_k \mathbf{w}_k^T \mathbf{w}_k = \lambda_k$ (6)

PCA solution is to find the eigenvector $\mathbf{w}_k$ and the corresponding eigenvalue λ_k, which provide the maximum variance of vector $\mathbf{x}$ in kth PC direction.

With PCA solution, two things need to be proved for the use of PCA solution in this approach. Firstly, the principal components from PCA solution indicates the membership of clusters for example the case of two classes of data sets for the clustering function. Also, the maximization of distance between two subsets always exist independently for the data set. The mathematical notations and theorems follow the works (Ding & He, 2004; Y. Zhang, Wu, & Cheng, 2012). The definition of K-means is then given by Eq.7 using number of K centroids to cluster the data:

$$J_K = \sum_{k=1}^{K} \sum_{i \in C_k} (\mathbf{x}_i - \mathbf{m}_k)^2$$ (7)

where $\{\mathbf{x}_i : \mathbf{x}_i \in C\}$, $\mathbf{X} = [\mathbf{x}_1, \mathbf{x}_2, ..., \mathbf{x}_n]^T$ is the data matrix for data set C, $\mathbf{m}_k = \sum_{i \in C_k} \mathbf{x}_i / n_k$ is the centroid of the subset C_k, n_k is the size of subset C_k and $\sum_{k=1}^{K} n_k = n$, K is the total number of all subsets, $\{C_k : C_k \in C\}$ and $C = C_1 \oplus C_2 ...... \oplus C_K$.

Let

$$d(C_k, C_l) = \sum_{i \in C_k} \sum_{j \in C_l} (\mathbf{x}_i - \mathbf{x}_j)^2 \tag{8}$$

be the sum of squared distance (SSD) between two subsets C_k and C_l. When $k = l$, SSD between individuals within one class becomes the deformation formula of covariance for one subset in Eq.9. The proof refers to (Y. Zhang et al., 2012).

$$\mathrm{var}(C_k, C_k) = \frac{1}{2n_k^2} \sum_{i=1}^{n_k} \sum_{j=1}^{n_k} (\mathbf{x}_i - \mathbf{x}_j)^2 \tag{9}$$

Here, the case of two classes of data set is considered. Although the case ($K=2$) can be extended for more general cases, the nonlinearity of multivariate will lower the credit of the data clusters as shown by the singularity of the centered matrix later. Now, denote C1 and C2 as two subsets, where $C_1 \oplus C_2 = C$. Also note that $n_1/n + n_2/n = 1$ where n1/n and n2/n are the class occurrence probabilities. It is obvious from the definition that SSD of the whole data set C can be calculated using SSD within each of two subsets and SSD between two subsets by Eq.10:

$$d(C, C) = d(C_1, C_1) + d(C_2, C_2) + 2d(C_1, C_2) \tag{10}$$

Substituting Eq.8 into Eq.9, the covariance of the whole data set C can be expressed by Eq.11:

$$\sigma_T^2 = \overline{\mathbf{y}^2} = \sum_i \mathbf{y}_i^T \mathbf{y}_i / n = \frac{1}{2n^2} d(C, C) \tag{11}$$

where σ_T^2 is the variance for the whole data set C, $\mathbf{y}_i = \mathbf{x}_i - \overline{\mathbf{x}}$ and $\overline{\mathbf{x}} = \sum_i \mathbf{x}_i / n$. With Eq.11, Eq.10 can be expressed by Eq.12:

$$2n^2 \sigma_T^2 = d(C_1, C_1) + d(C_2, C_2) + 2d(C_1, C_2) \tag{12}$$

Since the objective function J_K for K-means clustering is related to the within class variance for all subsets based on the definition, using Eq.9, J_K can be expressed by Eq.13:

$$J_K = \sum_{k=1}^{K} \sum_{i \in C_k} (\mathbf{x}_i - \mathbf{m}_k)^2 = \sum_{k=1}^{K} n_k \sigma_k^2 = \sum_{k=1}^{K} \frac{1}{2n_k} \sum_{i,j \in C_k} (\mathbf{x}_i - \mathbf{x}_j)^2 = \frac{1}{2n_1} d(C_1, C_1) + \frac{1}{2n_2} d(C_2, C_2) \tag{13}$$

where σ_k^2 is the within class variance for the subset C_k. Some algebra yields Eq.14 from Eq.12:

$$n\sigma_T^2 = \frac{1}{2n_1}(1-\frac{n_2}{n})d(C_1,C_1) + \frac{1}{2n_2}(1-\frac{n_1}{n})d(C_2,C_2) + \frac{1}{n}d(C_1,C_2)$$ (14)

After rearrangement of Eq.14, the objective function J_K can be re-expressed by Eq.15:

$$J_K = n\sigma_T^2 - \frac{n_1 n_2}{2n}(\frac{2d(C_1,C_2)}{n_1 n_2} - \frac{d(C_1,C_1)}{n_1^2} - \frac{d(C_2,C_2)}{n_2^2}) = n\sigma_T^2 - \frac{1}{2}J_D$$ (15)

where the right part is denoted as distance objective function,
$$J_D = \frac{n_1 n_2}{2n}(\frac{2d(C_1,C_2)}{n_1 n_2} - \frac{d(C_1,C_1)}{n_1^2} - \frac{d(C_2,C_2)}{n_2^2}).$$

On the other hand, the following relation always holds (Otsu, 1979):

$$\sigma_W^2 + \sigma_B^2 = \sigma_T^2$$ (16)

where σ_W^2 is the within class variance for two subsets, $\sigma_W^2 = \mu_1\sigma_1^2 + \mu_2\sigma_2^2$, and μ_1 and μ_2 are the class occurrence probability, here $\mu_1 = n_1/n$ and $\mu_2 = n_2/n$. The variables σ_1 and σ_2 are the variance of subset C_1 and C_2, and $\sigma_B^2 = \mu_1\mu_2(\mathbf{m}_1 - \mathbf{m}_2)^2$ is the between class variance, where $\mathbf{m}_1$ and $\mathbf{m}_2$ are the centroids of two subsets class.

By substituting σ_T^2, the total variance from Eq.16 into Eq.12 using Eq.9 for within class variance, it can be found that SSD between two subsets can be expressed by Eq.17:

$$\frac{1}{n_1 n_2}d(C_1,C_2) = \frac{1}{2n_1^2}d(C_1,C_1) + \frac{1}{2n_2^2}d(C_2,C_2) + (\mathbf{m}_1 - \mathbf{m}_2)^2$$ (17)

By substituting Eq.17 into J_D in Eq.15, J_D becomes Eq.18:

$$J_D = \frac{n_1 n_2}{n}(\mathbf{m}_1 - \mathbf{m}_2)^2$$ (18)

Eq.15 and Eq.18 indicate that the minimization of J_K is equivalent to the maximization of SSD between two subsets in the distance objective function J_D which is always positive, as given in Theorem 2.1.

Theorem 2.1 (Ding & He, 2004). For $K = 2$, the minimization of K-means cluster objective function J_K is equivalent to the maximization of the distance objective J_D, which is always positive.

Proof. The minimization of within class distance objective function in K-means is equivalent to the maximization of the between class distance objective function as shown in Eq.18. In addition, since $J_D > 0$, the maximization of J_D implies that the factor $n_1 n_2$ is maximized using the probability of occurrence for two subsets, that is the derivative gives the condition $n_1 = n_2 = 1/2$. Theorem 2.1 is important to show that the distance objective function J_D leads to the solution by the principal component. ÿ

Next thing is to show that the eigenvector subspace indicates the membership for K-means clusters. Before that, the theorem for singular value decomposition (SVD) is necessary. With data matrix $\mathbf{X}$, let $\mathbf{Y} = [\mathbf{y}_1, \mathbf{y}_2, ..., \mathbf{y}_n]^T$ be the centered data matrix, where $\mathbf{y}_i = \mathbf{x}_i - \bar{\mathbf{x}}$ and $\bar{\mathbf{x}} = \sum_i \mathbf{x}_i / n$. Then $\mathbf{A} = \sum_{ij} (\mathbf{x}_i - \bar{\mathbf{x}})(\mathbf{x}_j - \bar{\mathbf{x}})^T$ is the covariance matrix which can be expressed by $\mathbf{A} = \mathbf{U} \Sigma \mathbf{V}^T$, where $\mathbf{U}$ and $\mathbf{V}$ are two orthogonal matrix, with $rank(\mathbf{A}) = r$. Hence $\mathbf{A}$ is expressed by $\mathbf{A} = \sum_i \lambda_i \mathbf{u}_i \mathbf{v}_i^T$, where λ_i are singular values, $\mathbf{u}_i$ and $\mathbf{v}_i$ are principal directions and principal components respectively (Golub & Loan, 1996). The following theorem shows the connection between the clusters' membership indicator and PCA solution considering case of two classes of data sets.

Justification of Case of two Classes of Data Sets for Estimation Procedure

Theorem 2.2 (Ding & He, 2004). For K-means clustering where $K = 2$, the continuous solution of the cluster indicator vector is the principal component $\mathbf{v}_1$, i.e., clusters C_1, C_2 are given by

$$C_1 = \{i : \mathbf{v}_1(i) \leq 0\}, \quad C_2 = \{i : \mathbf{v}_2(i) > 0\} \tag{19}$$

The optimal value of K-means objective satisfies the bounds

$$n\overline{\mathbf{y}^2} - \lambda_1 < J_{K=2} < n\overline{\mathbf{y}^2} \tag{20}$$

Proof. The squared distance matrix is given by $\mathbf{D} = (d_{ij})$, where $d_{ij} = \|\mathbf{x}_i - \mathbf{x}_j\|^2$. Let the cluster indicator vector be

$$q(i) = \begin{cases} \sqrt{n_2/nn_1} & if \quad i \in C_1 \\ -\sqrt{n_1/nn_2} & if \quad i \in C_2 \end{cases} \tag{21}$$

The indicator satisfies the sum to zero and normalization condition: $\sum_i q(i) = 0$ and $\sum_i q^2(i) = 1$. The cluster indicator is applied as factor to the vector independently. Hence each element of the distance matrix has two indicator factors for two data instances. Recalling that the distance matrix includes three SSD as shown in Eq.10, the indicator factor can be assigned in vector $\mathbf{q}$ for each individual data instance. Also, the squared distance matrix $\mathbf{D}$ is symmetric. It can be seen that $\mathbf{q}^T \mathbf{D} \mathbf{q} = -J_D$. The value for elements of $\mathbf{q}$ can be relaxed into [-1, 1] to solve the minimization of $J(\mathbf{q}) = \mathbf{q}^T \mathbf{D} \mathbf{q} / \mathbf{q}^T \mathbf{q}$. Since $\mathbf{q}^T \mathbf{q} = 1$, the minimization of quadratic $\mathbf{q}^T \mathbf{D} \mathbf{q}$ becomes a standard eigenvector problem. The solution of minimization of $J(\mathbf{q})$ is the eigenvector corresponding to the lowest eigenvalue for the form $\mathbf{D}\mathbf{z} = \lambda\mathbf{z}$, where $\mathbf{z}$ is the eigenvector and λ is the corresponding eigenvalue. However, matrix $\mathbf{D}$ is not covariance based on the definition of distance. The way to use the covariance between data for the eigenvector solution is to transform the distance matrix $\mathbf{D}$ into the centered distance matrix without affecting the solution. Then to relax $\mathbf{q}$ into continuous solution, the centered matrix of $\mathbf{D}$ is used by subtracting the column and row means of $\mathbf{D}$. Let the centered matrix be $\hat{\mathbf{D}} = (\hat{d}_{ij})$, where

$$d_{ij}^E = d_{ij} - d_{i.}/n - d_{.j}/n + d_{..}/n^2 \tag{22}$$

where $d_{i.} = \sum_j d_{ij}$ is the sum of elements in each row of distance matrix $\mathbf{D}$, $d_{.j} = \sum_i d_{ij}$ is the sum of elements in each column of matrix $\mathbf{D}$, and $d_{..} = \sum_{ij} d_{ij}$ is the sum of all elements of matrix $\mathbf{D}$. The subtraction operation for the centered matrix is the row (and column) operation without changing the solution set. Since n and n^2 are constant for a given set in Eq.22, the operation is simply to replace the row (and column) with scaled of that and of others. Hence the solution set are same, for example the non-singular eigenvector for two matrices are coincident in the same direction, except the singular ones from the centered distance matrix (Ding & He, 2004). Now since the property of sum to zero, $\sum_i d_{ij} = 0$, $\forall j$, the centered distance matrix can be singular. Hence, by excluding the singular ones which correspond to zero eigenvalue, the solution for the minimization of $\mathbf{q}^T \mathbf{D}^E \mathbf{q}$ is the eigenvector corresponding to the lowest eigenvalue for $\mathbf{D}^E \mathbf{z} = \lambda \mathbf{z}$. Also, the singular eigenvector is orthogonal to the non-singular eigenvectors. The non-singular eigenvectors have property of sum to zero. Hence, the solution of principal component is indicator for the membership of the clusters for K-means function.

Next thing is to show that the eigenvector solution is for the covariance between any two of data instance from the centered distance matrix. With algebra using the squared distance for d_{ij}, the row sum is $d_{i.} = n\mathbf{x}_i^2 + n\overline{\mathbf{x}^2} + 2n\mathbf{x}_i^T \overline{\mathbf{x}}$, the column sum is $d_{.j} = n\mathbf{x}_j^2 + n\overline{\mathbf{x}^2} + 2n\mathbf{x}_j^T \overline{\mathbf{x}}$, and the total sum is $d_{..} = 2n^2 \overline{\mathbf{y}^2} = 2n^2 \sigma_T^2$, where $\overline{\mathbf{x}^2} = \sum_i \mathbf{x}_i^T \mathbf{x}_i / n$ and $\overline{\mathbf{x}} = \sum_i \mathbf{x}_i / n$. Substituting these equations into Eq.23, the element of centered matrix can be obtained

$$d_{ij}^E = -2(\mathbf{x}_i - \overline{\mathbf{x}})^T (\mathbf{x}_j - \overline{\mathbf{x}}) \tag{23}$$

Eq.23 gives the centered distance matrix by $\mathbf{D}^E = -2\mathbf{y}_i^T \mathbf{y}_j$, where $\mathbf{y}_i^T \mathbf{y}_j$ is Gram matrix for the inner product of two centered data. Therefore, the continuous solution for cluster indicator vector is the eigenvector corresponding to the largest (positive) eigenvalue of the Gram matrix $\mathbf{y}_i^T \mathbf{y}_j$, which is precisely the principal component $\mathbf{v}_1$ as defined. Clearly, $J_D < 2\lambda_1$ where λ_1 is the corresponding principal eigenvalue of the covariance matrix. Through Eq.15, the bound on the sum of squared errors J_K (Eq.20) is obtained. ÿ

The covariance matrix is constructed by the sum of centered data for each variable. The credit for the nonlinear classes of data is lowered as the number of variables is increased. Also, the centered distance matrix can be singular. Then only the case of at least two ($K = 2$) classes of data set is considered with confidence in the proposed method. Note that the case can be extended to more general case with $K > 2$ (Ding & He, 2004). The existence of maximization between two independent subsets is given as follows.

Theorem 2.3. For $K = 2$ case with the probability of class occurrence for two data subsets, the maximization of the between class distance always exist.

Proof. The maximization of SSD between two subsets in the distance objective J_D in Eq.18 is equivalent to the maximization of $\sigma_B^2 = \mu_1 \mu_2 (\mathbf{m}_1 - \mathbf{m}_2)^2$. Hence the range of thresholding t is sought to maximize:

$$T = \{t : \mu_1 \mu_2 = \mu(t)[1 - \mu(t)]\} \tag{24}$$

There are two situations only. If all the data belong to one class, then factor $\mu(t)$ is zero or one which means no subsets in the data set. Otherwise $0 < \mu(t) < 1$ is true, then $0 < 1 - \mu(t) < 1$, hence $0 < \mu(t)[1 - \mu(t)] < 1$ is true. Therefore, the maximum always exists. ÿ

Theorem 2.1 and theorem 2.2 have shown the connection between PCA solution and the clusters' membership for K-means function. The indication for minimum two classes of data subsets with maximization of the between class distance is guaranteed. With the mathematical connection, the estimation method is proposed as follows.

Use of PCA Solution in Hierarchy to Estimate Initial Parameters for Clustering

With the multicolor image data, the use of color space can be extended since the size of the covariance matrix for PCA solution is decided by the number of variables. The selection of the coordinate component from the color space is decided the perceptual value with contrast by research. In this approach, the procedure for PCA solution starts with a construction of vector consisting of coordinates of a*and b* from CIELAB space and H (Hue) from HSV space as follows:

$$\mathbf{a} = \left[a_{11}, a_{12}, ..., a_{1n}, a_{21}, a_{22}, ..., a_{2n}, ..., a_{m1}, a_{m2}, ..., a_{mn}\right]^T \tag{25}$$

$$\mathbf{b} = \left[b_{11}, b_{12}, ..., b_{1n}, b_{21}, b_{22}, ..., b_{2n}, ..., b_{m1}, b_{m2}, ..., b_{mn}\right]^T \tag{26}$$

$$\mathbf{h} = \left[h_{11}, h_{12}, ..., h_{1n}, h_{21}, h_{22}, ..., h_{2n}, ..., h_{m1}, h_{m2}, ..., h_{mn}\right]^T \tag{27}$$

where the size of image is $n \times m$, the size of $\mathbf{a}$, $\mathbf{b}$, and $\mathbf{h}$ vectors is ($n \times m$, 1). The image data are rearranged as in Eq.28 and denoted as a matrix $\mathbf{X}$:

$$\mathbf{X} = \begin{bmatrix} \mathbf{x}_1 & \mathbf{x}_2 & \mathbf{x}_3 \end{bmatrix} = \begin{bmatrix} x_{11} & x_{12} & x_{13} \\ x_{21} & x_{22} & x_{23} \\ \vdots & \vdots & \vdots \\ x_{mn} & x_{mn} & x_{mn} \end{bmatrix} = [\mathbf{a}, \mathbf{b}, \mathbf{h}] = \begin{bmatrix} a_{11} & b_{11} & h_{11} \\ a_{12} & b_{12} & h_{12} \\ \vdots & \vdots & \vdots \\ a_{mn} & b_{mn} & h_{mn} \end{bmatrix} \tag{28}$$

where each row represents the three intensity values of a*, b* and H for one pixel, i.e., $\left[a_{ij}, b_{ij}, h_{ij}\right]$, $i = 1, ..., m$; $j = 1, ..., n$, and the size of this matrix is ($n \times m$, 3). The expectation of the population in each coordinate is calculated by $v_l = \sum_{i=1}^{mn} pt_{il}$, $p = \dfrac{1}{mn}$, assuming that each event of the population has the same prior probability, where $l = 1, 2, 3$. The centered population is obtained by subtracting the mean of the corresponding original population in each coordinate by $\mathbf{x}_l = \mathbf{t}_l - \left[v_l, ..., v_l\right]^T_{\dim(\mathbf{t}_l)}$. In here, $\mathbf{x}_1$ is the vector of centered population of the coordinate a*, and $\mathbf{x}_2$ and $\mathbf{x}_3$ are those for the coordinate b*, and H, respectively. The covariance matrix is constructed using the sum of centered population of three coordinates a*, b*, and H. Hence, the dimension of this covariance matrix with sum of centered population is only decided by the number of variables and not by the size of data instance using affinity matrix (Xiang & Gong, 2008). PCs can be found by several approaches, for example single value decomposition (SVD), QL factorization, and the neural network based methods (Du & Swamy, 2006; Jolliffe, 2002). When image data set is fully presented, Gauss Jordan (GJ) elimination is convenient to find the eigenvector and the corresponding eigenvalue efficiently. The maximal eigenvector gives the direction to split the data into two data subsets.

On the other hand, the subsets need to be evaluated for termination with certain geometrical property for PCA solution. Under the condition that $\mathbf{x}$ has a normal distribution, i.e., the ellipsoids given in Eq.29 which define contours of constant probability for the distribution of $\mathbf{x}$, the following property shows that PCs of such ellipsoids represents the axes which can provide the maximal statistical variation and those axes are orthogonal from each other.

Property 2.1 (Jolliffe, 2002). Considering the p-dimensional ellipsoids

$$\mathbf{x}^T \Sigma^{-1} \mathbf{x} = constant \tag{29}$$

then the PCs define the principal axes of these ellipsoids, where $\mathbf{x}$ is the variable and Σ is the covariance matrix of the elements of vector $\mathbf{x}$.

Proof. The PC is an orthonormal linear transform and the eigenvectors are uncorrelated with each other (Jolliffe, 2002). By following the definition in Eq.1 and expressing the number of eigenvectors in a matrix form $\mathbf{W}$, the characteristic function becomes Eq.30:

$$\Sigma \mathbf{W} - \Lambda \mathbf{W} = 0 \tag{30}$$

where Λ is the diagonal matrix whose kth diagonal element is λ_k corresponding to the kth eigenvalue of Σ. With normalization constraints, the orthogonality of $\mathbf{W}$ gives another form by $\mathbf{W}^T \Sigma \mathbf{W} = \Lambda$ using the inverse form of $\mathbf{W}$.

Now consider the p-dimensional ellipsoids which is given in Eq.29. With Eq.1, the inverse transformation is $\mathbf{x} = \mathbf{W}\mathbf{y}$, where the number of PCs is given by vector $\mathbf{y}$, where $\mathbf{y} = \left[y_1, y_2, ..., y_p \right]$. Substituting this into Eq.29 gives Eq.31:

$$\left(\mathbf{W}\mathbf{y} \right)^T \Sigma^{-1} \left(\mathbf{W}\mathbf{y} \right) = constant = \mathbf{y}^T \mathbf{W}^T \Sigma^{-1} \mathbf{W}\mathbf{y} \tag{31}$$

Since the eigenvectors of Σ^{-1} and Σ are truly the same and the eigenvalues are the reciprocals of each other (Jolliffe, 2002), Eq.31 can be expressed by Eq.32:

$$\mathbf{y}^T \mathbf{W}^T \Sigma^{-1} \mathbf{W}\mathbf{y} = \mathbf{y}^T \Lambda^{-1} \mathbf{y} = \sum_{k=1}^{p} \frac{y_k^2}{\lambda_k} \tag{32}$$

Eq.32 is the equation for the ellipsoid referred to the fact that the half-lengths of principal axes are proportional to the square root of those eigenvalues (Jolliffe, 2002). This geometric property of ellipsoids is of statistical relevance if the distribution of $\mathbf{x}$ is assumed as multivariate normal (Jolliffe, 2002). Using this property, the transforming PCs can be substituted into the principal axes of ellipsoids. However, the thresholds on the projection data on the maximal eigenvector generally become less credible as the number of classes to be separated increases nonlinearly (Sezgin & Sankur, 2004). When the variance exists in one major eigenvector direction, the original data can be split into two data subsets with the global threshold on the projection data in the maximal eigenvector subspace (Otsu, 1979). However, the subsets can be processed with PC solution in the same way to reveal the hidden clusters in hierarchy. ÿ

With the definition and property described, the method to estimate initial parameters for K-means function using PCA solution is proposed graphically in Figure 1. The process starts with the rearrangement of the frame of image data with Eq.28. Then the PCA is applied to this rearranged data to find the solution. The termination criterion is measured in the standard deviation on each data subset. If the deviation is lower than certain small value, the corresponding image data set is considered covered by a unimodal ellipsoid, i.e., belongs to one cluster. Otherwise, the corresponding image will be projected onto the major eigenvector subspace. The projected data is split into two sub-images by a global threshold (Otsu, 1979). The whole process will be iterated in hierarchy procedure until all sub-images meet the termination criterion. Finally, the centroids of the number of clusters are used as initial parameters for K-means function.

Figure 1. Procedure to estimate initial parameters for K-means using PCA solution in hierarchy

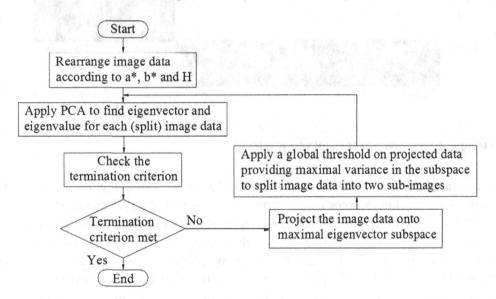

To visualize the procedure graphically, Figure 2 shows an example in which the image consists of 6 blobs with different colors and some white color noises. Firstly, the image is projected into the 1st PC and the global threshold t_1 is applied to split the image into two sub-images. Secondly, the same procedure is applied to the two split sub-images. As expected, the termination criterion will not be satisfied in this level. Hence the process is repeated into these two sub-images individually and split each sub-image into two subsequent sub-images. This process is iterated until it reaches step 6, where each color blob and white noise are correctly clustered as shown. Note that for the real-time images, there is a higher possibility to end up in over clustering. However, the redundant clusters such as noise clusters are initialized and refined by K-means function as the independent clusters such as the white noise in this example. In this way, the initial parameters are estimated close to the local optima for K-means function. The estimation procedure has been approached in classification application with some color image database in comparison with some classical methods.

Figure 2. Example of estimation process for initial parameters in steps

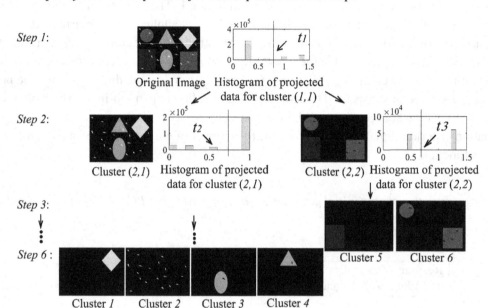

SOLUTIONS AND RECOMMENDATIONS

The estimation method for K-means function is approached on two types of color image data bank. In the first step, some benchmark color images from Columbia multispectral image database (Asuni & Giachetti, 2014) are selected and used. Then, some real time images such as citrus fruit images and plant images are used in the validation study. Also, the effectiveness of the proposed estimation method is compared to another two selected classical methods, namely Ward's method (Steinley & Brusco, 2007; Ward & Jr, 1963) and Sujatha's method (Sujatha & Sona, 2013). The Ward's method is an agglomerative hierarchical procedure with the objective function of the error sum of square measure by

$$ESS = \sum_{i=1}^{n} x_i^2 - (1/n)\left(\sum_{i=1}^{n} x_i\right)^2$$ (Steinley & Brusco, 2007; Ward & Jr, 1963), where x_i is the score of

ith individual dataset and n is the number of data. Since Ward's method merges pair of clusters at each step, it is selected as an agglomerative hierarchical based method to compare with the proposed method. On the other hand, Sujatha's method derives the initial partition along the data axis with the highest variation (Sujatha & Sona, 2013). The total clustering error is measured on the partitioned clusters by

$centroidDist = \left(\sum_{i=1}^{n} dsum_i\right)\Big/ n$ for the case with the total number of data points as n, where $dsum_i = \sum_{j=1}^{i} D_j$

and $D_j = d(c_j, c_{j+1})^2$ is the Euclidean of adjacent points on data axis, and n is the number of data points. Hence, Sujatha's method is selected as a projection based method for comparison purpose.

The accuracy of the results obtained is measured by Rand index (RI) (Hubert & Arabie, 1985; Rand, 1971). Rand index is a measure of agreement for similarity to check the accuracy of image clustering. By given two partitions, U and V, with the assumption that U is the reference and V is the clustering result, RI is given by Eq.33:

$$RI = \frac{(a+d)}{(a+b+c+d)} \tag{33}$$

where *a* is the number of pairs of objects that are placed in the same class in U and in the same cluster in V (i.e., true positive), *b* is the number of pairs of objects in the same class in U but not in the same cluster in V (i.e., false positive), *c* is the number of pairs of objects in the same cluster in V but not in the same class in U (i.e., false negative) and *d* is the number of pairs of objects in different classes and different clusters in both partitions (i.e., true negative). RI is ranged from 0 to 1, where the higher index the more accurate. With a reference image created manually and the clustering result, the nonzero pixels from two clusters images can be used to determine the dissimilarity between two partitions using this measure. The error contained in the manual reference would be insignificant when the clustering results are measured with the same reference.

Efficiency is also compared in the study. Ward's method searches the nearest cluster with merging of the nearest cluster pair. The complexity for Ward's method is $O(N^3)$ in the worst case, where N is the number of points to be classified. With more efficient approach, it could be improved to be $O(N^2\log(N))$ (Kurita, 1991). For Sujatha's method, the computational complexity of finding the optimal point is $O(N^2)$, where N is the total number of data points to be partitioned. For the proposed method, the complexity of solving GJ elimination by the rows reduction operation to find n unknown echelon equations is approximately $O(n^3)$ operation and the construction of the covariance matrix is $O(mn^2)$, where n is the dimension of the covariance matrix and m is the size of cluster data. The complexity of the global threshold for histogram is $O(L^2)$, where L is the grayscale of the histogram which depends on the spectra of the image and the size of the cluster data. With the size of echelon fixed, the efficiency of the proposed method is affected by the size of the data partially with the dimension of echelon in the construction of the covariance matrix and the grayscale of the histogram of the projected data. Hence in a hierarchical divisive procedure, the worst case is when the pixels of image data have variant grayscale in a color component. The speed of Ward's method will be lowered for the large data during the agglomerative hierarchical procedure. The Sujatha's approach should be fast for the hierarchical divisive procedure along one data axis (Sujatha & Sona, 2013). However, the efficiency is compromised with the accuracy in the experiment.

Figure 3 shows some of images used in the study. The images from Columbia multispectral image database [50] are selected and grouped into two types: one with simple color bars or blobs and the others with more feature-fluent real objects as shown by a(.) and b(.). Due to the difficulties in creation of the corresponding manual references for all clusters, only the salient clusters with unique colors are made as the reference cluster for the dissimilarity measure while the remaining backgrounds are ignored. The last row in Figure 3 shows some real-time images used including the citrus fruit images and the plant images. Normally the background of the real time image is feature fluent. Hence, only the clusters of the objects with interest are selected for the dissimilarity measure. Later, Figure 6 show the manually created reference images used in the study. The size of the real time images is 1304 by 976 for the citrus fruit images and 800 by 600 for the plant images. Averagely 30 images for each type of image bank are randomly selected from the image database for processing.

Figure 3. Image data used for validation of the proposed method:
(a1) Color_bars1; (a2) Clay; (a3) Color_bars2; (a4) Glass_tiles; (a5) Paints; (a6) Sponges;
(b1) Balloons; (b2) Beads; (b3) Feathers; (b4) Jelly_beans; (b5) Pompoms; (b6) Supperballs;
(c1) Citrus fruit image1; (c2) Citrus fruit image2; (c3) Plant image1; (c4) Plant image2

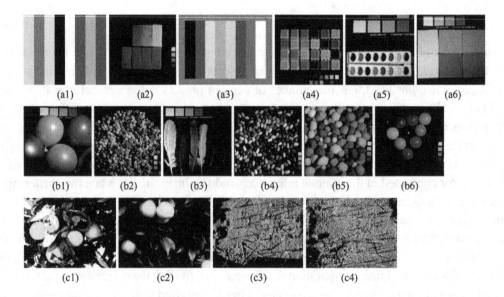

The evaluation study is conducted with MATLAB (9.4.0.813654 (R2018a)) on a computer of 64-bit operating system with Intel(R) Core(TM) i7-4790 CPU @ 3.60GHz and 8GB RAM. Three estimation methods: Ward's method, Sujatha's method, and the proposed method have been approached to find the initial parameters for K-means batch clustering (Linde, Buzo, & Gray, 1980). After the clustering converges to the finite minimum, the refined centroids are used to classify the original image. The classified salient cluster images are used to check the dissimilarity with the manually created reference cluster images using RI index. In implementation, the confidence level is set experimentally smaller to control the clusters for the initial parameters, for example, one percentage of the accumulated total variation of the transformed image data. As a result, the clusters generated from the simple color images are comparable. As for the feature-fluent color images, the proposed method generates less redundant number of clusters. In the study, the proposed method gives fewer redundant noise clusters to the other two methods.

As result, the closeness to the better local optima is shown by an example in Figure 5 namely "Pompoms" ((b5) in Figure 3). The first row is the reference cluster images by manual while the second row includes the results using initial parameters from Ward's method, the third row gives the results with Sujatha's method, and the last row shows the results with the proposed method respectively. The closeness to the ideal optima can be observed by RI values by the samples of processed database images in Table 1 and graphically in Figure 4. For those simple images (a(.)), RI value of three methods show little differences. However, in the feature-fluent images (b(.)), improvement of performance by the proposed method can be observed. The number of clusters with the proposed method is much closer to the value shown in the references than those obtained with the other two methods. A similar outcome has been observed in the real time images as shown by example in Figure 7. The first column in the figure presents the original images while the second column shows the manual reference. The results by approached methods are given in the other columns respectively. The resultant clusters by the proposed method is closer to the reference clusters as shown by the average of RI value obtained from 30 images of different types in Table 3 and graphically in Figure 6. The dissimilarity measure also illustrates the local optima as the non-homogenous spectra of the natural image on results from the approached estimation methods. Even with error included in the same manual reference, the dissimilarity measure is still comparable for all results by the approached methods empirically. In terms of processing time (see Table 2 and Table 3), Ward's method is slower while Sujatha's method is faster than the proposed method as expected. However, fast convergence is often compromised with accuracy. The RI value with Sujathas' method is lower than the value with the proposed method. The results from the experiment have shown the importance of the initial parameters for the clustering function to converge to the proper local optima.

Table 1. RI value for color image database using three estimation methods

Method	Indices	(a1)	(a2)	(a3)	(a4)	(a5)	(a6)	(b1)	(b2)	(b3)	(b4)	(b5)	(b6)
Ward's method	RI	1	0.96	0.90	0.99	0.96	0.99	0.92	0.92	0.94	0.91	*0.95*	0.92
	No. of clusters	8	23	31	20	25	22	24	22	21	15	*25*	21
Sujatha's method	RI	1	0.94	0.90	0.99	0.95	0.98	0.95	0.94	0.94	0.93	*0.95*	0.98
	No. of clusters	8	15	7	20	32	15	26	25	22	20	*22*	21
Propose method	RI	1	0.96	0.90	0.99	0.96	1	0.99	0.96	0.96	0.99	*0.99*	0.99
	No. of clusters	8	17	7	21	28	9	9	12	12	7	*11*	16

Simple images: (a1) Color_bars1; (a2) Clay; (a3) Color_bars2; (a4) Glass_tiles; (a5) Paints; (a6) Sponges; Feature-fluent images: (b1) Balloons; (b2) Beads; (b3) Feathers; (b4) Jelly_beans; (b5) Pompoms; (b6) Supperballs;

Table 2. Processing time for color image database with three estimation methods and K-means function

Processing time (Second)	Ward's method	Sujatha's method	Proposed method
Time for initial parameter estimation	10.00	0.83	4.18
Time of K-means convergence	5.69	4.30	4.19

FUTURE RESEARCH DIRECTIONS

The proposed estimation method has been implemented and compared to some classical methods in some classification applications. Also, the probability to improve the efficiency of the subsequent clustering has been identified when the outcome is close to the proper local optima of the nonlinear clusters. Hence, the estimation procedure originated based on the variance of information is feasible. Also, the probability to approach close to the real variables of the nonlinear clusters can be interesting, for example, the measure of the closeness between the estimated and the real variables and the chance to promote the probability to approach to the real variables.

Figure 4. RI value for some color image database with estimation methods and K-means batch clustering (a(.) and b(.) see Table 2.)

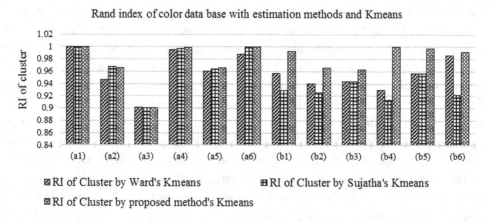

Figure 5. Reference clusters for image of "Pompoms" from (a1) to (a6); Resultant clusters by Ward's method from (b1) to (b6); Resultant clusters by Sujatha's method from (c1) to (c6); Resultant clusters by PCA based method from (d1) to (d6)

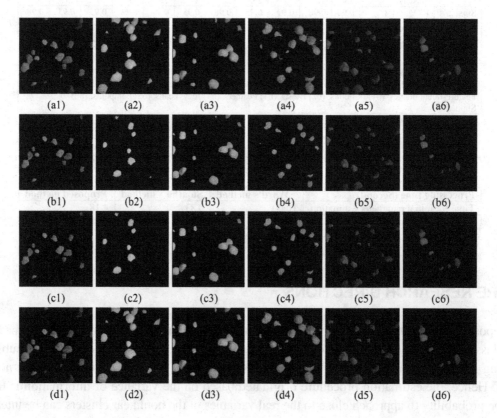

Table 3. Processing indices for citrus fruit and plant image

Estimation approach	Ward's method		Sujatha's method		Proposed method	
Types of citrus color image	Citrus image	Plant image	Citrus image	Plant image	Citrus image	plant image
Time for initial parameter estimation	61.79	10.98	1.77	0.74	10.37	3.81
Time of K-means convergence	50.88	12.68	13.06	3.47	75.84	20.31
No. of clusters estimated	27	33	32	38	20	15
RI measure	0.57	0.49	0.52	0.44	0.61	0.58

Figure 6. RI for citrus fruit and plant image with estimation methods and K-means batch clustering

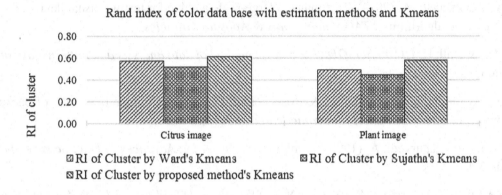

Figure 7. Citrus image (a1) and plant image (b1), reference for citrus image (a2) and plant image (b2), Ward's resultant cluster for citrus image (a3) and plant image (b3), Sujatha's resultant cluster for citrus image (a4) and plant image (b4), PCA based resultant cluster for citrus image (a5) and plant image (b5)

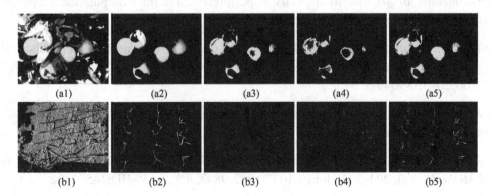

CONCLUSION

This chapter has proposed an estimation method to find the initial parameters automatically for K-means clustering function. The estimation method uses the statistical PCA solution in a hierarchy manner considering two classes of data sets covered by two ellipsoids. Each data set including the subsets split in maximal subspace is evaluated by the ellipsoidal conformation criterion with an appropriate confidence level. In this way, the nonlinear clusters with contrast can be revealed in a hierarchical manner iteratively. The mathematical verification for the connection between PCA solution and the clusters membership shows the confidence for the case of two classes of data sets in the estimation procedure. The proposed estimation method is evaluated with the dissimilarity measure using Rank index against another two selected typical methods on some different color image data banks. The validation results have shown the effectiveness and the significant feasibility of the proposed method to estimate the core parameters for clustering function.

REFERENCES

Asuni, N., & Giachetti, A. (2014). Testimage: a large-scale archive for testing visual devices and basic image processing algorithms. *STAG: Smart Tools & Apps for Graphics*.

Ball, G. H., & Hall, D. J. (1965). *ISODATA, a novel method of data analysis and pattern classification*. Academic Press.

Benezeth, Y., Jodoin, P.-M., Emile, B., & Rosenberger, C. (2010). Comparative study of background subtraction algorithms. *Journal of Electronic Imaging, 19*(3).

Carroll, J. D., & Chaturvedi, A. (1998). K-midranges clustering. *Advances in Data Science and Classification*, 3-14.

Chen, B., Tai, P. C., Harrison, R., & Pan, Y. (2005). *Novel hybrid hierarchical-K-means clustering method (H-K-means) for microarray analysis*. Paper presented at the 2005 IEEE Computational Systems Bioinformatics Conference - Workshops (CSBW'05).

Chen, B., Tai, P. C., Harrison, R., & Pan, Y. (2005). *Novel Hybrid Hierarchical-K-means Clustering Method (H-K-means) for Microarray Analysis*. Paper presented at the Computational Systems Bioinformatics Conference 2005, Stanford University.

Chiang, M. M.-T., & London, B. U. (2010). Intelligent choice of the number of clusters in K-means clustering: An experimental study with different cluster spreads. *Journal of Classification, 27*(1), 3–40. doi:10.100700357-010-9049-5

Ding, C., & He, X. (2004). K-means Clustering via Principal Component Analysis. *Proceedings of the 21st International Conference on Machine Learning*.

Douglas, S. (2003). Local Optima in K-Means Clustering: What You Don't Know May Hurt You. *Psychological Methods, 8*(3), 294–304. doi:10.1037/1082-989X.8.3.294 PMID:14596492

Du, K.-L., & Swamy, M. N. S. (2006). *Neural Networks in a Soft computing Framework*. Springer-Verlag London Limited.

Duda, R. O., Hart, P. E., & Stork, D. G. (2000). *Pattern Classification* (2nd ed.). Wiley-Interscience.

Dudoit, S., & Fridlyand, J. (2002). A prediction-based resampling method for estimating the number of clusters in a dataset. *Genome Biology, 3*(7), 1–21. doi:10.1186/gb-2002-3-7-research0036 PMID:12184810

Feng, Y., & Harmerly, G. (2007). *PG-means: learning the number of clusters in data.* Paper presented at the Advances in Neural Information Processing Systems, Cambridge, MA.

Golub, G. H., & Loan, C. F. V. (1996). Matrix Computations (3rd ed.). The Johns Hopkins University Press.

Huang, Z., & Ng, M. K. (2003). A note on K-modes clustering. *Journal of Classification, 23*(2), 257–261. doi:10.100700357-003-0014-4

Hubert, L., & Arabie, P. (1985). Comparing Partitions. *Journal of Classification, 2*(1), 193–218. doi:10.1007/BF01908075

Ishioka, T. (2005). *An expansion of X-means for automatically determining the optimal number of clusters.* Paper presented at the Fourth IASTED International Conference Computation Intelligence, Calgary, Alberta, Canada.

Jain, A. K. (2010). Data clustering: 50 years beyond K-means. *Pattern Recognition Letters, 31*(8), 651–666. doi:10.1016/j.patrec.2009.09.011

Ji, J., Pang, W., Zheng, Y., Wang, Z., & Ma, Z. (2015). An Initialization Method for Clustering Mixed Numeric and Categorical Data Based on the Density and Distance. *International Journal of Pattern Recognition and Artificial Intelligence, 29*(7), 1550024. Advance online publication. doi:10.1142/S021800141550024X

Ji, J., Pang, W., Zheng, Y., Wang, Z., Ma, Z., & Zhang, L. (2015). A Novel Cluster Center Initialization Method for the k_Prototypes Algorithms using Centrality and Distance. *Applied Mathematics & Information Sciences, 9*(6), 2933–2942. doi:10.12785/amis/090621

Jimenez, A. R., Ceres, R., & Pons, J. L. (2000). A Survey of Computer Vision Methods for Locating Fruit on Trees. *Transactions of the ASAE. American Society of Agricultural Engineers, 43*(6), 1911–1920. doi:10.13031/2013.3096

Jolliffe, I. T. (2002). Principal Component Analysis (2nd ed.). New York: Springer.

Kaufman, L., & Rousseeuw, P. J. (1990). *Finding Groups in Data: An Introduction to Cluster Analysis.* John Wiley & Sons, Inc. doi:10.1002/9780470316801

Khan, F. (2012). An initial seed selection algorithm for k-means clustering of georeferenced data to improve replicability of cluster assignments for mapping application. *Applied Soft Computing, 12*(11), 3698–3700. doi:10.1016/j.asoc.2012.07.021

Kumar, K. M., & Reddy, A. R. M. (2017). An efficient k-means clustering filtering algorithm using density based initial cluster centers. *Information Sciences, 418-419*, 286–301. doi:10.1016/j.ins.2017.07.036

Kurita, T. (1991). An efficient agglomerative clustering algorithm using a heap. *Pattern Recognition, 24*(3), 205–209. doi:10.1016/0031-3203(91)90062-A

LeCun, Y., Bengio, Y., & Hinton, G. (2015). Deep learning. *Nature*, *521*(7553), 436–444. doi:10.1038/nature14539 PMID:26017442

Li, R., Chen, Y., & Zhang, X. (2006). Fast robust eigen-background updating for foreground detection. *Proc. Int. Conf. on Image Processing*. 10.1109/ICIP.2006.312836

Linde, Y., Buzo, A., & Gray, R. M. (1980). An Algorithm for Vector Quantizer Design. *IEEE Transactions on Communications*, *COM-28*(1), 84–95. doi:10.1109/TCOM.1980.1094577

Lyakh, Y., Gurianov, V., Gorshkov, O., & Vihovanets, Y. (2012). Estimating the number of data clusters via the contrast statistic. *Journal of Biomedical Science and Engineering*, *5*(02), 95–99. doi:10.4236/jbise.2012.52012

Meila, M., & Heckerman, D. (1998). *An experimental comparison of several clustering and initialization methods*. Retrieved from Redmond.

Nidheesh, N., Nazeer, K. A. A., & Ameer, P. M. (2018). A Hierarchical Clustering Algorithm Based on Silhouette Index for Cancer Subtype Discovery from Omics Data. *bioRxiv*. Advance online publication. doi:10.1101/309716

Otsu, N. (1979). A threshold selection method from gray-level histograms. *IEEE Transactions on Systems, Man, and Cybernetics*, *SMC-9*(1), 62–66. doi:10.1109/TSMC.1979.4310076

Pena, J. M., Lozano, J. A., & Larranaga, P. (1999). An empirical comparison of four initialization methods for the K-Means algorithm. *Pattern Recognition Letters*, *20*(10), 1027–1040. doi:10.1016/S0167-8655(99)00069-0

Rand, W. M. (1971). Objective Criteria for the Evaluation of Clustering Methods. *Journal of the American Statistical Association*, *66*(336), 846–850. doi:10.1080/01621459.1971.10482356

Rao, K. R., & Yip, P. C. (2001). *The transform and data compression handbook*. CRC Press LLC.

Sezgin, M., & Sankur, B. (2004). Survey over image thresholding techniques and quantitative performance evaluation. *Journal of Electronic Imaging*, *13*(1), 146–165. doi:10.1117/1.1631315

Steinley, D. (2006). K-means clustering: A half-century synthesis. *British Journal of Mathematical & Statistical Psychology*, *57*(1), 1–34. doi:10.1348/000711005X48266 PMID:16709277

Steinley, D., & Brusco, M. J. (2007). Initializing K-means batch cluster: A critical evaluation of several teqhniques. *Journal of Classification*, *24*(1), 99–121. doi:10.100700357-007-0003-0

Su, M.-C., & Chou, C.-H. (2001). A modified version of the K-means algorithm with a distance based on cluster symmetry. *IEEE Transactions on Pattern Analysis and Machine Intelligence*, *23*(6), 674–680. doi:10.1109/34.927466

Su, T., & Dy, J. G. (2007). In search of deterministic methods for initializing k-means and Gaussian mixture clustering. *Intelligent Data Analysis*, *11*(4), 319–338. doi:10.3233/IDA-2007-11402

Sugar, C. A., & James, G. M. (2003). Finding the number of clusters in a dataset: An information-theoretic approach. *Journal of the American Statistical Association*, *98*(463), 750–763. doi:10.1198/016214503000000666

Sujatha, S., & Sona, A. S. (2013). New fast K-means clustering algorithm using modified centroid selection method. *International Journal of Engineering Research & Technology (Ahmedabad)*, 2(2), 1–9.

Tibshirani, R., & Walther, G. (2005). Cluster validation by prediction strength. *Journal of Computational and Graphical Statistics*, 14(3), 511–528. doi:10.1198/106186005X59243

Tibshirani, R., Walther, G., & Hastie, T. (2001). Estimating the number of clusters in a data set via the gap statistic. *Journal of the Royal Statistical Society. Series B. Methodological*, 63(2), 411–423. doi:10.1111/1467-9868.00293

Tzortzis, G., & Likas, A. (2014). The MinMax k-Means clustering algorithm. *Pattern Recognition*, 47(7), 2505–2516. doi:10.1016/j.patcog.2014.01.015

Wang, C.-W., Jeng, J.-H., Yang, W.-S., & Hsieh, J.-G. (2016). PCA image coding with iterative clustering. *Multidimensional Systems and Signal Processing*, 27(3), 647–666. doi:10.100711045-015-0357-0

Ward, J. H. Jr. (1963). Hierarchical grouping to optimize an objective function. *Journal of the American Statistical Association*, 58(301), 236–244. doi:10.1080/01621459.1963.10500845

Willigan, G. W., & Sokol, L. M. (1980). A two-stage clustering algorithm with robust recovery characteristics. *Educational and Psychological Measurement*, 40(3), 755–759. doi:10.1177/001316448004000320

Wong, M. A. (1982). A hybrid clustering method for identifying high-density clusters. *Journal of the American Statistical Association*, 77(380), 841–847. doi:10.1080/01621459.1982.10477896

Xiang, T., & Gong, S. (2008). Spectral clustering with eigenvector selection. *Pattern Recognition*, 41(3), 1012–1029. doi:10.1016/j.patcog.2007.07.023

Xu, R., & Wunsch, D. II. (2005). Survey of Clustering Algorithms. *IEEE Transactions on Neural Networks*, 16(3), 645–678. doi:10.1109/TNN.2005.845141 PMID:15940994

Zhang, B., Hsu, M., & Dayal, U. (1999). *K-harmonic means - A data clustering algorithm*. Academic Press.

Zhang, T., Cheng, L., & Ma, F. (2014). A modified rough cmeans clustering algorithm based on hybrid imbalanced measure of distance and density. *International Journal of Approximate Reasoning, 55*(8), 1805-1818.

Zhang, Y., Wu, H., & Cheng, L. (2012). Some new deformation formulas about variance and covariance. *Proceedings of 2012 International Conference on Modelling, Identification and Control*.

Zhang, Y.-J., & Liu, Z.-Q. (2002). Self-Splitting competitive learning: A new on-line clustering paradigm. *IEEE Transactions on Neural Networks*, 13(2), 369–380. doi:10.1109/72.991422 PMID:18244438

ADDITIONAL READING

Ding, C., & He, X. (2004). K-means Clustering via Principal Component Analysis. Paper presented at the Proceedings of the 21st International Conference on Machine Learning, Banff, Canada.

Gonzalez, R. C., Woods, R. E., & Eddins, S. L. (2004). *Digital Image Processing Using MATLAB*. Pearson Education, Inc.

Jain, A. K. (2010). Data clustering: 50 years beyond K-means. *Pattern Recognition Letters*, *31*(8), 651–666. doi:10.1016/j.patrec.2009.09.011

Jolliffe, I. T. (2002). Principal Component Analysis (2nd Edition ed.). New York: Springer.

LeCun, Y., Bengio, Y., & Hinton, G. (2015). Deep learning. *Nature*, *521*(7553), 436–444. doi:10.1038/nature14539 PMID:26017442

Sezgin, M., & Sankur, B. (2004). Survey over image thresholding techniques and quantitative performance evaluation. *Journal of Electronic Imaging*, *13*(1), 146–165. doi:10.1117/1.1631315

Wang, C.-W., Jeng, J.-H., Yang, W.-S., & Hsieh, J.-G. (2016). PCA image coding with iterative clustering. *Multidimensional Systems and Signal Processing*, *27*(3), 647–666. doi:10.100711045-015-0357-0

Xu, R., & Wunsch, D. II. (2005). Survey of Clustering Algorithms. *IEEE Transactions on Neural Networks*, *16*(3), 645–678. doi:10.1109/TNN.2005.845141 PMID:15940994

Zhang, Y., Wu, H., & Cheng, L. (2012). Some new deformation formulas about variance and covariance. Paper presented at the Proceedings of 2012 International Conference on Modelling, Identification and Control, Wuhan, China.

KEY TERMS AND DEFINITIONS

Classification: Classification is an application of pattern recognition by the assignment of the data instance with label. The assignment is realized by the measurement using certain dissimilarity metrics function.

Clustering: Clustering is a procedure to group the different objects into the same category which has similar properties measured by the specific metrics.

Image Segmentation: Image segmentation subdivides the image into constituent features with certain dissimilarity properties using the measuring metrics from each other.

Initial Parameters: When a function such as clustering function contains multi-variable or multi-factor, the number of variables and the initial values for the variables or factor are defined as initial parameters.

Supervised Learning: The supervised learning is the common machine learning in which the training samples with credit are used to find the parameters namely weights of a such as hyperplane for the subsequent classification application.

Thresholding: Thresholding is method to segment image data with hyperplane.

Unsupervised Learning: Unsupervised learning is a kind of self-mapping or self-organized learning procedure to group the different patterns without pre-learned parameters or labels.

Chapter 11
Some Algorithms on Detection of Corner Points for Digital Images

Muhammad Sarfraz

ⓘ https://orcid.org/0000-0003-3196-9132

Kuwait University, Kuwait

ABSTRACT

Detecting corner points for the digital images is based on determining significant geometrical locations. Corner points lead and guide for providing significant clues for shape analysis and representation. They actually provide significant features of an object, which can be used in different phases of processing. In shape analysis problems, for example, a shape can be efficiently reformulated in a compact way and with sufficient accuracy if the corners are properly located. This chapter selects seven well referred algorithms from the literature to review, compare, and analyze empirically. It provides an overview of these selected algorithms so that users can easily pick an appropriate one for their specific applications and requirements.

INTRODUCTION

Corner detection is a computer vision approach which is used to extract certain kinds of features and infer the contents of an image. It is very frequently used for various applications in real life. These applications include object reconstruction, motion detection, image mosaicking, panorama stitching, image registration, video tracking, object recognition and others. "A corner can be defined as the intersection of two edges. A corner can also be defined as a point for which there are two dominant and different edge directions in a local neighborhood of the point. An interest point is a point in an image which has a well-defined position and can be robustly detected. This means that an interest point can be a corner but it can also be, for example, an isolated point of local intensity maximum or minimum, line endings, or a point on a curve where the curvature is locally maximal" (Wikipedia, 2020).

DOI: 10.4018/978-1-7998-4444-0.ch011

In general, most of the corner detection methods detect interest points practically. As a matter of fact, the term "corner" and "interest point" are used interchangeably (Willis and Sui, 2009). Hence, if only corners are to be detected, it is necessary to do a local analysis of detected interest points, this will determine which of these are real corners. "Examples of edge detection that can be used with post-processing to detect corners are the Kirsch operator and the Frei-Chen masking set" (Wikipedia, 2020; Shapiro and Stockman, 2001).

Corner detection approaches for binary images usually involve segmenting the image into regions and extracting boundaries from those regions that contain them. The techniques for gray level images can be categorized into two classes: (a) Template based and (b) gradient based. The template based technique utilizes correlation between a sub image and a template of a given angle. A corner point is selected by finding the maximum of the correlation output. Gradient based techniques require computing curvature of an edge that passes through a neighborhood in a gray level image.

Corner detection schemes can be broadly divided into two categories based on their applications: gray level (suitable for gray level images); and binary (suitable for binary images). For gray level schemes, for brevity, the reader is referred to (Moravec, 1980; Harris & Stephens 1988; Kitchen & Rosenfeld, 1982; Noble, 1988; 1989; Lindeberg & Li, 1997; Smith & Brady, 1995; Sánchez et al., 2018; Shi & Tomasi, 1994; Förstner & Gülch, 1987; Kitchen & Rosenfeld, 1982; Koenderink & Richards, 1988; Mikolajczyk & Schmid, 2004; Bretzne & Lindeberg, 1998; Lindeberg, 1994, 1998, 2013, 2015; Lowe, 2004; Lindeberg, 1993, 1994, 1998, 2008; Mikolajczyk & Schmid, 2004; Wikipedia, 2020; Lindeberg and Garding 1997). For binary schemes, for brevity, the reader is referred to (Beus & Tiu, 1987; Chetverikov & Szabo, 1999; Freeman & Davis, 1977; Harris & Stephens 1988; Liu & Srinath, 1990; Pritchard et el., 1993; Rosenfeld & Weszka, 1975; Sarfraz et el., 2006, Sarfraz, 2014). Figure 1 provides an overview of various algorithms suitable for gray level images as well as binary images. This figure also reflects various applications related to corner detection algorithms in different times. This chapter is the extension of the article (Sarfraz, 2014) and mainly deals with techniques adopted for binary approach to detect corners.

OVERVIEW OF THE STUDY

Visually, corners are the endpoints of straight line segments of polygonal shapes. But, it is difficult and complicated to determine corners in case of non-parametric curves as well as outlines of natural objects especially when the noise is carried. In general, corners represent significant features of an object which human beings would perceive as the meaningful points. Detection of these points is not an easy job since accuracy of detected corners is gauged purely by human judgment and no standard definition/criteria exists. In order to compute the corners, it is important to give them some mathematical representation. In the literature, different authors have described them in different ways. Abe et el (Abe et el., 1993) described corners as local maxima points. They proposed a method for decomposing curves into straight segments and curved arcs, based on the slope at each point. Guru et. al., (Guru et. al., 2004) smoothed the boundary curve and found difference at each curve point called as "cornerity index". The larger values of cornerity index were taken as corners.

Rosenfeld and Johnston (Rosenfeld & Johnston, 1973) took curvature maxima points using k-cosine as corners. Rosenfeld and Weszka (Rosenfeld & Weszka, 1975) proposed a modification of (Rosenfeld & Johnston, 1973) in which averaged k-cosines were used. Freeman and Davis (Freeman & Davis 1977) found corners at maximum curvature change in which a straight line segment moves along the curve. Angular difference between successive segments was used to measure local curvature. Beus and Tiu

(Beus & Tiu, 1987) algorithm was similar to (Freeman & Davis 1977) except they proposed arm cutoff parameter τ to limit length of straight line. Davies (Devies, 1988) has described a method for detecting corners using Hough transform. Chetverikov and Szabo (Chetverikov & Szabo, 1999) located corners at significant change in curve slope. In their algorithm, corners are the locations where a triangle of specified size and opening angle can be inscribed in a curve. Pritchard et. al., (Pritchard et. al., 1993) used similar triangles, as in (Chetverikov & Szabo, 1999), to identify the corners in which they compared area of triangle with actual area under the curve.

Figure 1. A survey for Corner detection and applications.

Wikipedia, 2020 — Detecting corner points from images	Sánchez et al., 2018 — Detecting corner points from grayscale images	Lindeberg, 2015 — Scale-space interest point detection	Sarfraz, 2014 — Detection of corner points	Lindeberg, 2013 — Scale-space interest point detection	Willis & Sui, 2009 — Corner detection
Lindeberg, 2008 — Blob detection	Sarfraz et el., 2006 — Detection of corner points	Vincent & Laganiere, 2005 — Image matching	Sarfraz et el., 2004b — Image outline capture	Sarfraz et el., 2004a — Image outline capture	Mikolajzcyk and Schmid, 2004 — Detection of interest points
Guru at el., 2004 — Shape representation & image interpretation	Lowe, 2004 — Blob detection	Vincent & Laganire, 2001 — Stereo vision	Chetverikov & Szabo, 1999 — Detection of corner points	Smith et el., 1998 — Image matching	Lindeberg, 1998 — Blob detection
Bretzne & Lindeberg, 1998 — Detecting corner points from grayscale images	Smith & Brady, 1995 — Detecting corner points from grayscale images	Shi & Tomasi, 1994 — Detecting corner points from grayscale images	Lindeberg, 1994 — Blob detection	Lindeberg 1993 — Detection of interest points	Abe et el., 1993 — Decomposing or describing the curve
Zoghlami et el., 1997 — Building 2D mosaics	Pritchard et. al., 1993 — Detection of corner points	Liu & Srinath, 1990 — Detection of corner points	Kasturi et el., 1990 — Document image analysis	Deriche & Giraudon, 1990 — Use in scale space theory	Deriche & Faugeras, 1990 — Stereo vision
Lindeberg & Li, 1997 — Geon-based object recognition	Rattarangsi & Chin, 1992 — Scale-Based Detection of Corners	Cabrelli & Molter, 1990 — Image representation	Koenderink & Richards, 1988 — Detecting corner points from grayscale images	Harris & Stephens, 1988 — Detecting corner points from grayscale images	Förstner & Gülch, 1987 — Detecting corner points from grayscale images
Lindeberg & Garding, 1997 — Detection of interest points	Mokhtarian & Mackworth, 1992 — Use in scale space theory	Noble, 1989 — Detecting corner points from grayscale images	Asada and Brady, 1986 — Shape perception	Dreschler & Nagel, 1982 — Motion tracking	Moravec, 1980 — Detecting corner points from grayscale images
Wang & Brady, 1995 — Motion tracking	Teh & Chin, 1990 — Detection of dominant points on digital curves	Noble, 1988 — Detecting corner points from grayscale images	Kitchen & Rosenfeld, 1982 — Detecting corner points from grayscale images	Freeman & Davis, 1977 — Detection of corner points / Rosenfeld & Weszka, 1975 — Detection of corner points	Attneave, 1954 — Understa... human perception of objects

Another approach for detection of corner points in planar curves was presented in (Sarfraz et el., 2006). In this approach, detection of corner point is based on calculation of distances from the straight line joining two contour points on two sides of that corner. The developed algorithm performs quite satisfactorily on noisy shapes, it is also simple and efficient. Later, Sarfraz and Swati (Sarfraz & Swati, 2013) introduced an idea of a corner detection algorithm which uses combination of one rectangle and two ellipses. In this algorithm, a smaller ellipse is embedded in a bigger ellipse and the two ellipses are embedded in a rectangle. This combination of geometries slides along the boundary of the targeted shape. It keeps an eye over number of boundary points in the set of geometries of Rectangle and ellipses. It, ultimately, locates the best candidate point as the corner point. This algorithm is very close to natural way of looking for corners and quite resembles to the human vision system.

This chapter is devoted to seven algorithms in the literature which evolved with a variation of different times. These are based on the studies in (Rosenfeld & Johnston, 1973; Rosenfeld & Weszka, 1975; Freeman & Davis, 1977; Beus & Tiu, 1987; Chetverikov & Szabo, 1999; Sarfraz et el., 2006; Sarfraz & Swati, 2013). Since, these algorithms will be described and mentioned again and again in the rest of the chapter, let us provide acronyms to each of them for the sake of convenience as shown in Table 1. This table also specifies the Titles of the papers together with their author names and date of publications.

Table 1. Seven algorithms with their acronyms.

#	Reference	Paper Title	Acronym
1.	Rosenfeld & Johnston, 1973	Angle Detection on Digital Curves	RJ
2.	Rosenfeld & Weszka, 1975	An Improved Method of Angle Detection on Digital Curves	RW
3.	Freeman & Davis, 1977	A Corner Finding Algorithm for Chain Coded Curves	FD
4.	Beus & Tiu, 1987	An Improved Corner Detection Algorithm based on Chain Coded Plane Curves	BT
5.	Chetverikov & Szabo, 1999	A Simple and Efficient Algorithm for Detection of High Curvature Points in Planner Curves	CS
6.	Sarfraz et el., 2006	A new approach to corner detection	SMA
7.	Sarfraz & Swati, 2013	Mining Corner Points on the Generic Shapes	REE

In general, accuracy of any corner detection algorithm changes with noise, size and resolution of input shape and nature of corner (sharpness). It may perform well for a particular shape and display poor results for others. This does not happen in case of human judgment because they are gifted with adaptive nature and automatically adapt themselves to the changing environment. Study of this human behavior may lead to the developments of adaptive algorithms. Various parameters are generally introduced to compensate for such variations. But, it would be preferable if one can go for an algorithm that covers wide range of shape variations without changing its parameters.

This chapter is devoted to seven algorithms in the literature which evolved with a variation of different times. These are based on the studies in). Since, these algorithms will be described and mentioned again and again in the rest of the chapter, let us provide acronyms to each of them for the sake of convenience as shown in Table 1. This table also specifies the Titles of the papers together with their author names and date of publications.

Accuracy of any corner detector can be judged only if the actual corner positions are already known. A set of outlines of eight test shapes, see Figure 2, has been chosen. Let us call them as im1, im2, ..., im8 throughout this Chapter. These are available in various references including (Rosenfeld & Johnston, 1973; Rosenfeld & Weszka, 1975; Freeman & Davis, 1977; Beus & Tiu, 1987; Chetverikov & Szabo, 1999; Sarfraz et el., 2006; Sarfraz & Swati, 2013; Sarfraz, 2014). Seven corner detection algorithms, as mentioned in Table 1, have been implemented and tested on the shapes im1, im2, ..., im8. These algorithms are explained and tested, in the coming sections, for the corners depicted according to human visual system as shown in Figure 3. A detailed analysis, together with tabular data and graphical displays, also makes an essential part of this study.

Figure 2. Shapes used in the tests.

Figure 3. Test shapes marked with actual corner points

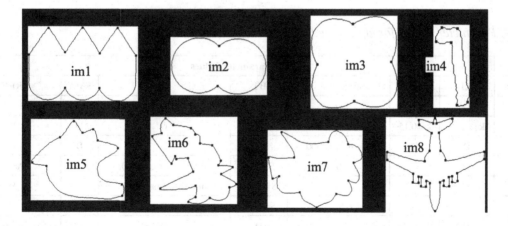

Seven Commonly Referred Corner Detectors

This section is devoted for the summary and implementation of seven corner detection algorithms namely RJ, RW, FD, BT, CS, SMA and REE. This is based on the survey (Sarfraz, 2014) extended by an additional algorithm in (Sarfraz et el., 2006). Each algorithm inputs contour of an image in the form of a digital curve that is converted into a sequence of points $P_i = (x_i, y_i)$, $i = 1, 2, ..., N$. When processing a point P_i as a potential corner in P_i, the algorithms mostly consider two sets of points: a subsequent set of points; and a set of previous points. These sets act like arms to provide an amount of strength for a point P_i to be a corner point. Let us define, for a positive integer k, the forward and the backward *k-vectors* at point P_i as follows:

$$a_{ik} = \left(x_i - x_{i+k}, \ y_i - y_{i+k} \right) = \left(X_{ik}^+, Y_{ik}^+ \right), \tag{1}$$

$$b_{ik} = \left(x_i - x_{i-k}, \ y_i - y_{i-k} \right) = \left(X_{ik}^-, Y_{ik}^- \right), \tag{2}$$

where X_{ik}^+, Y_{ik}^+ and X_{ik}^-, Y_{ik}^- are the components of a_{ik} and b_{ik}, respectively.

Each of the algorithms RJ, RW, FD, BT, CS, SMA and REE will be briefly discussed as far as their construction is concerned. For further details of the algorithms, the reader is referred to the sources in (Rosenfeld & Johnston, 1973; Rosenfeld & Weszka, 1975; Freeman & Davis, 1977; Beus & Tiu, 1987; Chetverikov & Szabo, 1999; Sarfraz et el., 2006; Sarfraz & Swati, 2013). There are specific parameters in each algorithm to determine the strength of corner depending on the geometry adopted. Table 2 demonstrates a variety of those parameters for each implementation. Default values of these parameters are denoted by 'D' whereas the deviations from the D's are presented specifically otherwise. Demonstration of the implementations of the algorithms, for the shapes im1, im2, ..., im8, is avoided due to unnecessary length. However, individual results of each implementation are made in the data tables of Figure 5 and Figure 6. The proposed algorithms yield, reasonable to promising, results at the shown values for all the 8 shapes.

Table 2. Parameter values for eight tested shapes and seven algorithms.

Images	Parameter Values						
	RJ	**RW**	**FD**	**BT**	**CS**	**SMA**	**REE**
im1	D	D	D	D	D	D	B=1.7
im2	k = 0.15	k =0.15	k = 7, S =2500	D	D	D	D
im3	D	D	S = 6, K= 2500	D	D	D	D
im4	D	D	k= 5, S= 500	S =500	dmin=8, αmax=140	d=3	A=18
im5	k =.06	k=.07	D	S =1000	dmin=8, αmax=140	D	D
im6	D	D	k= 7, S =1000	S=1300	D	R=13	D
im7	D	D	D	D	D	D	A=16, B=2.42
im8	D	D	D	S =1000	D	R=7	A=10

Algorithm 1: Rosenfeld and Johnston 73 (RJ)

The algorithm in (Rosenfeld & Johnston, 73) uses the idea of k-cosine of the angle between the k-vectors to determine the corner strength. Equation (3) defines it mathematically as follows:

$$c_{ik} = \frac{(a_{ik} \cdot b_{ik})}{|a_{ik}||b_{ik}|}.$$

(3)

Equations (1) and (2) simply define the terms a_{ik} and b_{ik} respectively. The corner points are selected by a procedure as follows. Starting from $m = kN$, k is decremented until c_{ik} stops to increase as follows:

$$c_{im} < c_{i,m-1} < ... < c_{in} \not< ci, n-1.$$

Then, the best value for the ith point is selected by $k = n$. A corner is indicated in i if $c_{in} > c_{jp}$ for all j such that $|i - j| \leq n/2$, where p is the best value of k for the jth point. The single parameter κ specifies the maximum considered value of k as a fraction of the total number of curve points N. This limits the length of an arm at κN. The default value is taken as $\kappa = 0.05$.

Algorithm 2: Rosenfeld and Weszka 75 (RW)

The algorithm in (Rosenfeld & Weszka, 75) uses averaged k-cosine of the angle between the k-vectors to determine the corner strength. It is defined as follows:

$$\bar{c}_{ik} = \begin{cases} \dfrac{2}{k+2} \displaystyle\sum_{t=k/2}^{k} c_{it}, & \text{if } k \text{ is even,} \\ \dfrac{2}{k+3} \displaystyle\sum_{t=(k-1)/2}^{k} c_{it}, & \text{if } k \text{ is odd,} \end{cases}$$

Here c_{it} are same as in Equation (3). The criteria for the selection corner points, in this algorithm, is same as that in RJ. However, it is performed for $\bar{c}_{ik}$. In the same manner, the choice of parameter is also similar to that of RJ. The default value is also assumed $\kappa = 0.05$ as that in RJ.

Algorithm 3: Freeman and Davis 77 (FD)

Freeman and Davis (Freeman & Davis, 77) have determined the corner strength at the ith point. They have proposed the angle between the x-axis and the backward k-vector, defined in Equation (2), as follows:

$$\theta_{ik} = \theta_{ik} = \begin{cases} \tan^{-1}\left(Y_{ik}^{-} / X_{ik}^{-}\right), & \text{if } |X_{ik}^{-}| \geq |Y_{ik}^{-}|, \\ \cot^{-1}\left(X_{ik}^{-} / Y_{ik}^{-}\right), & \text{otherwise.} \end{cases}$$

The incremental curvature is then defined as

$$\delta_{ik} = \theta_{i+1,k} - \theta_{i-1,k}.$$ (4)

Finally, the k-strength in i is computed as

$$S_{ik} = \ln t_1 . \ln t_2 \sum_{j=i}^{i+k} \delta_{jk},$$ (5)

where

$$t_1 = \max\left\{ t : \delta_{i-v,k} \in (-\Delta, \Delta), \forall\, 1 \leq \upsilon \leq t \right\},$$

and

$$t_2 = \max\left\{ t : \delta_{i+k+v,k} \in (-\Delta, \Delta), \forall\, 1 \leq \upsilon \leq t \right\},$$

account for the effect of the forward and backward arms as the maximum spacings (numbers of steps from i) that still keep the incremental curvature δ_{ik}, within the limit $\pm \Delta$. The Δ is set as follows:

$$\Delta = \arctan(1 / (k-1)).$$ (6)

The selection procedure for the corner points is as follows. The ith point is selected as a corner if S_{ik} exceeds a given threshold S and individual corners are separated by a spacing of at least $k + 1$ steps. There is an involvement of two parameters for the procedure. These parameters are the spacing k and the corner strength threshold S. The default values for the parameters are set as $k = 5$ and $S = 1500$.

Algorithm 4: Beus and Tiu 87 (BT)

Beus and Tiu (Beus & Tiu, 87) proposes to determine the corner strength in a similar way as in FD. However, they have suggested some modifications in their algorithm. They have introduced an arm cutoff parameter τ which specifies the upper limit for t_1 and t_2 as a fraction of N. This explains as follows:

$$t_1 = \max\left\{ t : \delta_{i-v,k} \in (-\Delta, \Delta), \forall\, 1 \leq \upsilon \leq t, \text{ and } t \leq \tau N \right\},$$

and

$$t_2 = \max\left\{ t : \delta_{i+k+v,k} \in (-\Delta, \Delta), \forall\, 1 \leq \upsilon \leq t, \text{ and } t \leq \tau N \right\},$$

where δ_{ik} and Δ are given by Equations (4) and (6), respectively. The corner strength is obtained by averaging Equation (5) between two values k_1 and k_2 as follows:

$$S_i = (\sum_{k=k_1}^{k_2} S_{ik}) / (k_2 - k_1 + 1).$$

The selection procedure is not different than that in FD77. The procedure involves two parameters which are the averaging limits k_1 and k_2. It also involves the arm cutoff parameter τ and the corner strength threshold S. The values of $k_1 = 4$, $k_2 = 7$, $\tau = 0.05$, and $S = 1500$ are set as default values for these parameters.

Algorithm 5: Chetverikov and Szabo 99 (CS)

The algorithm of Chetverikov and Szabo (Chetverikov & Szabo, 1999) is a two pass algorithm. They have defined a corner point as that point for which the triangle of specified angle can be inscribed within a specified distance from its neighbor points. They also predefine the number of neighbor points to be checked.

This algorithm, in the first pass, scans the sequence of points and selects those points which act as candidate corner points. In each curve point P, the detector tries to inscribe in the curve a variable triangle (P^-, P, P^+) constrained by a set of simple rules. For each point P_i, it is checked if triangle of specified size and angle is inscribed or not.

The second pass is post-processing to remove superfluous candidates. A candidate corner point P from the first pass is discarded if it has a sharper valid neighbor. The values d_{min}, d_{max} and a_{max} are the parameters of the algorithm. Small values of d_{min} respond to fine corners. The upper limit d_{max} is necessary to avoid false sharp triangles formed by distant points in highly varying curves. The a_{max} is the angle limit that determines the minimum sharpness accepted as high curvature.

Algorithm 6: (Sarfraz, Masood & Asim, 2006) SMA

The algorithm SMA in (Sarfraz et el., 2006) is divided into two passes. The first pass is to detect candidate corner points. For $1 \le i \le n$, where n is the number of contour points in a closed loop, the contour point P_k is given as:

if $(i + L) \le n$ then $P_k = P_{i+L}$ else $P_k = P_{(i+L)-n}$.

Sometimes, corners are not the sharp angle points and hence allowing superfluous candidate corner to be detected. Second pass is devoted to discard such points. The candidate corner is superfluous if any other candidate is in the range R. For any candidate corner point to stay, it must be the strongest corner among the R number of points on its both sides.

This algorithm possesses three parameters namely L, d & R. The parameter L stands for the length parameter, it takes into consideration the object scaling as well as resolution. The most suitable default value for L is 14. Straight line $P_i P_k$ will always join the two contour points, L points apart. The local sharpness and opening angle corners are checked by the distance parameter d. It also helps to control the false selection of corners due to noise and other irregularities. Any point is considered as a candidate corner point if its distance from the straight line P_iP_k goes beyond d. The selection of $d = 2.6$ is set as the default value. Sometimes local sharpness of a corner is not high enough but a global view of shape identifies it as a valid corner. Such corners are also detected successfully with this method at the cost of some additional (superfluous) corners. These corners are removed/discarded using range parameter R. Default value of R is same as L. However, it is preferable to give it a lower value to enable detection of closely located corners.

Algorithm 7: (Sarfraz & Swati, 2013) REE

In the algorithm by Sarfraz and Swati (Sarfraz & Swati, 2013), corner detection is based on rectangle R and two ellipses E_1 and E_2 sliding along the given curve. The geometry of R, E_1 and E_2 is constructed in such a way that R contains E_1 and E_1 contains E_2. Mathematically, it is expressed as $R \supset E_1 \supset E_2$. Pictorially, this geometry is demonstrated in Figure 4. It can be seen that the rectangle and ellipses have common center at p_i. It helps to collect information about the locality of neighboring curve points.

Figure 4. Geometrical structure of REE Algorithm.

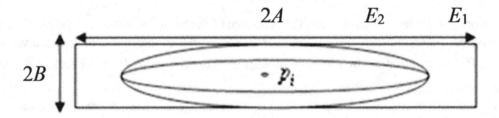

The geometric structure of Figure 4 has been adopted in such a way that the length and width of the rectangle R are considered to be $2A$ and $2B$ respectively. The semi minor axis and semi major axis of the ellipse E_1 are considered to be the lengths $3A/4$ and B respectively. The semi minor axis and semi major axis of the ellipse E_2 are considered to be the lengths $3A/4$ and $B/2$ respectively. The combination of R and two ellipses E_1 and E_2 slides along the boundary of the targeted shape contour. It remembers the number of boundary points in the set of geometries of Rectangle and the two ellipses. It, ultimately, locates the best candidate point as the corner point. This algorithm is very close to natural way of looking for corners and quite resembles to the human vision system.

In this algorithm, default value of A is 14. The values of $A/8$ and $3A/4$ are assigned to B and η respectively. All other parameters are relative to A. Value of parameter A depends upon the size of boundary, noise, and resolution of image. Assigned values to semi major axis, semi minor axis, length, and width of ellipses and rectangle are suitable to a certain range of size and resolution, which covers all demonstrated shapes in this Chapter. These sizes were found after extensive testing on many images of similar size and resolution. The relationship between relative size of ellipses and rectangle is set (again with extensive testing) for convenience of using these parameters. The user needs to tune only one parameter i.e. A instead of three. However, accuracy can improve by assigning independent sizes, but this would be at the cost of complex tuning of parameters.

Figure 5. Display of numerical data of correctly detected corner points.

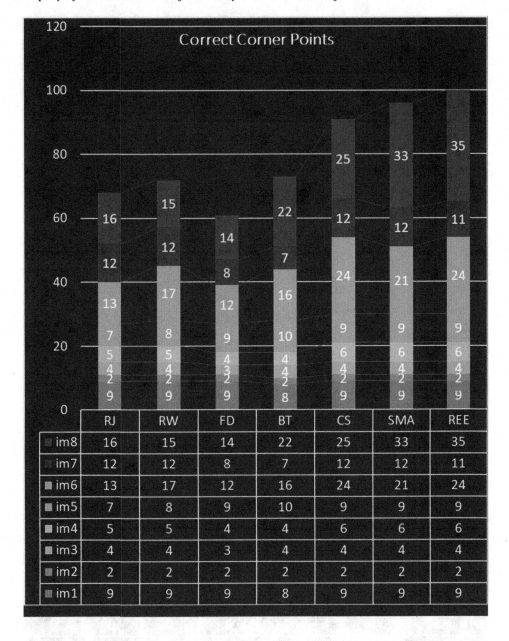

	RJ	RW	FD	BT	CS	SMA	REE
■ im8	16	15	14	22	25	33	35
■ im7	12	12	8	7	12	12	11
■ im6	13	17	12	16	24	21	24
■ im5	7	8	9	10	9	9	9
■ im4	5	5	4	4	6	6	6
■ im3	4	4	3	4	4	4	4
■ im2	2	2	2	2	2	2	2
■ im1	9	9	9	8	9	9	9

IMPLEMENTATION & DISCUSSIONS

Data tables in Figure 5 and Figure 6 together with Table 3 demonstrate numerical presentation for corner points in all the eight images using all the seven algorithms. Data tables in Figure 5 and Figure 6, respectively, describe the number of correct and incorrect corner points for all the eight images using all the seven algorithms. These figures provide overviews for correctly and incorrectly detected corners by a single algorithm for all the images as well as correctly and incorrectly detected corners by a single image for all the algorithms. Table 3 sums up all the corner points (correct and incorrect) for each image

Figure 6. Display of numerical data of correctly detected corner points.

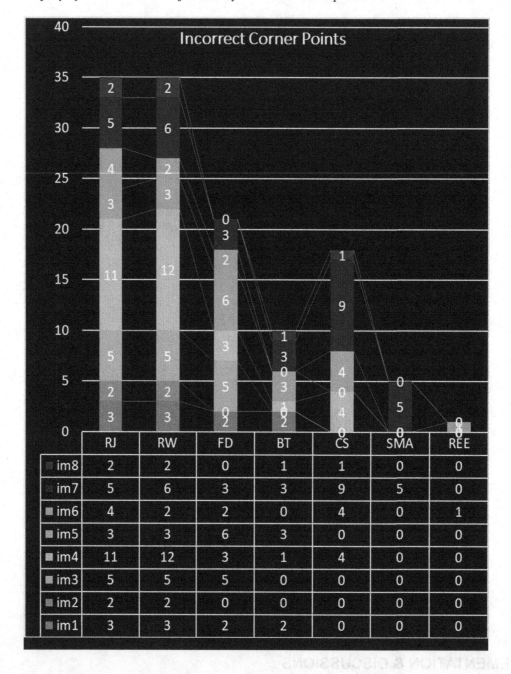

	RJ	RW	FD	BT	CS	SMA	REE
■ im8	2	2	0	1	1	0	0
■ im7	5	6	3	3	9	5	0
■ im6	4	2	2	0	4	0	1
■ im5	3	3	6	3	0	0	0
■ im4	11	12	3	1	4	0	0
■ im3	5	5	5	0	0	0	0
■ im2	2	2	0	0	0	0	0
■ im1	3	3	2	2	0	0	0

corresponding to each of the algorithms RJ, RW, FD, BT, CS, SMA and REE. It provides an overall view for the total number of correct and incorrect detected corners by a single algorithm for all the images. Table 4 presents percentage of correct and incorrect corners. Figure 7 and Figure 8, respectively, represent the results of correct and incorrect corner points to have visual analytical look. Following observations can be very clearly made from these figures and tables:

- For RJ and RW, somewhat better results can be obtained when the parameters are slightly modified.
- For stable performance, FD and BT need more frequent modifications of their parameters.
- In case of BT, only S needed to be varied.
- CS mainly depends on default values of parameters. However, values of dmin and dmax can be varied to produce better results in some cases.
- SMA depends mostly on default values of parameters. However, values of d and R can be very slightly varied to produce better results in some cases.
- REE depends mostly on default values of parameters. However, values of A and B can be very slightly varied to produce better results in some cases.
- CS outperforms RJ, RW, FD and BT.
- SMA outperforms RJ, RW, FD, BT and CS.
- REE outperforms RJ, RW, FD, BT, CS and SMA.
- REE detects highest number (99.01%) of correct corner points.
- REE detects lowest number (0.99%) of incorrect corner points.
- RJ detects lowest number (66.02%) of correct corner points.
- RJ detects highest number (33.98%) of incorrect corner points.

Hence, it can be concluded that REE is the best algorithm for correct corner detection whereas RJ is the worst. Table 4 reflects SMA as the second best algorithm for corner detection. It detects second highest number (95.05%) of correct corner points and second lowest number (4.95%) of incorrect corner points. Table 4 also indicates that CS is the third best corner detector after SMA as it detects third highest number (83.49%) of correct corner points and second lowest number (16.51%) of incorrect corner points.

Table 3. Total number of correct and incorrect detected corners by each algorithm.

	RJ	RW	FD	BT	CS	SMA	REE
Correct	68	72	61	73	91	96	100
Incorrect	35	35	21	10	18	5	1
Total	103	107	82	83	109	101	101

CONCLUDING REMARKS

Corners are not simply the local maxima, high curvature or dominant points. Points of abrupt change from where the shape can be segmented and which human beings perceive as meaningful points are the true corners. Seven corner detection approaches namely RJ, RW, FD, BT, CS, SMA and REE have been discussed, experimented, and analyzed. REE algorithm has been found most accurate and efficient. A comparative study, based on proposed parameters, shows that REE algorithm has various advantages over previous techniques. Some of the advantages are that it is: (1) most consistent with human judgment of corners; (2) ratio of false detection is extremely low; (3) computationally efficient; (4) invariant to transformation changes; (5) highly insensitive to noise/irregularities along the curve; (6) robust to minor changes in size and resolution; and (7) very suitable for natural shapes/objects. Independent tuning of the parameters can further fine tune the results if needed in some extreme case.

Figure 7. Correct and incorrect detected corners by each algorithm.

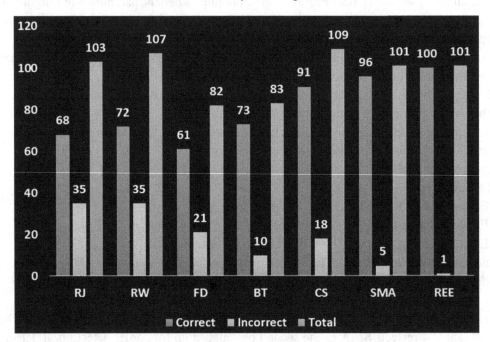

Table 4. Percentage of correct and incorrect detected corners by each algorithm.

	RJ	RW	FD	BT	CS	SMA	REE
Correct %	66.02	67.29	74.39	87.95	83.49	95.05	99.01
Incorrect %	33.98	32.71	25.61	12.05	16.51	4.95	0.99

Figure 8. Percentage of correct and incorrect detected corners by each algorithm.

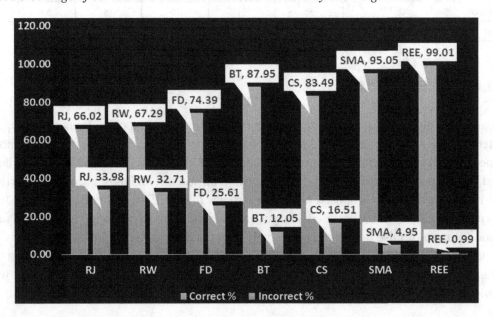

REFERENCES

Abe, K., Morii, R., Nishida, K., & Kadonaga, T. (1993). Comparison of Methods for Detecting Corner Points From Digital Curves—A Preliminary Report. In *Proceedings of International Conference on Document Analysis and Recognition*. Tsukuba Science City, Japan: IEEE. 10.1109/ICDAR.1993.395603

Asada, H., & Brady, M. (1986). The curvature primal sketch. *IEEE Transactions on Pattern Analysis and Machine Intelligence*, *8*(1), 2–4. doi:10.1109/TPAMI.1986.4767747 PMID:21869318

Attneave, F. (1954). Some Informational Aspects of Visual Perception. *Psychological Review*, *61*(3), 183–193. doi:10.1037/h0054663 PMID:13167245

Beus, H. L., & Tiu, S. S. H. (1987). An Improved Corner Detection Algorithm based on Chain Coded Plane Curves. *Pattern Recognition*, *20*(3), 291–296. doi:10.1016/0031-3203(87)90004-5

Bretzner, L., & Lindeberg, T. (1998). Feature tracking with automatic selection of spatial scales. *Computer Vision and Image Understanding*, *71*(3), 385–392. doi:10.1006/cviu.1998.0650

Cabrelli, C. A., & Molter, U. M. (1990). Automatic representation of binary images. *IEEE Transactions on Pattern Analysis and Machine Intelligence*, *12*(12), 1190–1196. doi:10.1109/34.62608

Chetverikov, D., & Szabo, Z. (1999). A Simple and Efficient Algorithm for Detection of High Curvature Points in Planner Curves. In *Proceedings of 23rd Workshop of Australian Pattern Recognition Group*, (pp. 175-184). Academic Press.

Davies, E. R. (1988). Application of generalized Hough transform to corner detection. *IEE Proceedings, 135E*(1), 49-54.

Deriche, R., & Faugeras, O. D. (1990). 2D curve matching using high curvature points: Application to stereo vision. In *Proceedings of 10th International Conference on Pattern Recognition*. Atlantic City, NJ: IEEE.

Deriche, R., & Giraudon, G. (1990). Accurate corner detection: An analytical study. In *Proceedings of 3rd International Conference on Computer Vision*. Osaka, Japan: IEEE.

Dreschler, L., & Nagel, H. H. (1982). On the selection of critical points and local curvature extrema of region boundaries for interframe matching. In *Proceedings of International Conference on Pattern Recognition*. Munich, Germany: Springer.

Förstner, M. A., & Gülch, E. (1987). A Fast Operator for Detection and Precise Location of Distinct Points, Corners and Centers of Circular Features. *Proceedings of the ISPRS Intercommission Conference on Fast Processing of Phonogrammic Data*, 281-305.

Freeman, H., & Davis, L. S. (1977). A Corner Finding Algorithm for ChainCoded Curves. *IEEE Transactions on Computers*, *26*(3), 297–303. doi:10.1109/TC.1977.1674825

Guru, D. S., Dinesh, R., & Nagabhushan, P. (2004). Boundary based corner detection and localization using new 'cornerity' index: a robust approach. In *Proc. 1st Canadian Conference on Computer and Robot Vision*. London, Canada: IEEE. 10.1109/CCCRV.2004.1301477

Harris, C., & Stephens, M. (1988). A combined corner and edge detector. In *Proceedings of the Fourth Alvey Vision Conference*. Manchester, UK: Alvety Vision Club.

Kadonaga, T., & Abe, K. (1996). Comparison of Methods for Detecting Corner Points from Digital Curves, Graphics Recognition Methods and Applications. *Lecture Notes in Computer Science*, *1072*, 23–34. doi:10.1007/3-540-61226-2_3

Kasturi, R., Siva, S., & O'Gorman, L. (1990). Techniques for line drawing interpretation: an overview. In *Proc. IAPR Workshop on Machine Vision Applications*. IAPR.

Kitchen, L., & Rosenfeld, A. (1982). Gray-level corner detection. *Pattern Recognition Letters*, *1*(2), 95–102. doi:10.1016/0167-8655(82)90020-4

Koenderink, J. J., & Richards, W. (1988). Two-dimensional curvature operators. *Journal of the Optical Society of America. A, Optics and Image Science*, *5*(7), 1136–1141. doi:10.1364/JOSAA.5.001136

Lindeberg, T. (1994). *Scale-Space Theory in Computer Vision*. Springer. doi:10.1007/978-1-4757-6465-9

Lindeberg, T. (1998). Feature detection with automatic scale selection. *International Journal of Computer Vision*, *30*(2), 77–116.

Lindeberg, T. (2008). Scale-Space. In B. Wah (Ed.), *Wiley Encyclopedia of Computer Science and Engineering. IV* (pp. 2495–2504). John Wiley and Sons., doi:10.1002/9780470050118.ecse609

Lindeberg, T. (2013). Scale selection properties of generalized scale-space interest point detectors. *Journal of Mathematical Imaging and Vision, Volume*, *46*(2), 177–210. doi:10.100710851-012-0378-3

Lindeberg, T. (2015). Image matching using generalized scale-space interest points. *Journal of Mathematical Imaging and Vision*, *52*(1), 3–36. doi:10.100710851-014-0541-0

Lindeberg, T., & Garding, J. (1997). Shape-adapted smoothing in estimation of 3-D depth cues from affine distortions of local 2-D structure. *Image and Vision Computing*, *15*(6), 415–434. doi:10.1016/S0262-8856(97)01144-X

Lindeberg, T., & Li, M.-X. (1997). Segmentation and classification of edges using minimum description length approximation and complementary junction cues. *Computer Vision and Image Understanding*, *67*(1), 88–98. doi:10.1006/cviu.1996.0510

Liu, H. C., & Srinath, L. S. (1990). Corner Detection from Chain-Code. *Pattern Recognition*, *23*(1-2), 51–68. doi:10.1016/0031-3203(90)90048-P

Lowe, D. (2004). Distinctive Image Features from Scale-Invariant Keypoints. *International Journal of Computer Vision*, *60*(2), 91. doi:. doi:10.1023/B:VISI.0000029664.99615.94

Mikolajczyk, K., & Schmid, C. (2004). Scale and affine invariant interest point detectors. *International Journal of Computer Vision*, *60*(1), 63–86. doi:10.1023/B:VISI.0000027790.02288.f2

Mokhtarian, F., & Mackworth, A. K. (1992). A Theory of Multiscale, Curvature-Based Shape Representation for Planar Curves. *IEEE Transactions on Pattern Analysis and Machine Intelligence*, *14*(8), 789–805. doi:10.1109/34.149591

Moravec, H. (1980). *Obstacle Avoidance and Navigation in the Real World by a Seeing Robot Rover.* Tech Report CMU-RI-TR-3 Carnegie-Mellon University, Robotics Institute.

Noble, J. A. (1988). Finding corners. *Image and Vision Computing, 6*(2), 121–128. doi:10.1016/0262-8856(88)90007-8

Noble, J. A. (1989). *Descriptions of Image Surfaces (Ph.D.).* Department of Engineering Science, Oxford University.

Pritchard, A. J., Sangwine, S. J., & Horne, R. E. N. (1993). Corner and curve detection along a boundary using line segment triangles. *Electronics Division Colloquium on Hough Transforms, 106,* 1–4.

Rattarangsi, A., & Chin, R. T. (1992). Scale-Based Detection of Corners of Planar Curves. *IEEE Transactions on Pattern Analysis and Machine Intelligence, 14*(4), 430–449. doi:10.1109/34.126805

Ray, B. K., & Pandyan, R. (2003). ACORD – an adaptive corner detector for planar curves. *Pattern Recognition, 36*(3), 703–708. doi:10.1016/S0031-3203(02)00084-5

Rosenfeld, A., & Johnston, E. (1973). Angle Detection on Digital Curves. *IEEE Transactions on Computers, 22*(9), 875–878. doi:10.1109/TC.1973.5009188

Rosenfeld & Weszka. (n.d.). An Improved Method of Angle Detection on Digital Curves. *IEEE Transactions on Computers, 24,* 940-941.

Rutkowski, W. S., & Rosenfeld, A. (1978). *A comparison of corner-detection techniques for chain-coded curves (TR-623).* Computer Science Center, University of Maryland.

Sánchez, J., Monzón, N., & Salgado, A. (2018). An Analysis and Implementation of the Harris Corner Detector. *Image Processing on Line, 8,* 305–328. doi:10.5201/ipol.2018.229

Sarfraz, M. (2014). Detecting Corner Features of Planar Objects. In M. Sarfraz (Ed.), *Computer Vision and Image Processing in Intelligent Systems and Multimedia Technologies* (pp. 262–279). IGI Global. doi:10.4018/978-1-4666-6030-4.ch015

Sarfraz, M., Asim, M. R., & Masood, A. (2004a). Capturing Outlines using Cubic Bezier Curves. In *Proc. of IEEE 1st International Conference on Information & Communication Technologies: from Theory to Applications.* IEEE.

Sarfraz, M., Asim, M. R., & Masood, A. (2004b). A Web Based System for Capturing Outlines of 2D Objects. In *Proceedings of The International Conference on Information and Computer Science,* (pp. 575 – 586). King Fahd University of Petroleum and Minerals.

Sarfraz, M., Masood, A., & Asim, M. R. (2006). A new approach to corner detection. In K. Wojciechowski, B. Smolka, H. Palus, R. S. Kozera, W. Skarbek, & L. Noakes (Eds.), *Computer vision and graphics* (pp. 528–533). Springer. doi:10.1007/1-4020-4179-9_75

Sarfraz, M., & Swati, Z. N. K. (2013). Mining Corner Points on the Generic Shapes. *Ozean Journal of Applied Sciences, 3*(01, 1B), 10–15. doi:10.4236/ojapps.2013.31B003

Shapiro, L. G., & Stockman, G. C. (2001). *Computer Vision.* Prentice Books.

Shi, J., & Tomasi, C. (June 1994). Good Features to Track. *9th IEEE Conference on Computer Vision and Pattern Recognition. Springer.* 593–600. doi:10.1109/CVPR.1994.323794

Smith, P., Sinclair, D., Cipolla, R., & Wood, K. (1998). Effective Corner Matching. In *Proceedings of the 9th British Machine Vision Conference*, (vol. 2, pp. 545-556). BMVA Press.

Smith, S., & Brady, J. (1995). SUSAN— A new approach to low level image processing. *International Journal of Computer Vision, 23*(1), 45–78. doi:10.1023/A:1007963824710

Teh, C. H., & Chin, R. (1990). On the detection of dominant points on digital curves. *IEEE Transactions on Pattern Analysis and Machine Intelligence, 11*(8), 859–873. doi:10.1109/34.31447

Tomasi, C. & Kanade, T. (1991). *Detection and Tracking of Point Features* (Technical report). School of Computer Science, Carnegie Mellon University. CMU-CS-91-132.

Vincent, E., & Laganiere, R. (2005). Detecting and matching feature points. *Journal of Visual Communication and Image Representation, 16*(1), 38–54. doi:10.1016/j.jvcir.2004.05.001

Vincent, E., & Laganire, R. (2001). Matching feature points in stereo pairs: A comparative study of some matching strategies. *Machine Graphics and Vision, 10*, 237–259.

Wang, H., & Brady, M. (1995). Real-time corner detection algorithm for motion estimation. *Image and Vision Computing, 13*(9), 695–703. doi:10.1016/0262-8856(95)98864-P

Wikipedia. (2020). *Corner Detection*. https://en.wikipedia.org/wiki/Corner_detection

Willis, A., & Sui, Y. (2009). An Algebraic Model for fast Corner Detection. *2009 IEEE 12th International Conference on Computer Vision*, 2296–2302. doi:10.1109/ICCV.2009.5459443

Zoghlami, I., Faugeras, O., & Deriche, R. (1997). Using geometric corners to build a 2D mosaic from a set of images. In *Proceedings of the Conference on Computer Vision and Pattern Recognition*. IEEE Computer Society. 10.1109/CVPR.1997.609359

Chapter 12
Use of Deep Neural Network for Optical Character Recognition

Abhishek Das

ITER, Siksha O Anusandhan (Deemed), India

Mihir Narayan Mohanty

ITER, Siksha O Anusandhan (Deemed), India

ABSTRACT

In this chapter, the authors have given a detailed review on optical character recognition. Various methods are used in this field with different accuracy levels. Still there are some difficulties in recognizing handwritten characters because of different writing styles of different individuals even in a particular language. A comparative study is given to understand different types of optical character recognition along with different methods used in each type. Implementation of neural network in different forms is found in most of the works. Different image processing techniques like OCR with CNN, RNN, combination of CNN and RNN, etc. are observed in recent research works.

1. INTRODUCTION

Documents with printed text are vastly used in our day to day life. Starting from the morning to night we are coming across different form of text data. The text data may be in printed or hand written form. The printed form of text is not limited to paper related documents but also it includes number plates, shop hoardings, metal stampings, TV scene etc. In this digital world still some documents are there which are manually filled for safety purpose. One example of such document is bank check. In which a person have to write the amount in words as well as in numbers and have to put his/her signature by hand. Similarly different forms are being filled by hand, handwritten reports are being collected for office work. There are many ancient handwritten documents which are to be restored in typed form so that it will be easy to read. In mobile phones handwritten keyboards are available which convert handwritten input to typed output. So development of handwritten character recognition is required for better accuracy.

DOI: 10.4018/978-1-7998-4444-0.ch012

Character recognition is broadly classified as Online and Offline character recognition as shown in fig.1. Online means the user will write the characters on mobile screen or by any other source and the characters will be recognized simultaneously. Offline means the images of the documents containing either printed or handwritten characters will be used for recognition.

Figure 1. Classification of Optical Character Recognition

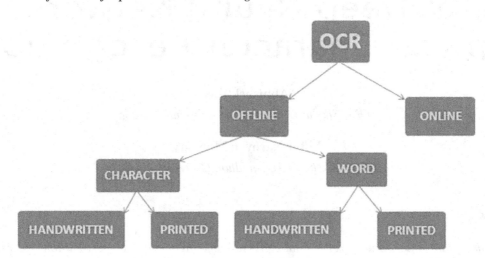

2. LITERATURE SURVEY

Human beings can easily identify the characters in any format but how the computers will understand the characters that is the topic of research. Different researchers have adopted different techniques for feature extraction, classification to improve the accuracy of recognition and also keeping the time constraint in mind. Deep learning is the method which is vastly being used by researchers now a day as the feature extraction part is not to be done by the programmer but the deep neural network will do this job by itself. Some other aspects of character recognition like template matching, ANN etc are also used. A detailed study of different approaches is presented here method wise.

2.1 Using CNN Only

Image classification is a part of optical character recognition if the image consists of different characters in it. Convolutional neural network (CNN) is used for image classification (Xin & Wang, 2019) and it shows better performance. In this work the authors have used MNIST dataset for numeral classification and CIFAR-10 dataset for classification of airplane, automobile, bird, cat, deer, dog, frog, horse, ship, truck. They have analyzed the cross entropy and M^3CE results. To get better result they have combined cross entropy and M^3CE.In the network of CNN the authors have used convolutional layer with pooling activation function and the n they have taken fully connected layers for classification on input images. The system architecture of proposed method is shown in figure 2.

Figure 2. Proposed CNN architecture

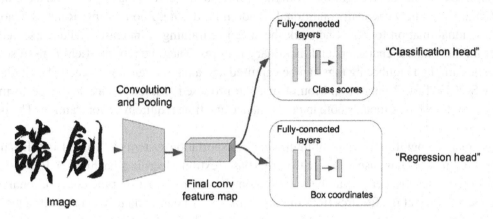

Medicine prescription recognition (Peilun Wu, Wang, & Liu, 2018) is another form of hand written character recognition. In this work Peilun Wu et. al have integrated three different classifiers. The three classifiers are CNN, PCA and KNN. A voting method is used to select the best features extractor from the different filters. Authors have taken 13 prescriptions for the recognition. All the prescriptions consist of English, Chinese alphabets and numbers. They have individually considered the classifiers and compared the results with the multi-classifier network. The accuracy obtained from this multi-classifier method is 99.1% which is found to be better than single classifier systems.

Figure 3. Proposed RD-CNN-CRF model

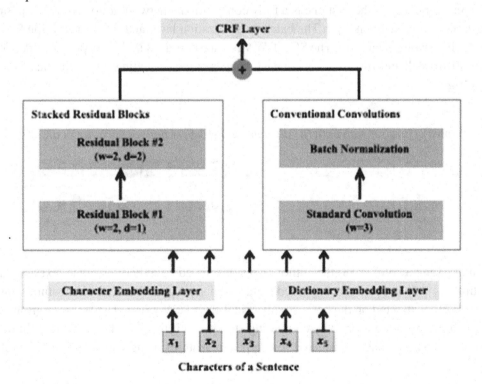

For Chinese clinical data recognition from the report Jiahui Qiu et. al have proposed a method using convolutional neural network with conditional Random field (Qiu, Zhou, Wang, Ruan, & Gao, 2019). By using residual dilation for CNN network the speed of training is increased. The dense vectors are formed from the Chinese characters and dictionary features. Then the random field is used so that the dependencies among neighboring tags can be captured and a tag sequence is formed. The authors have used CCKS-2017 Task 2 dataset and found that the proposed method results better performance in comparison to RNN based models both in performance and time requirement for training. The proposed architecture is shown in fig. 3.

License plate recognition is a part of intelligent transportation system (Y. Yang, Li, & Duan, 2017). The authors of this work have used CNN with kernel based extreme learning machines (KELM) to classify the Chinese characters as well as numbers written on number plate. At first the convolutional layers of CNN are used to extract the features from the input images of license plate. Then the extracted features of CNN layer are used as input for KELM classifier in which the classification is done. The activation function used in CNN layer of proposed method is sigmoid activation function. According to the author the CNN with KELM gives better result in comparison to CNN with softmax activation function and other classifiers as SVM as well as ELM only. The authors have used the dataset collected by them which consists of 15600 numbers of license plate images. All the images are divided into two parts, one part for training purpose with 12480 images and second part for testing the architecture performance with remaining 3120 numbers of images. The testing accuracy obtained in the proposed method is 96.38%.

Convolutional Neural network is one of the methods applied for water meter number reading. Fan Yang et. al.(F. Yang, Jin, Lai, Gao, & Li, 2019) have used fully convolutional neural networks for this purpose. AugLoss objective function is used for better performance. This function manages the intermediary states of the digits of the meter reading and helps in improving the overall performance. The stochastic gradient descent was used to minimize the objective function. The projected FCSRN is having three main components: the first one is a fully convolutional network followed by temporal mapper and the last one is transcription layer. The batch normalization layer and ReLU activation functions are used after each convolutional layer. The SCUT-WMN dataset is used in this proposed work. The dataset contains 5000 difficult and 1000 numbers of easy images of meter readings. The sample of such dataset is shown in fig.4.

Figure 4. Samples of dataset with both (a) difficult and (b) easy images (F. Yang et al., 2019)

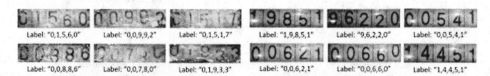

In (Youbao Tang & Wu, 2018) the authors have developed a method for scene text detection using stroke features as well as deep learning based features. In superpixel-based stroke feature transform the character region is extracted on the basis of superpixel-based clustering. The text regions are extracted and the remaining parts are refined by computing stroke width maps of the characters. In deep learning approach the authors have considered four types of features using Convolutional Neural network followed by fully connected network for better computation which consists of color features, geometric features, texture features and deep features. Color features are used to distinguish texts from the background. Texture features are used to distinguish character region from background. As we know that texts are having different geometry in comparison to other objects in the image the geometry features are used to distinguish characters from background. The authors have used ICDAR2011, ICDAR2013 and SVT datasets for this approach and the F-measure values achieved in this work is 0.876, 0.855 and 0.631 respectively.

License plate recognition is the primary part of character recognition from the vehicles. Once the license plate is localized the characters and numbers written in the plate can be extracted through different procedures. In (Bulan, Kozitsky, Ramesh, & Shreve, 2017) Orhan Bulan et. al. have proposed a method without segmentation and annotation for license plate recognition. In this method the input image first passes through the SNoW classifier to extract the candidate region and then filtered them through strong convolutional neural network. Once the location of license plate is found it is then gone through segmentation and optical character recognition which uses the method of probabilistic inference (based on hidden markov model). The Viterbi algorithm is used to determine the code sequence. The performance evaluation for the proposed method is carried out using license plate images captured under realistic conditions in US.

Prasun Roy et. al. have used Convolutional neural network for air writing recognition for English, Bengali and Devanagari languages (Roy, Ghosh, & Pal, 2018). The air writing involves a video captured in front of a camera and we know that videos are nothing but the continuous change of image frames. In this method a marker of a particular color is used to create gestures of different numerals in front of generic video camera which is correlated with convolutional neural network for recognition. The accuracy obtained for English, Bengali and Devanagari languages are 97.7%, 95.4% and 93.7%. The steps followed in this proposed method are: Marker segmentation, marker tip identification, trajectory approximation and finally the character recognition. Marker segmentation is done by using generic color segmentation method. Marker tip identification is done by calculating the top most point of the detected marker with highest y-coordinate. The trajectory is computed using dx and dy values i.e. change in x and y coordinates. The video frames captured by the camera are then converted to two dimensional images which is fed to the CNN layer for image recognition.

In (Liang, Jin, Xie, Xiao, & Huang, 2017) the authors have given comprehensive analysis of the results misclassified by the CNN model. The result of misclassification by the CNN is compared with human recognition results using top-1 voting system. The reasons found in misclassification are: a) some of the images from the dataset are wrongly labeled b) some of the samples with different confidence are having different characteristics c) some samples are wrongly written or having heavy cursive appearance. This study helps to understand the error found in computing and evaluating a CNN model.

Thanh-Nga Nguyen et. al. have used CNN for Vietnamese car plate recognition (Nguyen & Nguyen, 2018). In this work they have gone through plate detection, character segmentation and character recognition. The architecture in this method consists of three convolutional layers, three pooling layers and two fully connected layers. The output layer is having only one node. ReLU activation function is used in convolutional layers. To define the loss function the authors have used cross entropy algorithm. The network is trained with SGD algorithm. The precision, recall and f-measure values obtained in this method are 98.5%, 99.3% and 98.9% respectively.

For Bangladeshi license plate recognition (Dhar, Guha, Biswas, & Abedin, 2018) Prasengit Dhar et. al. have used Convolutional Neural Network. The input images are gone through different steps like: 1) preprocessing 2) edge detection 3) morphological dilation and 4) filtering for plate detection in the image of the car. Once the plate is detected by using distance to the borders (DtBs) algorithm the shape of the plate is verified. Then the characters are segmented from the license plate and fed to the CNN layers for automatic features extraction and recognition. Due to unavailability of Bangladeshi license plate dataset the authors have captured images and generated some synthetic images for this purpose. The system is simulated using MATLAB and after 15 epochs the accuracy achieved is 99.6%.

Birhanu Hailu Belay et. al. have utilized the beauty of CNN in recognizing Amharic characters (Belay, Habtegebrial, & Stricker, 2018). The dataset used for this work is having 80000 numbers of Amharic characters. The authors have generated the Amharic text lines, characters using OCRopus. The whole dataset is divided as 70% for training, 10% for validation and 20% for testing. In the CNN architecture they have used two sets of two consecutive conlolutional layers followed by max-pooling layer, then a single convolutional layer followed by max-pooling layer, two fully connected layers with Softmax layer at the end of the network. The accuracy level achieved in this method is 92.71%.

K-CNN based medical sheet recognition (Duan, Li, Wang, Zhang, & Cao, 2017) is one of the applications of deep learning. In this work the authors have proposed a model which utilizes both KNN based features and CNN based features for character recognition in medical sheets which is found to be having better result in comparison to tesseract open source recognition engine. The local features are extracted through KNN algorithm and deep features are extracted through CNN algorithm. The whole process includes preprocessing, zone cutting, features extraction and clustering and finally recognition.

Optical character recognition is used for retail food packaging in (Ribeiro et al., 2018). The different data related to food packaging are name of the product, price, ingredients, expiry dates etc. The authors have used CNN and fully connected network (FCN) to apply filters on blurry & valid images and to detect the date respectively. The first part of the network is a convolutional network which detects the quality of the input images. It uses different filters on blurry images and it checks whether the image contains the date or not. If no date is present in the image then it discards that image from the pipeline. The valid results of this network are then fed to the FCN network for date recognition. Two datasets with 1404 and 6739 images of packaged food products are used for this method. The accuracy level achieved on these datasets are 98% and 97.10% respectively.

Restaurant menus recognition (Swastika, Setiawan, & Subianto, 2017) is another application of optical character recognition in which the authors have used the concept of Deep learning. Especially a convolutional neural network is used in this approach. The work is developed by keeping in the mind that tourist can use this method through an application in the android mobile phones to know the details about any food printed in menu. The steps followed in this proposed method is as follows: the image of the menu will be captured by the camera of mobile phone, then it will go through preprocessing for gray scaling, noise removal & binarization and finally recognition through CNN. Once the food item will be recognized the app will show the details about that food item from the database. The accuracy obtained for Sans Serif Font in 100% but for Times New Roman it is only 56%.

In (Mondal, Mondal, Saha, & Chattopadhyay, 2017) authors have used the convolutional neural network for recognition of automatic number plat. The main purpose of this recognition is to know the State to which the vehicle belongs to. In the architecture of CNN convolutional neural network with ReLU activation function is used. After this layer max-pooling layer and fully connected layers are used for classification. The authors have tested the proposed architecture on four states i.e. Tamil Nadu, Maharashtra, West Bengal and Jharkhand.

Different researches have been done on Bangla handwritten digit recognition. In (Saha, Faisal, & Rahman, 2019) the authors have used an improved version of CNN architecture which consists of 7 layers including convolutional layer, max pooling layer and fully connected layer. The CMATERdb 3.1.1 dataset having 6000images of Bangla digits is used to implement the proposed method. The testing accuracy obtained in this method is 97.6%. The proposed work is implemented using Keras framework with Tensorflow as backend.

Recognizing handwritten data is the primary part of OCR. In (Ding, Chen, Hu, Cai, & Huo, 2018) authors have used CNN-DBLSTM combination to recognize and extract the text from the handwritten data. The first CNN part of the proposed method is named as teacher and the second Deep bidirectional LSTM part is named as student. In this work the authors have calculate the word error rate and character error rate to evaluate the performance of this method. The CNN part of this method is designed based on VGG network, so it is also named as VGG-DBLSTM.

Handwritten Chinese character recognition and based on it different fonts are printed in (Zhuang, Li, & Zhou, 2018). For the recognition part the authors have used convolutional neural network(CNN). Once a handwritten character is recognized it is used for printing different handwritten fonts. In this work Chairman Mao's handwritten font is printed from the recognized characters. A total of 50 different fonts are printed in this method. To train the convolutional layers the CASIA offline handwritten dataset is used and for testing purpose the ICDAR-2013 dataset is used. The proposed CNN architecture is of 12 layers including 5 convolutional layers, 5 maxpooling layer and two fully connected layers. The accuracy obtained in this method is 97.29%.

Data pre-selection is an approach to reduce the size of datasets used to train a model. Frederic Rayar et. al. have proposed a method (Rayar, Goto, & Uchida, 2018) based on bridge vectors using related neighborhood graph for selection of closely related datasets so that the noise, training time and memory requirement will be less. To implement this method the authors have done experiment on MNIST and HW_O RID dataset which are having 60000 and 740438 numbers of images respectively. Once the pre-selection is done the results of this procedure are fed to CNN for hand written character recognition.

Image improvement is some time required when the dataset available is not having high values of resolution. This technique is applied by Haochen Zhang et. al. using CNN (H. Zhang, Liu, & Xiong, 2017). In this work the authors have developed a new loss function by modifying the existing MSE loss function and named it as weighted-MSE. In MSE loss function each pixel pf an image is given same priority but in this work the authors have given higher priority to some pixels than others. The accuracy in getting super resolution using ICDAR 2015 dataset is 78.10% which is said to be remarkable improvement in comparison to the existing methods.

Abnormality detection is an approach in OCR in which the characters are detected and then the large variation from the general characters is detected. In (T.-Q. Wang & Liu, 2018) the authors have used deep learning to detect abnormality in Handwritten Chinese characters. Stroke level detection is used after skeletonization of the characters. The impact of abnormal strokes on the classification is evaluated to know the presence of abnormality. The authors have developed a dataset which is template free and named as SA-CASIA-HW. The dataset contains 3696 handwritten characters with different stroke abnormalities.

Now a day mobile phones are having online handwritten character input capability. To recognize the character different algorithms are being used. In (Xiao, Yang, Ahmad, Jin, & Chang, 2017) authors have used CNN model for online handwritten recognition. The Dropweight and global pooling concept is used in this approach. Dropweight means the weights of different layers are pruned if it does not achieve a threshold value. It helps in reducing the memory requirement. Global average pooling is used in the place of last pooling and fully connected layers in order to reduce the size as well as memory. The authors have designed three types of networks and have compared the results. The first network is a CNN model which consists of convolutional layers followed by max pooling and fully connected layers. The second network consists of residual network and the third one is the Inception-v4 network. The storage requirement I this approach is 0.57 MB which is very less in comparison to existing methods.

To detect the character and boundary of modern Japanese documents the authors in (Watanabe et al., 2018) have used a fully connected convolutional neural network (CNN). The input image to the network is a scanned image of official Japanese document from which the boundary of each character is obtained and it is gone through character recognition procedures. The authors have used 38 pairs of such data to train the model and achieved the fitness ratio and recall ratio as 98% and 975 respectively.

Hiroya Yatsuyanagi et. al. in (Yatsuyanagi, Fuchida, Okayasu, & Nakamura, 2017) have used CNN for word recognition which are printed on the surface of various retail products. In this approach the authors have used two types of font styles namely MS Mincho and MS Gothic which are broadly used to print the information about the products. Each font types are having 2228 numbers og images. To train the CNN with large dataset the authors have generated 4types of images from the present images by blurring, changing the color and background. After recognition through CNN the extracted characters are converted to their respective words by calculating the distance among the characters to form a word. The recognition accuracy in this approach reached 96.7%.

Bangla isolated handwritten compound character recognition is done (Fanany, 2017) using a convolutional neural network. In this work the authors have used CMATERdb 3.2.3.3 dataset for training and testing. The accuracy value obtained in this approach is 95.5%. A comparison among the proposed method and other existing methods is shown in this work. In this approach the authors have focused on isolated compound characters only. The CNN architecture contains 8 convolutional layers. After each two consecutive convolutional layer a max-pooling layer is used. In this way there are a total of 4 max-pooling layers used in this network. At the end part two fully connected layers are used.

For Javanese character recognition Mohammad Agung Wibowo have used the concept of deep learning in (Wibowo, Soleh, Pradani, Hidayanto, & Arymurthy, 2017). The authors have especially used Convolutional Neural Network (CNN) with two convolutional layers, two max-pooling layers and two fully connected layer. Sofmax function is used for classification from the features. The dataset was created by the authors by collecting data from the students of University of Indonesia which contains 11000 Javanese characters. The accuracy obtained in this approach is 94.57%.

The investigation of local discriminant training as well as global optimization used in CNN architecture is done by Xiangsheng Zeng et. al (Zeng, Xiang, Peng, Liu, & Ding, 2017) on Chinese characters. The triplet loss is utilized before the last fully connected layer for local discriminant training. The Conditional Random Field(CRF) is used for global optimization. The last layer of the proposed network is Softmax with CTC loss. In this approach the CASIA offline dataset (HWDB-1.0-1.1) is used to train the network. The ICDAR-2013 offline dataset is used to test the network accuracy.

Samad Roohi et. al have used convolutional neural network for Persian handwritten character recognition (Alizadehashraf & Roohi, 2017). The authors have designed and compared three networks for comparison purpose on the same datasets. The three networks are:1) Softmax based Linear classification, 2) Single CNN based on Lenet-5 and 3) Ensemble learning based CNN. The comparison among these networks show that the ECNN gives highest accuracy among three networks. The accuracy level achieved in designed first, second and third models are 86.3%, 96.9% and 97.1% respectively.

Printed Thai characters are gone through segmentation and recognition (Chomphuwiset, 2017) by Phatthanaphong Chomphuwiset using convolutional neural network (CNN). The whole work is based on two processes i.e. segmentation of characters and recognition. The character boundaries are obtained using connected compound analysis method. Then the segmented characters are gone through CNN for recognition which architecture is shown in the fig.5. The dataset contains 66 classes of characters including special characters along with Thai characters. The accuracy obtained in this approach is 98%. For classification and error evaluation logistic Softmax function is used. Stochastic gradient descent is used for optimization.

Figure 5. Proposed CNN architecture (Chomphuwiset, 2017)

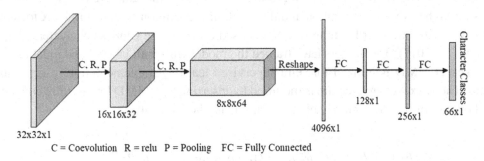

Chinese character recognition based on radial region features (Weike & Sei-Ichiro, 2017) in CNN is another approach of OCR in which to train the network both local and global features are used at a time. Radial region features are based on structural characteristics i.e. it gives the information about left, right, top as well as bottom radical regions as shown in fig.6. To improve the accuracy a multi supervised learning method is adopted. The results of both local and global features are concatenated to get a single feature vector which is used to train the network for better accuracy. The CASIA dataset is used to train the model. The accuracy and error rate calculated in this approach are 97.42% and 2.58% respectively.

Figure 6. Regional based segmentation (Weike & Sei-Ichiro, 2017)

To recognize cursive Hanja characters Sangwon Lee in (Lee & Jang, 2017) have used a residual network based on ResNet along with CNN architecture. The authors have used Chaucer dataset having 240000 data among which 824 are Chinese characters from the old dictionary of Korean studies portal. The accuracy value achieved in this work is 94.7%. The experiments are done on three different models which are based on VGGnet, VGG-Resnet and Resnet. Adam optimizer is used to update the weights.

In (Peiqi Wu, Huang, & Li, 2017) the authors have tried to improve the accuracy of Chinese license plate recognition by improving and using convolutional neural network. The images dataset is first gone through salt and pepper addition and affine transformation to train the model with more critical images. The CNN network consists of three convolutional layers, two max-pooling layers and two fully connected layers.

Math formula recognition (Liu et al., 2017) is another approach in OCR. The authors have proposed a new type of over segmentation method to separate highly compound characters and the extracted characters will pass through CNN network for recognition. Due to limited data on math formula the authors have developed their own dataset and named it as MFR-100 which contains 100 numbers of images captured by smart phones. The F-measure in this dataset is found to be 0.85. The adhesive characters are segmented based on candidate segment (vertical) lines. Once the adhesive characters are separated it will pass through CNN for recognition and the result of recognition is shown in latex format.

A semi-supervised transfer learning in CNN is used to recognize Chinese characters (Yejun Tang, Wu, Peng, & Liu, 2017). The authors have trained the model with both labeled and unlabeled datasets. The Multi kernel MMD is utilized for semi-supervised learning implementation in fine-tunes CNN architecture. The Alex Net architecture is modified by inserting MK MMD loss in fully connected layer which is shown in fig.7. The accuracy obtained in this method is 92.4%.

Figure 7. a) Alex Net b) Modified network as in (Yejun Tang et al., 2017)

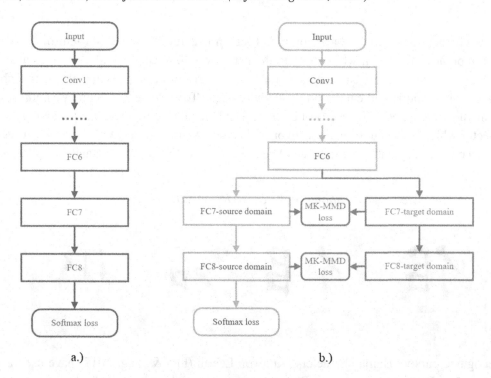

Orthogonal subspace filters (Gatto, dos Santos, & Fukui, 2017) are used as feature extractor in convolutional layers. It decreases the distance between classes and it creates the cluster of classes with very less space. From the less occupied subspaces the kernels of convolutional layers are constructed which are used for feature extraction. In this way the authors have decreased the memory space required to store the networks for wide range of applications. To investigate the effectiveness of this method the authors have used four datasets i.e. USPS dataset of 9298 handwritten digits, MNIST, CIFAR-10 and LFW face images for recognition.

Convolutional neural network is broadly used in character recognition. In (Hu, Wei, & Liu, 2017) the Hongwei Hu et. al have used CNN architecture to recognize machine printed Mongolian characters which is shown in fig.8. In this work the authors have taken three convolutional layers, two sub sampling layers and single fully connected layer for recognition. The sub sampling layer consists of S2 and S4 layers. The dataset used in this method consists of 20000 Mongolian characters. After 10 epochs the accuracy achieved in this procedure is 99.91%. The authors have given a comparison of CNN with BP network. The accuracy obtained in BP network is 95.45% which is less in comparison to CNN model.

Figure 8. Proposed architecture (Hu et al., 2017)

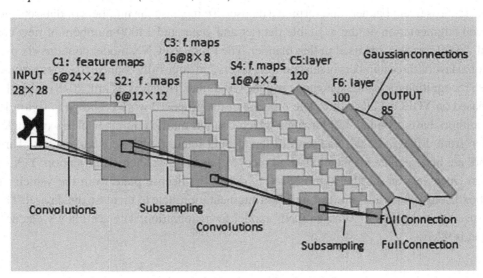

To recognize the serial number printed on RMB(The currency of China) Nannan Zhao et.al in (Zhao, Zhang, Ouyang, Lv, & Zang, 2018) have used convolutional neural network. The first step of recognition is the segmentation of characters from detected rows. To detect the characters the window moving operation is applied in this work as the numbers are of same size, same font and are having same gap between them which is as shown in the fig.9. A two level CNN model is designed to carry out the recognition. The first level works on all the letters and digits but the second level is working on the similar letter and numbers like 4 & A, 3 & B etc. The CNN network is trained with the sample images of banknotes. The accuracy achieved in this method is found to be 99.99% and the time of recognition is 5 msec.

In (Ali, Pickering, & Shafi, 2018) Asghar Ali et. al. have used convolutional neural network to recognize the Urdu characters from the captured natural scenes. To train the CNN model the authors have extracted 14000 numbers of characters from the images captured from sign boards, shop scenes, street

Figure 9. Window Design (Zhao et al., 2018)

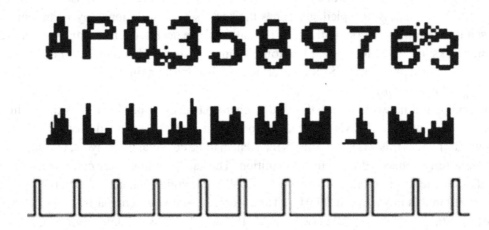

scenes and advertisement banners and formed a dataset. To increase the numbers of datasets the authors have applied augmentation on the available dataset and generated 14000 numbers of new characters. So in total 28000 images were used in this manner. The Proposed CNN model contains six numbers of convolutional layers, three numbers of max pooling layers and three fully connected layers for recognition.

License recognition for Bangla language is done (Abdullah, Hasan, & Islam, 2018) using three stage network based on YOLOv3 algorithm. The pipeline of the proposed work is shown in figure 10. In this work the authors have captured 1500 images which contain multiple number plates or single number plate, taken from different angles and with different light intensities to generate dataset. Three stages in this work are license plate localization, digit recognition and character identification. YOLOv3 (You Only Learn Once version 3) algorithm is used to detect the license plate from the vehicle. Then the bounded box license plates are gone through data augmentation state to increase the dataset. The formed dataset is used to train ResNet20 based CNN model for recognition. The accuracy value achieved in this method is 92.7%.

Figure 10. Pipeline of Three stage network (Abdullah et al., 2018)

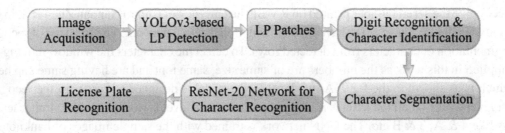

String detection is one of the applications of optical character recognition. In (Zhan, Lyu, & Lu, 2018) the authors have used CNN only to recognize the handwritten digit strings instead of CNN-RNN which consumes more times in comparison to CNN only. There are three parts in the proposed network. The layers are feature extraction layer, then the feature dimension transcription and finally an output layer. Dense blocks are used to extract the features. CTC is used for loss evaluation and decoding of features. The model is tested on ORAND-CAR-A and ORAND-XAR-B database which resulted the recognition rates of 92.2% and 94.02% respectively. The architecture of this work is shown in fig.11.

Figure 11. Proposed Network (Zhan et al., 2018)

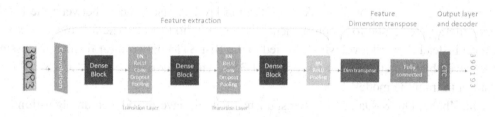

In (Lu, Sun, Chu, Huang, & Yu, 2018) WEI LU et. al. have proposed a corner response and deep CNN based video text detection and recognition. In this approach the corner response is used as feature mapping to detect the text regions on the video scene. Then by using projection analysis the test lines are detected. Then they have constructed a network for classification which consists of the transferred parameters of Residual Network-50(ResNet50), VGG16 and Inception V3 in order to reduce the false positives. Finally a fuzzy c-means based approach is utilized to get the text later from the background so that the text will be recognized by using any available OCR software.

2.2 Using RNN Only

Another aspect of character recognition is to first draw the characters using recurrent neural network and recognize those generated characters also using RNN (X.-Y. Zhang et al., 2017). The authors of this work have used the combination of LSTM and GRU along with bidirectional RNN for drawing and recognizing Chinese characters. For the same purpose if CNN is used then one extra step is to be followed i.e. the drawn characters as shown in fig.12 will be converted to images. But this step is excluded in RNN as it deals with end to end sequential data of characters.

Figure 12. Three Chinese characters draw online (the numbers represent the sequence of strokes) (X.-Y. Zhang et al., 2017)

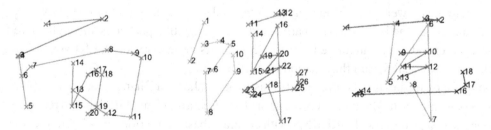

The sequential data considered in this works are the XY-coordinates for each time the pen is moved and the serial number of each stroke of a character. The author have used ICDAR-2013 competition database and achieved accuracy. Xu-Yao Zhang et. al. have designed 6 different network with different number of stacked layers of LSTM and GRU. The accuracy for the different network is found to be different with very less variation. But there is a huge difference among training time with different networks.

Optical character recognition is applied in the field of clinical named entity recognition (G. Wu, Tang, Wang, Zhang, & Wang, 2019). In this work Guohua Wu et. al have used bidirectional LSTM network along with conditional random field to recognize the words related to health issues i.e. body parts, different diseases, symptoms etc. A self attention layer is also used in between the LSTM and CRF layers which is the reason for improvement in the simulation result. The features are extracted in character level instead of word level which are fed to the Bi-LSTM network for further processing. The accuracy achieved by the authors for F1 score is 91.35%. The authors have used CCKS-2017 (Shared Task-2) dataset to train the model.

In (Jianshu Zhang, Du, & Dai, 2018) Jianshu Zhang et. al. have introduced an algorithm based on tracking and parsing to recognize online handwritten mathematical expressions. They have used bi-directional recurrent neural network with gated recurrent unit to trace the expressions and GRU with Guided Hybrid Attention (GHA) to generate the traced notations. GHA comprises of coverage based spatial attention and temporal attention. The authors have demonstrated the basic difference between static images in offline handwritten recognition and the ink-trajectory based online information using fully convolutional based watcher in this TAP mechanism. The accuracy achieved in this method are 61.16% using CROHME2014 and 57.02% using CROHME2016 offline datasets.

Deep learning is used for Nastaliq text recognition (Naz et al., 2016). In this work the authors have recognized Nastaliq texts which is somehow different from Arabic scripts as the alphabets are written from right to left with some slope. The layers used in the neural network are multi-dimensional long short term memory. By using MD-LSTM the authors achieved an accuracy of 98%. A pixel based MDLSTM is used for this purpose. The hidden layer of this system consists of 3 LSTM fully connected layers. Different steps followed in this work are: preprocessing, feature extraction, features are then fed to MDLSTN layers and then the recognition is done. In the preprocessing stage the Urdu scripts are first converted to gray scale with height normalized to 46 pixels. Then these outputs are gone through feature extraction by 4x1 patches which are then fed to MDLSTM layer for further processing. A text line version of UPTI dataset is used. This dataset consists of 10000 numbers of text lines. These 10000 datasets are used for training, validation and testing. The testing dataset consists of 1600 numbers of images.

Lei Shao et. al have proposed a design for an intelligent system based on attention GAN (Shao et al., 2019). The architecture of proposed attention based GAN is shown in fig.13. Both printed and handwritten texts are recognized in this work. First the printed texts are removed from the images using attention GAN and then handwritten texts are generated in the place of removed texts. The remaining handwritten texts are used as training data. YOLOv3 network is used to recognize the handwritten characters and the place where the answers will be generated. O the whole system is divided into two parts, one is generative part and other one is the discriminative part. The generative part consists of attentive RNN and contextual auto-encoder. The attentive RNN model consists of deep residual, LSTM and Convoluional layers. The accuracy achieved in this method is 91.34%.

Online mathematical expression recognition is done in (Jianshu Zhang, Du, & Dai, 2017) using an encoder-decoder approach. The encoder consists of Gated Recurrent Unit (GRU) based recurrent network. The decoder is also comprises of GRURNN with coverage based attention model. After recognizing the

Figure 13. Proposed Architecture of Attention GAN-Based method (Shao et al., 2019)

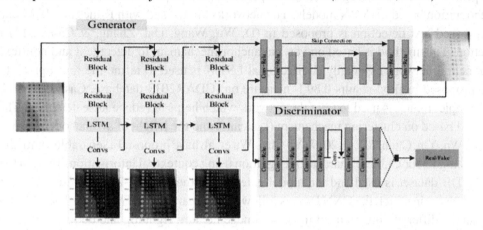

symbols and characters in the expression the result is shown in LaTeX format. The proposed method is validated using the competition task of CROHME 2014. The accuracy obtained in this method is 52.43%. The input sequence to the GRU layers are the coordinate point and the pen strokes.

For in-air Chinese handwritten recognition (Ren, Wang, Lu, Zhou, & Yuan, 2017) Haiqing Ren et. al. have used Recurrent neural network as we know that sequence data can be processed easily using RNN. The X and Y coordinates of the dot locations are used as sequential data for RNN network. It consists of input layer followed by five RNN layers, a dropout layer and finally a fully connected layer. After the fully connected layer a softmax layer is used to compare the probability distribution to recognize which class it belongs to. The proposed network is tested with IAHCC-UCAS2016 dataset and the accuracy result was found to be 91.84%.

To recognize the Arabic text data present in the TV screen for news channels Oussama Zayene et. al. have utilized the concept of RNN (Zayene, Amamou, & BenAmara, 2017). Especially the Multi Dimensional LSTM with CTC(Connectionist Temporal Clasification) are used in this proposed work. To test the network AcTIV-R dataset is used. The system is based on two steps i.e. 1)Preprocessing and 2) Recognition. In preprocessing the images are converted to gray scale of particular pixel values. Then normalization on the datasets is applied. The normalized images are fed to the MDLSTM network followed by CTC and the last layer is softmax layer.

Kyuyeon Hwang et. al. have used hierarchical recurrent neural network for character level recognition (Hwang & Sung, 2017) and it is found to be more efficient in comparison to word level recognition. By using external clock and reset signals a simple RNN model is converted to hierarchical RNN. The architecture of this proposed model is having different layers of RNN. The higher level RNNs are having slower clock signal in comparison to lower level layers of RNNs. The proposed method is tested with Wall Street Journal corpus and One billion word benchmark to compare the character level and word level recognition.

Theodore Bluche et. al in (Bluche, Kermorvant, Touzet, & Glotin, 2017) have proposed a cortical based open Bigram for handwritten word recognition using BLSTM. It is based on the concept that normally people read the word without reading the each character. The words are recognized by their open Bigrams. To predict the open-Bigrams from the word the authors have used LSTM recurrent neural network. Then from the bigrams the respective words are predicted by applying cosine similarity measure on the bigram representation and the bagged recurrent predictions. The proposed method is compared with the simple recognition based on RNN models. The networks are trained with Rimes and IAM databases.

A strip based text detection is proposed in (D. Wu, Wang, Dai, Zhang, & Cao, 2017) for scene text detection. This method is based on vertical anchor mechanism to detect text and non-text regions. Recurrent neural network especially Bidirectional LSTM is used to refine the result predicted as text area. The proposed method results 0.89 F measure on ICDAR2013 database. Cascade learning based on hard example mining is used to train the network which helps to reduce false detection. The anchors are generated based on clustering mechanism (k-means) and the height of all anchors is also measured.

In (Y.-C. Wu, Yin, Chen, & Liu, 2017) Yi-Chao Wu et. al. have proposed a separable multi dimensional LSTM-RNN model for Chinese character recognition using contextual information. To train the network CASIA-HWDB dataset is used and the model is tested on the ICDAR-2013 dataset. The architecture consists of 7 layers in which the CNN layer is followed by separable LSTM layers. The SMDLSTMs are used to scan the different directions of the input image i.e. left, right top and bottom. The transcription is done to convert the sequence data into a labeled output using CTC layer.

Online handwritten recognition on Devanagari scripts have been developed by Rajib Ghosh et. al. in (Keshri, Kumar, & Ghosh, 2018). The authors have considered the strokes present in writing the scripts as sequential data to the RNN network. The LSTM and Bidirectional LSTM models are used for this work. First of all the upper lines (Sirolekha) are removed which are common to all characters in Devanagari. Using local zone the strokes are detected from which dominant points are considered in terms of slope angle. The characters are broken into numbers of basic strokes. The x and y coordinates of pen tips are used as sequential data. There are 73 basic strokes in Devanagari scripts. So the output layer consists of 73 nodes. The proposed method is developed with 10k different words in the lexicon.

Xin Xu et. al. have designed a model based on residual network along with Bidirectional GRU and CTC (X. Xu, Zhou, & Zhang, 2018) for screen rendered text recognition for Chinese and English languages. The first step in this recognition is to extract the text lines for feature sequence storage. Then the sequence data is transferred through the bidirectional RNN (GRU) is to extract contextual features for recognition. Loss is calculated using connectionist temporal classification. The model is tested with ORAND-CAR-A and ORAND-CAR-B dataset and the recognition accuracy found are 91.89%, 93.79% respectively. An overview of this method is shown in figure 14.

Figure 14. The proposed architecture for screen rendered text recognition (X. Xu et al., 2018)

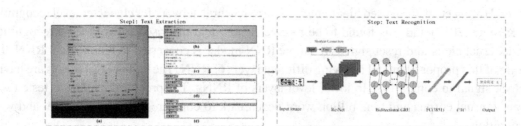

Font recognition is also an interesting part which is based on the optical character recognition. The authors Dapeng Tao et al. (Tao, Lin, Jin, & Li, 2015) have used principal component based long short term memory network for recognition of characters and to determine the font information i.e. whether the character is of normal, bold, italic or bold-italic fonts. In this approach the basic strokes present in Chinese characters are taken into consideration. The noise present in the input data are removed using principal component convolution and the recognition is done through 2-domentional LSTM module which accept the contextual features in the direction of scanning which is useful to contrast the text trajectory from the background.

2.3 Combined use of CNN-RNN

Optical character recognition is also used in the field of arithmetic operation recognition (Jiang, Dong, & El Saddik, 2018) which is somehow different from simple character recognition as different arithmetic symbols are used along with the numbers and characters. The authors in this work have designed two networks for arithmetic operation recognition. One is Deep Convolutional Neural Network (DCNN) for simple arithmetic operations as shown in figure 15(a) and the second one is the convolutional Recurrent neural Network(CRNN) for complex arithmetic operations as shown in figure 15(b).

Figure 15. Examples of (a) simple and (b) complex arithmetic operations. (Jiang et al., 2018)

Using DCNN they achieved the accuracy of 99.985% and in that of CRNN they got 98.087% of accuracy. In DCNN, authors have used 5 numbers of convolutional layer with ReLU activation function followed by Max-Pooling layer, a flatten layer and at the end they have used dense layer. The output of each dense layer is either a numerical value or any symbols like + or – or brackets etc.

Scene text recognition (F. Wang, Guo, Lei, & Zhang, 2017) uses the concept of optical character recognition in which the main objective is to extract text data from the images of different scenes. The authors have designed a Recurrent Neural Network to recognize and extract the text without segmenting the characters. The features extracted from a convolution layer are used as sequential input for recurrent layer. A hidden markov model is used to supervise the training procedure in CNN part. The datasets used in this work are: ICDAR(2011),IIIT5K-word and SVT. They achieved the accuracy of 92.5%,86.7%,90.2%,91.6% and 86.9% by using IIIT5K-50, IIIT5K-1000, SVT-50, 1C11-50 and IC11-FULL datasets respectively. A sample of SVT dataset is shown in figure. 16

Figure 16. Sample of SVT dataset (F. Wang et al., 2017)

License plate localization (Jingjing Zhang, Li, Li, Xun, & Shan, 2019) is done using the combination of CNN and RNN. In this work authors have only developed an algorithm for localization of number plate but they have gone through character extraction. This method can be used for optical character recognition in which once the number plate is located it will be used for character extraction. The presence of characters is checked using convolutional neural network. Once all the characters are detected the segments are joined by the vertical anchor mechanism. Then the number plate is correctly detected by the continuous presence of characters which is verified with the help of bidirectional-LSTM. They have applied their algorithm on Chinese as well as other different language based number plates and got the average precision of 99.10% and 97.11% respectively. The results of this work is shown in fig.17.

Figure 17. Number plate localization. (Jingjing Zhang et al., 2019)

Natural scene text detection is one of the applications of Deep learning. To detect the texts in the images taken from different scenes authors in (Zuo, Sun, Mao, Qi, & Jia, 2019) have used CNN and Bidirectional LSTM for feature extraction and sequential coding of features respectively. The whole system is divided into two parts i.e. encoder and decoder for scene text recognition. The encoder consists of the input layer to which images will be fed, then the convolutional layer is used for feature extraction followed by bidirectional long short term memory (BD-LSTM) for sequential operation on the features.

The decoder consists of a combination of CTC and attention layer followed by LSTM layer to decode the text. In this work the authors have used Synth90k dataset -10 for training and ICDAR 2003, SVT, ICDAR 2013, IIIT5K dataset for testing. The accuracy obtained in this method is 98.2% for SVT dataset (with 50 test images) which is seen to be highest among other datasets used.

Authors in (Ding et al., 2017) have designed an offline hand written recognition system using CNN-Deep Bidirectional LSTM combination. Tucker decomposition is used to decompose the pre-trained weights followed by fine tuning. Tucker decomposition is having 4 way tensors which is a higher version of SVD decomposition with 2 way tensors. The CNN part is based on the VGG architecture. A PCA-DBLSTM model is designed by the authors to verify the effectiveness of the proposed CNN-DBLSTM. Two evaluate the two techniques the authors have conducted test in a large scale English offline handwritten task. It is found that the tucker transformation gives better result when used alone to build a CNN-DBLSTM architecture.

For online Chinese handwritten character recognition Kai Chen et. al. (Chen et al., 2017) have used the combination of CNN and deep bidirectional LSTM. Authors in this work have used CASIA-OLHWDB database to train the model with connectionist temporal classification principle. In this approach the pen-tip movements are recorded as path features which are then converted to image and fed to the CNN for further feature extraction. The features extracted which are then fed to the LSTM layer as sequence vector. The preprocessing of raw data follows slope reduction, core region estimation, size normalization and pen speed normalization. A s the optimization method the authors have used stochastic gradient descent based on mini batches.

Cheng-Hung Lin et. al. in (Lin & Li, 2019) have proposed a method based on masked R-CNN for license plate recognition. Authors have focused on the images which are taken by using wide range cameras, the images of vehicles taken with higher shooting angle and more slanted images. The whole procedure includes three steps i.e. 1) vehicle detection, 2) license plate detection and 3) character recognition as shown in fig. 18.

Figure 18. Steps of number plate recognition (Lin & Li, 2019)

To detect the vehicle in the image YOLOv2 is adopted in this work. To detect the license plate from the detected vehicle again the YOLOv2 is adopted. In the final step to recognize the characters on the detected license plate thr proposed masked R-CNN is used. For different shooting angle they got different accuracy levels.

Combination of CNN and RNN for character recognition is seen in recent works. In (Dutta, Krishnan, Mathew, & Jawahar, 2018) Kartik Dutta et. al. have used this combination for both line and word recognition. For pre-processing the authors have used image slant as well as slant normalization methods. The proposed network is pre-trained with synthetic data of IIIT-HWS dataset. To train and test the network the available dataset is augmented to generate more data by using different augmentation techniques like affine transformation, elastic distortion and multi-scale transformation. The authors have calculated character error rate (CER) and word error rate (WER) for comparison purpose with existing methods. Different components of the proposed network are spatial transformer network, then residual convolutional layers, BDLSTM and at the end CTC loss.

Liangcai Gao et. al have proposed a method based on combination of CNN-RNNN (Gao et al., 2017) for mathematical formula detection in pdf documents. First the PDF information is obtained from the input PDF document. The information includes the images, characters, paths present on the page. To obtain the formula region the authors have used both top-down and bottom- up approach. Once the region of formula is extracted it passes through the CNN- RNN network for recognition. CNN part of the network extract the visual features and the RNN is used to extract the sequential features from the input images. The authors have generated a dataset and also used the Marmot dataset for comparison. It is found that when the Marmot dataset is applied to the proposed CNN-RNN network the f1 measure value is 93.4% and by using their own dataset the F1 value is 88.7% which are better in comparison to state of the art methods.

Yuxin Zhang et. al. have used the combination of CNN and RNN (Y. Zhang & Huang, 2019) to detect and recognize the Chinese license plates. The authors have used CCPD –Rotate and CCPD-Tilt sub-dataset to train and test the proposed network. The process involves no segmentation and fixed length license plates. Accuracy values obtained using the two datasets are 92.7% and 93.5% respectively. The detection is done based on the shape of the number plate so that affine linear transformation is used. Once the License plate is detected it is fed to the CRNN model which consists of CNN, BiRNN and CTC.

Scene text recognition is also an application of OCR. By using CNN-RNN Combination Minesh Mathew et. al (Mathew, Jain, & Jawahar, 2017) have designed a network to recognize the Devanagari, Telugu and Malayalam texts from the different scenes like name plates, shop hoardings, bank hoardings etc. In this approach the CRNN network is used followed by softmax and CTT for probability distribution and loss calculation respectively. The IIIT-ILST dataset is used to train the model. The following image shows the result from this network on the images having three languages.

Figure 19. Result obtained from the Proposed Method (Mathew et al., 2017)

In (Jaramillo, Murillo-Fuentes, & Olmos, 2018) the authors have proposed a method for handwritten text recognition in which a CRNN architecture is used. The method uses the comparison of the effect of large dataset and small dataset and the authors have tried to find out which layer is not retrained due to small dataset. The network is trained by IAM dataset and a small Washington dataset for this comparison. When the training is transferred from large dataset to small dataset it is found to be more effective in comparison to training from the scratch. The character error rate (CER) is found to be 3.3% for transfer learning mechanism where as CER value is 18.2% for training from scratch.

2.4 Using methods other than DNN:

G. Pirlo and D. Impedovo have given zoning based classification (Pirlo & Impedovo, 2011) for hand written characters. They have used fuzzy-membership functions and genetic algorithm which are real-coded. Voronoi based zoning is given in Fig.5 in which feature are extracted from handwritten number 5 where P_1, P_2, P_3 etc are the voronoi points. The membership function in this method is used to represent the features from different zones of the character. It is found in this approach that optimal FMF based zoning gives better result in comparison to the models using other membership functions.

Fig.20. Voronoi-based zoning (Pirlo & Impedovo, 2011)

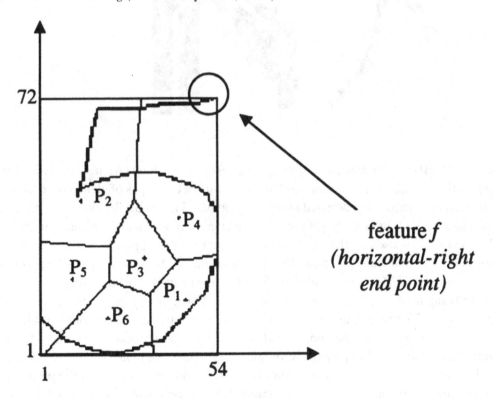

In (L. Xu, Wang, Li, & Pan, 2019), LIANG XU et.al have used concept learning to recognize Chinese handwritten characters. They developed a meta-stroke information library. The strokes from different characters are extracted for concept learning. Bayesian extraction program is applied for this method. Using Monte Carlo Markov based chain sampling the characters are generated for conceptual learning. They have used ICDAR-2013 dataset to test the performance of the proposed network. Stroke extraction from Chinese characters is shown as in figure 6.

Figure 21.Stroke extraction from Chinese alphabet. (L. Xu et al., 2019)

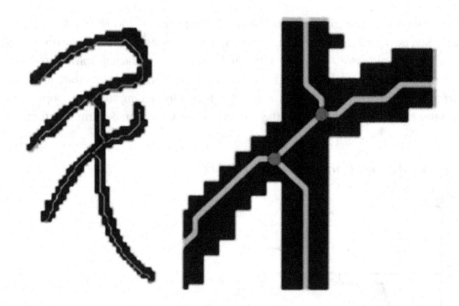

FAIZ ALOTAIBI et. al. have used the concept of similarity matching (Alotaibi et al., 2017) to detect and recognize the Quranic texts. The texts of Quran consists of two types of elements i.e. diacritics and the characters. The diacritics are detected using a region based method. The characters are recognized using projection method. In order to get the higher recognition ratio an optimization technique is applied. Modified KNN is used as classifier. The experiment for this approach is done using MATLAB and the result is compared with existing KNN based algorithms. The accuracy percentages are found to be 96.4268% and 92.3077% for recognition of diacritics and characters respectively.

Qiu-Feng Wang have proposed a context based (Q.-F. Wang, Yin, Liu, & intelligence, 2011) Chinese handwritten offline recognition system. The three parameters are taken into consideration. The parameters are candidate path evaluation, second one is the path search and the last one is the parameter estimation. To evaluate candidate path the Bayesian decision view is adopted and the path search is done on the basis of modified beam search algorithm. To increase the performance of the proposed method data augmentation is applied on characters for training. The experiment is done the Chinese handwritten dataset CASIA-HWDB and the result was found with 91.39% correct rate and 90.75% accurate rate.

In (Shi et al., 2015), Cun-Zhao Shi et.al. have used the concept of stroke detection for character recognition. They have used CVLSD dataset for handwritten recognition. In this work the authors have given a comparative analysis on three different architectures i.e. tree-structured recognition, multi stroke based discriminative model and dictionary embedded learning-based recognition. The accuracy level was found to be 95.5% on ICDAR-2013 dataset in case of Dictionary embedded system. They have also applied this method of recognition on MNIST dataset. The strokes obtained from handwritten data are shown in figure 22.

Figure 22. Stroke detection on handwritten data (Shi et al., 2015)

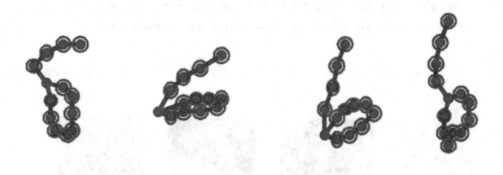

Xiang Bai et. al. have proposed a strokelet based approach (Bai, Yao, & Liu, 2016) for scene test recognition. The strokelet is the information about strokes present is the character. By decomposing the characters into number of strokes and then getting the information of each stroke represents the class of the character. The experiment is carried out using different public datasets like IIIT-5K word, ICDAR-2013 and SVT. The accuracy values are 82.64% on ICDAR-2013 (Full), 90.27% on ICDAR-2013 (50) and 80.99% on using SVT dataset.

Majid Sepahvand et. al. have utilized the structural properties (Sepahvand, Abdali-Mohammadi, & Mardukhi, 2016) of character to recognize Perian/Arabic characters online. The inertial sensor based pen is used to reconstruct the trajectory of the characters so that it will be used for feature extraction. The position of the pen tip is calculated using inertial position navigation strategy. The position information is utilized to get high level features for accuracy improvement. An algorithm based on genetic program-

Figure 23. Reconstructed Persian/Arabic digits (Sepahvand et al., 2016)

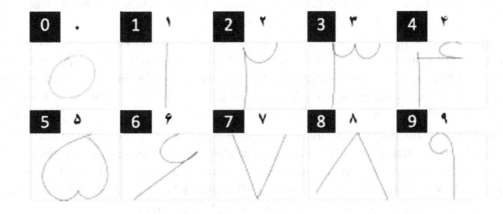

ming is used to calculate the characteristic function for all the characters so that it will help in classifying the characters. Some examples of reconstructed Persian/Arabic digits are shown in fig. 3. The GP

In order to recognize the characters present in any video or scene Yirui Wu et. al. have proposed a contour restoration based model (Y. Wu et al., 2016). The contour means shape of the gray scaled images from different videos or scenes are considered as input to the system instead of binary images. To identify the stroke candidate pixels the authors have used the zero crossing points resulted from the Laplacian application. Fourier phase-angles and gradient magnitude based symmetry features are utilized for all the SPC pairs so that the probable stroke-candidate pairs (PSCP) will be identified. The proposed method is tested on the ICDAR, SVD and MSRA datasets and the result obtained is found to be better than state of the art methods. The effect of applying Laplacian is shown in fig.24.

Figure 24. (a)The input image (b) Canny Edge images (c) Multi-directional and Laplacian images (Y. Wu et al., 2016)

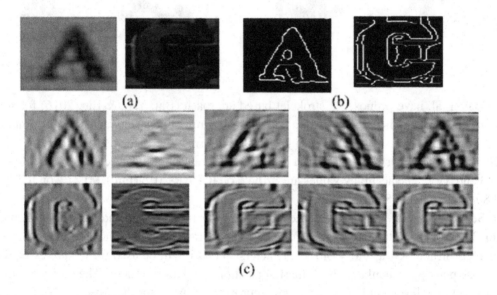

Application of Artificial neural network with Hidden Markov Model is seen in (Kishna & Francis, 2017). In this work the authors have utilized the neural network with HMM to recognize Malayalam cursive handwritten characters. The input images are gone through different steps before feature extraction. The first step is common for all process i.e. the image acquisition. Then the image captured is gone through preprocessing to remove noise, skewness present in the image etc. Then the image is segmented based on the character presence. The features are extracted using median filters. Then the extracted features are fed to ANN and HMM for classification. The accuracy value obtained in this method is 93.4%.

Character segmentation and recognition from Indian document images is done in (Sahare & Dhok, 2018) by using the SVM and KNN classifiers. The authors have first segmented the joined characters using graph distane method and the result of segmentation is verified by the support vector machine (SVM) classifier. For character recognition geometrical shape based three features are considered. The first and second features are based on the center pixel values of a character and the third feature is based on neighborhood information. The characters are classified using KNN-Classifier. The accuracy percentage obtained in this method is 98.86% for segmentation and 99.84% for recognition.

Devanagari and Tamil word recognition (Bharath, Madhvanath, & intelligence, 2011) is done using both lexicon based and lexicon free Hidden Markov model. In this work the lexicon driven means the prior knowledge of the words is considered as features. The writing order, symbol order etc are considered as lexicon based features. The lexicon free means there is no information about the symbol sequence or writing order. A large number of images are used directly as bag-of-Symbol inputs. The accuracy percentage obtained for Devanagari and Tami languages are 87.13% and 91.8% respectively when the system is tested using 20000 words lexicon.

Semi-Markov CRF (Conditional Random fields) based Chinese/ Japanese character recognition is done in (Zhou et al., 2013). Xiang-Dong Zhou et. al. have used the CRF on the lattice which contains all possible segmentation and recognition hypothesis for a string. The linguistic and geometric features are used as feature functions. To optimize the fusion parameters the negative log likelihood loss with the margin term is minimized. To reduce the complexity related to computation a forward and backward lattice pruning is proposed. Beam search algorithm is used to increase the speed of training. The proposed method is tested using two databases i.e. CASIA-OLHWDB and TUAT Kondate. The accuracy percentage are 94.54%, and 94.55% respectively.

Qi Li et. al have designed a recognition tool based on Tesseract (Li, An, Zhou, & Ma, 2016) for recognizing offline Chinese handwritten characters. The first step in this approach is ti develop a Chinese handwritten library which is independent of the user's writing methods. The second step is to preprocess the input images and adjustment of the parameters of Tesseract tool. The obtained accuracy of recognition in this method is 88%.

Feature fusion based Bangla handwritten character recognition is seen in (Bipu & Afroge, 2018).In this approach the features are extracted by combining Histogram of Oriented Gradients (HOG) and Gabor filter. The results are obtained from individual methods and compared with the fusion based system and it is found that the result of fusion mechanism results better that individual systems. The recognition accuracy for HOG, Gabor filter and the combined system are found to be 90.5%, 91.2% and 96.1% respectively. The block diagram of the proposed fusion based method of recognition is shown in fig.25.

Figure 25. Proposed fusion based model (Bipu & Afroge, 2018)

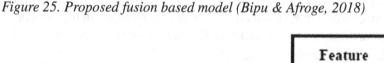
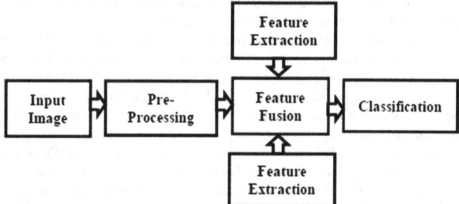

Use of K nearest neighbor (KNN) for character recognition is seen in (Hazra, Singh, & Daga, 2017) In this approach the authors have used KNN as the classifier for custom images. The images are first converted to gray scale images. Then blurred, threshold is done and is converted to a flattened image so that the features will be extracted to distinguish characters from the background. From the contour the features are extracted which are stored in a numpy array. Then these array are concatenated with labels an d are stored in a text file. The KNN classifier is trained with text files and the next step is for testing. The network is trained with MNIST and Chars74K dataset.

By recognizing the patterns present in a paragraph the character recognition become easier. The authors in (Pachpande & Chaudhari, 2017) have used horizontal histogram for line segmentation and by using vertical histogram the words are separated. Before passing through the image segmentation preprocessing is done to remove the noise, skewness present in the Devanagari script image. The median filter is used on binarized image to remove the distortions present in the image. By using convex-hull technique the features are extracted. The work is specially based on segmentation into words. The accuracy value for word segmentation is found to be 98.1%

Optical character recognition based on structural information is found in (Khaustov, Spitsyn, & Maksimova, 2016). In this approach the strokes and their composite edge points are considered. The joint points are termed as bend points which are used as features. If the structural components are considered then according to the authors of this work the result will be better whether less amount of images are available for training. The performance of this method is verified using MNIST dataset. The authors have given a comparison based study with other methods like Intersection method, SVM and Probabilistic neural network and it is found that the proposed method gives better result. The accuracy after 5 iterations was found to be 95.1% which is better in comparison to other methods.

Artificial neural network based classification of English alphabet is done in (Katiyar & Mehfuz, 2016) with multiple features. The features are extracted from seven feature extractors to reduce the time consumption and to increase the accuracy of recognition. The best features are then selected by using genetic algorithm. Seven features considered in this approach are based on geometry features, moment features, distance based features and finally the local features. The performance of the proposed system is checked using CEDAR dataset of English Handwritten alphabets. Before the feature extraction the input images are gone through preprocessing step which includes image binarization, slant correction, smoothing, noise removal and size normalization. The accuracy of recognition in this approach is found to be 94.65% for capital alphabets and 91.115 for small alphabets.

Segmentation free ligature based Urdu Nastaliq recognition is done in (Din, Siddiqi, Khalid, Azam, & Processing, 2017). The ligatures are composed of main body and dots with diacritics. In this approach the dots and diacritics are separated from the main body to be recognized separately. Then the two recognitions are combined to recognize the ligature as a whole. The hidden markov model is used to classify the ligatures based Urdu printed characters. The performance of the proposed method is verified by using UPTI database and the ligature recognition accuracy value was found to be 92%.

Textline detection from degraded ancient documents (Ahn, Ryu, Koo, Cho, & Processing, 2017) is done by Byeongyong Ahn et. al.. The authors have followed two steps. First one is the binarization of the input image and second step is to extract the text line from the preprocessed image. The main paragraph is detected by removing some meta data present in the page. By using projection profile mechanism the main block i.e. a paragraph is detected. Then the Connected Component (CC) algorithm is adopted to extract the textlines from the paragraph. The skew error present in the paragraph is also considered for better output. ICDAR 2015 dataset is used for both training and testing. The detection rate, recognition accuracy and the F-measure values for the proposed method are found to be 71.49%, 73.06% and 72.27% respectively.

HD cameras are used for better recognition of number plates. Ali Farhat et. al. have used the concept of template matching for number plate recognition (Farhat et al., 2018). In this approach the input image is gone through preprocessing i.e. resizing the image, morphology and application of connected component analysis. OpenCV is used to apply CCA in both detection and recognition stages. The features used in this method are based on zoning, vector crossing and the combined zoning-vector crossing. The performance of the designed architecture is verified using MATLAB and the hardwire implementation is also done using system on Chip (SoC). The So platform used is Xilinx Zynq-7000 which is connected to ARM processor. The implemented system recognize each character in 0.63ms. The accuracy of recognition is 99.5%.

Character recognition from metal stamping is done in (Xiang et al., 2018). The recognition is based on image fusion of multi directional illumination. In this approach four gray scale images are taken from four different directions b using four bar sized light sources. Then those images are used for comparison based on stamped depression zones and flat portions for background detection and removal. Then the images are fused and passed through mean filter application, binarization process and morphological closing steps in order to detect and segment the characters from the string of fused images. Then the normalized characters are recognized using back propagation based artificial neural network and histogram analysis method. 99.6% of accuracy value is obtained in this method to recognize the characters from metal stamping. The samples of metal stamping are shown in the fig.15.

Figure 26. Samples of colored metal stampings (Xiang et al., 2018)

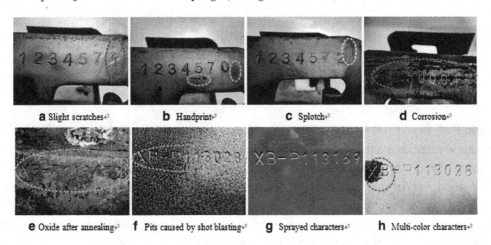

A combined feature based strategy for handwritten recognition is done in (Sharma, 2015). The static and dynamic properties are considered for better recognition. The static properties are the white pixels, the horizontal, vertical and diagonal angles from the binary image. The dynamic properties include the drawing order. From each image feature of length 356 is extracted. The support vector machine is used to classify the characters. The MNIST dataset is used and the overall error rate found in this approach is 0.73% which is very less in comparison to state of the art methods.

For Chinese scene text recognition in (X. Ren et al., 2017) Xiaohang Ren et. al. have used text structure details as feature. The text structural component detection (TSCD) along with a residual network is used for feature extraction from the input image. It helps in both text detection and text recognition. An unified Chinese features are extracted using two convolutional layers followed by TSCD layer. To classify the detected characters the fullyconnected layers and Softmax layer are used. In order to increase the numbers of training dataset the authors have synthesized the high quality Chinese handwritten characters by the use of neural networks. The precision, recall and f-measure results from the proposed method are found to be 0.87. 0.82 and 0.84 respectively. The basic layer diagram of this proposed method is shown in fig.27.

Figure 27. The proposed method for recognition based on TSCD (X. Ren et al., 2017)

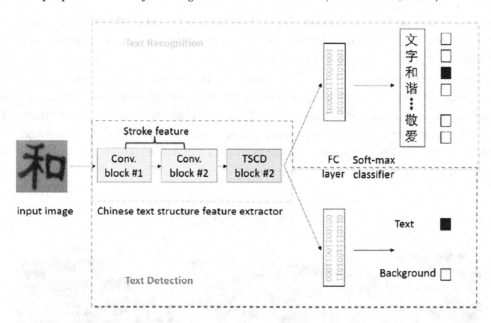

Optimum Path Forest (OPF) classifier is used in (Lopes, da Silva, Rodrigues, & Reboucas Filho, 2016) for handwritten character recognition. The features considered in this method are the signatures of characters which is a new approach in feature extraction. The proposed method is tested on Manhattan distance stood_out database which results an accuracy of 99.53%. The testing and training times are lower in comparison to state of the art methods due to the use of Optimum Path forest classifier.

Application of optical character recognition with wearable devices which consume less energy is found in (Son, So, Kim, Choi, & Lee, 2015). The researchers have taken time factor as well as accuracy value into consideration for better user satisfaction. In order to achieve this higher accuracy and less time with less energy the authors have used OCR with selected features on Tesseract platform which consumes 48.25% less energy in comparison to state of the art methods. A linear regression is carried to model the execution time.

3. Summary

Character recognition is associated with the image containing characters. So the effectiveness of the result of OCR first depends on the image quality. Different noise removal methods are available. But if the degradation in the image will be more then that will affect the result. The methods used to extract the characters from the image i.e. the segmentation are also having greater impact when the cursive handwritten character is used. Number of dataset for training plays an important role in the recognition depending upon the method chosen. The present scenario in OCR includes primitive methods which require less dataset to the current trend in OCR with large datasets of printed as well as handwritten datasets in case of deep learning. The application of OCR in banking sector, office automation and educational institute has been increased because of its effectiveness in converting hardcopies to soft copies for further processing. In future the OCR may replace the human efforts in different fields of intelligence which is a topic for consideration.

REFERENCES

Abdullah, S., Hasan, M. M., & Islam, S. M. S. (2018). *YOLO-Based Three-Stage Network for Bangla License Plate Recognition in Dhaka Metropolitan City.* Paper presented at the 2018 International Conference on Bangla Speech and Language Processing (ICBSLP). 10.1109/ICBSLP.2018.8554668

Ahn, B., Ryu, J., Koo, H. I., Cho, N. I. J. E. J. o. I., & Processing, V. (2017). *Textline detection in degraded historical document images.* Academic Press.

Ali, A., Pickering, M., & Shafi, K. (2018). *Urdu natural scene character recognition using convolutional neural networks.* Paper presented at the 2018 IEEE 2nd international workshop on Arabic and derived script analysis and recognition (ASAR). 10.1109/ASAR.2018.8480202

Alizadehashraf, B., & Roohi, S. (2017). *Persian handwritten character recognition using convolutional neural network.* Paper presented at the 2017 10th Iranian Conference on Machine Vision and Image Processing (MVIP). 10.1109/IranianMVIP.2017.8342359

Alotaibi, F., Abdullah, M. T., Abdullah, R. B. H., Rahmat, R. W. B. O., Hashem, I. A. T., & Sangaiah, A. K. J. I. A. (2017). *Optical character recognition for quranic image similarity matching.* Academic Press.

Bai, X., Yao, C., & Liu, W. J. I. T. o. I. P. (2016). *Strokelets: A learned multi-scale mid-level representation for scene text recognition.* Academic Press.

Belay, B. H., Habtegebrial, T. A., & Stricker, D. (2018). *Amharic character image recognition.* Paper presented at the 2018 IEEE 18th International Conference on Communication Technology (ICCT). 10.1109/ICCT.2018.8599888

Bharath, A., Madhvanath, S. J. I. t. o. p. a., & Intelligence, m. (2011). *HMM-based lexicon-driven and lexicon-free word recognition for online handwritten Indic scripts.* Academic Press.

Bipu, M. M. C., & Afroge, S. (2018). *A feature fusion based approach for handwritten Bangla character recognition using extreme learning machine.* Paper presented at the 2018 International Conference on Computer, Communication, Chemical, Material and Electronic Engineering (IC4ME2).

Bluche, T., Kermorvant, C., Touzet, C., & Glotin, H. (2017). *Cortical-Inspired Open-Bigram Representation for Handwritten Word Recognition.* Paper presented at the 2017 14th IAPR International Conference on Document Analysis and Recognition (ICDAR). 10.1109/ICDAR.2017.21

Bulan, O., Kozitsky, V., Ramesh, P., & Shreve, M. J. I. T. o. I. T. S. (2017). *Segmentation-and annotation-free license plate recognition with deep localization and failure identification.* Academic Press.

Chen, K., Tian, L., Ding, H., Cai, M., Sun, L., Liang, S., & Huo, Q. (2017). *A compact cnn-dblstm based character model for online handwritten chinese text recognition.* Paper presented at the 2017 14th IAPR International Conference on Document Analysis and Recognition (ICDAR). 10.1109/ICDAR.2017.177

Chomphuwiset, P. (2017). *Printed thai character segmentation and recognition.* Paper presented at the 2017 IEEE 4th International Conference on Soft Computing & Machine Intelligence (ISCMI). 10.1109/ISCMI.2017.8279611

Dhar, P., Guha, S., Biswas, T., & Abedin, M. Z. (2018). *A system design for license plate recognition by using edge detection and convolution neural network.* Paper presented at the 2018 International Conference on Computer, Communication, Chemical, Material and Electronic Engineering (IC4ME2). 10.1109/IC4ME2.2018.8465630

Din, I. U., Siddiqi, I., Khalid, S., Azam, T. J. E. J. o. I., & Processing, V. (2017). *Segmentation-free optical character recognition for printed Urdu text.* Academic Press.

Ding, H., Chen, K., Hu, W., Cai, M., & Huo, Q. (2018). *Building Compact CNN-DBLSTM Based Character Models for Handwriting Recognition and OCR by Teacher-Student Learning.* Paper presented at the 2018 16th International Conference on Frontiers in Handwriting Recognition (ICFHR). 10.1109/ICFHR-2018.2018.00033

Ding, H., Chen, K., Yuan, Y., Cai, M., Sun, L., Liang, S., & Huo, Q. (2017). *A compact CNN-DBLSTM based character model for offline handwriting recognition with Tucker decomposition.* Paper presented at the 2017 14th IAPR International Conference on Document Analysis and Recognition (ICDAR). 10.1109/ICDAR.2017.89

Duan, P., Li, Z., Wang, Y., Zhang, B., & Cao, Y. (2017). *An effective recognition method for medical sheet based on deep learning approach.* Paper presented at the 2017 12th International Conference on Computer Science and Education (ICCSE). 10.1109/ICCSE.2017.8085516

Dutta, K., Krishnan, P., Mathew, M., & Jawahar, C. (2018). *Improving CNN-RNN hybrid networks for handwriting recognition.* Paper presented at the 2018 16th International Conference on Frontiers in Handwriting Recognition (ICFHR). 10.1109/ICFHR-2018.2018.00023

Fanany, M. I. (2017). *Handwriting recognition on form document using convolutional neural network and support vector machines (CNN-SVM).* Paper presented at the 2017 5th international conference on information and communication technology (ICoIC7).

Farhat, A., Hommos, O., Al-Zawqari, A., Al-Qahtani, A., Bensaali, F., Amira, A., . . . Processing, V. (2018). *Optical character recognition on heterogeneous SoC for HD automatic number plate recognition system.* Academic Press.

Gao, L., Yi, X., Liao, Y., Jiang, Z., Yan, Z., & Tang, Z. (2017). *A deep learning-based formula detection method for PDF documents.* Paper presented at the 2017 14th IAPR International Conference on Document Analysis and Recognition (ICDAR). 10.1109/ICDAR.2017.96

Gatto, B. B., dos Santos, E. M., & Fukui, K. (2017). *Subspace-based convolutional network for handwritten character recognition.* Paper presented at the 2017 14th IAPR international conference on document analysis and recognition (ICDAR). 10.1109/ICDAR.2017.173

Hazra, T. K., Singh, D. P., & Daga, N. (2017). *Optical character recognition using KNN on custom image dataset.* Paper presented at the 2017 8th Annual Industrial Automation and Electromechanical Engineering Conference (IEMECON). 10.1109/IEMECON.2017.8079572

Hu, H., Wei, H., & Liu, Z. (2017). *The CNN based machine-printed traditional Mongolian characters recognition.* Paper presented at the 2017 36th Chinese Control Conference (CCC). 10.23919/ChiCC.2017.8027973

Hwang, K., & Sung, W. (2017). *Character-level language modeling with hierarchical recurrent neural networks.* Paper presented at the 2017 IEEE International Conference on Acoustics, Speech and Signal Processing (ICASSP). 10.1109/ICASSP.2017.7953252

Jaramillo, J. C. A., Murillo-Fuentes, J. J., & Olmos, P. M. (2018). *Boosting handwriting text recognition in small databases with transfer learning.* Paper presented at the 2018 16th International Conference on Frontiers in Handwriting Recognition (ICFHR).

Jiang, Y., Dong, H., & El Saddik, A. J. I. A. (2018). *Baidu Meizu deep learning competition: arithmetic operation recognition using end-to-end learning OCR technologies.* Academic Press.

Katiyar, G., & Mehfuz, S. J. S. (2016). *A hybrid recognition system for off-line handwritten characters.* Academic Press.

Keshri, P., Kumar, P., & Ghosh, R. (2018). *Rnn based online handwritten word recognition in devanagari script.* Paper presented at the 2018 16th International Conference on Frontiers in Handwriting Recognition (ICFHR). 10.1109/ICFHR-2018.2018.00096

Khaustov, P., Spitsyn, V., & Maksimova, E. (2016). *Algorithm for optical handwritten characters recognition based on structural components extraction.* Paper presented at the 2016 11th International Forum on Strategic Technology (IFOST). 10.1109/IFOST.2016.7884126

Kishna, N. T., & Francis, S. (2017). *Intelligent tool for Malayalam cursive handwritten character recognition using artificial neural network and Hidden Markov Model.* Paper presented at the 2017 International Conference on Inventive Computing and Informatics (ICICI). 10.1109/ICICI.2017.8365201

Lee, S., & Jang, G.-J. (2017). *Recognition model based on residual networks for cursive hanja recognition.* Paper presented at the 2017 International Conference on Information and Communication Technology Convergence (ICTC). 10.1109/ICTC.2017.8191045

Li, Q., An, W., Zhou, A., & Ma, L. (2016). *Recognition of offline handwritten Chinese characters using the Tesseract open source OCR engine.* Paper presented at the 2016 8th International Conference on Intelligent Human-Machine Systems and Cybernetics (IHMSC). 10.1109/IHMSC.2016.239

Liang, K., Jin, L., Xie, Z., Xiao, X., & Huang, W. (2017). *A Comprehensive Analysis of Misclassified Handwritten Chinese Character Samples by Incorporating Human Recognition*. Paper presented at the 2017 14th IAPR International Conference on Document Analysis and Recognition (ICDAR). 10.1109/ICDAR.2017.82

Lin, C.-H., & Li, Y. (2019). *A License Plate Recognition System for Severe Tilt Angles Using Mask R-CNN*. Paper presented at the 2019 International Conference on Advanced Mechatronic Systems (ICAMechS). 10.1109/ICAMechS.2019.8861691

Liu, N., Zhang, D., Xu, X., Guo, L., Chen, L., Liu, W., & Ke, D. (2017). *Robust math formula recognition in degraded chinese document images*. Paper presented at the 2017 14th IAPR International Conference on Document Analysis and Recognition (ICDAR). 10.1109/ICDAR.2017.27

Lopes, G. S., da Silva, D. C., Rodrigues, A. W. O., & Reboucas Filho, P. P. J. I. L. A. T. (2016). *Recognition of handwritten digits using the signature features and Optimum-Path Forest Classifier*. Academic Press.

Lu, W., Sun, H., Chu, J., Huang, X., & Yu, J. J. I. A. (2018). *A novel approach for video text detection and recognition based on a corner response feature map and transferred deep convolutional neural network*. Academic Press.

Mathew, M., Jain, M., & Jawahar, C. (2017). *Benchmarking scene text recognition in devanagari, telugu and malayalam*. Paper presented at the 2017 14th IAPR International Conference on Document Analysis and Recognition (ICDAR). 10.1109/ICDAR.2017.364

Mondal, M., Mondal, P., Saha, N., & Chattopadhyay, P. (2017). *Automatic number plate recognition using CNN based self synthesized feature learning*. Paper presented at the 2017 IEEE Calcutta Conference (CALCON). 10.1109/CALCON.2017.8280759

Naz, S., Umar, A. I., Ahmed, R., Razzak, M. I., Rashid, S. F., & Shafait, F. J. S. (2016). *Urdu Nasta'liq text recognition using implicit segmentation based on multi-dimensional long short term memory neural networks*. Academic Press.

Nguyen, T.-N., & Nguyen, D.-D. (2018). *A new convolutional architecture for Vietnamese car plate recognition*. Paper presented at the 2018 10th International Conference on Knowledge and Systems Engineering (KSE). 10.1109/KSE.2018.8573375

Pachpande, S., & Chaudhari, A. (2017). *Implementation of devanagri character recognition system through pattern recognition techniques*. Paper presented at the 2017 International Conference on Trends in Electronics and Informatics (ICEI). 10.1109/ICOEI.2017.8300796

Pirlo, G., & Impedovo, D. J. I. T. o. F. S. (2011). *Fuzzy-zoning-based classification for handwritten characters*. Academic Press.

Qiu, J., Zhou, Y., Wang, Q., Ruan, T., & Gao, J. J. I. T. o. N. (2019). *Chinese clinical named entity recognition using residual dilated convolutional neural network with conditional random field*. Academic Press.

Rayar, F., Goto, M., & Uchida, S. (2018). *CNN training with graph-based sample preselection: application to handwritten character recognition*. Paper presented at the 2018 13th IAPR International Workshop on Document Analysis Systems (DAS). 10.1109/DAS.2018.10

Ren, H., Wang, W., Lu, K., Zhou, J., & Yuan, Q. (2017). *An end-to-end recognizer for in-air handwritten Chinese characters based on a new recurrent neural networks.* Paper presented at the 2017 IEEE International Conference on Multimedia and Expo (ICME). 10.1109/ICME.2017.8019443

Ren, X., Zhou, Y., Huang, Z., Sun, J., Yang, X., & Chen, K. J. I. A. (2017). *A novel text structure feature extractor for Chinese scene text detection and recognition.* Academic Press.

Ribeiro, F. D. S., Gong, L., Calivá, F., Swainson, M., Gudmundsson, K., Yu, M., . . . Kollias, S. (2018). *An end-to-end deep neural architecture for optical character verification and recognition in retail food packaging.* Paper presented at the 2018 25th IEEE International Conference on Image Processing (ICIP).

Roy, P., Ghosh, S., & Pal, U. (2018). *A CNN based framework for unistroke numeral recognition in air-writing.* Paper presented at the 2018 16th International Conference on Frontiers in Handwriting Recognition (ICFHR). 10.1109/ICFHR-2018.2018.00077

Saha, C., Faisal, R. H., & Rahman, M. M. (2019). *Bangla handwritten digit recognition using an improved deep convolutional neural network architecture.* Paper presented at the 2019 International Conference on Electrical, Computer and Communication Engineering (ECCE). 10.1109/ECACE.2019.8679309

Sahare, P., & Dhok, S. B. J. I. A. (2018). *Multilingual character segmentation and recognition schemes for Indian document images.* Academic Press.

Sepahvand, M., Abdali-Mohammadi, F., & Mardukhi, F. J. I. t. o. c. (2016). *Evolutionary metric-learning-based recognition algorithm for online isolated Persian/Arabic characters, reconstructed using inertial pen signals.* Academic Press.

Shao, L., Liang, C., Wang, K., Cao, W., Zhang, W., Gui, G., & Sari, H. J. I. A. (2019). *. . Attention GAN-Based Method for Designing Intelligent Making System.*, 7, 163097–163104.

Sharma, A. J. V. J. o. C. S. (2015). *A combined static and dynamic feature extraction technique to recognize handwritten digits.* Academic Press.

Shi, C.-Z., Gao, S., Liu, M.-T., Qi, C.-Z., Wang, C.-H., & Xiao, B.-H. J. I. T. o. I. P. (2015). *Stroke detector and structure based models for character recognition: A comparative study.* Academic Press.

Son, S., So, H., Kim, J., Choi, D., & Lee, H.-J. J. E. L. (2015). *Energy-efficient adaptive optical character recognition for wearable devices.* Academic Press.

Swastika, W., Setiawan, H., & Subianto, M. (2017). *Android based application for recognition of Indonesian restaurant menus using convolution neural network.* Paper presented at the 2017 International Conference on Sustainable Information Engineering and Technology (SIET). 10.1109/SIET.2017.8304104

Tang, Y., Wu, B., Peng, L., & Liu, C. (2017). *Semi-supervised transfer learning for convolutional neural network based Chinese character recognition.* Paper presented at the 2017 14th IAPR International Conference on Document Analysis and Recognition (ICDAR). 10.1109/ICDAR.2017.79

Tang, Y., & Wu, X. J. I. T. o. M. (2018). *Scene text detection using superpixel-based stroke feature transform and deep learning based region classification.* Academic Press.

Tao, D., Lin, X., Jin, L., & Li, X. J. I. t. o. c. (2015). *Principal component 2-D long short-term memory for font recognition on single Chinese characters.* Academic Press.

Wang, F., Guo, Q., Lei, J., & Zhang, J. J. I. C. V. (2017). *Convolutional recurrent neural networks with hidden Markov model bootstrap for scene text recognition.* Academic Press.

Wang, Q.-F., Yin, F., Liu, C.-L. J. I. t. o. p. a., & Intelligence, M. (2011). *Handwritten Chinese text recognition by integrating multiple contexts.* Academic Press.

Wang, T.-Q., & Liu, C.-L. (2018). *DeepAD: A Deep Learning Based Approach to Stroke-Level Abnormality Detection in Handwritten Chinese Character Recognition.* Paper presented at the 2018 IEEE International Conference on Data Mining (ICDM). 10.1109/ICDM.2018.00176

Watanabe, K., Takahashi, S., Takagi, Y., Yamada, M., Mekada, Y., Hasegawa, J., . . . Miyazaki, S. (2018). *Detection of Characters and their Boundary from Images of Modern Japanese Official Documents using Fully CNN-based Filter.* Paper presented at the 2018 Nicograph International (NicoInt). 10.1109/NICOINT.2018.00024

Weike, L., & Sei-Ichiro, K. (2017). *Radical Region Based CNN for Offline Handwritten Chinese Character Recognition.* Paper presented at the 2017 4th IAPR Asian Conference on Pattern Recognition (ACPR). 10.1109/ACPR.2017.76

Wibowo, M. A., Soleh, M., Pradani, W., Hidayanto, A. N., & Arymurthy, A. M. (2017). *Handwritten Javanese character recognition using descriminative deep learning technique.* Paper presented at the 2017 2nd International conferences on Information Technology, Information Systems and Electrical Engineering (ICITISEE). 10.1109/ICITISEE.2017.8285521

Wu, D., Wang, R., Dai, P., Zhang, Y., & Cao, X. (2017). *Deep strip-based network with cascade learning for scene text localization.* Paper presented at the 2017 14th IAPR International Conference on Document Analysis and Recognition (ICDAR). 10.1109/ICDAR.2017.140

Wu, G., Tang, G., Wang, Z., Zhang, Z., & Wang, Z. J. I. A. (2019). . . *An Attention-Based BiLSTM-CRF Model for Chinese Clinic Named Entity Recognition.*, *7*, 113942–113949.

Wu, P., Huang, Z., & Li, D. (2017). *Research on the character recognition for Chinese license plate based on CNN.* Paper presented at the 2017 3rd IEEE International Conference on Computer and Communications (ICCC). 10.1109/CompComm.2017.8322820

Wu, P., Wang, F., & Liu, J. (2018). *An Integrated Multi-Classifier Method for Handwritten Chinese Medicine Prescription Recognition.* Paper presented at the 2018 IEEE 9th International Conference on Software Engineering and Service Science (ICSESS). 10.1109/ICSESS.2018.8663789

Wu, Y., Shivakumara, P., Lu, T., Tan, C. L., Blumenstein, M., & Kumar, G. H. J. I. T. o. I. P. (2016). *Contour restoration of text components for recognition in video/scene images.* Academic Press.

Wu, Y.-C., Yin, F., Chen, Z., & Liu, C.-L. (2017). *Handwritten chinese text recognition using separable multi-dimensional recurrent neural network.* Paper presented at the 2017 14th IAPR International Conference on Document Analysis and Recognition (ICDAR). 10.1109/ICDAR.2017.22

Xiang, Z., You, Z., Qian, M., Zhang, J., Hu, X. J. E. J. o. I., & Processing, V. (2018). *Metal stamping character recognition algorithm based on multi-directional illumination image fusion enhancement technology.* Academic Press.

Xiao, X., Yang, Y., Ahmad, T., Jin, L., & Chang, T. (2017). *Design of a very compact cnn classifier for online handwritten chinese character recognition using dropweight and global pooling.* Paper presented at the 2017 14th IAPR International Conference on Document Analysis and Recognition (ICDAR). 10.1109/ICDAR.2017.150

Xin, M., & Wang, Y. (2019). Research on image classification model based on deep convolution neural network. *EURASIP Journal on Image and Video Processing, 2019*(1), 40. doi:10.118613640-019-0417-8

Xu, L., Wang, Y., Li, X., & Pan, M. J. I. A. (2019).. . *Recognition of Handwritten Chinese Characters Based on Concept Learning.*, 7, 102039–102053.

Xu, X., Zhou, J., & Zhang, H. (2018). *Screen-rendered text images recognition using a deep residual network based segmentation-free method.* Paper presented at the 2018 24th International Conference on Pattern Recognition (ICPR). 10.1109/ICPR.2018.8545678

Yang, F., Jin, L., Lai, S., Gao, X., & Li, Z. J. I. A. (2019). *Fully convolutional sequence recognition network for water meter number reading.* Academic Press.

Yang, Y., Li, D., & Duan, Z. J. I. I. T. S. (2017). *Chinese vehicle license plate recognition using kernel-based extreme learning machine with deep convolutional features.* Academic Press.

Yatsuyanagi, H., Fuchida, M., Okayasu, K., & Nakamura, A. (2017). *Development of a specific word recognition system for the visually handicapped—Character recognition based on dataset generated from font data.* Paper presented at the 2017 IEEE/SICE International Symposium on System Integration (SII). 10.1109/SII.2017.8279305

Zayene, O., Amamou, S. E., & BenAmara, N. E. (2017). *Arabic Video Text Recognition Based on Multi-Dimensional Recurrent Neural Networks.* Paper presented at the 2017 IEEE/ACS 14th International Conference on Computer Systems and Applications (AICCSA). 10.1109/AICCSA.2017.126

Zeng, X., Xiang, D., Peng, L., Liu, C., & Ding, X. (2017). *Local discriminant training and global optimization for convolutional neural network based handwritten Chinese character recognition.* Paper presented at the 2017 14th IAPR International Conference on Document Analysis and Recognition (ICDAR). 10.1109/ICDAR.2017.70

Zhan, H., Lyu, S., & Lu, Y. (2018). *Handwritten digit string recognition using convolutional neural network.* Paper presented at the 2018 24th International Conference on Pattern Recognition (ICPR). 10.1109/ICPR.2018.8546100

Zhang, H., Liu, D., & Xiong, Z. (2017). *CNN-based text image super-resolution tailored for OCR.* Paper presented at the 2017 IEEE Visual Communications and Image Processing (VCIP). 10.1109/VCIP.2017.8305127

Zhang, J., Du, J., & Dai, L. (2017). *A gru-based encoder-decoder approach with attention for online handwritten mathematical expression recognition.* Paper presented at the 2017 14th IAPR International Conference on Document Analysis and Recognition (ICDAR). 10.1109/ICDAR.2017.152

Zhang, J., Du, J., & Dai, L. J. I. T. o. M. (2018). *Track, attend, and parse (tap): An end-to-end framework for online handwritten mathematical expression recognition.* Academic Press.

Zhang, J., Li, Y., Li, T., Xun, L., & Shan, C. J. I. S. J. (2019). *License plate localization in unconstrained scenes using a two-stage CNN-RNN.* Academic Press.

Zhang, X.-Y., Yin, F., Zhang, Y.-M., Liu, C.-L., Bengio, Y. J. I. t. o. p. a., & Intelligence, M. (2017). *Drawing and recognizing chinese characters with recurrent neural network.* Academic Press.

Zhang, Y., & Huang, C. (2019). *A Robust Chinese License Plate Detection and Recognition Systemin Natural Scenes.* Paper presented at the 2019 IEEE 4th International Conference on Signal and Image Processing (ICSIP). 10.1109/SIPROCESS.2019.8868545

Zhao, N., Zhang, Z., Ouyang, X., Lv, N., & Zang, Z. (2018). *The recognition of RMB serial number based on CNN.* Paper presented at the 2018 Chinese Control And Decision Conference (CCDC). 10.1109/CCDC.2018.8407694

Zhou, X.-D., Wang, D.-H., Tian, F., Liu, C.-L., Nakagawa, M. J. I. t. o. p. a., & Intelligence, M. (2013). *Handwritten Chinese/Japanese text recognition using semi-Markov conditional random fields.* Academic Press.

Zhuang, H., Li, C., & Zhou, X. (2018). *CCRS: web service for Chinese character recognition.* Paper presented at the 2018 IEEE International Conference on Web Services (ICWS). 10.1109/ICWS.2018.00010

Zuo, L.-Q., Sun, H.-M., Mao, Q.-C., Qi, R., & Jia, R.-S. J. I. A. (2019). *Natural scene text recognition based on encoder-decoder framework.* Academic Press.

Chapter 13
Search–Based Classification for Offline Tifinagh Alphabets Recognition

Mohammed Erritali
iD https://orcid.org/0000-0002-1672-8085
Sultan Moulay Slimane University, Morocco

Youssef Chouni
iD https://orcid.org/0000-0002-4469-082X
Sultan Moulay Slimane University, Morocco

Youssef Ouadid
iD https://orcid.org/0000-0002-0493-5028
Sultan Moulay Slimane University, Morocco

ABSTRACT

The main difficulty in developing a successful optical character recognition (OCR) system lies in the confusion between the characters. In the case of Amazigh writing (Tifinagh alphabets), some characters have similarities based on rotation or scale. Most of the researchers attempted to solve this problem by combining multiple descriptors and / or classifiers which increased the recognition rate, but at the expense of processing time that becomes more prohibitive. Thus, reducing the confusion of characters and their recognition times is the major challenge of OCR systems. In this chapter, the authors present an off-line OCR system for Tifinagh characters.

1 INTRODUCTION

A large number of populations all over the world, especially in North Africa, speak Amazigh language. Since its normalization in 2001, efforts of research centers have manifested themselves in numerous and in-depth studies on the promotion of this alphabet and the widening of its scope. This has led to the

DOI: 10.4018/978-1-7998-4444-0.ch013

appearance of Amazigh documents written in Amazigh. From then on, the automatic processing and recognition of these documents became a very active field of research. Even though the OCR research is well advanced for Arabic, Latin and Chinese scripts, research on Amazigh scripts OCR s is still in the infancy stage. The goal is to elaborate a fast and accurate OCR to convert the text of such documents into a machine- readable representation easily reproducible by computers.

The main difficulty in developing an efficient OCR system is the confusion between characters. Indeed, the automatic recognition of characters consists in describing the content of the images automatically by features through an analysis of their visual content.

This analysis is confronted by: the noise produced during acquisition and the problem of shape variability that can come from scale and rotation changes. This accentuates the problem of intra-class variation and inter-class resemblance. This visual variation creates complicated relationships between character classes and their visual content, which leads to confusion between the characters and makes the recognition problem very difficult to solve. Most of the researchers attempted to solve this problem by combining multiple descriptors and / or classifiers which increased the recognition rate, but at the expense of processing time that becomes more prohibitive.

Oulamara et al. (Oulamara and Duvernoy, 1988) used the Hough transform to extract straight segments with their attributes (length and orientation). By analyzing the characters in the parametric space, a reading matrix is constructed containing the feature vectors of the reference images in the learning phase. Using a local database, the authors achieved interesting results. However, according to Djematene et al. (Djematen et al., 1998), this technique is not appropriate because the segmentation by the Hough transform does not produce a correct segmentation.

Ait Ouguengay et al. (Ait Ouguengay and Taalabi, 2009a) have proposed a recognition system based on multilayer artificial neural networks (RNA) with a single hidden layer to classify characteristic vectors composed of geometric properties (horizontal and vertical projections, centers of gravity in x and y, perimeter, area, compactness and central moments of order 2). Interesting results are obtained by testing the system on a local database.

Amrouch et al. (Amrouch et al., 2009) proposed an approach based on the extraction of directional information from the Hough transformation of each character in the form of a vector of observations. This information feeds a hidden Markov model (HMM). The results obtained are promising. However, the discrimination of these models is not very good because in the learning phase each character, according to the authors, is represented by a single reference image. To remedy this issue, Amrouch et al. (Amrouch et al., 2012) have replaced the Hough transform with a new technique to express a set of structural features from the contour of the character based on points that have maximum deviation. In the learning and classification phase, they combined dynamic programming with continuous HMMs. This approach has the advantage of being independent of the number of recognition classes (in terms of memory and speed) since the model is built for all classes. The results, which are quite encouraging, have shown that continuous HMMs are more robust. However, the disadvantages of this approach are the detection of the points that have the maximum deviation for the features extraction phase that seem restrictive for some fonts of the Amazigh writing.

In an attempt to solve orientation and size change problems, El Ayachi et al. (El Ayachi et al., 2014) compared two robust descriptors. These are the invariant moments and the transform of Walsh. The authors presented two systems containing the same preprocessing and classification techniques. Using dynamic programming in the classification phase, the authors concluded that the invariant moments are greater than the Walsh transform in terms of execution time and discrimination. In order to improve the recognition rate, El Ayachi et al. (Ayachi et al., 2011) have replaced the dynamic programming method with a single hidden layer neural network. The system gave a better recognition rate compared to dynamic programming and neural networks with 2 or 3 hidden layers. Recently, in (El Ayachi et al., 2014) the authors used their systems to display the braille code adapted to Tifinagh characters. The braille system is a system adopted to help blind and partially sighted people integrate into different areas of life.

Es Saady et al. (Es Saady et al., 2008) proposed a syntactical approach for the recognition of printed Tifinagh characters. This is done by representing the character images using Freeman coding. The classification is performed using the finite automata. An automaton is built from the specific automata of each image of the printed Tifinagh character. According to the authors, the tests carried out show the robustness of the system. However, the problem with this approach is that it does not deal with circular characters. To remedy this, the authors used the horizontal and vertical symmetry of the spelling of the Tifinagh alphabet. Indeed, the authors presented in (Es Saady et al., 2010) a system based on the position of the central lines of each character. The features are extracted based on the density of the pixels contained in a sliding window in the image of the character. According to the authors, this approach has proved its power of discrimination by testing it on a local database.

In order to complement the limits of the previous systems facing the problems of rotation and size change, Bencharef et al. (Bencharef et al., 2011) proposed an approach based on a geometric description using geodetic descriptors. These descriptors served as input to the hybrid classification process that combines neural networks and decision trees. The success of Bencharef's approach has motivated Oujaoura et al. to go in the same direction. In a first approach (Mustapha Oujaoura et al., 2013), the authors performed a comparison between the Walsh transform, GIST and texture using Bayesian networks as classifiers. The tests of these descriptors on a local database showed the superiority of the GIST method in terms of recognition rate and computation time. In a second approach (M. Oujaoura et al., 2013), the authors have proposed a system that combines Zernike moments, Legendre moments, Hu moments, Walsh and GIST transforms in the feature extraction phase; As well as the neuron networks, SVM and NN in the classification phase. The results obtained are excellent in terms of recognition rate. However, the system is quite slow in terms of computation time.

Table 1. The official directory of the alphabet Tifinagh- IRCAM with their correspondents in Latin characters

1	ya	ꙩ	12	yaḥ	ᴧ	23	yaṛ	Q
2	yab	⊖	13	yaԐ	ᕼ	24	yaɣ	Ԡ
3	yag	X	14	yax	X	25	yas	⊙
4	yagᵂ	Ẍ	15	yaq	ⵇ	26	yaṣ	Ø
5	yad	Λ	16	yi	Ɛ	27	yac	Ç
6	yaḍ	E	17	yaj	I	28	yat	†
7	yey	⁝	18	yal	‖	29	yaṭ	E
8	yaf	Ж	19	yam	⊏	30	yaw	Ц
9	yak	ⵗ	20	yan	I	31	yay	ⵚ
10	yakᵂ	ⵗ̈	21	yu	⁝	32	yaz	✳
11	yah	ⵁ	22	yar	O		yaẓ	✳

Authors developed an OCR system based on exact graph matching described by incidence matrices (Ouadid et al., 2014). Graphs are constructed using the key points, extracted from the skeletons of the different characters, by the neighborhood algorithm. Then, in order to improve the recognition rate of this system, in (Y. Ouadid et al., 2016) they adapted the thinning algorithm to their needs then they used Harris method to extract the key points. At the classification level, inexact graph matching is applied. It is based on a spectral approach that represent and distinguish the structural properties of graphs using the eigenvectors and eigenvalues of their adjacency matrices. The evaluation of the system thus carried out, using a database of printed characters (Ait Ouguengay and Taalabi, 2009b), highlighted the good performances of this system in terms of recognition rate and execution time.

Properties of Amazigh scripts Tifinagh alphabet is composed of 33 graphemes corresponding to the 33 phonemes of the standard Amazigh. The following table, presents these 33 characters as well as their Latin correspondents.

Amazigh script is written from left to right. Unlike Arabic and Latin language, it does not have the notion of uppercase and lowercase, nor that of pseudo-word. However, it includes the same punctuation marks as the Latin one. It is a non-cursive writing which facilitates the process of segmentation. This justifies the fact that most of the research done on this writing is focused on character recognition since existing works on the segmentation of Latin script documents are viable for that of the Amazigh.

As for the graphic models of characters, their shapes are composed of dots, small circles and straight segments. Indeed, we can divide these characters into three classes:

- Linear letters: ⵝ, ⵠ, ⴻ, ⵂ, ⵔ, ⵯ, ⵅ, ⴽ, ⵀ, ⵏ, ⵉ,

  ⵗ, ⵕ, ⵛ, ⴳ, ⵜ, ⴻ, ⵓ, ⵚ, ⵯ;

- Circular letters: ⵔ, ⴻ, ⵊ, ⵙ, ⵗ, ⵔ, ⵕ, ⵔ, ⵔ;
- Other: ⵙ, ⵅ, ⴳ.

Ignoring the criteria of the orientation and the size in the graphical models of the characters, some characters are similar such as: (ⴻ and ⵙ), (ⵛ and ⵓ), (ⵔ and ⵔ). It is important to note that most charactersare composed of a single connected component except for (ⵯ, ⵯ, ⵊ, ⵙ, ⵔ) alphabets.

The paper is structured as follows: section 1 gives a brief introduction about the offline character recognition domain. The architecture of the proposed system is introduced in section 2. The experiments and results obtained are presented in section 3. Finally, section 4 concludes the paper.

2 METHODOLOGY

The proposed system consists of three main phases: preprocessing, feature extraction and classification. The scanned image is first preprocessed to produce a clean version by removing as much unwanted information as possible. In the feature extraction, preprocessed image is divided into several segments using a proposed key point extraction algorithm. Then structural properties are represented by a feature vector containing segments properties and a graph representation using an incidence matrix. The incidence matrix of test images are compared with their counterpart in reference images. In case if the exact comparison output produces multiple classes, feature vector is then classified using normal distance criteria. The architecture of the proposed system is shown in figure 1.

2.1 Pre-processing

In order to reduce as much distortion as possible, the Otsu's global thresholding (Xu et al., 2011) is applied to the scanned image. Since the operations applied in the proposed system are structural and pixel type ones to the image are pixel type ones, the gap between image borders and the smallest rectangle containing the character is removed first.

Then, the character skeleton is extracted using Zhang- Suen thinning algorithm (Zhang and Suen, 1984). To ensure that no relevant information is removed after thinning, Zhang-Suen algorithm is applied to the 8- connected components of the image. This will allow us to keep all components composing the character such as the filled hole in yas character (☉) as shown in figure 2. The character skeleton is then smoothed by removing pixels that have differences between the numbers of foreground pixels and the number of transitions from a background pixel with a foreground pixel. This operation is applied in the 8-neighborhood of every foreground pixel in the image. Figure 3 show results of skeleton smoothing further details can be found in (Youssef Ouadid et al., 2016).

Figure 1. Proposed system architecture

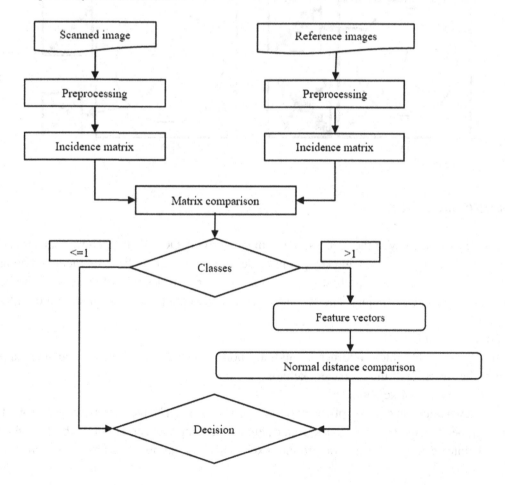

Figure 2. Thinning enhancement: (a) Zhang-Suen applied on the image, (b) Zhang-Suen applied to the 8-connected component of the image

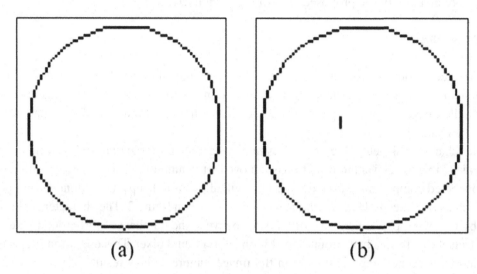

(a)   (b)

Figure 3. Skeleton smoothing: (a) Before smoothing, (b) After smoothing

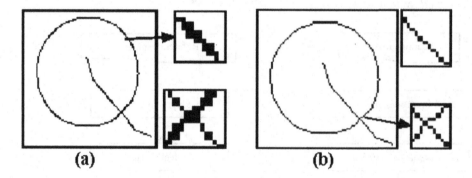

(a)   (b)

2.2 Feature extraction

Feature extraction is the key of the success rate of the underlying OCR system. Here, character skeleton is divided into several segments using key points as delimiters. Based on these segment and points sets, two feature sets are extracted. The first set is incidence matrix. It describes the relationship between extracted segments and key points. The second set is a vector containing the length and orientation of every segment.

Key points extraction

Key points (so-called interest/corner points), are point-like features where fast change happens in direction in the structure of the character skeleton.

There are two types of key points:

Primary key points that consists of end and intersection points. The end points are foreground pixels where the number of transitions (from background neighbor to foreground neighbor) in the 8-neighborhood is equal to 1. Intersection points are foreground pixels where the number of transitions is more than 2.

Secondary key points are points where the change of direction happens in the curved parts of character skeleton.

The proposed algorithm for the extraction of key points is well described in [14]. It is proceeded as follows:

a. Based on the skeleton of the character, extract primary key points;
b. Divide the skeleton into segments using primary key points as delimiters;
c. c. Check the level of curvature of every segment using the threshold k where (distance refers to Euclidian distance):

$$k = \text{segment length} / \text{distance between segment ends} \tag{1}$$

d. If the threshold is bigger than an emperically chosen value, then secondary key points is required;
e. If a secondary key point is required, then choose the pixel that have the biggest orthogonal distance from the straight line connecting segment ends as a key point;
f. Update key points list and repeat steps 1 to 5 till no secondary key point is required;

2.3 Incidence matrix

Incidence matrix is a way to define the graphical representation of the character. A graph is a formal mathematical representation of a set of objects and their relationships. Each object is called a vertex. Relationships between objects are called edges. More formally, we define a graph G as an ordered pair of G = (V, E) where V is a set of vertices, E is a set of edges and each edge is a pair of vertices.

Incidence matrix is fast and compact representation of a graph. It is a m × n matrix M where m is the number of nodes and n is the number of edges. The entry in row i and column j is non-zero, if and only if, the vertex i is incident at the edge j, which means:

$$M(i, j) = 1 \text{ si node i is incident to the edge j } \{M(i, j) = 0 \text{ else}} \tag{2}$$

In this work, the nodes represent key points and the edges represent segments linking these points in pairs.

2.4 Feature vector

As it is said earlier, the feature vector represents the orientation and length of every segment. Since the graphical representation deals with most of orientation problems, length is given more weight than the orientation as follow:

$$\text{segment feature} = 2 \times \text{Length} + \text{Orientation}$$

The size of the feature vector depends on the number of segments of the character.

2.5 Classification

In this phase, the resulting graphical representation of input images are compared with the reference images. In order to benefit from the representational potency of graphs and the reliability of statistical classification techniques in a timely manner, we propose a flexible hybrid classification based on matrix matching and Bayesian naïve classification. This hybridization is performed sequentially as indicated in Figure 1.

Alternatively, if the search results provide images with multiple classes, features vectors are compared using Euclidian distance and input image is affected to the closest class. The reason behind using such a simple way to classify is the fact that the number of observations is very small to build and compared to other classifier such as Naïve Bayes are almost the same. The algorithm is proceeded as follows:

a. **Input 1:** A cell array (2475x3) that contains required information (Incidence matrix, feature vector and class label (1 to 33)) for trainning dataset;

b. **Input 2:** A cell array (825x3) that contains required information (Incidence matrix, feature vector and Actual class label) for test dataset;

c. **Output:** 2D array (825x2) that represents actual and predicted classes.

d. **For** each incidence matrix of the test cell array is compared to all incidence matrices of trainning cell array;

e. Two incidence matrices are similar if they have the same size and the same values;

f. **If** a similar incidence matrix is found, its row coordinate is stored in an array; So its related informations such as class label and feature vector are accessible when needed;

g. Once the comparison is done. The number of class labels of similar incidence matrices are verified;

h. **If** all labels predicted the same class; then the actual class and predicted class are affected to the output array;

i. **Else if** the prediction gave several class labels; then their feature vectors are compared with test feature vector using Euclidian distance; the class label of the closest vector is designed as the predicted class;

j. **Else** if both options (h and i) are not available then the predicted class is zeros label defining a rejection case;

k. This steps are repeated till all elements of test dataset are processed.

3 RESULTS AND DISCUSSION

3.1 Experimentations Setup

Several experimentations have been conducted under a compatible Dell Precision 5520 with the following configuration:

- Quad core processor intel i7 6820hq 2.7 GHz;
- 16 Gb RAM DDR4;
- Implementation under MATLAB programing langage.

As said earlier, the threshold that allow us to divide the character skeleton is calculated empirically. Accuracy, All possible threshold within the interval [0.1,0.3].

3.2 Database

In order to evaluate the performance of the proposed system, A database provided by (Ait Ouguengay and Taalabi, 2009b) is used. It's composed of 3300 images; every alphabet is represented by 100 images with variable scale. Training dataset is composed of 2475 images and test dataset is composed of 825 images. A random selection is performed in the process of splitting database into training and test sets.

3.3 Classification Performance

After performing Feature Engineering, Extraction and getting output in the forms of a class, the next step is to see how effective is the classifier test dataset. In Machine Learning, there are several performance metrics to evaluate algorithms. The Confusion matrix (also know as the Contingency Table) is of simplest metrics used for determining the effectiveness of the classifier which record actual and predicted classes. Table 2 illustrates the Confusion Matrix of a binary classification and some performance measurements. The Contingency table in itself is not a performance metric as such, but almost all of the performance metrics are based on it and the numbers inside it. An example of metrics are Precision, Recall, Accuracy and F-measure which can be used for sorting algorithms primarily used by search engines.

Where:

$$\text{Precision} = \text{PPV} = \text{TP} / \text{TP} + \text{FN} \tag{3}$$

$$\text{Accuracy} = \text{TN} + \text{TP} / \text{TP} + \text{FP} + \text{FN} + \text{FP} \tag{4}$$

$$\text{Recall} = \text{Sensitivity} = \text{TP} / \text{TP} + \text{FP} \tag{5}$$

$$\text{Specificity} = \text{TN} / \text{TN} + \text{FP} \tag{6}$$

$$\text{F} - \text{measure} = 2 * \text{Precision} * \text{Recall} / \text{Precision} + \text{Recall} \tag{7}$$

Table 2. Confusion Matrix of a binary classification and some performance measurements

		Actual	
		Positives	**Negatives**
Predicted	Positives	True Positive (TP)	True Negative (TN)
	Negatives	False Negative (FN)	False Positive (FP)

Table 3. Classifier Performance metrics based on Threshold value 0.21

Metrics	Accuracy (%)	Precision (%)	F-measure (%)	Recall (%)	F-measure2 (%)	Test Time (s)
Results	99.967806	99.519425	99.9833557	99.510101	99.5099007	0.8882479

Figure 4. Contingency Table based on thresholds best value (Alphabets numbered from 1 to33)

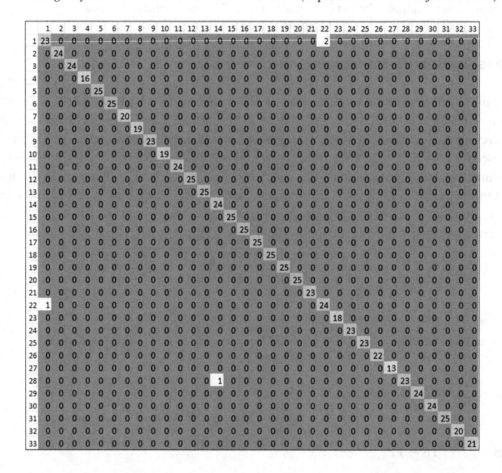

Figure 5. Accuracy measurement per threshold

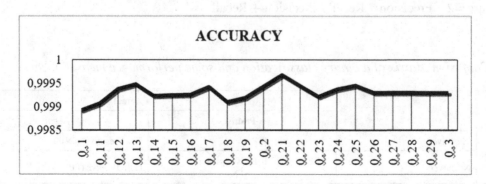

Figure 6. Precision measurement per threshold

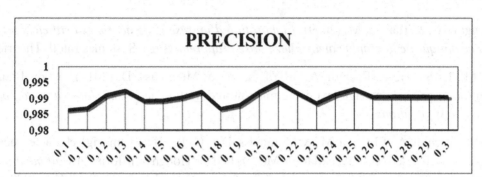

Figure 7. F-measure measurement per threshold

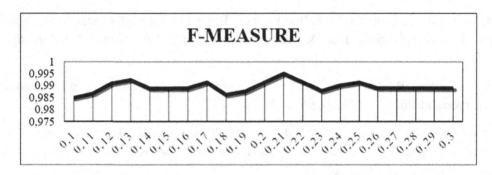

For the threshold of feature extraction process, we performed a series of runs by changing the threshold value starting from 0.1 till 0.3. The starting value is minimums value that produce a reasonable number of key points. As shown in figures 5-9 the value 0.21 produced the best results in term of Accuracy, Precision, Recall, Specificity and F-measure. Figure 4 illustrates contingency table based of the best value. Based on this value learning process of 3300 images is elapsed in 61 sec and an accuracy of 99.97% while 8.7% of images are reject in the search phase. Rejection can be minimized using an alternative classifier on rejected images. Tables presents the overall performance of the proposed system.

4 CONCLUSION

An effort is made to provide a fast and accurate Amazigh OCR system without relying on the parallel combination of multiple descriptors/classifiers. The idea is to use the simplest ways to achieve our goal. It consists on structural information in the form of incidence matrix, then a search of similar images is performed based on simple comparison between the graphical representation of input images and their counterpart in training dataset. Then alternatively, Euclidian distance is used to refine the search.

According to the analyzes, the proposed system gives good results in term confusion. Yet, due to the rejection rate the proposed system is far from perfection. In future work, refinement will be applied to this system in order to minimize rejection without affecting performance.

REFERENCES

Ait Ouguengay, Y., & Taalabi, M. (2009). *Elaboration d'un réseau de neurones artificiels pour la reconnaissance optique de la graphie amazighe: Phase d'apprentissage*. Systèmes Intell.-Théories Appl.

Amrouch, M., Es-Saady, Y., Rachidi, A., El-Yassa, M., & Mammass, D. (2012). A novel feature set for recognition of printed amazigh text using maximum deviation and hmm. *International Journal of Computers and Applications*, 44.

Amrouch, M., Rachidi, A., El Yassa, M., & Mammass, D. (2009). Printed amazigh character recognition by a hybrid approach based on Hidden Markov Models and the Hough transform. In *Multimedia Computing and Systems, 2009. ICMCS'09. International Conference On*. IEEE. 10.1109/MMCS.2009.5256672

Ayachi, R. E., Fakir, M., & Bouikhalene, B. (2011). Recognition of TIFINAGHE Characters Using A multilayer Neural Network. *Int. J. Image Process. IJIP*, *5*, 109.

Bencharef, O., Fakir, M., Minaoui, B., & Bouikhalene, B. (2011). Tifinagh Character Recognition Using Geodesic Distances, Decision Trees & Neural Networks. *Int. J. Adv. Comput. Sci. Appl. Spec. Issue Artif. Intell.*, 1–5.

Djematen, A., Taconet, B., & Zahour, A. (1998). Une méthode statistique pour la reconnaissance de caractères berbères manuscrits. *CIFED*, *98*, 170–178.

El Ayachi, R., Oujaoura, M., Fakir, M., & Minaoui, B. 2014. Code Braille et la reconnaissance d'un document écrit en Tifinagh. *Proceedings of the International Conference on Information and Communication Technologies for the Amazigh*.

Es Saady, Y., Rachidi, A., El Yassa, M., & Mammas, D. (2010). Printed Amazigh Character Recognition by a Syntactic Approach using Finite Automata. *Int. J. Graph. Vis. Image Process.*, *10*, 1–8.

Es Saady, Y., Rachidi, A., Elyassa, M., & Mammass, D. (2008). Une méthode syntaxique pour la reconnaissance de caractères Amazighes imprimés. *CARI'08*.

Ouadid, Y., Fakir, M., & Minaoui, B. (2016). Tifinagh Printed Character Recognition through Structural Feature Extraction. Int. J. Comput. Vis. Image Process. *IJCVIP*, *6*, 42–53.

Ouadid, Y., Minaoui, B., & Fakir, M. (2016). Spectral Graph Matching for Printed Tifinagh Character. *Computer Graphics, Imaging and Visualization (CGiV), 2016 13th International Conference On*, 105–111. 10.1109/CGiV.2016.29

Ouadid, Y., Minaoui, B., Fakir, M., & Abouelala, O. (2014). *New Approach of Tifinagh Character Recognition using Graph Matching*. Academic Press.

Oujaoura, M., Minaoui, B., & Fakir, M. (2013). Walsh, Texture and GIST Descriptors with Bayesian Networks for Recognition of Tifinagh Characters. *International Journal of Computers and Applications*, 81.

Oujaoura, M., El Ayachi, R., Minaoui, B., Fakir, M., Bouikhalene, B., & Bencharef, O. (2013). Invariant descriptors and classifiers combination for recognition of isolated printed Tifinagh characters. *Third International Symposium on Automatic Amazigh Processing (SITACAM'13)*. 10.14569/SpecialIssue.2013.030205

Oulamara, A., & Duvernoy, J. (1988). An application of the Hough transform to automatic recognition of Berber characters. *Signal Processing, 14*(1), 79–90. doi:10.1016/0165-1684(88)90045-X

Xu, X., Xu, S., Jin, L., & Song, E. (2011). Characteristic analysis of Otsu threshold and its applications. *Pattern Recognition Letters, 32*(7), 956–961. doi:10.1016/j.patrec.2011.01.021

Zhang, T. Y., & Suen, C. Y. (1984). A fast parallel algorithm for thinning digital patterns. *Communications of the ACM, 27*(3), 236–239. doi:10.1145/357994.358023

Chapter 14

A Perceptually Optimized Foveation Wavelet Visible Difference Predictor Quality Metric Based on Psychovisual Properties of the Human Visual System (HVS):
Region of Interest Image Coding Quality Visual Metric

Abderrahim Bajit

National School of Applied Sciences, Ibn Toufail University, Morocco

ABSTRACT

Region of interest (ROI) image and video compression techniques have been widely used in visual communication applications in an effort to deliver good quality images and videos at limited bandwidths. Foveated imaging exploits the fact that the spatial resolution of the human visual system (HVS) is highest around the point of fixation (foveation point) and decreases dramatically with increasing eccentricity. Exploiting this fact, the authors have developed an appropriate metric for the assessment of ROI coded images, adapted to foveation image coding based on psycho-visual quality optimization tools, which objectively enable us to assess the visual quality measurement with respect to the region of interest (ROI) of the human observer. The proposed metric yields a quality factor called foveation probability score (FPS) that correlates well with visual error perception and demonstrating very good perceptual quality evaluation.

DOI: 10.4018/978-1-7998-4444-0.ch014

1. INTRODUCTION

The foveated image compression algorithm is motivated because there are considerable high-frequency information redundancy in the peripheral regions, so much more efficient representation of images can be obtained by removing or reducing such information redundancy, based on the foveation point(s) and the viewing distances (Chang, 1998; Chang et al., 2000; Wang and Bovik, 2001; Wang and Bovik, 2001; Lee, et al., 2001). The first aim of that algorithm is foveation filtering, which foveate a uniform resolution image, such that when to get an eyeful at the point of fixation, we cannot distinguish between the original and the foveated versions of that image. In order to assess or compare image compression techniques, we need to reliably measure the quality of foveated images by taking into account the observer mean opinion score (MOS). Many mathematical metrics are simple functions of the analysed images and are often used such as mean squared error (MSE), the mean absolute error (MAE) and peak signal to noise ratio (PSNR). While these measures are simple to calculate and facilitate efficient mathematical optimization, but they often have a poor correlation with MOS and functions, that take advantage of properties of the human visual system (HVS) (Gaudart, et al., 1993), are often incorporated to improve their performance. Recently, techniques based on multiple channel models of the HVS have been shown to improve correlation to MOS (Larson and Chandler, 2010). From these HVS models it is possible to predict, on a pixel by pixel basis, if the noise introduced in the compressed image will be visible to a human observer. The Daly Visible Differences Predictor (VDP) (Daly, 1993) is one of perceptual image quality metrics attempt to quantify the errors in a way that simulates human visual error sensitivity features. The wavelet transform is one of the most powerful techniques for image decomposition, because of its similarities to the multiple channel models of the HVS. The DWT (Mallat, 2002; Cohen, et al., 1992) decomposes the image into a limited number of spatial frequency channels. Despite this limitation, the quality measure still a goal of the wavelet visible difference predictor (WVDP) (Bradley, 1999) to visually optimize image compression scheme.

Great success has been obtained recently by a class of wavelet image quality and fidelity assessor oriented region of interest (ROI), such as the foveation wavelet quality index FWQI proposed in (Wang and Bovik, 2001). This model is based on a foveation masking and distortion prediction with respect to traditional thresholds and a classical psychometric function. In the latter scheme the integration of interesting HVS features are not considered, like luminance and contrast masking or threshold elevation (Chandler and Hemami, 2005; Jia, et al., 2006; Liu, et al., 2006; Daly, et al., 2000), whose particular feature is to adapt spatially the image luminance and reshape unmasked frequencies to the human visual cortex. Exploiting this fact, we can adapt image contrast (luminance masking and contrast masking), to adapt masked frequencies with respect to the wavelet JND threshold and still assess efficiently the perceptual quality in the region of interest.

The proposed metric is the foveated Wavelet Visible Difference Predictor FWVDP. This model is based both on traditional psychometric function and the model Visible Difference Predictor (VDP). and integrates various psychovisual models (foveation, luminance and contrast masking). It plays an important role and demonstrates very good performance in foveation image coding quality assessment.

The subsection II-A presents the foveation masking setup. Adopted visual models in our algorithm are wavelet JND (wavelet just noticeable difference) thresholds developed in subsection II-B. The objective quality metrics is detailed in section III. Section IV presents the used experimental methods for subjective quality metric. In section V, obtained results are presented and discussed. The last section concludes.

Figure 1. Foveation Filter error sensitivity mask inthe DWT domain. The top-left, top-right, bottom left and bottom-right Figures: V = 1, 3, 6 and 10.

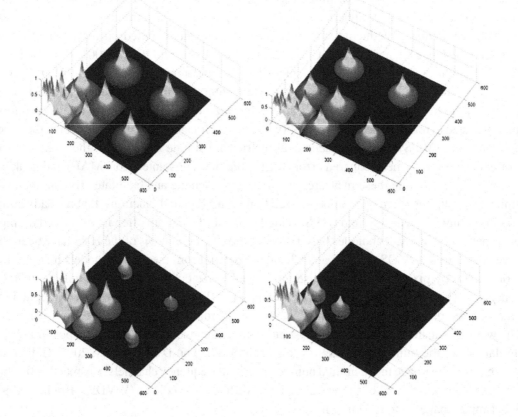

2. PSYCHOVISUAL TOOLS USED INTO THE METRICS

1.1. Foveation Masking SetUp

In this operation, we locate the foveation point to determine the foveation mask to weight the decomposed image; as a result frequencies around the region of interest will be either reduced or removed from the image spectrum (Chang, 1998; Chang et al., 2000). The borders foveation filtering shape determinates the region of interest in the DWT domain. This region with respect to DWT decomposition level and orientations limits the frequencies located around the fixation point that will be weighted by the filter mask. In first levels, a great amount of frequencies are removed, but approximately the whole low frequencies are taken into account in coding. The best parameters can be obtained in (Wang and Bovik, 2001; Lee, et al., 2001).

This foveation filter mask depends on many essential parameters like the display Nyquist and cut-off frequencies (Wang and Bovik, 2001). The first one expresses the visible frequencies towards the fixation region of interest; the second one shows the limits of visible frequencies without a display aliasing in the human visual cortex. The minimum of them determinates the final visible frequency spectrum in the area of interest. Other feature of the foveation filter is it's modification of the spectrum occupation depending on the viewing observation distance V. This shape eliminates progressively higher frequencies with observation distance increase as illustrate in Figure 1. As a result, observer is progressively unable to detect high frequencies in image when distance increases.

1.2. Wavelet Just Noticeable Difference Thresholds

The perceptual quantization is the operation used to quantize the foveation based wavelets coefficients in order to reduce the entropy manifested by the required bits budget to transmit the compressed image. Compression is achieved by quantization and entropy coding of the DWT coefficients. Typically, a uniform quantize (Chandler and Hemami, 2005) is used, implemented by division by a factor Q and rounding to the nearest integer. The factor Q may differ for different bands. Quantization of a single DWT coefficient in band will generate an artifact in the reconstructed image. A particular quantization factor in one band will result in coefficient errors in that band that are approximately uniformly distributed over the interval. The error image will be the sum of a lattice of basis functions with amplitudes proportional to the corresponding coefficient errors (Jia, et al., 2006).

Table 1. Contrast Sensitivity in DWT Domain for V = 4.

Orientation	DWT Decompostion Level				
	1	2	3	4	5
A	0.0859	0.1304	0.1613	0.1600	0.1226
H,D	0.0976	0.1311	0.1416	0.1148	0.0734
V	0.0904	0.1010	0.0895	0.0597	0.0280

Figure 2. Wavelet Error Sensitivity WES for viewing distance V = 4.

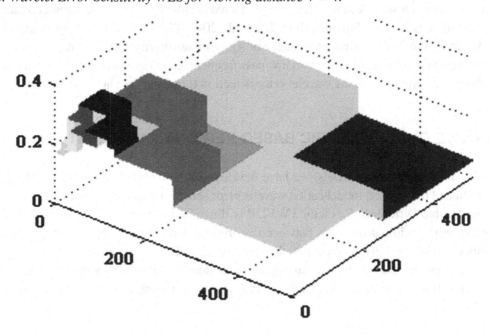

Figure 3. Detection thresholds for viewing distance V=4.

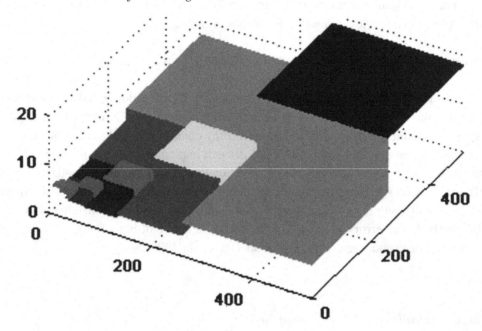

Thus, to predict the visibility of the error due to a particular quantization step, we must measure the visibility thresholds for individual basis function and error ensembles. The wavelet coefficients at different subbands and locations supply information of variable perceptual importance to the HVS. In order to develop a good wavelet-based image coding algorithm that considers HVS features, we need to measure the visual importance of the wavelet coefficients. Psychovisual experiments were conducted to measure the visual sensitivity in wavelet decompositions. Noise was added to the wavelet coefficients of a blank image with uniform mid-gray level. After the inverse wavelet transform, the noise threshold in the spatial domain was tested. A model that provided a reasonable fit to the experimental data is shown in Table 1 and ((Chandler and Hemami, 2005; Jia, et al., 2006; Liu, et al., 2006; Daly, et al., 2000).

As shown in Figure 2 (for a viewing distance of 4), error sensitivity increases rapidly with wavelet spatial frequency, and with orientation from low pass frequencies to horizontal/vertical to diagonal orientations. Its reverse form yields the wavelet error detection thresholds as shown in Figure 3.

3. OBJECTIVE QUALITY METRIC BASED REGION OF INTEREST

Based on the multiple channel models, we have developed a new objective metric based on wavelet decomposition and the Watson model called wavelet error sensitivity model. This metric called Foveation Wavelet Visible Difference Predictor FWVDP is illustrated in Figure 4. The FWVDP is used in this paper to predict visible differences between the original and degraded images with respect to the detect ability of errors for a given perceptual threshold of the WES model within each wavelet channel. For each wavelet coefficient within all channels and error detection probability is then computed based on psychometric function (Robson and Graham, 1981), and then using a Minkowski summation of all error probabilities from low to high frequencies we obtain a visible difference map VDM, which yields a quality measure scale called the foveation probability scale FPS.

In addition to the block called "Foveated Point and ROI Setup" which operates for configuring perceptual models of region of interest from the fixed point (Xf, Yf) on the foveated image and the block called "Wavelet JND Thresholds" cited previously in section II, the FWVDP model is based also on the critical block called "Threshold elevation". In the latter, we alter the amount of masking in each frequency level of the decomposition. This is necessary in the case of the critically sampled wavelet transform to reflect the fact that coefficients at higher levels in the decomposition represent increasingly larger spatial areas and therefore have a reduced masking effect. Typical values for a 5 level decomposition are b(f) = [4; 2; 1; 0:5; 0:25] for decomposition levels 1; 2; 3; 4; 5 respectively. In addition, there is a factor of two difference in the masking effect for positive and negative coefficients, i.e., bneg = 2:bpos . This allows the model to account for the fact that masking is more reliable on the dark side of edges, i.e., for negative coefficients (Wang and Bovik, 2001). The alteration routine, for the original image for example, respects the following law (Equation 1):

$$Alter(\lambda, \theta, i, j) = \begin{cases} b(f) \cdot C_{\lambda,\theta,i,j} & if\ C_{\lambda,\theta,i,j} > 0, \\ 2b(f) \left\| C_{\lambda,\theta,i,j} \right\| & if\ C_{\lambda,\theta,i,j} < 0. \end{cases} \tag{1}$$

Then, the threshold elevation t(_; _; i; j) express the wavelet coefficient ratios against the contrast mean Vmean (128 for 8 bits gray level image), which depends on the image size. This parameter is given by the following expression (Equation 2). C are the coefficients in the DWT domain.

$$t(\lambda, \theta, i, j) = \left| \frac{C(\lambda, \theta, i, j)}{V_{mean}} \right|^{aT} \tag{2}$$

It adjusted by the factor at which determines the masking phenomenon. Ahumada and Peterson (1992) suggest taking the value 0:649.

The threshold elevations T (Equation 3) and b T are calculated as follows:

$$T_{(\lambda,\theta,i,j)} = \max(JND_{(\lambda,\theta,i,j)}, Alter_{(\lambda,\theta,i,j)} \tag{3}$$

Where $JND_{(\lambda,\theta,i,j)} = \dfrac{1}{t_{(\lambda,\theta,i,j)}}$

The mutual masking Mm is the minimum of the two threshold elevations and respects the following relation (Equation 4):

$$\tag{4}$$

An improved psychometric function (Equation 3) is then applied to estimate the error detection probabilities for each wavelet coefficient and convert these differences, as a ratio of the wavelet JND thresholds, to sub-band detection probabilities.

This factor means the ability of detecting a distortion in a subband (_; _) at location (i; j) in the DWT field. The Equation 5 express this probability.

$$M_m(\lambda, \theta, i, j) = \min(T_{(\lambda,\theta,i,j)}, \hat{T}_{(\lambda,\theta,i,j)}) \tag{5}$$

where

- The errors D(_;_;i;j) = C(_;_;i;j) b C(_;_;i;j) denote the distortion at location decomposition (_; _; i; j);

  -The ROI(_;_;i;j) denotes the DWT region of interest with respect to the fixation point;
  -The parameter _ is chosen to maximize the correspondence of the DWT probability error FPb(_;_;i;j) and the probability summation (Robson and Graham, 1981);
  -The decision threshold _ is estimated between 1 and 1:5 (Robson and Graham, 1981). In this paper, we use _=2 and _=1.06.

The output of the model FWVDP is a probability map, i.e.,the detection probability at each pixel in the image. Therefore, the probability of detection in each of the sub-bands (channels) must be combined for every spatial location in the image. This is done using a product series (Daly, 1993; Bradley, 1999). This map called the "Visible Difference Map" VDM is given by the following algorithm as illustrated by Equation 6.

$$FPb_{(\lambda,\theta,i,j)} = 1 - \exp\left(-\left|\frac{ROI_{(\lambda,\theta,i,j)} \cdot D_{(\lambda,\theta,i,j)}}{\left(M_m(\lambda,\theta,i,j)\right)^{\alpha}}\right|^{\beta}\right) \tag{6}$$

Finally, to confirm the subjective quality ordering of the images we also defined a simple score FPS for the MXN image size as calculated by Equation 7.

$$VDM = FPd_{(\lambda,\theta,i,j)} = 1 - \prod_b \left(1 - FPb_{(\lambda,\theta,i,j)}\right) \tag{7}$$

Note that the FPS values vary between 0 and 1 included.

4. SUBJECTIVE QUALITY METRIC

4.1. Conditions of Subjective Quality Evaluation

The subjective quality evaluation is normalized by the recommendations of the CCIR (1982). However, these recommendations are designed, originally, for the television image without taking into account the measure of the degradations with the original image.

Our purpose is to measure the distortions between two images instead of the quality of a single image by adopting the tests of comparative measures: We suppose furthermore that the images can be edited, zoomed and observed at the lowest possible distance. Therefore, we refer to the conditions of evaluation which were used by Fr'anti where the recommendations of the CCIR are partially respected in Table 2.

The room of evaluation is normalized in order to make tests without introducing errors relative to the study environment. All the light sources, other than those used for the lighting of the room are avoided because they degrade significantly the image quality. The screen is positioned so that no light source as, a lamp or a window, affects directly the observer's vision field, or causes reflections on the some surfaces on the screen. The subjective measure serves only, in our study, to estimate the objective measures in terms of the coefficient of correlation which will be described in the following paragraph.

Table 2. Conditions of Subjective Quality Evaluation

Image Quality	Photographic Images
Observation Conditions	Environment of Normal Desk
Viewing Distance V	In the free Appreciation of the Observer
Observation Duration	Unlimited
Number of Observers	Between 15 and 39
Scale	The MOS Scale Interval (between 0 and 10)

4.2. The Objective Measure Correlation Coefficients

To determine the objective measure correlation (noted by the vector X) with the subjective measure (noted by the observation vector Y), we use the correlation coefficient which is defined by the following Equation 8:

$$FPS = \frac{1}{MN} \sum_{i,j}^{M,N} FPd_{(\lambda,\theta,i,j)} \tag{8}$$

where Xi and Yi, i = 1 to n, are respectively, the components of vectors X and Y . n represents the number of values used in the measure. X and Y represent, respectively, values average of vectors X and Y, given according to the following formula 9:

$$p(X,Y) = \frac{\sum_{i=1}^{n}(X_i - \bar{X})(Y_i - \bar{Y})}{\sqrt{\sum_{i=1}^{n}(X_i - \bar{X})^2}\sqrt{\sum_{i=1}^{n}(Y_i - \bar{Y})^2}} \tag{9}$$

We agree to associate the variance value determined by the relation 10 with every MOS average.

$$\bar{X} = \frac{1}{n}\sum_{i=1}^{n}X_i \tag{10}$$

5. EXPERIMENTAL RESULTS AND DISCUSSION

The test images are shown on a screen CRT of PC, with 10.5 cm x 10.5 cm (512 X 512 pixels images) (Jia, et al., 2006; Liu, et al., 2006). The MOS scale extends from 0 to 10 (2: very annoying degradation, 4: annoying, 6: a little bit annoying, 8: perceptible, but not annoying, 10: Imperceptible). We also tuned the possibility to the observers to give notes by half-values. To calculate the final subjective measure of a foveated image, we determine the average of notes given by the observers. If the correlation is used through a single type of image, n will take the value 8 (POEFIC 512 X 512 coded images at 0.0078125, 0.015625, 0.03125, 0.0625, 0.125, 0.25, 0.5 and 1 bpp). If the correlation is used through all the types of image, n will take the value of the total number of images (16 POEFIC 512X512 coded images). Figure 4 presents the foveated "Zelda" and "Mandrill" images at (Xf, Yf)=(280,280) and (253,60) respectively. Note that the observer specifies the Region Of Interest ROI on the image and assumes the viewing distance which equal V times screen height.

Figure 4. Foveated (Region Of Interest) "Zelda" and "Mandrill" test images.

In Figures 5 and 6, we plot the MOS subjective measures vs the FPS objective measures for the foveated POEFIC (Bajit, et al., 2007) images at observation viewing distance V=4. Let observe that the evolution of the FPS factors is quasi-linear according to that of the MOS observer notes. Finally, the

Figure 5. MOS subjective measures vs FPS objective measures for POEFIC coded "Zelda" images at 0.0078125, 0.015625, 0.03125, 0.0625, 0.125, 0.25, 0.5 and 1 bpp; viewing distance V = 4; 24 observers.

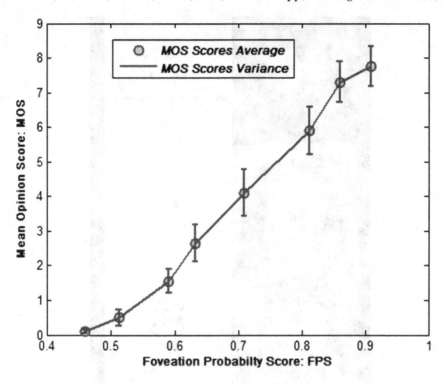

Figure 6. MOS subjective measures vs FPS objective measures for POEFIC coded "Mandrill" images at 0.0078125, 0.015625, 0.03125, 0.0625, 0.125, 0.25, 0.5 and 1 bpp; viewing distance V = 4; 24 observers.

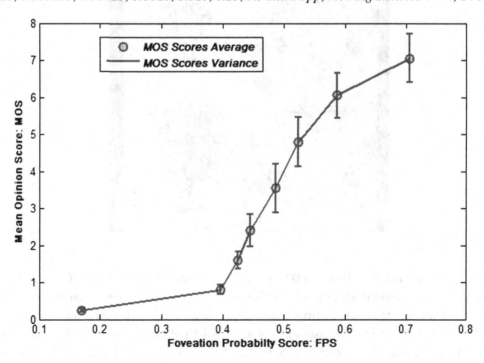

Figure 7. POEFIC Compressed "Mandrill" Images (left column) at 0.0078125, 0.015625, 0.03125, 0.0625, 0.125 bpp and IFA Maps (right column) for observation distance V = 4.

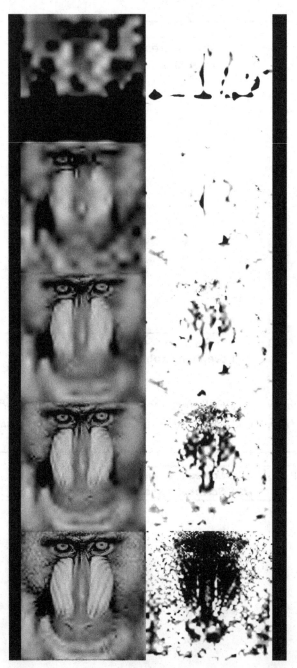

correlation coefficients reach 0:9948 and 0:9179 through 8 images coded POEFIC coder for "Zelda" and "Mandrill" images respectively; by the FWVDP metric. Its reach 0:8199 through 16 images.

Figures 7 and 8 show the spatial errors maps (differences between original and foveated images) namely called IFA (Image Fidelity Assessor) given by FWVDP model for POEFIC coded images at 0.0078125, 0.015625, 0.03125, 0.0625, 0.125, 0.25, 0.5 and 1 bpp. Note that if the IFA map is totally

Figure 8. POEFIC compressed "Mandrill" Images (left column) at 0.25, 0.5 and 1 bpp and IFA Maps (right column) for observation distance V = 4.

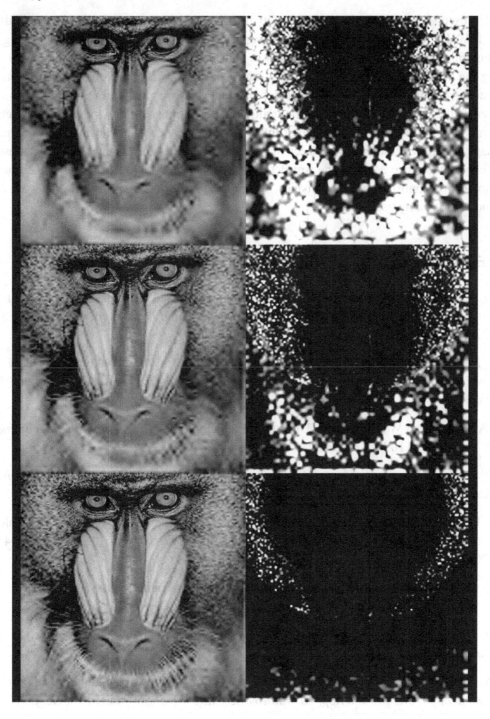

black, i.e it is no difference between original and foveated images. The IFA maps follow the image nature, and represent faithfully the visible error structures. Generally, the FWVDP metric predicts more or less the same perceived quality evaluation.

6. CONCLUSION

This work presents a new method of image quality metric called Foveation Wavelet Visible Differences Predictor FWVDP which has demonstrated the superiority for image assessment by proving its best correlation with the Mean Opinion Score MOS in consideration to other models commonly used for evaluating the image perceived distortions. This metric exploits a various Human Visual System HVS model to achieve the aim of improving the perceptual quality assessment for the foveated reconstructed images versus the measures obtained by the traditional algorithms. simply apply for this metric, two parameters as inputs that are 1) the Region of Interest on image and 2) the viewing distance, regardless of the image coding type, so that it provides maps of spatial errors IFA (Image Fidelity Assessor) and VDM (Visible Difference Map) in the wavelet domain. Indeed, the proposed quality measure shows to perform well on almost all foveated images. We are also exploring extensions of this work for color images and video quality assessment.

REFERENCES

Ahumada, A. J., & Peterson, H. A. (1992). Luminance-model-based DCT quantization for color image compression, *Proc. SPIE on Human Vision, Visual Processing and Digital Display III*, 1666, 365-374. 10.1117/12.135982

Bajit, A., Nahid, M., Tamtaoui, A., & Bouyakhf, E. H. (2007). A Perceptually Optimized Foveation based Wavelet Embedded Zerotree Image Coding. *International Journal of Computational Science*, 2(4), 229–234.

Bradley, A. P. (1999). A Wavelet Visible Difference Predictor. *IEEE Transactions on Image Processing*, 8(5), 717–730. doi:10.1109/83.760338 PMID:18267486

CCIR. (1982). *Method for the Subjective Assessment of the Quality of Television Picture, Recommendations et Rapports du CCIR. Rec.* Genve.

Chandler, D. M., & Hemami, S. S. (2005). Dynamic contrast-based quantization for lossy wavelet image compression. *IEEE Transactions on Image Processing*, 14(4), 397–410. doi:10.1109/TIP.2004.841196 PMID:15825476

Chang, E. C. (1998). *Foveation techniques and scheduling issues in thin wire visualization* (Ph.D. dissertation). New York Univ.

Chang, E. C., Mallat, S., & Yap, C. (2000). *Wavelet Foveation.* Available: http://www.comp.nus.edu.sg/ changec/publications/

Cohen, A., Daubechies, I., & Feauveau, J. C. (1992). Biorthogonal bases of compactly supported wavelets. *Communications on Pure and Applied Mathematics*, 45(5), 485–560. doi:10.1002/cpa.3160450502

Daly, S. (1993). The visible differences predictor: An algorithm for the assessment of image fidelity. In *Digital Images and Human Vision* (pp. 179–205). MIT Press.

Daly, S., Zeng, W., Li, J., & Lei, S. (2000). Visual masking in wavelet compression for JPEG 2000. *Proceedings of IS&T/SPIE Conference on Image, Video Communications and Processing, 3974.*

Gaudart, L., Grebassa, T., & Petrakian, J. P. (1993). Wavelet transform in human visual channels. *Applied Optics, 32*(22), 4119–4127. doi:10.1364/AO.32.004119 PMID:20830054

Jia, V., Lin, W., & Kassim, A. A. (2006). Estimating Just-Noticeable Distortion for Video. *IEEE Transactions on Circuits and Systems for Video Technology, 16*(7), 820–829. doi:10.1109/TCSVT.2006.877397

Larson, E. C., & Chandler, D. M. (2010). Most apparent distortion: Full-reference image quality assessment and the role of strategy. *Journal of Electronic Imaging, 19*(1), 011006. doi:10.1117/1.3267105

Lee, S., Pattichis, M. S., & Bovik, A. C. (2001). Foveated video compression with optimal rate control. *IEEE Transactions on Image Processing, 10*(7), 977–992. doi:10.1109/83.931092 PMID:18249671

Liu, Z., Karam, L. J., & Watson, A. B. (2006). JPEG2000 Encoding With Perceptual Distortion Control. *IEEE Transactions on Image Processing, 15*(7).

Mallat, S. (2002). A wavelet Tour of Signal and Image Processing (Edition 2002). Academic Press.

Robson, J. G., & Graham, N. (1981). Probability summation and regional variation in contrast sensitivity across the visual field. *Vision Research, 21*(3), 409–418. doi:10.1016/0042-6989(81)90169-3 PMID:7269319

Wang, Z., & Bovik, A. C. (2001). Embedded Foveation Image Coding. *IEEE Transactions on Image Processing, 10*(10). PMID:18255485

Wang, Z., Lu, L., & Bovik, A. C. (2003). Foveation Scalable Video Coding with Automatic Fixation Selection. *IEEE Transactions on Image Processing, 12*(2). PMID:18237905

282

Compilation of References

Abbas, S., Hussain, M., & Irshad, M. (2017). Trigonometric spline for medical image interpolation. *Journal of the National Science Foundation of Sri Lanka, 45*(1), 33. doi:10.4038/jnsfsr.v45i1.8036

Abdullah, S., Hasan, M. M., & Islam, S. M. S. (2018). *YOLO-Based Three-Stage Network for Bangla License Plate Recognition in Dhaka Metropolitan City.* Paper presented at the 2018 International Conference on Bangla Speech and Language Processing (ICBSLP). 10.1109/ICBSLP.2018.8554668

Abe, K., Morii, R., Nishida, K., & Kadonaga, T. (1993). Comparison of Methods for Detecting Corner Points From Digital Curves—A Preliminary Report. In *Proceedings of International Conference on Document Analysis and Recognition.* Tsukuba Science City, Japan: IEEE. 10.1109/ICDAR.1993.395603

Ahn, B., Ryu, J., Koo, H. I., Cho, N. I. J. E. J. o. I., & Processing, V. (2017). *Textline detection in degraded historical document images.* Academic Press.

Ahumada, A. J., & Peterson, H. A. (1992). Luminance-model-based DCT quantization for color image compression, *Proc. SPIE on Human Vision, Visual Processing and Digital Display III*, 1666, 365-374. 10.1117/12.135982

Aigner, W., Miksch, S., Schumann, H., & Tominski, C. (2011). *Visualization of Time-Oriented Data.* Springer. doi:10.1007/978-0-85729-079-3

Ait Ouguengay, Y., & Taalabi, M. (2009). *Elaboration d'un réseau de neurones artificiels pour la reconnaissance optique de la graphie amazighe: Phase d'apprentissage.* Systèmes Intell.-Théories Appl.

Alam, J., Hassan, M., Khan, A., & Chaudhry, A. (2015). Robust fuzzy RBF network based image segmentation and intelligent decision making system for carotid artery ultrasound images. *Neurocomputing, 151*, 745–755. doi:10.1016/j.neucom.2014.10.027

Ali, A., Pickering, M., & Shafi, K. (2018). *Urdu natural scene character recognition using convolutional neural networks.* Paper presented at the 2018 IEEE 2nd international workshop on Arabic and derived script analysis and recognition (ASAR). 10.1109/ASAR.2018.8480202

Aliabadian, A. (2013). A Robust Clustering Approach Based on KNN and Modified C-Means Algorithm. *World Applied Sciences Journal, 25*(4), 585–591.

Alizadehashraf, B., & Roohi, S. (2017). *Persian handwritten character recognition using convolutional neural network.* Paper presented at the 2017 10th Iranian Conference on Machine Vision and Image Processing (MVIP). 10.1109/IranianMVIP.2017.8342359

Al-masni, M. A., Al-antari, M. A., Park, J. M., Gi, G., Kim, T. Y., Rivera, P., Valarezo, E., Choi, M.-T., Han, S.-M., & Kim, T. S. (2018). Simultaneous detection and classification of breast masses in digital mammograms via a deep learning YOLO-based CAD system. *Computer Methods and Programs in Biomedicine*, *157*, 85–94. doi:10.1016/j.cmpb.2018.01.017 PMID:29477437

Alotaibi, F., Abdullah, M. T., Abdullah, R. B. H., Rahmat, R. W. B. O., Hashem, I. A. T., & Sangaiah, A. K. J. I. A. (2017). *Optical character recognition for quranic image similarity matching*. Academic Press.

Al-Zubi, S., Brömme, A., & Tönnies, K. (2003). Using an active shape structural model for biometric sketch recognition. In *Joint Pattern Recognition Symposium* (pp. 187-195). Springer Berlin Heidelberg. 10.1007/978-3-540-45243-0_25

Amrouch, M., Rachidi, A., El Yassa, M., & Mammass, D. (2009). Printed amazigh character recognition by a hybrid approach based on Hidden Markov Models and the Hough transform. In *Multimedia Computing and Systems, 2009. ICMCS'09. International Conference On*. IEEE. 10.1109/MMCS.2009.5256672

Amrouch, M., Es-Saady, Y., Rachidi, A., El-Yassa, M., & Mammass, D. (2012). A novel feature set for recognition of printed amazigh text using maximum deviation and hmm. *International Journal of Computers and Applications*, 44.

Andrienko, G. L., Andrienko, N. V., Budziak, G., von Landesberger, T., & Weber, H. (2018). Exploring pressure in football. *Proceedings of the 2018 International Conference on Advanced Visual Interfaces, AVI*, 54:1–54:3.

Ardianto, S., Chen, C.-J., & Hang, H.-M. (2017). Real-time traffic sign recognition using color segmentation and SVM. *International Conference on Systems, Signals and Image Processing (IWSSIP)*, 1-5. 10.1109/IWSSIP.2017.7965570

Argamon, S., Šarić, M., & Stein, S. S. (2003). Style mining of electronic messages for multiple authorship discrimination: first results. In *Proceedings of the Ninth ACM SIGKDD International Conference on Knowledge Discovery and Data Mining* (pp. 475-480). ACM. 10.1145/956750.956805

Arumugadevi, S., & Seenivasagam, V. (2015). Comparison of clustering methods for segmenting color images. *Indian Journal of Science and Technology*, *8*(7), 670–677. doi:10.17485/ijst/2015/v8i7/62862

Asada, H., & Brady, M. (1986). The curvature primal sketch. *IEEE Transactions on Pattern Analysis and Machine Intelligence*, *8*(1), 2–4. doi:10.1109/TPAMI.1986.4767747 PMID:21869318

Asuni, N., & Giachetti, A. (2014). Testimage: a large-scale archive for testing visual devices and basic image processing algorithms. *STAG: Smart Tools & Apps for Graphics*.

Athanasiou, L. S., Karvelis, P. S., Tsakanikas, V. D., Naka, K. K., Michalis, L. K., Bourantas, C. V., & Fotiadis, D. I. (2012). A Novel Semiautomated Atherosclerotic Plaque Characterization Method Using Grayscale Intravascular Ultrasound Images: Comparison With Virtual Histology. *IEEE Transactions on Information Technology in Biomedicine*, *16*(3), 391–400. doi:10.1109/TITB.2011.2181529 PMID:22203721

Attneave, F. (1954). Some Informational Aspects of Visual Perception. *Psychological Review*, *61*(3), 183–193. doi:10.1037/h0054663 PMID:13167245

Ayachi, R. E., Fakir, M., & Bouikhalene, B. (2011). Recognition of TIFINAGHE Characters Using A multilayer Neural Network. *Int. J. Image Process. IJIP*, *5*, 109.

Azam, S., & Gavrilova, M. (2017). Person identification using discriminative visual aesthetic. In *Canadian Conference on Artificial Intelligence* (pp. 15-26). Springer.

Bai, X., Yao, C., & Liu, W. J. I. T. o. I. P. (2016). *Strokelets: A learned multi-scale mid-level representation for scene text recognition*. Academic Press.

Bajit, A., Nahid, M., Tamtaoui, A., & Bouyakhf, E. H. (2007). A Perceptually Optimized Foveation based Wavelet Embedded Zerotree Image Coding. *International Journal of Computational Science*, 2(4), 229–234.

Bakelman, N., Monaco, J. V., Cha, S. H., & Tappert, C. C. (2013). Keystroke biometric studies on password and numeric keypad input. In *Proceedings of Intelligence and Security Informatics Conference (EISIC)* (pp. 204-207). IEEE. 10.1109/EISIC.2013.45

Balafar, M. (2011). Spatial based expectation maximizing (EM). *Diagnostic Pathology*, 6(1), 103. doi:10.1186/1746-1596-6-103 PubMed

Ball, G. H., & Hall, D. J. (1965). *ISODATA, a novel method of data analysis and pattern classification*. Academic Press.

Banerjee, B., Bhattacharjee, T., & Chowdhury, N. (2010). Color Image Segmentation Technique Using "Natural Grouping" of Pixels. *International Journal of Image Processing*, 4(4), 320–328.

Bazazian, S., & Gavrilova, M. (2015). A hybrid method for context-based gait recognition based on behavioral and social traits. In M. Gavrilova, C. Tan, K. Saeed, N. Chaki, & S. Shaikh (Eds.), *Transactions on Computational Science XXV* (Vol. 9030, pp. 115–134). Springer. doi:10.1007/978-3-662-47074-9_7

Belay, B. H., Habtegebrial, T. A., & Stricker, D. (2018). *Amharic character image recognition*. Paper presented at the 2018 IEEE 18th International Conference on Communication Technology (ICCT). 10.1109/ICCT.2018.8599888

Benaichouche, A., Oulhadj, H., & Siarry, P. (2013). Improved spatial fuzzy c-means clustering for image segmentation using PSO initialization, Mahalanobis distance and post-segmentation correction. *Digital Signal Processing*, 23(5), 1390–1400. doi:10.1016/j.dsp.2013.07.005

Bencharef, O., Fakir, M., Minaoui, B., & Bouikhalene, B. (2011). Tifinagh Character Recognition Using Geodesic Distances, Decision Trees & Neural Networks. *Int. J. Adv. Comput. Sci. Appl. Spec. Issue Artif. Intell.*, 1–5.

Benezeth, Y., Jodoin, P.-M., Emile, B., & Rosenberger, C. (2010). Comparative study of background subtraction algorithms. *Journal of Electronic Imaging*, 19(3).

Bertalmio, M., Caselles, V., & Provenzi, E. (2009). Issues about retinex theory and contrast enhancement. *International Journal of Computer Vision*, 83(01), 101–119. doi:10.100711263-009-0221-5

Bertin, E., & Arnouts, S. (1996). SExtractor: Software for source extraction. *Astronomy & Astrophysics. Supplement Series*, 117(2), 393–404. doi:10.1051/aas:1996164

Beus, H. L., & Tiu, S. S. H. (1987). An Improved Corner Detection Algorithm based on Chain Coded Plane Curves. *Pattern Recognition*, 20(3), 291–296. doi:10.1016/0031-3203(87)90004-5

Bharath, A., Madhvanath, S. J. I. t. o. p. a., & Intelligence, m. (2011). *HMM-based lexicon-driven and lexicon-free word recognition for online handwritten Indic scripts*. Academic Press.

Bingley, F. (1957). *Color vision and colorimetry*. McGraw Hill.

Bipu, M. M. C., & Afroge, S. (2018). *A feature fusion based approach for handwritten Bangla character recognition using extreme learning machine*. Paper presented at the 2018 International Conference on Computer, Communication, Chemical, Material and Electronic Engineering (IC4ME2).

Bluche, T., Kermorvant, C., Touzet, C., & Glotin, H. (2017). *Cortical-Inspired Open-Bigram Representation for Handwritten Word Recognition*. Paper presented at the 2017 14th IAPR International Conference on Document Analysis and Recognition (ICDAR). 10.1109/ICDAR.2017.21

Bo, C., Zhang, L., Li, X. Y., Huang, Q., & Wang, Y. (2013). SilentSense: Silent user identification via touch and movement behavioral biometrics. In *Proceedings of the 19th Annual International Conference on Mobile Computing & Networking* (pp. 187-190). ACM. 10.1145/2500423.2504572

Bora, V. B., Kothari, A. G., & Keskar, A. G. (2016). Robust Automatic Pectoral Muscle Segmentation from Mammograms Using Texture Gradient and Euclidean Distance Regression. *Journal of Digital Imaging*, 29(1), 115–125. doi:10.1007/s10278-015-9813-5 PubMed

Boucher, A., Jouve, P., Cloppet, F., & Vincent, N. (2009). Segmentation du muscle pectoral sur une mammographie. ORASIS'09 - Congrès des jeunes chercheurs en vision par ordinateur, 2009, Trégastel, France. https://hal.inria.fr/inria-00404631/document

Bours, P. (2012). Continuous keystroke dynamics: A different perspective towards biometric evaluation. *Information Security Technical Report*, 17(1), 36–43. doi:10.1016/j.istr.2012.02.001

Bouti, V., Mahraz, M. A., Riffi, J., & Tairi, V. (2017). Robust system for road sign detection and recognition using template matching. *2017 Intelligent Systems and Computer Vision (ISCV)*, 1-4. doi:10.1109/ISACV.2017.8054966

Bradley, A. P. (1999). A Wavelet Visible Difference Predictor. *IEEE Transactions on Image Processing*, 8(5), 717–730. doi:10.1109/83.760338 PMID:18267486

Bretzner, L., & Lindeberg, T. (1998). Feature tracking with automatic selection of spatial scales. *Computer Vision and Image Understanding*, 71(3), 385–392. doi:10.1006/cviu.1998.0650

Briggs, K. C., & Myers, I. B. (2017). *Myers–Briggs Type Indicator (MBTI) Myers-Briggs Personality Type* [Dataset]. https://www.kaggle.com/datasnaek/mbti-type

Brkić, K., Šegvić, S., Kalafatić, Z., Sikirić, I., & Pinz, A. (2010). Generative modeling of spatio-temporal traffic sign trajectories. *2010 IEEE Computer Society Conference on Computer Vision and Pattern Recognition - Workshops*, 25-31. 10.1109/CVPRW.2010.5543888

Bulan, O., Kozitsky, V., Ramesh, P., & Shreve, M. J. I. T. o. I. T. S. (2017). *Segmentation-and annotation-free license plate recognition with deep localization and failure identification*. Academic Press.

Burch, M., & Weiskopf, D. (2011). Visualizing dynamic quantitative data in hierarchies - TimeEdgeTrees: Attaching dynamic weights to tree edges. *IMAGAPP & IVAPP 2011 - Proceedings of the International Conference on Imaging Theory and Applications and International Conference on Information Visualization Theory and Applications*, 177–186.

Cabrelli, C. A., & Molter, U. M. (1990). Automatic representation of binary images. *IEEE Transactions on Pattern Analysis and Machine Intelligence*, 12(12), 1190–1196. doi:10.1109/34.62608

Camilus, K. S., Govindan, V., & Sathidevi, P. (2010). Computer-Aided Identification of the Pectoral Muscle in Digitized Mammograms. *Journal of Digital Imaging*, 23(5), 562–580. doi:10.1007/s10278-009-9240-6 PubMed

Carroll, J. D., & Chaturvedi, A. (1998). K-midranges clustering. *Advances in Data Science and Classification*, 3-14.

CCIR. (1982). *Method for the Subjective Assessment of the Quality of Television Picture, Recommendations et Rapports du CCIR. Rec.* Genve.

Chaiyakhan, K., Hirunyawanakul, A., Chanklan, R., Kerdprasop, K., & Kerdprasop, N. (2015). Traffic Sign Classification using Support Vector Machine and Image Segmentation. *Proc. Of the 3rd International Conference on Industrial Application Engineering*. 10.12792/iciae2015.013

Chandler, D. M., & Hemami, S. S. (2005). Dynamic contrast-based quantization for lossy wavelet image compression. *IEEE Transactions on Image Processing*, *14*(4), 397–410. doi:10.1109/TIP.2004.841196 PMID:15825476

Chang, E. C. (1998). *Foveation techniques and scheduling issues in thin wire visualization* (Ph.D. dissertation). New York Univ.

Chang, E. C., Mallat, S., & Yap, C. (2000). *Wavelet Foveation*. Available: http://www.comp.nus.edu.sg/ changec/publications/

Chang, C.-C., & Lin, C.-J. (2011). LIBSVM: A library for support vector machines. *ACM Transactions on Intelligent Systems and Technology*, *2*(3), 27. doi:10.1145/1961189.1961199

Chang, C., Hu, W., Hsieh, J., & Chen, Y. (2002). Shadow Elimination for Effective Moving Object Detection with Gaussian Models. *IEEE Conference on Pattern Recognition*, 540-543. 10.1109/ICPR.2002.1048359

Chatzidimitriou, K., Diamantopoulos, T., Papamichail, M., & Symeonidis, A. (2018). Practical Machine Learning in R. https://leanpub.com/practical-machine-learning-r

Chawla, N. V., Bowyer, K. W., Hall, L. O., & Kegelmeyer, W. P. (2002). SMOTE: Synthetic minority over-sampling technique. *Journal of Artificial Intelligence Research*, *16*, 321–357. doi:10.1613/jair.953

Cheikhrouhou, I. (2012). Description et classification des masses mammaires pour le diagnostic du cancer du sein [Description and classification of breast masses for the diagnosis of breast cancer] (Doctoral Thesis). University of Évry Val d'Essonne, France. https://dblp.org/rec/phd/hal/Cheikhrouhou12

Chen, B., Tai, P. C., Harrison, R., & Pan, Y. (2005). *Novel hybrid hierarchical-K-means clustering method (H-K-means) for microarray analysis*. Paper presented at the 2005 IEEE Computational Systems Bioinformatics Conference - Workshops (CSBW'05).

Chen, B., Tai, P. C., Harrison, R., & Pan, Y. (2005). *Novel Hybrid Hierarchical-K-means Clustering Method (H-K-means) for Microarray Analysis*. Paper presented at the Computational Systems Bioinformatics Conference 2005, Stanford University.

Chen, C., & Aggarwal, J. (2010). Human shadow removal with unknown light source. *International Conference on Pattern Recognition*, 2407-2410. 10.1109/ICPR.2010.589

Chen, K., Tian, L., Ding, H., Cai, M., Sun, L., Liang, S., & Huo, Q. (2017). *A compact cnn-dblstm based character model for online handwritten chinese text recognition*. Paper presented at the 2017 14th IAPR International Conference on Document Analysis and Recognition (ICDAR). 10.1109/ICDAR.2017.177

Chen, J., Chi, M., Chen, M., & Hsu, C. (2003). ROI video coding based on H2.63+ with robust skin-color detection technique. *IEEE Transactions on Consumer Electronics*, *49*(03), 724–730. doi:10.1109/TCE.2003.1233810

Chen, T., & Lu, S. (2016). Accurate and efficient traffic sign detection using discriminative adaboost and support vector regression. *IEEE Transactions on Vehicular Technology*, *65*(6), 4006–4015. doi:10.1109/TVT.2015.2500275

Chen, W., Lao, T., Xia, J., Huang, X., Zhu, B., Hu, W., & Guan, H. (2016). Gameflow: Narrative visualization of NBA basketball games. *IEEE Transactions on Multimedia*, *18*(11), 2247–2256. doi:10.1109/TMM.2016.2614221

Chen, Y., Wang, J. Z., & Krovetz, R. (2005). CLUE: Cluster-based retrieval of images by unsupervised learning. *IEEE Transactions on Image Processing*, *14*(8), 1187–1201. doi:10.1109/TIP.2005.849770 PMID:16121465

Chetverikov, D., & Szabo, Z. (1999). A Simple and Efficient Algorithm for Detection of High Curvature Points in Planner Curves. In *Proceedings of 23rd Workshop of Australian Pattern Recognition Group*, (pp. 175-184). Academic Press.

Chiang, M. M.-T., & London, B. U. (2010). Intelligent choice of the number of clusters in K-means clustering: An experimental study with different cluster spreads. *Journal of Classification*, 27(1), 3–40. doi:10.100700357-010-9049-5

Chi, D., & Chenge, W. (2010). A Hybrid Clustering Method for Automatic Medical Image Segmentation. *Journal of Computer Information Systems*, 6, 1983–1993.

Chitade, A. Z., & Katiyar, S. (2010). Colour based image segmentation using k-means clustering. *International Journal of Engineering Science and Technology*, 1(2), 5319–5325.

Choi, S.-S., Cha, S.-H., & Tappert, C. C. (2010). A Survey of Binary Similarity and Distance Measures. *Journal of Systemics, Cybernetics and Informatics*, 8(1), 43–48.

Chomphuwiset, P. (2017). *Printed thai character segmentation and recognition.* Paper presented at the 2017 IEEE 4th International Conference on Soft Computing & Machine Intelligence (ISCMI). 10.1109/ISCMI.2017.8279611

Chung, K., Lin, Y., & Huang, Y. (2009a). *The Algorithm program.* Retrieved from http://140.118.175.164/Huang/STS-BasedAlgorithm.zip

Chung, K., Lin, Y., & Huang, Y. (2009b). Efficient Shadow Detection of Color Aerial Images Based on Successive Thresholding Scheme. *IEEE Transactions on Geoscience and Remote Sensing*, 47(02), 671–682. doi:10.1109/TGRS.2008.2004629

Cleveland, W. S., & McGill, R. (1986). An experiment in graphical perception. *International Journal of Man-Machine Studies*, 25(5), 491–501. doi:10.1016/S0020-7373(86)80019-0

Cohen, A., Daubechies, I., & Feauveau, J. C. (1992). Biorthogonal bases of compactly supported wavelets. *Communications on Pure and Applied Mathematics*, 45(5), 485–560. doi:10.1002/cpa.3160450502

Consultative Committee for Space Data Systems. (2018). *Tracking Data Message.* Pink Book.

Csurka, G., Larlus, D., & Perronnin, F. (2013). What is a good evaluation measure for semantic segmentation? The Proceedings of the British Machine Vision Conference (BVMC 2013), 32.1-32.11. doi:10.5244/C.27.32

Dalal, N., & Triggs, B. (2005). Histograms of oriented gradients for human detection. *2005 IEEE Computer Society Conference on Computer Vision and Pattern Recognition (CVPR'05)*, 886-893. 10.1109/CVPR.2005.177

Daly, S. (1993). The visible differences predictor: An algorithm for the assessment of image fidelity. In *Digital Images and Human Vision* (pp. 179–205). MIT Press.

Daly, S., Zeng, W., Li, J., & Lei, S. (2000). Visual masking in wavelet compression for JPEG 2000. *Proceedings of IS&T/SPIE Conference on Image, Video Communications and Processing, 3974.*

Dattner, Y., & Yadid-Pecht, O. (2011). High and low light CMOS imager employing wide dynamic range expansion and low noise readout. *IEEE Sensors Journal*, 12(6), 2172–2179. doi:10.1109/JSEN.2011.2179290

Davies, E. R. (1988). Application of generalized Hough transform to corner detection. *IEE Proceedings, 135E*(1), 49-54.

Davis, J. W., & Keck, M. A. (2005, January). A two-stage template approach to person detection in thermal imagery. In *Seventh IEEE Workshops on Applications of Computer Vision (WACV/MOTION'05)-Volume 1* (Vol. 1, pp. 364-369). IEEE.

De Oliveira, D. C., & Wehrmeister, M. A. (2016, May). Towards real-time people recognition on aerial imagery using convolutional neural networks. In *IEEE 19th International Symposium on Real-Time Distributed Computing (ISORC)* (pp. 27-34). IEEE.

Delgado-Gómez, D., Sukno, F., Aguado, D., Santacruz, C., & Artés-Rodriguez, A. (2010). Individual identification using personality traits. *Journal of Network and Computer Applications*, 33(3), 293–299. doi:10.1016/j.jnca.2009.12.009

Deriche, R., & Faugeras, O. D. (1990). 2D curve matching using high curvature points: Application to stereo vision. In *Proceedings of 10th International Conference on Pattern Recognition*. Atlantic City, NJ: IEEE.

Deriche, R., & Giraudon, G. (1990). Accurate corner detection: An analytical study. In *Proceedings of 3rd International Conference on Computer Vision*. Osaka, Japan: IEEE.

Dhar, P., Guha, S., Biswas, T., & Abedin, M. Z. (2018). *A system design for license plate recognition by using edge detection and convolution neural network*. Paper presented at the 2018 International Conference on Computer, Communication, Chemical, Material and Electronic Engineering (IC4ME2). 10.1109/IC4ME2.2018.8465630

Din, I. U., Siddiqi, I., Khalid, S., Azam, T. J. E. J. o. I., & Processing, V. (2017). *Segmentation-free optical character recognition for printed Urdu text*. Academic Press.

Ding, H., Chen, K., Hu, W., Cai, M., & Huo, Q. (2018). *Building Compact CNN-DBLSTM Based Character Models for Handwriting Recognition and OCR by Teacher-Student Learning*. Paper presented at the 2018 16th International Conference on Frontiers in Handwriting Recognition (ICFHR). 10.1109/ICFHR-2018.2018.00033

Ding, H., Chen, K., Yuan, Y., Cai, M., Sun, L., Liang, S., & Huo, Q. (2017). *A compact CNN-DBLSTM based character model for offline handwriting recognition with Tucker decomposition*. Paper presented at the 2017 14th IAPR International Conference on Document Analysis and Recognition (ICDAR). 10.1109/ICDAR.2017.89

Ding, C., & He, X. (2004). K-means Clustering via Principal Component Analysis. *Proceedings of the 21st International Conference on Machine Learning*.

Divivier, A., Trieb, R., Ebert, A., Hagen, H., Gross, C., Fuhrmann, A., & Luckas, V. (2004). *Virtual try-on topics in realistic, individualized dressing in virtual reality*. Academic Press.

Djematen, A., Taconet, B., & Zahour, A. (1998). Une méthode statistique pour la reconnaissance de caractères berbères manuscrits. *CIFED*, *98*, 170–178.

Dong, G., & Xie, M. (2005). Color clustering and learning for image segmentation based on neural networks. *IEEE Transactions on Neural Networks*, *16*(4), 925–936. doi:10.1109/TNN.2005.849822 PMID:16121733

Dong, H., Liang, X., Shen, X., Wang, B., Lai, H., Zhu, J., ... Yin, J. (2019). Towards multi-pose guided virtual try-on network. In *Proceedings of the IEEE International Conference on Computer Vision* (pp. 9026-9035). IEEE.

Dong, H., Liang, X., Shen, X., Wu, B., Chen, B. C., & Yin, J. (2019). FW-GAN: Flow-navigated Warping GAN for Video Virtual Try-on. In *Proceedings of the IEEE International Conference on Computer Vision* (pp. 1161-1170). 10.1109/ICCV.2019.00125

Dongxiang, C., Ming, L., & Ying, Z. (2011). A Hybrid Clustering Method for Automatic Medical Image Segmentation. *Computer Applications and Software*, *8*, 141–145.

Douglas, S. (2003). Local Optima in K-Means Clustering: What You Don't Know May Hurt You. *Psychological Methods*, *8*(3), 294–304. doi:10.1037/1082-989X.8.3.294 PMID:14596492

Dreschler, L., & Nagel, H. H. (1982). On the selection of critical points and local curvature extrema of region boundaries for interframe matching. In *Proceedings of International Conference on Pattern Recognition*. Munich, Germany: Springer.

Drucker, H., Burges, C. J. C., Kaufman, L., Smola, A., & Vapnik, V. (1996). Support vector regression machines. In *Proceedings of the 9th International Conference on Neural Information Processing Systems (NIPS'96)* (pp. 155–161). MIT Press. https://dl.acm.org/doi/10.5555/2998981.2999003

Duan, P., Li, Z., Wang, Y., Zhang, B., & Cao, Y. (2017). *An effective recognition method for medical sheet based on deep learning approach.* Paper presented at the 2017 12th International Conference on Computer Science and Education (ICCSE). 10.1109/ICCSE.2017.8085516

Duda, R. O., & Hart, P. E. (1971). Use of the Hough transformation to detect lines and curves in pictures (No. SRI-TN-36). Sri International Menlo Park Ca Artificial Intelligence Center.

Duda, R. O., Hart, P. E., & Stork, D. G. (2000). *Pattern Classification* (2nd ed.). Wiley-Interscience.

Dudoit, S., & Fridlyand, J. (2002). A prediction-based resampling method for estimating the number of clusters in a dataset. *Genome Biology*, *3*(7), 1–21. doi:10.1186/gb-2002-3-7-research0036 PMID:12184810

Du, K.-L., & Swamy, M. N. S. (2006). *Neural Networks in a Soft computing Framework*. Springer-Verlag London Limited.

Dutta, K., Krishnan, P., Mathew, M., & Jawahar, C. (2018). *Improving CNN-RNN hybrid networks for handwriting recognition.* Paper presented at the 2018 16th International Conference on Frontiers in Handwriting Recognition (ICFHR). 10.1109/ICFHR-2018.2018.00023

Eastwood, S. C., Shmerko, V. P., Yanushkevich, S. N., Drahansky, M., & Gorodnichy, D. O. (2015). Biometric-enabled authentication machines: A survey of open-set real-world applications. *IEEE Transactions on Human-Machine Systems*, *46*(2), 231–242. doi:10.1109/THMS.2015.2412944

El Ayachi, R., Oujaoura, M., Fakir, M., & Minaoui, B. 2014. Code Braille et la reconnaissance d'un document écrit en Tifinagh. *Proceedings of the International Conference on Information and Communication Technologies for the Amazigh.*

El-Dahshan, E. A., Mohsen, H. M., Revett, K., & Salem, A. M. (2014). Computer-aided diagnosis of human brain tumor through MRI: A survey and a new algorithm. *Expert Systems with Applications*, *41*(11), 5526–5545. doi:10.1016/j.eswa.2014.01.021

Ellahyani, A., El Ansari, M., & El Jaafari, I. (2016). Traffic sign detection and recognition based on random forests. *Applied Soft Computing*, *46*, 805–815. doi:10.1016/j.asoc.2015.12.041

Es Saady, Y., Rachidi, A., Elyassa, M., & Mammass, D. (2008). Une méthode syntaxique pour la reconnaissance de caractères Amazighes imprimés. *CARI'08.*

Es Saady, Y., Rachidi, A., El Yassa, M., & Mammas, D. (2010). Printed Amazigh Character Recognition by a Syntactic Approach using Finite Automata. *Int. J. Graph. Vis. Image Process.*, *10*, 1–8.

Fanany, M. I. (2017). *Handwriting recognition on form document using convolutional neural network and support vector machines (CNN-SVM).* Paper presented at the 2017 5th international conference on information and communication technology (ICoIC7).

Fang, L., Qiong, W., & Sheng, Y. (2008). A method to segment moving vehicle cast shadow based on wavelet transform. *Pattern Recognition Letters*, *29*(16), 2182–2188. doi:10.1016/j.patrec.2008.08.009

Faraji, M., Cheng, I., Naudin, I., & Basu, A. (2018). Segmentation of arterial walls in intravascular ultrasound cross-sectional images using extremal region selection. *Ultrasonics*, *84*, 356–365. doi:10.1016/j.ultras.2017.11.020 PMID:29241056

Farhat, A., Hommos, O., Al-Zawqari, A., Al-Qahtani, A., Bensaali, F., Amira, A., . . . Processing, V. (2018). *Optical character recognition on heterogeneous SoC for HD automatic number plate recognition system.* Academic Press.

Feng, Y., & Harmerly, G. (2007). *PG-means: learning the number of clusters in data.* Paper presented at the Advances in Neural Information Processing Systems, Cambridge, MA.

Feng, W., Zhang, C., Zhang, W., Han, J., Wang, J., Aggarwal, C., & Huang, J. (2015). STREAMCUBE: Hierarchical spatio-temporal hashtag clustering for event exploration over the twitter stream. In *Proceedings of the 31st International Conference on Data Engineering* (pp. 1561-1572). IEEE. 10.1109/ICDE.2015.7113425

Fernandez-Moral, E., Martins, R., Wolf, D., & Rives, P. (2018). A New Metric for Evaluating Semantic Segmentation: Leveraging Global and Contour Accuracy. 2018 IEEE Intelligent Vehicles Symposium (IV), 1051-1056. doi:10.1109/IVS.2018.8500497

Ferrari, R. J., Rangaraj, M., Desautels, J. E. L., Borges, R. A., & Frere, A. F. (2004). Automatic identification of the pectoral muscle in mammograms. *IEEE Transactions on Medical Imaging*, *23*(2), 232–245. doi:10.1109/TMI.2003.823062 PubMed

Fiedler, H., Herzog, J., Hinze, A., Prohaska, M., Schildknecht, T., & Weigel, M. (2018). *SMARTnet-Evolution and Results*. Academic Press.

Fiedler, H., Herzog, J., Prohaska, M., Schildknecht, T., & Weigel, M. (2017). SMARTnet (TM)-Status and Statistics. *International Astronautical Congress 2017, IAC 2017*.

Förstner, M. A., & Gülch, E. (1987). A Fast Operator for Detection and Precise Location of Distinct Points, Corners and Centers of Circular Features. *Proceedings of the ISPRS Intercommission Conference on Fast Processing of Phonogrammic Data*, 281-305.

Frank, M., Biedert, R., Ma, E., Martinovic, I., & Song, D. (2012). Touchalytics: On the applicability of touchscreen input as a behavioral biometric for continuous authentication. *IEEE Transactions on Information Forensics and Security*, *8*(1), 136–148. doi:10.1109/TIFS.2012.2225048

Freeman, H., & Davis, L. S. (1977). A Corner Finding Algorithm for ChainCoded Curves. *IEEE Transactions on Computers*, *26*(3), 297–303. doi:10.1109/TC.1977.1674825

Galdran, A., Picón, A., Garrote, E., & Pardo, D. (2015). Pectoral muscle segmentation in mammograms based on cartoon-texture decomposition. In R. Paredes, J. Cardoso, & X. Pardo (Eds.), Lecture Notes in Computer Science: Vol. 9117. *Pattern Recognition and Image Analysis. IbPRIA 2015* (pp. 587–594). Springer., doi:10.1007/978-3-319-19390-8_66

Ganesan, K., Acharya, U. R., Chua, K. C., Min, L. C., & Abraham, K. T. (2013). Pectoral muscle segmentation: A review. *Computer Methods and Programs in Biomedicine*, *110*(1), 48–57. doi:10.1016/j.cmpb.2012.10.020 PubMed

Gao, L., Yi, X., Liao, Y., Jiang, Z., Yan, Z., & Tang, Z. (2017). *A deep learning-based formula detection method for PDF documents*. Paper presented at the 2017 14th IAPR International Conference on Document Analysis and Recognition (ICDAR). 10.1109/ICDAR.2017.96

Gao, S., Zhang, C., & Zhang, Y. (2009, May). A New Algorithm for Image Resizing Based on Bivariate Rational Interpolation. In *International Conference on Computational Science* (pp. 770-779). Springer. 10.1007/978-3-642-01973-9_86

Gao, S., Zhang, C., Zhang, Y., & Zhou, Y. (2008, December). Medical image zooming algorithm based on bivariate rational interpolation. In *International Symposium on Visual Computing* (pp. 672-681). Springer. 10.1007/978-3-540-89646-3_66

Gardezi, S. J. S., Adjed, F., Faye, I., Kamel, N., & Eltoukhy, M. M. (2018). Segmentation of pectoral muscle using the adaptive gamma corrections. *Multimedia Tools and Applications*, *77*(3), 3919–3940. doi:10.1007/s11042-016-4283-4

Gatto, B. B., dos Santos, E. M., & Fukui, K. (2017). *Subspace-based convolutional network for handwritten character recognition*. Paper presented at the 2017 14th IAPR international conference on document analysis and recognition (ICDAR). 10.1109/ICDAR.2017.173

Gatys, L. A., Ecker, A. S., & Bethge, M. (2016). Image style transfer using convolutional neural networks. In *Proceedings of the IEEE Conference on Computer Vision and Pattern Recognition* (pp. 2414-2423). 10.1109/CVPR.2016.265

Gaudart, L., Grebassa, T., & Petrakian, J. P. (1993). Wavelet transform in human visual channels. *Applied Optics*, *32*(22), 4119–4127. doi:10.1364/AO.32.004119 PMID:20830054

Ge, Y., Zhang, R., Wang, X., Tang, X., & Luo, P. (2019). DeepFashion2: A Versatile Benchmark for Detection, Pose Estimation, Segmentation and Re-Identification of Clothing Images. In *Proceedings of the IEEE Conference on Computer Vision and Pattern Recognition* (pp. 5337-5345). 10.1109/CVPR.2019.00548

Gligorić, K., Anderson, A., & West, R. (2018). How constraints affect content: The case of Twitter's switch from 140 to 280 characters, In *Twelfth International AAAI Conference on Web and Social Media* (pp. 596–599). AAAI.

Glossary. (2019). https://help.twitter.com/en/glossary

Golub, G. H., & Loan, C. F. V. (1996). Matrix Computations (3rd ed.). The Johns Hopkins University Press.

Gómez-Adorno, H., Posadas-Durán, J. P., Sidorov, G., & Pinto, D. (2018). Document embeddings learned on various types of n-grams for cross-topic authorship attribution. *Computing*, *100*(7), 741–756. doi:10.100700607-018-0587-8

Gong, K., Liang, X., Zhang, D., Shen, X., & Lin, L. (2017). Look into Person: Self-Supervised Structure-Sensitive Learning and a New Benchmark for Human Parsing. *2017 IEEE Conference on Computer Vision and Pattern Recognition (CVPR)*. 10.1109/CVPR.2017.715

Gonzalez, R., & Woods, R. (2002). *Digital Image Processing* (2nd ed.). Prentice Hall.

Goodfellow, I., Pouget-Abadie, J., Mirza, M., Xu, B., Warde-Farley, D., Ozair, S., Courville, A., & Bengio, Y. (2014). Generative adversarial nets. In Advances in neural information processing systems (pp. 2672-2680). Academic Press.

Gouws, S., Metzler, D., Cai, C., & Hovy, E. (2011). Contextual bearing on linguistic variation in social media. In *Proceedings of the Workshop on Languages in Social Media* (pp. 20-29). ACM.

Green, R. M., & Sheppard, J. W. (2013). Comparing frequency-and style-based features for Twitter author identification. In *Proceedings of the Twenty-Sixth International FLAIRS Conference* (pp. 64–69). AAAI.

Gronemann, M., Jünger, M., Liers, F., & Mambelli, F. (2016). Crossing minimization in storyline visualization. *Proceedings of 24th International Symposium of Graph Drawing and Network Visualization*, 367–381. 10.1007/978-3-319-50106-2_29

Gubern-Mérida, A., Kallenberg, M., Martí, R., & Karssemeijer, N. (2012). Segmentation of the Pectoral Muscle in Breast MRI Using Atlas-Based Approaches. In N. Ayache, H. Delingette, P. Golland, & K. Mori (Eds.), Medical Image Computing and Computer-Assisted Intervention: Vol. 7511. MICCAI 2012. MICCAI 2012. Lecture Notes in Computer Science. Springer. doi:10.1007/978-3-642-33418-4_46

Guo, Y., Yang, L., Ding, X., Han, J., & Liu, Y. (2013). OpenSesame: Unlocking smart phone through handshaking biometrics. In Proceedings IEEE INFOCOM (pp. 365-369). IEEE.

Guo, Y., Zhao, W., Li, S., Zhang, Y., & Lu, Y. (2020). Automatic segmentation of the pectoral muscle based on boundary identification and shape prediction. *Physics in Medicine and Biology*, *65*(4), 045016. Advance online publication. doi:10.1088/1361-6560/ab652b PubMed

Guru, D. S., Dinesh, R., & Nagabhushan, P. (2004). Boundary based corner detection and localization using new 'cornerity' index: a robust approach. In *Proc. 1st Canadian Conference on Computer and Robot Vision*. London, Canada: IEEE. 10.1109/CCCRV.2004.1301477

Guven, M., & Cengizler, C. (2014). Data cluster analysis-based classification of overlapping nuclei in Pap smear samples. *Biomedical Engineering Online, 13*(1), 1. doi:10.1186/1475-925X-13-159 PMID:25487072

Habibi, A. H., Jahani, H. E., & Domenec, P. (2016). A practical approach for detection and classification of traffic signs using Convolutional Neural Networks. *Robotics and Autonomous Systems, 84*, 97–112.

Han, J., Zhang, D., Cheng, G., Liu, N., & Xu, D. (2018). Advanced deep-learning techniques for salient and category-specific object detection: A survey. *IEEE Signal Processing Magazine, 35*(1), 84–100. doi:10.1109/MSP.2017.2749125

Han, X., Wu, Z., Wu, Z., Yu, R., & Davis, L. S. (2018). Viton: An image-based virtual try-on network. In *Proceedings of the IEEE Conference on Computer Vision and Pattern Recognition* (pp. 7543-7552). IEEE.

Harris, C., & Stephens, M. (1988). A combined corner and edge detector. In *Proceedings of the Fourth Alvey Vision Conference*. Manchester, UK: Alvety Vision Club.

Hatwar, M. C., & Dhengre, S. (2016). Segmentation & Classification Of MR Images of Brain Tissue Using IFCM & K-NN Algorithm. *International Journal of Scientific Engineering and Applied Science, 2*(3), 464–467.

Hazra, T. K., Singh, D. P., & Daga, N. (2017). *Optical character recognition using KNN on custom image dataset.* Paper presented at the 2017 8th Annual Industrial Automation and Electromechanical Engineering Conference (IEMECON). 10.1109/IEMECON.2017.8079572

Healey, C. G., & Enns, J. T. (2012). Attention and visual memory in visualization and computer graphics. *IEEE Transactions on Visualization and Computer Graphics, 18*(7), 1170–1188. doi:10.1109/TVCG.2011.127 PMID:21788672

Hong, W., Li, M., Geng, J., & Zhang, Y. (2019). Novel chaotic bat algorithm for forecasting complex motion of floating platforms. *Applied Mathematical Modelling, 72*, 425–443. doi:10.1016/j.apm.2019.03.031

Horprasert, T., Harwood, D., & Davis, L. (1999). A statistical approach for real-time robust background subtraction and shadow detection. In *IEEE ICCV'99 Frame-Rate Workshop*. University of Maryland.

Hsieh, J., Hu, W., Chang, C., & Chen, Y. (2003). Shadow elimination for effective moving object detection by Gaussian shadow modeling. *Image and Vision Computing, 21*(06), 505–516. doi:10.1016/S0262-8856(03)00030-1

Hsu, G. S. J., Ambikapathi, A., & Chen, M. S. (2017). Deep learning with time-frequency representation for pulse estimation from facial videos. In *Proceedings of International Joint Conference on Biometrics (IJCB)* (pp. 383-389). IEEE. 10.1109/BTAS.2017.8272721

Hsu, G. S. J., Cheng, Y. T., Ng, C. C., & Yap, M. H. (2017). Component biologically inspired features with moving segmentation for age estimation. In *Proceedings of IEEE Conference on Computer Vision and Pattern Recognition Workshops (CVPRW)* (pp. 540-547). IEEE. 10.1109/CVPRW.2017.81

Hsu, G. S. J., Huang, W. F., & Kang, J. H. (2018). Hierarchical network for facial palsy detection. *IEEE/CVF Conference on Computer Vision and Pattern Recognition Workshops (CVPRW)* (pp. 693-699). IEEE.

Hu, H., Wei, H., & Liu, Z. (2017). *The CNN based machine-printed traditional Mongolian characters recognition.* Paper presented at the 2017 36th Chinese Control Conference (CCC). 10.23919/ChiCC.2017.8027973

Huang, S., Lin, H., & Chang, C. (2017). An in-car camera system for traffic sign detection and recognition. *2017 Joint 17th World Congress of International Fuzzy Systems Association and 9th International Conference on Soft Computing and Intelligent Systems (IFSA-SCIS)*, 1-6. doi: 10.1109/IFSA-SCIS.2017.8023239

Huang, J., & Chen, C. (2009). Moving cast shadow detection using physics-based features. *IEEE Conference on Computer Vision and Pattern Recognition*, 2310-2317. 10.1109/CVPR.2009.5206629

Huang, J., Xie, W., & Tang, L. (2004). Detection and compensation for shadows in colored urban aerial images. *5th World Congr. Intell. Control Autom*, 3098-3100. 10.1109/WCICA.2004.1343090

Huang, Z., & Ng, M. K. (2003). A note on K-modes clustering. *Journal of Classification, 23*(2), 257–261. doi:10.100700357-003-0014-4

Hubert, L., & Arabie, P. (1985). Comparing Partitions. *Journal of Classification, 2*(1), 193–218. doi:10.1007/BF01908075

Huynh-Thu, Q., & Ghanbari, M. (2012). The accuracy of PSNR in predicting video quality for different video scenes and frame rates. *Telecommunication Systems, 49*(1), 35–48. doi:10.1007/s11235-010-9351-x

Hwang, K., & Sung, W. (2017). *Character-level language modeling with hierarchical recurrent neural networks.* Paper presented at the 2017 IEEE International Conference on Acoustics, Speech and Signal Processing (ICASSP). 10.1109/ICASSP.2017.7953252

Idris, I., Selamat, A., Nguyen, N. T., Omatu, S., Krejcar, O., Kuca, K., & Penhaker, M. (2015). A combined negative selection algorithm–particle swarm optimization for an email spam detection system. *Engineering Applications of Artificial Intelligence, 39*, 33–44. doi:10.1016/j.engappai.2014.11.001

Idrissi, N. (2008). La navigation dans les bases d'images: prise en compte des attributs de texture (Ph.D. Thesis). University Mohamed V and Nantes University.

Igarashi, K., Miyajima, C., Itou, K., Takeda, K., Itakura, F., & Abut, H. (2004). Biometric identification using driving behavioral signals. In *Proceedings of the International Conference on Multimedia and Expo (ICME)* (Vol. 1, pp. 65-68). IEEE.

Ishioka, T. (2005). *An expansion of X-means for automatically determining the optimal number of clusters.* Paper presented at the Fourth IASTED International Conference Computation Intelligence, Calgary, Alberta, Canada.

Isola, P., Zhu, J. Y., Zhou, T., & Efros, A. A. (2017). Image-to-image translation with conditional adversarial networks. In *Proceedings of the IEEE conference on computer vision and pattern recognition* (pp. 1125-1134). IEEE.

Jain, A. K. (2010). Data clustering: 50 years beyond K-means. *Pattern Recognition Letters, 31*(8), 651–666. doi:10.1016/j.patrec.2009.09.011

Jain, A. K., Dass, S. C., & Nandakumar, K. (2004). Soft biometric traits for personal recognition systems. In *Biometric Authentication* (pp. 731–738). Springer Berlin Heidelberg. doi:10.1007/978-3-540-25948-0_99

Jain, A. K., Flynn, P., & Ross, A. A. (2008). *Handbook of Biometrics.* Springer Science & Business Media. doi:10.1007/978-0-387-71041-9

Jain, A. K., Nandakumar, K., & Ross, A. (2016). 50 years of biometric research: Accomplishments, challenges, and opportunities. *Pattern Recognition Letters, 79*, 80–105. doi:10.1016/j.patrec.2015.12.013

Jain, A. K., Ross, A., & Pankanti, S. (2006). Biometrics: A tool for information security. *IEEE Transactions on Information Forensics and Security, 1*(2), 125–143. doi:10.1109/TIFS.2006.873653

Jamshidi, O., Pilevar, A.H. (2013). Automatic segmentation of medical images using fuzzy c-means and the genetic algorithm. *Journal of Computational Medicine.* doi:10.1155/2013/972970

Jaramillo, J. C. A., Murillo-Fuentes, J. J., & Olmos, P. M. (2018). *Boosting handwriting text recognition in small databases with transfer learning.* Paper presented at the 2018 16th International Conference on Frontiers in Handwriting Recognition (ICFHR).

Jeong, D., Kim, M., Kim, K., Kim, T., Jin, J., Lee, C., & Lim, S. (2018). Real-time driver identification using vehicular big data and deep learning. In *International Conference on Intelligent Transportation Systems* (pp. 123-130). IEEE. 10.1109/ITSC.2018.8569452

Jetchev, N., & Bergmann, U. (2017). The conditional analogy gan: Swapping fashion articles on people images. In *Proceedings of the IEEE International Conference on Computer Vision* (pp. 2287-2292). 10.1109/ICCVW.2017.269

Jiang, Y., Dong, H., & El Saddik, A. J. I. A. (2018). *Baidu Meizu deep learning competition: arithmetic operation recognition using end-to-end learning OCR technologies.* Academic Press.

Jiang, W., Xiang, J., Liu, L., Zha, D., & Wang, L. (2013). From mini house game to hobby-driven behavioral biometrics-based password. In *Proceedings of the 12th International Conference on Trust, Security and Privacy in Computing and Communications* (pp. 712-719). IEEE. 10.1109/TrustCom.2013.86

Jia, V., Lin, W., & Kassim, A. A. (2006). Estimating Just-Noticeable Distortion for Video. *IEEE Transactions on Circuits and Systems for Video Technology, 16*(7), 820–829. doi:10.1109/TCSVT.2006.877397

Ji, J., Pang, W., Zheng, Y., Wang, Z., & Ma, Z. (2015). An Initialization Method for Clustering Mixed Numeric and Categorical Data Based on the Density and Distance. *International Journal of Pattern Recognition and Artificial Intelligence, 29*(7), 1550024. Advance online publication. doi:10.1142/S021800141550024X

Ji, J., Pang, W., Zheng, Y., Wang, Z., Ma, Z., & Zhang, L. (2015). A Novel Cluster Center Initialization Method for the k_Prototypes Algorithms using Centrality and Distance. *Applied Mathematics & Information Sciences, 9*(6), 2933–2942. doi:10.12785/amis/090621

Jimenez, A. R., Ceres, R., & Pons, J. L. (2000). A Survey of Computer Vision Methods for Locating Fruit on Trees. *Transactions of the ASAE. American Society of Agricultural Engineers, 43*(6), 1911–1920. doi:10.13031/2013.3096

Johnson, J., Alahi, A., & Fei-Fei, L. (2016, October). Perceptual losses for real-time style transfer and super-resolution. In *Proceedings of the European Conference on Computer Vision (ECCV)* (pp. 694-711). Springer. 10.1007/978-3-319-46475-6_43

John, V., Mita, S., Liu, Z., & Qi, B. (2015, May). Pedestrian detection in thermal images using adaptive fuzzy C-means clustering and convolutional neural networks. In *14th IAPR International Conference on Machine Vision Applications (MVA)* (pp. 246-249). IEEE. 10.1109/MVA.2015.7153177

Jolliffe, I. T. (2002). Principal Component Analysis (2nd ed.). New York: Springer.

Jong, A., & Moh, T. S. (2019). Short video datasets show potential for outfits in virtual reality. *Proceedings of the IEEE International Conference on High Performance Computing & Simulation (HPCS).*

Jorgensen, Z., & Yu, T. (2011). On mouse dynamics as a behavioral biometric for authentication. In *Proceedings of the 6th ACM Symposium on Information, Computer and Communications Security* (pp. 476-482). ACM. 10.1145/1966913.1966983

Juang, L.-H., & Wu, M.-N. (2010). MRI brain lesion image detection based on color-converted K-means clustering segmentation. *Measurement, 43*(7), 941–949. doi:10.1016/j.measurement.2010.03.013

Judge, T. A., Higgins, C. A., Thoresen, C. J., & Barrick, M. R. (1999). The big five personality traits, general mental ability, and career success across the life span. *Personnel Psychology, 52*(3), 621–652. doi:10.1111/j.1744-6570.1999.tb00174.x

Kachouane, M., Sahki, S., Lakrouf, M., & Ouadah, N. (2012, December). HOG based fast human detection. In *2012 24th International Conference on Microelectronics (ICM)* (pp. 1-4). IEEE. 10.1109/ICM.2012.6471380

Kadonaga, T., & Abe, K. (1996). Comparison of Methods for Detecting Corner Points from Digital Curves, Graphics Recognition Methods and Applications. *Lecture Notes in Computer Science, 1072*, 23–34. doi:10.1007/3-540-61226-2_3

Kalyani, S., & Swarup, K. S. (2011). Particle swarm optimization based K-means clustering approach for security assessment in power systems. *Expert Systems with Applications, 38*(9), 10839–10846. doi:10.1016/j.eswa.2011.02.086

Kang, X., Huang, Y., Li, S., Lin, H., & Benediktsson, J. (2018). Extended Random Walker for Shadow Detection in Very High Resolution Remote Sensing Images. *IEEE Transactions on Geoscience and Remote Sensing, 56*(02), 867–876. doi:10.1109/TGRS.2017.2755773

Kaplan, B. S., Huseyin, G., Ozgur, O., & Cuneyt, A. (2016). On circular traffic sign detection and recognition. *Expert Systems with Applications, 48*, 67–75. doi:10.1016/j.eswa.2015.11.018

Karim, S. A. A., & Saaban, A. (2017). Shape Preserving Interpolation Using Rational Cubic Ball Function and Its Application in Image Interpolation. Mathematical Problems in Engineering.

Karim, S. A. A. (2015). Shape preserving by using rational cubic ball interpolant. *Far East Journal of Mathematical Sciences, 96*(2), 211–230. doi:10.17654/FJMSJan2015_211_230

Kasturi, R., Siva, S., & O'Gorman, L. (1990). Techniques for line drawing interpretation: an overview. In *Proc. IAPR Workshop on Machine Vision Applications*. IAPR.

Katiyar, G., & Mehfuz, S. J. S. (2016). *A hybrid recognition system for off-line handwritten characters*. Academic Press.

Katouzian, A., Baseri, B., Konofagou, E. E., & Laine, A. F. (2008). Texture-driven coronary artery plaque characterization using wavelet packet signatures. *2008 5th IEEE International Symposium on Biomedical Imaging: From Nano to Macro*, 197-200. doi: 10.1109/ISBI.2008.4540966

Kaufman, L., & Rousseeuw, P. J. (1990). *Finding Groups in Data: An Introduction to Cluster Analysis*. John Wiley & Sons, Inc. doi:10.1002/9780470316801

Kaur, A., & Singh, M. (2012). An overview of pso-based approaches in image segmentation. *Int J Eng Technol, 2*(8), 1349–1357.

Kaur, P., Soni, A. K., & Gosain, A. (2012). Novel intuitionistic fuzzy C-means clustering for linearly and nonlinearly separable data. *WSEAS Transactions on Computers, 11*(3), 65–76.

Keim, D. A. (2012). Solving problems with visual analytics: Challenges and applications. *Proceedings of Machine Learning and Knowledge Discovery in Databases - European Conference*, 5–6.

Keller, B., Nathan, D., Wang, Y., Zheng, Y., Gee, J., Conant, E., & Kontos, D. (2011). Adaptive Multi-cluster Fuzzy C-Means Segmentation of Breast Parenchymal Tissue in Digital Mammography. In G. Fichtinger, A. Martel, & T. Peters (Eds.), Medical Image Computing and Computer-Assisted Intervention: Vol. 6893. MICCAI 2011. MICCAI 2011. Lecture Notes in Computer Science (pp. 562–569). Springer. doi:10.1007/978-3-642-23626-6_69

Keshri, P., Kumar, P., & Ghosh, R. (2018). *Rnn based online handwritten word recognition in devanagari script*. Paper presented at the 2018 16th International Conference on Frontiers in Handwriting Recognition (ICFHR). 10.1109/ICFHR-2018.2018.00096

Khalid, N. E. A., Ibrahim, S., & Manaf, M. (2011). Brain abnormalities segmentation performances contrasting: adaptive network-based fuzzy inference system (ANFIS) vs K-nearest neighbors (k-NN) vs fuzzy c-means (FCM). *15th WSEAS International Conference on Computers*.

Khan, F. (2012). An initial seed selection algorithm for k-means clustering of georeferenced data to improve replicability of cluster assignments for mapping application. *Applied Soft Computing*, *12*(11), 3698–3700. doi:10.1016/j.asoc.2012.07.021

Khaustov, P., Spitsyn, V., & Maksimova, E. (2016). *Algorithm for optical handwritten characters recognition based on structural components extraction.* Paper presented at the 2016 11th International Forum on Strategic Technology (IFOST). 10.1109/IFOST.2016.7884126

Khoulqi, I., & Idrissi, N. (2019). Breast cancer image segmentation and classification. *Proceedings of the 4th International Conference on Smart City Applications (SCA '19)*, 1–9. 10.1145/3368756.3369039

Khoulqi, I., & Idrissi, N. (2020). Split and Merge-Based Breast Cancer Segmentation and Classification. In M. Sarfraz (Ed.), *Critical Approaches to Information Retrieval Research* (pp. 225–238). IGI Global., doi:10.4018/978-1-7998-1021-6.ch012.

Kishna, N. T., & Francis, S. (2017). *Intelligent tool for Malayalam cursive handwritten character recognition using artificial neural network and Hidden Markov Model.* Paper presented at the 2017 International Conference on Inventive Computing and Informatics (ICICI). 10.1109/ICICI.2017.8365201

Kitchen, L., & Rosenfeld, A. (1982). Gray-level corner detection. *Pattern Recognition Letters*, *1*(2), 95–102. doi:10.1016/0167-8655(82)90020-4

Klinkrad, H. (2010). Space debris. Encyclopedia of Aerospace Engineering.

Koenderink, J. J., & Richards, W. (1988). Two-dimensional curvature operators. *Journal of the Optical Society of America. A, Optics and Image Science*, *5*(7), 1136–1141. doi:10.1364/JOSAA.5.001136

Kok, C. W., & Tam, W. S. (2019). *Digital Image Interpolation in Matlab.* John Wiley & Sons. doi:10.1002/9781119119623

Kouprianov, V. (2008). Distinguishing features of CCD astrometry of faint GEO objects. *Advances in Space Research*, *41*(7), 1029–1038. doi:10.1016/j.asr.2007.04.033

Krinidis, S., & Chatzis, V. (2010). A robust fuzzy local information C-means clustering algorithm. *IEEE Transactions on Image Processing*, *19*(5), 1328–1337. doi:10.1109/TIP.2010.2040763 PMID:20089475

Kumar, K. M., & Reddy, A. R. M. (2017). An efficient k-means clustering filtering algorithm using density based initial cluster centers. *Information Sciences*, *418-419*, 286–301. doi:10.1016/j.ins.2017.07.036

Kumar, K. P., & Gavrilova, M. L. (2019). Personality Traits Classification on Twitter. In *Proceedings of International Conference on Advanced Video and Signal Based Surveillance (AVSS)* (pp. 1-8). IEEE.

Kummer, H. (1987). The consultative committee for space data systems (CCSDS) planned and potential use of the recommendations. *Acta Astronautica*, *16*, 199–205. doi:10.1016/0094-5765(87)90106-8

Kurita, T. (1991). An efficient agglomerative clustering algorithm using a heap. *Pattern Recognition*, *24*(3), 205–209. doi:10.1016/0031-3203(91)90062-A

Kwok, S. M., Chandrasekhar, R., Attikiouzel, Y., & Rickard, M. T. (2004). Automatic Pectoral Muscle Segmentation on Mediolateral Oblique View Mammograms. *IEEE Transactions on Medical Imaging*, *23*(9), 1129–1140. doi:10.1109/TMI.2004.830529 PubMed

Lai, K., Kanich, O., Dvořák, M., Drahanský, M., Yanushkevich, S., & Shmerko, V. (2017). Biometric-enabled watchlists technology. *IET Biometrics*, *7*(2), 163–172. doi:10.1049/iet-bmt.2017.0036

Lampprecht, T., Salb, D., Mauser, M., van de Wetering, H., Burch, M., & Kloos, U. (2019). Information Visualization - Biomedical Visualization and Geometric Modelling and Imaging, IV 2019. Piscataway: Institute of Electrical and Electronics Engineers.

Lang, D., Hogg, D. W., Mierle, K., Blanton, M., & Roweis, S. (2010). Astrometry. net: Blind astrometric calibration of arbitrary astronomical images. *The Astronomical Journal, 139*(5), 1782–1800. doi:10.1088/0004-6256/139/5/1782

Larson, E. C., & Chandler, D. M. (2010). Most apparent distortion: Full-reference image quality assessment and the role of strategy. *Journal of Electronic Imaging, 19*(1), 011006. doi:10.1117/1.3267105

Layton, R., Watters, P., & Dazeley, R. (2010). Authorship attribution for twitter in 140 characters or less. In *Cybercrime and Trustworthy Computing Workshop (CTC)* (pp. 1-8). IEEE. 10.1109/CTC.2010.17

LeCun, Y., Bengio, Y., & Hinton, G. (2015). Deep learning. *Nature, 521*(7553), 436–444. doi:10.1038/nature14539 PMID:26017442

Lecun, Y., Bottou, L., Bengio, Y., & Haffner, P. (1998). Gradient-based learning applied to document recognition. *Proceedings of the IEEE, 86*(11), 2278–2324. doi:10.1109/5.726791

Lee, S., & Jang, G.-J. (2017). *Recognition model based on residual networks for cursive hanja recognition.* Paper presented at the 2017 International Conference on Information and Communication Technology Convergence (ICTC). 10.1109/ICTC.2017.8191045

Lee, C.-Y., & Lee, Z.-J. (2012). A novel algorithm applied to classify unbalanced data. *Applied Soft Computing, 12*(8), 2481–2485. doi:10.1016/j.asoc.2012.03.051

Lee, S., Pattichis, M. S., & Bovik, A. C. (2001). Foveated video compression with optimal rate control. *IEEE Transactions on Image Processing, 10*(7), 977–992. doi:10.1109/83.931092 PMID:18249671

Leone, A., & Distante, C. (2007). Shadow detection for moving objects based on texture analysis. *Pattern Recognition, 40*(04), 1222–1233. doi:10.1016/j.patcog.2006.09.017

Li, Q., An, W., Zhou, A., & Ma, L. (2016). *Recognition of offline handwritten Chinese characters using the Tesseract open source OCR engine.* Paper presented at the 2016 8th International Conference on Intelligent Human-Machine Systems and Cybernetics (IHMSC). 10.1109/IHMSC.2016.239

Liang, K., Jin, L., Xie, Z., Xiao, X., & Huang, W. (2017). *A Comprehensive Analysis of Misclassified Handwritten Chinese Character Samples by Incorporating Human Recognition.* Paper presented at the 2017 14th IAPR International Conference on Document Analysis and Recognition (ICDAR). 10.1109/ICDAR.2017.82

Liang, X., Gong, K., Shen, X., & Lin, L. (2019). Look into Person: Joint Body Parsing & Pose Estimation Network and a New Benchmark. *IEEE Transactions on Pattern Analysis and Machine Intelligence, 41*(4), 871–885. doi:10.1109/TPAMI.2018.2820063 PMID:29994083

Li, H., He, H., & Wen, Y. (2015). Dynamic particle swarm optimization and K-means clustering algorithm for image segmentation. *Optik (Stuttgart), 126*(24), 4817–4822. doi:10.1016/j.ijleo.2015.09.127

Li, H., Zhang, L., & Shen, H. (2012). A perceptually inspired variational method for the uneven intensity correction of remote sensing images. *IEEE Transactions on Geoscience and Remote Sensing, 50*(08), 3053–3065. doi:10.1109/TGRS.2011.2178075

Li, J. S., Chen, L. C., Monaco, J. V., Singh, P., & Tappert, C. C. (2017). A comparison of classifiers and features for authorship authentication of social networking messages. *Concurrency and Computation, 29*(14), e3918. doi:10.1002/cpe.3918

Lillesand, T., & Kiefer, R. (2000). *Remote Sensing and Image Interpretation* (4th ed.). Wiley.

Lillo-Castellano, J. M., Mora-Jiménez, I., Figuera-Pozuelo, C., & Rojo-Álvarez, J. L. (2015). Traffic sign segmentation and classification using statistical learning methods. *Neurocomputing, 153,* 286–299. doi:10.1016/j.neucom.2014.11.026

Lin, C.-H., & Li, Y. (2019). *A License Plate Recognition System for Severe Tilt Angles Using Mask R-CNN*. Paper presented at the 2019 International Conference on Advanced Mechatronic Systems (ICAMechS). 10.1109/ICAMechS.2019.8861691

Lindeberg, T. (1994). *Scale-Space Theory in Computer Vision*. Springer. doi:10.1007/978-1-4757-6465-9

Lindeberg, T. (1998). Feature detection with automatic scale selection. *International Journal of Computer Vision, 30*(2), 77–116.

Lindeberg, T. (2008). Scale-Space. In B. Wah (Ed.), *Wiley Encyclopedia of Computer Science and Engineering. IV* (pp. 2495–2504). John Wiley and Sons., doi:10.1002/9780470050118.ecse609

Lindeberg, T. (2013). Scale selection properties of generalized scale-space interest point detectors. *Journal of Mathematical Imaging and Vision, Volume, 46*(2), 177–210. doi:10.100710851-012-0378-3

Lindeberg, T. (2015). Image matching using generalized scale-space interest points. *Journal of Mathematical Imaging and Vision, 52*(1), 3–36. doi:10.100710851-014-0541-0

Lindeberg, T., & Garding, J. (1997). Shape-adapted smoothing in estimation of 3-D depth cues from affine distortions of local 2-D structure. *Image and Vision Computing, 15*(6), 415–434. doi:10.1016/S0262-8856(97)01144-X

Lindeberg, T., & Li, M.-X. (1997). Segmentation and classification of edges using minimum description length approximation and complementary junction cues. *Computer Vision and Image Understanding, 67*(1), 88–98. doi:10.1006/cviu.1996.0510

Linde, Y., Buzo, A., & Gray, R. M. (1980). An Algorithm for Vector Quantizer Design. *IEEE Transactions on Communications, COM-28*(1), 84–95. doi:10.1109/TCOM.1980.1094577

Li, R., Chen, Y., & Zhang, X. (2006). Fast robust eigen-background updating for foreground detection. *Proc. Int. Conf. on Image Processing.* 10.1109/ICIP.2006.312836

Liu, K., Chen, T., & Chen, C. (2016). MVC: A Dataset for View-Invariant Clothing Retrieval and Attribute Prediction. *ICMR '16.*

Liu, N., Zhang, D., Xu, X., Guo, L., Chen, L., Liu, W., & Ke, D. (2017). *Robust math formula recognition in degraded chinese document images.* Paper presented at the 2017 14th IAPR International Conference on Document Analysis and Recognition (ICDAR). 10.1109/ICDAR.2017.27

Liu, D., Chin, T., & Rowntree, T. (2019). Optical Detection of Geostationary Objects Using End-To-End Deep Learning. *Proceedings of International Astronautical Conference 2019.*

Liu, H. C., & Srinath, L. S. (1990). Corner Detection from Chain-Code. *Pattern Recognition, 23*(1-2), 51–68. doi:10.1016/0031-3203(90)90048-P

Liu, Y., Chen, W., Liu, L., & Lew, M. S. (2019). SwapGAN: A Multistage Generative Approach for Person-to-Person Fashion Style Transfer. *IEEE Transactions on Multimedia, 21*(9), 2209–2222. doi:10.1109/TMM.2019.2897897

Liu, Z.-G., Pan, Q., & Dezert, J. (2014). Classification of uncertain and imprecise data based on evidence theory. *Neurocomputing, 133,* 459–470. doi:10.1016/j.neucom.2013.12.009

Liu, Z., Karam, L. J., & Watson, A. B. (2006). JPEG2000 Encoding With Perceptual Distortion Control. *IEEE Transactions on Image Processing, 15*(7).

Liu, Z., Luo, P., Qiu, S., Wang, X., & Tang, X. (2016). Deepfashion: Powering robust clothes recognition and retrieval with rich annotations. In *Proceedings of the IEEE conference on computer vision and pattern recognition* (pp. 1096-1104). 10.1109/CVPR.2016.124

Lopes, G. S., da Silva, D. C., Rodrigues, A. W. O., & Reboucas Filho, P. P. J. I. L. A. T. (2016). *Recognition of handwritten digits using the signature features and Optimum-Path Forest Classifier.* Academic Press.

Lowe, D. (2004). Distinctive Image Features from Scale-Invariant Keypoints. *International Journal of Computer Vision, 60*(2), 91. doi:. doi:10.1023/B:VISI.0000029664.99615.94

Lu, W., Sun, H., Chu, J., Huang, X., & Yu, J. J. I. A. (2018). *A novel approach for video text detection and recognition based on a corner response feature map and transferred deep convolutional neural network.* Academic Press.

Lukies, M. (n.d.). *Normal pelvis and both hips: Radiology Case.* Retrieved August 26, 2019, from https://radiopaedia.org/cases/normal-pelvis-and-both-hips

Lyakh, Y., Gurianov, V., Gorshkov, O., & Vihovanets, Y. (2012). Estimating the number of data clusters via the contrast statistic. *Journal of Biomedical Science and Engineering, 5*(02), 95–99. doi:10.4236/jbise.2012.52012

Macleod, N., & Grant, T. (2012). Whose Tweet? Authorship analysis of micro-blogs and other short-form messages. In *International Association of Forensic Linguists' Tenth Biennial Conference* (pp. 210–224). Academic Press.

MacQueen, J. B. (1967). Some methods for classification and analysis of multivariate observations. *Proceedings of the Fifth Berkeley Symposium on Mathematical Statistics and Probability,* 281-297.

Madhukumar, S., & Santhiyakumari, N. (2015). Evaluation of K-means and fuzzy C-means segmentation on MR images of brain. *The Egyptian Journal of Radiology and Nuclear Medicine, 46*(2), 475–479. doi:10.1016/j.ejrnm.2015.02.008

Maini, R., & Aggarwal, H. (2010). A Comprehensive Review of Image Enhancement Techniques. *Journal of Computing, 2*(3), 8–13. https://arxiv.org/ftp/arxiv/papers/1003/1003.4053.pdf

Maitra, I. K., Nag, S., & Bandyopadhyay, S. K. (2011). Detection and isolation of pectoral muscle from digital mammogram: An automated approach. *International Journal of Advanced Research in Computer Science, 2*(3), 375–380. http://www.ijarcs.info/index.php/Ijarcs/article/view/555/543

Mala, C., & Sridevi, M. (2014). Color Image Segmentation Using Hybrid Learning Techniques. *IT Convergence Practice, 2*(2), 21–42.

Mallat, S. (2002). A wavelet Tour of Signal and Image Processing (Edition 2002). Academic Press.

Mann, W. R. (1953). Mean value methods in iteration. *Proceedings of the American Mathematical Society, 4*(3), 506–510. doi:10.1090/S0002-9939-1953-0054846-3

Mathew, M., Jain, M., & Jawahar, C. (2017). *Benchmarking scene text recognition in devanagari, telugu and malayalam.* Paper presented at the 2017 14th IAPR International Conference on Document Analysis and Recognition (ICDAR). 10.1109/ICDAR.2017.364

Matthew, M., Felde, G., Golden, S., Gardner, J., & Anderson, G. (2000). An algorithm for de-shadowing spectral imagery. *Proceedings of SPIE - The International Society for Optical Engineering, 4816*(10), 203-210.

Ma, Y., & Huang, L. (2015). Hierarchical traffic sign recognition based on multi-feature and multi-classifier fusion, *Proc. of the First International Conference on Information Science and Electronic Technology (ISET).* 10.2991/iset-15.2015.15

Meiburger, K. M., Acharya, U. R., & Molinari, F. (2018). Automated localization and segmentation techniques for B-mode ultrasound images: A review. *Computers in Biology and Medicine, 92*, 210–235. doi:10.1016/j.compbiomed.2017.11.018 PMID:29247890

Meila, M., & Heckerman, D. (1998). *An experimental comparison of several clustering and initialization methods.* Retrieved from Redmond.

Meurie, C., Lebrun, G., & Lezoray, O. (2003). A. Elmoataz A *comparison of supervised pixels-based color image segmentation methods. application in cancerology. WSEAS Transactions on Computers, 2*(3), 739–744.

Mikolajczyk, K., & Schmid, C. (2004). Scale and affine invariant interest point detectors. *International Journal of Computer Vision, 60*(1), 63–86. doi:10.1023/B:VISI.0000027790.02288.f2

Mink, D. J. (1998, September). WCSTools: An image astrometry toolkit. *Bulletin of the American Astronomical Society, 30*, 1144.

Minor Planet Center. (2019). *Format for Astrometric Observations Of Comets, Minor Planets and Natural Satellites.* Retrieved from https://minorplanetcenter.net/iau/info/ObsFormat.html

Mirza, M., & Osindero, S. (2014). *Conditional generative adversarial nets.* arXiv preprint arXiv:1411.1784

Mokhtarian, F., & Mackworth, A. K. (1992). A Theory of Multiscale, Curvature-Based Shape Representation for Planar Curves. *IEEE Transactions on Pattern Analysis and Machine Intelligence, 14*(8), 789–805. doi:10.1109/34.149591

Molinara, M., Marrocco, C., & Tortorella, F. (2013). Automatic segmentation of the pectoral muscle in mediolateral oblique mammograms. Proceedings of the 26th IEEE International Symposium on Computer-Based Medical Systems, 506-509. doi:10.1109/CBMS.2013.6627852

Mo, N., Zhu, R., Yan, L., & Zhao, Z. (2018). Deshadowing of Urban Airborne Imagery Based on Object-Oriented Automatic Shadow Detection and Regional Matching Compensation. *IEEE Journal of Selected Topics in Applied Earth Observations and Remote Sensing, 11*(02), 585–605. doi:10.1109/JSTARS.2017.2787116

Mondal, M., Mondal, P., Saha, N., & Chattopadhyay, P. (2017). *Automatic number plate recognition using CNN based self synthesized feature learning.* Paper presented at the 2017 IEEE Calcutta Conference (CALCON). 10.1109/CALCON.2017.8280759

Monwar, M. M., & Gavrilova, M. (2013). Markov chain model for multimodal biometric rank fusion. *Signal, Image and Video Processing, 7*, 137–149. doi:10.100711760-011-0226-8

Mookiah, M. R. K., Acharya, U. R., Lim, C. M., Petznick, A., & Suri, J. S. (2012). Data mining technique for automated diagnosis of glaucoma using higher order spectra and wavelet energy features. *Knowledge-Based Systems, 33*, 73–82. doi:10.1016/j.knosys.2012.02.010

Moravec, H. (1980). *Obstacle Avoidance and Navigation in the Real World by a Seeing Robot Rover.* Tech Report CMU-RI-TR-3 Carnegie-Mellon University, Robotics Institute.

Mostafa, Y., & Abdelhafiz, A. (2017). Accurate Shadow Detection from High-Resolution Satellite Images. *IEEE Trans. on Geoscience and Remote Sensing Letters, 14*(4), 494-498.

Munroe, R. (2019). *XKCD number 657: Movie narrative charts.* https://xkcd.com/657

Murthy, D. (2018). *Twitter.* Polity Press.

Musleh, S., Sarfraz, M., & Niepel, L. (2018). A Comparative Study on Shadow Detection Methods Based on Features. *IEEE International Conference on Computing Sciences and Engineering (ICCSE).* 10.1109/ICCSE1.2018.8373992

Nair, A., Margolis, M. P., Kuban, B. D., & Vince, D. G. (2007). Automated coronary plaque characterisation with intravascular ultrasound backscatter: Ex vivo validation. *EuroIntervention, 3*(1), 113–120. PMID:19737694

Nair, V., Ram, P., & Sundararaman, S. (2019). Shadow detection and removal from images using machine learning and morphological operations. *ITE The Journal of Engineering, 2019*(01), 11–18. doi:10.1049/joe.2018.5241

Naz, S., Umar, A. I., Ahmed, R., Razzak, M. I., Rashid, S. F., & Shafait, F. J. S. (2016). *Urdu Nasta'liq text recognition using implicit segmentation based on multi-dimensional long short term memory neural networks.* Academic Press.

NCI (National Cancer Institute). (2016). Annual Report to the Nation: Cancer Death Rates Continue to Decline; Increase in Liver Cancer Deaths Cause For Concern. https://www.cancer.gov/news-events/press-releases/2016/annual-report-nation-1975-2012

Neal, T., Sundararajan, K., Fatima, A., Yan, Y., Xiang, Y., & Woodard, D. (2018). Surveying stylometry techniques and applications. *ACM Computing Surveys, 50*(6), 86. doi:10.1145/3132039

Ng, H. P., Ong, S. H., Foong, K. W. C., Goh, P. S., & Nowinski, W. L. (2006, March). Medical image segmentation using k-means clustering and improved watershed algorithm. In *IEEE Southwest Symposium on Image Analysis and Interpretation* (pp. 61-65). IEEE. 10.1109/SSIAI.2006.1633722

Nguyen, T.-N., & Nguyen, D.-D. (2018). *A new convolutional architecture for Vietnamese car plate recognition.* Paper presented at the 2018 10th International Conference on Knowledge and Systems Engineering (KSE). 10.1109/KSE.2018.8573375

Nicolas, H., & Pinel, J. (2006). Joint moving cast shadows segmentation and light source detection in video sequences. *Signal Processing Image Communication, 21*(1), 22–43. doi:10.1016/j.image.2005.06.001

Nidheesh, N., Nazeer, K. A. A., & Ameer, P. M. (2018). A Hierarchical Clustering Algorithm Based on Silhouette Index for Cancer Subtype Discovery from Omics Data. *bioRxiv.* Advance online publication. doi:10.1101/309716

Noble, J. A. (1988). Finding corners. *Image and Vision Computing, 6*(2), 121–128. doi:10.1016/0262-8856(88)90007-8

Noble, J. A. (1989). *Descriptions of Image Surfaces (Ph.D.).* Department of Engineering Science, Oxford University.

Nowozin, S. (2014). Optimal decisions from probabilistic models: the intersection-over-union case. In *Proceedings of the IEEE Conference on Computer Vision and Pattern Recognition* (pp. 548-555). 10.1109/CVPR.2014.77

Oak, R. (2018). A literature survey on authentication using behavioral biometric techniques. In *Proceedings of Intelligent Computing and Information and Communication* (pp. 173–181). Springer. doi:10.1007/978-981-10-7245-1_18

Oda, H., Yanagisawa, T., Kurosaki, H., & Tagawa, M. (2014, September). Optical observation, image-processing, and detection of space debris in geosynchronous Earth orbit. *Proceedings of the Advanced Maui Optical and Space Surveillance Technologies Conference.*

Ogawa, M., & Ma, K. (2010). Software evolution storylines. *Proceedings of the ACM Symposium on Software Visualization,* 35–42.

Ojo, J. A., Adepoju, T. M., Omdiora, E. O., Olabiyisi, O. S., & Bello, O. T. (2014). Pre-processing method for extraction of pectoral muscle and removal of artifacts in mammogram. IOSR Journal of Computer Engineering, 16(3), 6–9. doi:10.9790/0661-16350609

Olejnik, L., & Castelluccia, C. (2013). Towards web-based biometric systems using personal browsing interests. In *Proceedings of International Conference on Availability, Reliability and Security* (pp. 274-280). IEEE. 10.1109/ARES.2013.36

Oliver, A., Lladó, X., Torrent, A., & Martí, J. (2014). *One-shot segmentation of breast, pectoral muscle, and background in digitised mammograms. In 2014 IEEE International Conference on Image Processing (ICIP).* IEEE., doi:10.1109/ICIP.2014.7025183.

Orebaugh, A., & Allnutt, J. (2009). Classification of instant messaging communications for forensics analysis. *International Journal of Forensic Computer Science, 1,* 22–28. doi:10.5769/J200901002

Othman, K., & Ahmad, A. (2016). New Embedded Denotes Fuzzy C-Mean Application for Breast Cancer Density Segmentation in Digital Mammograms. IOP Conference Series: Materials Science and Engineering, 160:012105, International Engineering Research and Innovation Symposium (IRIS), Melaka, Malaysia. DOI: 10.1088/1757-899X/160/1/012105

Otsu, N. (1979). A threshold selection method from gray level histograms. *IEEE Transactions on Systems, Man, and Cybernetics, 9*(01), 62–69. doi:10.1109/TSMC.1979.4310076

Ouadid, Y., Fakir, M., & Minaoui, B. (2016). Tifinagh Printed Character Recognition through Structural Feature Extraction. Int. J. Comput. Vis. Image Process. *IJCVIP, 6,* 42–53.

Ouadid, Y., Minaoui, B., & Fakir, M. (2016). Spectral Graph Matching for Printed Tifinagh Character. *Computer Graphics, Imaging and Visualization (CGiV), 2016 13th International Conference On,* 105–111. 10.1109/CGiV.2016.29

Ouadid, Y., Minaoui, B., Fakir, M., & Abouelala, O. (2014). *New Approach of Tifinagh Character Recognition using Graph Matching.* Academic Press.

Oujaoura, M., Minaoui, B., & Fakir, M. (2013). Walsh, Texture and GIST Descriptors with Bayesian Networks for Recognition of Tifinagh Characters. *International Journal of Computers and Applications, 81.*

Oujaoura, M., El Ayachi, R., Minaoui, B., Fakir, M., Bouikhalene, B., & Bencharef, O. (2013). Invariant descriptors and classifiers combination for recognition of isolated printed Tifinagh characters. *Third International Symposium on Automatic Amazigh Processing (SITACAM'13).* 10.14569/SpecialIssue.2013.030205

Oulamara, A., & Duvernoy, J. (1988). An application of the Hough transform to automatic recognition of Berber characters. *Signal Processing, 14*(1), 79–90. doi:10.1016/0165-1684(88)90045-X

Pachpande, S., & Chaudhari, A. (2017). *Implementation of devanagri character recognition system through pattern recognition techniques.* Paper presented at the 2017 International Conference on Trends in Electronics and Informatics (ICEI). 10.1109/ICOEI.2017.8300796

Pal, M. (2016). Investigating Polynomial Interpolation Functions for Zooming Low Resolution Digital Medical Images. *International Journal of Computer and Information Engineering, 10*(2), 396–402.

Park, J. H., Yim, H. S., Choi, Y. J., Jo, J. H., Moon, H. K., Park, Y. S., Bae, Y.-H., Park, S.-Y., Roh, D.-G., Cho, S., Choi, E.-J., Kim, M.-J., & Choi, E. J. (2018). OWL-Net: A global network of robotic telescopes for satellite observation. *Advances in Space Research, 62*(1), 152–163. doi:10.1016/j.asr.2018.04.008

Park, S. Y., Choi, J., Roh, D. G., Park, M., Jo, J. H., Yim, H. S., Park, Y.-S., Bae, Y.-H., Park, J.-H., Moon, H.-K., Choi, Y.-J., Cho, S., & Choi, Y. J. (2016). Development of a data reduction algorithm for optical wide field patrol (OWL) II: Improving measurement of lengths of detected streaks. *Journal of Astronomy and Space Sciences, 33*(3), 221–227. doi:10.5140/JASS.2016.33.3.221

Pavan, A. L. M., Vacavant, A., Alves, A. F. F., Trindade, A. P., & de Pina, D. R. (2019). Automatic Identification and Extraction of Pectoral Muscle in Digital Mammography. *IFMBE Proceedings, 68*(1). doi:10.1007/978-981-10-9035-6_27

Pena, J. M., Lozano, J. A., & Larranaga, P. (1999). An empirical comparison of four initialization methods for the K-Means algorithm. *Pattern Recognition Letters, 20*(10), 1027–1040. doi:10.1016/S0167-8655(99)00069-0

Pennington, J., Socher, R., & Manning, C. (2014). Glove: Global vectors for word representation. *In Proceedings of the 2014 Conference on Empirical Methods in Natural Language Processing (EMNLP)* (pp. 1532-1543). ACL. 10.3115/v1/D14-1162

Pereira, D. C., Ramos, R. P., & do Nascimento, M. Z. (2014). Segmentation and detection of breast cancer in mammograms combining wavelet analysis and genetic algorithm. *Computer Methods and Programs in Biomedicine, 114*(1), 88–101. doi:10.1016/j.cmpb.2014.01.014 PubMed

Perin, C., Boy, J., & Vernier, F. (2016). Using gap charts to visualize the temporal evolution of ranks and scores. *IEEE Computer Graphics and Applications, 36*(5), 38–49. doi:10.1109/MCG.2016.100 PMID:28113147

Perin, C., Vuillemot, R., Stolper, C. D., Stasko, J. T., Wood, J., & Carpendale, S. (2018). State of the art of sports data visualization. *Computer Graphics Forum, 37*(3), 663–686. doi:10.1111/cgf.13447

Philipson, W. (1997). Manual of Photographic Interpretation (2nd ed.). Bethesda, MD: American Society Photogrammetry and Remote Sensing (ASPRS).

Pirlo, G., & Impedovo, D. J. I. T. o. F. S. (2011). *Fuzzy-zoning-based classification for handwritten characters.* Academic Press.

Polidorio, A., Flores, F., Imai, N., Tommaselli, A., & Franco, C. (2003). Automatic shadow segmentation in aerial color images. *XVI Brazilian Symp. Comput. Graph. Image Process*, 270-277. 10.1109/SIBGRA.2003.1241019

Portmann, J., Lynen, S., Chli, M., & Siegwart, R. (2014, May). People detection and tracking from aerial thermal views. *IEEE International Conference on Robotics and Automation*, •••, 1794–1800. doi:10.1109/ICRA.2014.6907094

Prati, A., Mikic, I., Trivedi, M., & Cucchiara, R. (2003). Detecting moving shadows: Algorithms and evaluations. *IEEE Transactions on Pattern Analysis and Machine Intelligence, 25*(07), 918–923. doi:10.1109/TPAMI.2003.1206520

Prescott, J. W., Pennell, M., Best, T. M., Swanson, M. S., Haq, F., Jackson, R., & Gurcan, M. N. (2009). An automated method to segment the femur for osteoarthritis research. In *Proceedings of the Annual International Conference of the IEEE Engineering in Medicine and Biology Society.* IEEE., doi:10.1109/IEMBS.2009.5333257.

Pritchard, A. J., Sangwine, S. J., & Horne, R. E. N. (1993). Corner and curve detection along a boundary using line segment triangles. *Electronics Division Colloquium on Hough Transforms, 106*, 1–4.

Punitha, S., Amuthan, A., & Joseph, K. S. (2018). Benign and malignant breast cancer segmentation using optimized region growing technique. Future Computing and Informatics Journal, 3(2), 348–358. doi:10.1016/j.fcij.2018.10.005

Qian, C., & Yang, X. (2018). An integrated method for atherosclerotic carotid plaque segmentation in ultrasound image. *Computer Methods and Programs in Biomedicine, 153*, 19–32. doi:10.1016/j.cmpb.2017.10.002 PMID:29157451

Qian, P., Zhao, K., Jiang, Y., Su, K.-H., Deng, Z., Wang, S., & Muzic, R. F. Jr. (2017). Knowledge-Leveraged Transfer Fuzzy C-Means for Texture Image Segmentation with Self-Adaptive Cluster Prototype Matching. *Knowledge-Based Systems, 130*, 33–50. doi:10.1016/j.knosys.2017.05.018 PMID:30050232

Qiao, J., Cai, X., Xiao, Q., Chen, Z., Kulkarni, P., Ferris, C., Kamarthi, S., & Sridhar, S. (2019). Data on MRI brain lesion segmentation using K-means and Gaussian Mixture Model-Expectation Maximization. *Data in Brief, 27*, 104628. Advance online publication. doi:10.1016/j.dib.2019.104628 PubMed

Qi, B., John, V., Liu, Z., & Mita, S. (2014, October). Pedestrian detection from thermal images with a scattered difference of directional gradients feature descriptor. In *17th International IEEE Conference on Intelligent Transportation Systems (ITSC)*(pp. 2168-2173). IEEE. 10.1109/ITSC.2014.6958024

Qiu, J., Zhou, Y., Wang, Q., Ruan, T., & Gao, J. J. I. T. o. N. (2019). *Chinese clinical named entity recognition using residual dilated convolutional neural network with conditional random field.* Academic Press.

Raba, D., Oliver, A., Martí, J., Peracaula, M., & Espunya, J. (2005). Breast Segmentation with Pectoral Muscle Suppression on Digital Mammograms. In J. S. Marques, N. Pérez de la Blanca, & P. Pina (Eds.), Lecture Notes in Computer Science: Vol. 3523. *Pattern Recognition and Image Analysis. IbPRIA 2005* (pp. 471–478). Springer., doi:10.1007/11492542_58.

Radford, A., Metz, L., & Chintala, S. (2015). *Unsupervised representation learning with deep convolutional generative adversarial networks.* arXiv preprint arXiv:1511.06434

Raj, A., Sangkloy, P., Chang, H., Lu, J., Ceylan, D., & Hays, J. (2018). Swapnet: Garment transfer in single view images. In *Proceedings of the European Conference on Computer Vision (ECCV)* (pp. 666-682). Academic Press.

Rampun, A., López-Linares, K., Morrow, P. J., Scotney, B. W., Wang, H., Ocaña, I. G., Maclair, G., Zwiggelaar, R., Ballester, M. A. G., & Macía, I. (2019). Breast pectoral muscle segmentation in mammograms using a modified holistically-nested edge detection network. *Medical Image Analysis*, *57*, 1–17. doi:10.1016/j.media.2019.06.007 PubMed

Rand, W. M. (1971). Objective Criteria for the Evaluation of Clustering Methods. *Journal of the American Statistical Association*, *66*(336), 846–850. doi:10.1080/01621459.1971.10482356

Rao, K. R., & Yip, P. C. (2001). *The transform and data compression handbook.* CRC Press LLC.

Rattarangsi, A., & Chin, R. T. (1992). Scale-Based Detection of Corners of Planar Curves. *IEEE Transactions on Pattern Analysis and Machine Intelligence*, *14*(4), 430–449. doi:10.1109/34.126805

Rayar, F., Goto, M., & Uchida, S. (2018). *CNN training with graph-based sample preselection: application to handwritten character recognition.* Paper presented at the 2018 13th IAPR International Workshop on Document Analysis Systems (DAS). 10.1109/DAS.2018.10

Ray, B. K., & Pandyan, R. (2003). ACORD – an adaptive corner detector for planar curves. *Pattern Recognition*, *36*(3), 703–708. doi:10.1016/S0031-3203(02)00084-5

Redmon, J., Divvala, S., Girshick, R., & Farhadi, A. (2016). You only look once: Unified, real-time object detection. In *Proceedings of the IEEE conference on computer vision and pattern recognition* (pp. 779-788). 10.1109/CVPR.2016.91

Ren, H., Wang, W., Lu, K., Zhou, J., & Yuan, Q. (2017). *An end-to-end recognizer for in-air handwritten Chinese characters based on a new recurrent neural networks.* Paper presented at the 2017 IEEE International Conference on Multimedia and Expo (ICME). 10.1109/ICME.2017.8019443

Ren, X., Zhou, Y., Huang, Z., Sun, J., Yang, X., & Chen, K. J. I. A. (2017). *A novel text structure feature extractor for Chinese scene text detection and recognition.* Academic Press.

Rezaei, Z., Kasmuni, M. D., Selamat, A., Rahim, M. S. M., Abaei, G., & Abdul Kadir, M. R. (2015). Comparitive Study Of clustering Algorithms In order To Virtual Histology (VH) Image Segmentation. *Jurnal Teknologi*, *75*(2), 133–139. doi:10.11113/jt.v75.4994

Rezaei, Z., Selamat, A., Taki, A., Mohd Rahim, M. S., Abdul Kadir, M. R., Penhaker, M., Krejcar, O., Kuca, K., Herrera-Viedma, E., & Fujita, H. (2018). Thin Cap Fibroatheroma Detection in Virtual Histology Images Using Geometric and Texture Features. *Applied Sciences (Basel, Switzerland)*, *8*(9), 1632. doi:10.3390/app8091632

Rezaei, Z., Selamat, A., Taki, A., Rahim, M. S. M., & Abdul Kadir, M. R. (2017). Automatic plaque segmentation based on hybrid fuzzy clustering and k nearest neighborhood using virtual histology intravascular ultrasound images. *Applied Soft Computing*, *53*, 380–395. doi:10.1016/j.asoc.2016.12.048

Ribeiro, F. D. S., Gong, L., Calivá, F., Swainson, M., Gudmundsson, K., Yu, M., . . . Kollias, S. (2018). *An end-to-end deep neural architecture for optical character verification and recognition in retail food packaging.* Paper presented at the 2018 25th IEEE International Conference on Image Processing (ICIP).

Robson, J. G., & Graham, N. (1981). Probability summation and regional variation in contrast sensitivity across the visual field. *Vision Research, 21*(3), 409–418. doi:10.1016/0042-6989(81)90169-3 PMID:7269319

Rocha, A., Scheirer, W. J., Forstall, C. W., Cavalcante, T., Theophilo, A., Shen, B., & Stamatatos, E. (2016). Authorship attribution for social media forensics. *IEEE Transactions on Information Forensics and Security, 12*(1), 5–33. doi:10.1109/TIFS.2016.2603960

Ronan, P. (2007). *Electromagnetic Spectrum.* Retrieved from http://www.kiwiwise.co.nz/photo/fantail-vector

Rosenberger, C., & Chehdi, K. (2000). Unsupervised clustering method with optimal estimation of the number of clusters: Application to image segmentation. In *Proceedings 15th International Conference on Pattern Recognition. ICPR-2000* (Vol. 1, pp. 656-659). IEEE. 10.1109/ICPR.2000.905473

Rosenfeld & Weszka. (n.d.). An Improved Method of Angle Detection on Digital Curves. *IEEE Transactions on Computers, 24*, 940-941.

Rosenfeld, A., & Johnston, E. (1973). Angle Detection on Digital Curves. *IEEE Transactions on Computers, 22*(9), 875–878. doi:10.1109/TC.1973.5009188

Rosenholtz, R., Li, Y., Mansfield, J., & Jin, Z. (2005). Feature congestion: A measure of display clutter. In *Proceedings of the SIGCHI Conference on Human Factors in Computing Systems,* (pp. 761–770). ACM. 10.1145/1054972.1055078

Roy, P., Ghosh, S., & Pal, U. (2018). *A CNN based framework for unistroke numeral recognition in air-writing.* Paper presented at the 2018 16th International Conference on Frontiers in Handwriting Recognition (ICFHR). 10.1109/ICFHR-2018.2018.00077

Rujikietgumjorn, S., & Watcharapinchai, N. (2017, August). Real-time hog-based pedestrian detection in thermal images for an embedded system. In *14th IEEE International Conference on Advanced Video and Signal Based Surveillance (AVSS)* (pp. 1-6). IEEE. 10.1109/AVSS.2017.8078561

Russell, A., & Zou, J. (2012). Vehicle detection based on color analysis. *IEEE Conf. on Communications and Information Technologies (ISCIT),* 620-625.

Russell, J. D., Weems, C. F., Ahmed, I., & Richard, G. G. III. (2017). Self-reported secure and insecure cyber behaviour: Factor structure and associations with personality factors. *Journal of Cyber Security Technology, 1*(3-4), 163–174. doi :10.1080/23742917.2017.1345271

Russell, M., Zou, J., & Fang, G. (2003). Real-time vehicle shadow detection. *IEEE Electronics Letters, 51*(16), 1253–1255. doi:10.1049/el.2015.1841

Rutkowski, W. S., & Rosenfeld, A. (1978). *A comparison of corner-detection techniques for chain-coded curves (TR-623).* Computer Science Center, University of Maryland.

Saha, C., Faisal, R. H., & Rahman, M. M. (2019). *Bangla handwritten digit recognition using an improved deep convolutional neural network architecture.* Paper presented at the 2019 International Conference on Electrical, Computer and Communication Engineering (ECCE). 10.1109/ECACE.2019.8679309

Sahare, P., & Dhok, S. B. J. I. A. (2018). *Multilingual character segmentation and recognition schemes for Indian document images.* Academic Press.

Sánchez, J., Monzón, N., & Salgado, A. (2018). An Analysis and Implementation of the Harris Corner Detector. *Image Processing on Line*, *8*, 305–328. doi:10.5201/ipol.2018.229

Sankari, L., & Chandrasekar, C. (2011). Semi Supervised Image Segmentation by Optimal Color Seed Selection using Fast Genetic Algorithm. *International Journal of Computers and Applications*, *26*(10), 13–18. doi:10.5120/3143-4340

Sarfraz, M. (2014). Detecting Corner Features of Planar Objects. In M. Sarfraz (Ed.), *Computer Vision and Image Processing in Intelligent Systems and Multimedia Technologies* (pp. 262–279). IGI Global. doi:10.4018/978-1-4666-6030-4.ch015

Sarfraz, M., Asim, M. R., & Masood, A. (2004a). Capturing Outlines using Cubic Bezier Curves. In *Proc. of IEEE 1st International Conference on Information & Communication Technologies: from Theory to Applications*. IEEE.

Sarfraz, M., Asim, M. R., & Masood, A. (2004b). A Web Based System for Capturing Outlines of 2D Objects. In *Proceedings of The International Conference on Information and Computer Science*, (pp. 575 – 586). King Fahd University of Petroleum and Minerals.

Sarfraz, M., Masood, A., & Asim, M. R. (2006). A new approach to corner detection. In K. Wojciechowski, B. Smolka, H. Palus, R. S. Kozera, W. Skarbek, & L. Noakes (Eds.), *Computer vision and graphics* (pp. 528–533). Springer. doi:10.1007/1-4020-4179-9_75

Sarfraz, M., & Swati, Z. N. K. (2013). Mining Corner Points on the Generic Shapes. *Ozean Journal of Applied Sciences*, *3*(01, 1B), 10–15. doi:10.4236/ojapps.2013.31B003

Sarkar, J. P., Saha, I., & Maulik, U. (2016). Rough Possibilistic Type-2 Fuzzy C-Means clustering for MR brain image segmentation. *Applied Soft Computing*, *46*, 527–536. doi:10.1016/j.asoc.2016.01.040

Sepahvand, M., Abdali-Mohammadi, F., & Mardukhi, F. J. I. t. o. c. (2016). *Evolutionary metric-learning-based recognition algorithm for online isolated Persian/Arabic characters, reconstructed using inertial pen signals*. Academic Press.

Sezgin, M., & Sankur, B. (2004). Survey over image thresholding techniques and quantitative performance evaluation. *Journal of Electronic Imaging*, *13*(1), 146–165. doi:10.1117/1.1631315

Shalhoub, G., Simon, R., Iyer, R., Tailor, J., & Westcott, S. (2010). Stylometry system–use cases and feasibility study. *Forensic Linguistics*, *1*(8).

Shao, L., Liang, C., Wang, K., Cao, W., Zhang, W., Gui, G., & Sari, H. J. I. A. (2019).. . *Attention GAN-Based Method for Designing Intelligent Making System.*, *7*, 163097–163104.

Shapiro, L. G., & Stockman, G. C. (2001). *Computer Vision*. Prentice Books.

Sharma, A. J. V. J. o. C. S. (2015). *A combined static and dynamic feature extraction technique to recognize handwritten digits*. Academic Press.

Shen, R., Yan, K., Xiao, F., Chang, J., Jiang, C., & Zhou, K. (2018). Automatic Pectoral Muscle Region Segmentation in Mammograms Using Genetic Algorithm and Morphological Selection. *Journal of Digital Imaging*, *31*(5), 680–691. doi:10.1007/s10278-018-0068-9 PubMed

Shi, C.-Z., Gao, S., Liu, M.-T., Qi, C.-Z., Wang, C.-H., & Xiao, B.-H. J. I. T. o. I. P. (2015). *Stroke detector and structure based models for character recognition: A comparative study*. Academic Press.

Shi, J., & Tomasi, C. (June 1994). Good Features to Track. *9th IEEE Conference on Computer Vision and Pattern Recognition. Springer.* 593–600. doi:10.1109/CVPR.1994.323794

Shneiderman, B. (1996). The eyes have it: A task by data type taxonomy for information visualizations. *Proceedings of the IEEE Symposium on Visual Languages*, 336–343. 10.1109/VL.1996.545307

Šilha, J. (2019). Slovak optical telescope and image processing pipeline for the space debris and NEA observations and research. ESA NEO and Debris Conference.

Silva, R. S., Laboreiro, G., Sarmento, L., Grant, T., Oliveira, E., & Maia, B. (2011). 'Twazn me! Automatic authorship analysis of micro-blogging messages. In *Natural Language Processing and Information Systems* (pp. 161–168). Springer. doi:10.1007/978-3-642-22327-3_16

Simi, V., & Joseph, J. (2015). Segmentation of Glioblastoma Multiforme from MR Images–A comprehensive review. *The Egyptian Journal of Radiology and Nuclear Medicine, 46*(4), 1105–1110. doi:10.1016/j.ejrnm.2015.08.001

Singh, Arun Pal, & Singh. (2019, July 30). *Normal Wrist X-Ray: Bone and Spine.* Retrieved August 26, 2019, from https://boneandspine.com/normal-wrist-x-ray/

Smith, H. (1992). Putting colors in order. *Dr. Dobb's Journal, 1993*(01), 40.

Smith, P., Sinclair, D., Cipolla, R., & Wood, K. (1998). Effective Corner Matching. In *Proceedings of the 9th British Machine Vision Conference*, (vol. 2, pp. 545-556). BMVA Press.

Smith, S., & Brady, J. (1995). SUSAN— A new approach to low level image processing. *International Journal of Computer Vision, 23*(1), 45–78. doi:10.1023/A:1007963824710

Snoek, J., Larochelle, H., & Adams, R. P. (2012). Practical bayesian optimization of machine learning algorithms. In Advances in neural information processing systems (pp. 2951-2959). Academic Press.

Son, S., So, H., Kim, J., Choi, D., & Lee, H.-J. J. E. L. (2015). *Energy-efficient adaptive optical character recognition for wearable devices.* Academic Press.

Song, H., Huang, B., & Zhang, K. (2014). Shadow Detection and Reconstruction in High-Resolution Satellite Images via Morphological Filtering and Example-Based Learning. *IEEE Transactions on Geoscience and Remote Sensing, 52*(05), 2545–2554. doi:10.1109/TGRS.2013.2262722

Song, Y., & Cai, W. (2017). Handling of Feature Space Complexity for Texture Analysis in Medical Images. In A. Depeursinge, O. S. Al-Kadi, & J. R. Mitchell (Eds.), *Biomedical Texture Analysis, Fundamentals, Tools and Challenges* (pp. 163–191). Academic Press., doi:10.1016/B978-0-12-812133-7.00006-5.

Spafford, E. H., & Weeber, S. A. (1993). Software forensics: Can we track code to its authors? *Computers & Security, 12*(6), 585–595. doi:10.1016/0167-4048(93)90055-A

Spinello, L., & Arras, K. O. (2011, September). People detection in RGB-D data. In *IEEE/RSJ International Conference on Intelligent Robots and Systems* (pp. 3838-3843). IEEE.

Sreedevi, S., & Sherly, E. (2015). A Novel Approach for Removal of Pectoral Muscles in Digital Mammogram. *Procedia Computer Science, 46*, 1724–1731. doi:10.1016/j.procs.2015.02.117

Stallkamp, J., Schlipsing, M., Salmen, J., & Igel, C. (2011). The German Traffic Sign Recognition Benchmark: A multi-class classification competition. *The 2011 International Joint Conference on Neural Networks*, 1453-1460. doi: 10.1109/IJCNN.2011.6033395

Steinley, D. (2006). K-means clustering: A half-century synthesis. *British Journal of Mathematical & Statistical Psychology, 57*(1), 1–34. doi:10.1348/000711005X48266 PMID:16709277

Steinley, D., & Brusco, M. J. (2007). Initializing K-means batch cluster: A critical evaluation of several teqhniques. *Journal of Classification, 24*(1), 99–121. doi:10.100700357-007-0003-0

Strutz, T. (2016). *Data Fitting and Uncertainty: A practical introduction to weighted least squares and beyond* (2nd ed.). Springer., doi:10.1007/978-3-658-11456-5.

Su, N., Zhang, Y., Tian, S., Yan, Y., & Miao, X. (2016). Shadow Detection and Removal for Occluded Object Information Recovery in Urban High-Resolution Panchromatic Satellite Images. *IEEE Journal on Geoscience and Remote Sensing, 9*(6), 2568-2582.

Suckling, J., Parker, J., Astley, S., Hutt, I. W., Boggis, C., Ricketts, I. W., Stamatakis, E., Cerneaz, N., Kok, S., Taylor, P., Betal, D., & Savage, J. (1994). The Mammographic Image Analysis Society Digital Mammogram Database. Exerpta Medica. *International Congress Series, 1069*, 375–378.

Sugar, C. A., & James, G. M. (2003). Finding the number of clusters in a dataset: An information-theoretic approach. *Journal of the American Statistical Association, 98*(463), 750–763. doi:10.1198/016214503000000666

Sujatha, S., & Sona, A. S. (2013). New fast K-means clustering algorithm using modified centroid selection method. *International Journal of Engineering Research & Technology (Ahmedabad), 2*(2), 1–9.

Sultana, M., & Gavrilova, M. (2018). Temporal pattern in tweeting behavior for persons' identity verification. In *Proceedings of International Conference on System, Men and Cybernetics (SMC)* (pp 2468-2473). IEEE. 10.1109/SMC.2018.00424

Sultana, M., Paul, P. P., & Gavrilova, M. (2014). A concept of social behavioral biometrics: motivation, current developments, and future trends. In *Proceedings of International Conference on Cyberworlds* (pp. 271-278). IEEE. 10.1109/CW.2014.44

Sultana, M., Paul, P. P., & Gavrilova, M. (2014). Mining social behavioral biometrics in Twitter. In *International Conference on Cyberworld* (pp. 293-299). IEEE.

Sultana, M., Paul, P. P., & Gavrilova, M. (2015). Social behavioral biometrics: An emerging trend. *International Journal of Pattern Recognition and Artificial Intelligence, 29*(08), 1556013. doi:10.1142/S0218001415560133

Sultana, M., Paul, P. P., & Gavrilova, M. L. (2014). Online user interaction traits in web-based social biometrics. In M. Sarfraz (Ed.), *Computer Vision and Image Processing in Intelligent Systems and Multimedia Technologies* (pp. 177–190). IGI Global. doi:10.4018/978-1-4666-6030-4.ch009

Sultana, M., Paul, P. P., & Gavrilova, M. L. (2017). Social behavioral information fusion in multimodal biometrics. *IEEE Transactions on Systems, Man, and Cybernetics. Systems, 48*(12), 2176–2187. doi:10.1109/TSMC.2017.2690321

Sultana, M., Paul, P. P., & Gavrilova, M. L. (2017). User recognition from social behavior in computer-mediated social context. *IEEE Transactions on Human-Machine Systems, 47*(3), 356–367. doi:10.1109/THMS.2017.2681673

Su, M.-C., & Chou, C.-H. (2001). A modified version of the K-means algorithm with a distance based on cluster symmetry. *IEEE Transactions on Pattern Analysis and Machine Intelligence, 23*(6), 674–680. doi:10.1109/34.927466

Su, T., & Dy, J. G. (2007). In search of deterministic methods for initializing k-means and Gaussian mixture clustering. *Intelligent Data Analysis, 11*(4), 319–338. doi:10.3233/IDA-2007-11402

Swastika, W., Setiawan, H., & Subianto, M. (2017). *Android based application for recognition of Indonesian restaurant menus using convolution neural network*. Paper presented at the 2017 International Conference on Sustainable Information Engineering and Technology (SIET). 10.1109/SIET.2017.8304104

Taki, A. (2010). *Improvement and Automatic Classification of IVUS-VH (Intravascular Ultrasound – Virtual Histology) Images. Technical University of Munich*. TUM.

Taki, A., Roodaki, A., Setarehdan, S. K., Avansari, S., Unal, G., & Navab, N. (2013). An IVUS image-based approach for improvement of coronary plaque characterization. *Computers in Biology and Medicine, 43*(4), 268–280. doi:10.1016/j.compbiomed.2012.12.008 PMID:23410676

Tang, Y., & Wu, X. J. I. T. o. M. (2018). *Scene text detection using superpixel-based stroke feature transform and deep learning based region classification.* Academic Press.

Tang, Y., Wu, B., Peng, L., & Liu, C. (2017). *Semi-supervised transfer learning for convolutional neural network based Chinese character recognition.* Paper presented at the 2017 14th IAPR International Conference on Document Analysis and Recognition (ICDAR). 10.1109/ICDAR.2017.79

Tan, K. S., & Isa, N. A. M. (2011). Color image segmentation using histogram thresholding–Fuzzy C-means hybrid approach. *Pattern Recognition, 44*(1), 1–15. doi:10.1016/j.patcog.2010.07.013

Tan, K. S., Isa, N. A. M., & Lim, W. H. (2013). Color image segmentation using adaptive unsupervised clustering approach. *Applied Soft Computing, 13*(4), 2017–2036. doi:10.1016/j.asoc.2012.11.038

Tan, K. S., Lim, W. H., & Isa, N. A. M. (2013). Novel initialization scheme for Fuzzy C-Means algorithm on color image segmentation. *Applied Soft Computing, 13*(4), 1832–1852. doi:10.1016/j.asoc.2012.12.022

Tao, D., Lin, X., Jin, L., & Li, X. J. I. t. o. c. (2015). *Principal component 2-D long short-term memory for font recognition on single Chinese characters.* Academic Press.

Teh, C. H., & Chin, R. (1990). On the detection of dominant points on digital curves. *IEEE Transactions on Pattern Analysis and Machine Intelligence, 11*(8), 859–873. doi:10.1109/34.31447

Teutsch, M., Muller, T., Huber, M., & Beyerer, J. (2014). Low resolution person detection with a moving thermal infrared camera by hot spot classification. In *Proceedings of the IEEE Conference on Computer Vision and Pattern Recognition Workshops* (pp. 209-216). 10.1109/CVPRW.2014.40

Tian, Y., Lu, M., & Hampapur, A. (2005). Robust and efficient foreground analysis for real-time video surveillance. *IEEE Conference on Computer Vision and Pattern Recognition*, 1182-1187.

Tibshirani, R., & Walther, G. (2005). Cluster validation by prediction strength. *Journal of Computational and Graphical Statistics, 14*(3), 511–528. doi:10.1198/106186005X59243

Tibshirani, R., Walther, G., & Hastie, T. (2001). Estimating the number of clusters in a data set via the gap statistic. *Journal of the Royal Statistical Society. Series B. Methodological, 63*(2), 411–423. doi:10.1111/1467-9868.00293

Tlig, L., Sayadi, V., & Fnaiech, F. (2012). A new fuzzy segmentation approach based on S-FCM type 2 using LBP-GCO features. *Signal Processing Image Communication, 27*(6), 694–708. doi:10.1016/j.image.2012.03.001

Tomasi, C. & Kanade, T. (1991). *Detection and Tracking of Point Features* (Technical report). School of Computer Science, Carnegie Mellon University. CMU-CS-91-132.

Tsai, V. (2006). A comparative study on shadow compensation of color aerial images in invariant color models. *IEEE Transactions on Geoscience and Remote Sensing, 44*(06), 1661–1671. doi:10.1109/TGRS.2006.869980

Tufte, E. R. (1992). *The Visual Display of Quantitative Information.* Graphics Press.

Tweedie, F. J., & Baayen, R. H. (1998). How variable may a constant be? Measures of lexical richness in perspective. *Computers and the Humanities, 32*(5), 323–352. doi:10.1023/A:1001749303137

Tzikopoulos, S. D., Mavroforakis, M. E., Georgiou, H. V., Dimitropoulos, N., & Theodoridis, S. (2011). A fully automated scheme for mammographic segmentation and classification based on breast density and asymmetry. *Computer Methods and Programs in Biomedicine*, *102*(1), 47–63. doi:10.1016/j.cmpb.2010.11.016 PubMed

Tzortzis, G., & Likas, A. (2014). The MinMax k-Means clustering algorithm. *Pattern Recognition*, *47*(7), 2505–2516. doi:10.1016/j.patcog.2014.01.015

Unar, J. A., Seng, W. C., & Abbasi, A. (2014). A review of biometric technology along with trends and prospects. *Pattern Recognition*, *47*(8), 2673–2688. doi:10.1016/j.patcog.2014.01.016

Vakhare, P. (2015). Shadow detection and elimination using geometric approach for static images. *IEEE Conference on Applied and Theoretical Computing and Communication Technology (iCATccT)*, 415-419. 10.1109/ICATCCT.2015.7456919

Vallado, D., Crawford, P., Hujsak, R., & Kelso, T. S. (2006, August). Revisiting spacetrack report #3. In AIAA/AAS Astrodynamics Specialist Conference and Exhibit (p. 6753). Academic Press.

van der Aalst, W. M. P. (2016). *Process Mining - Data Science in Action* (2nd ed.). Springer. doi:10.1007/978-3-662-49851-4

Van der Merwe, D., & Engelbrecht, A. P. (2003). Data clustering using particle swarm optimization. In *The 2003 Congress on Evolutionary Computation, Proceedings of the IEEE Congress on Evolutionary Computation, CEC 2003*. Canberra, Australia, IEEE. DOI: 10.1109/CEC.2003.1299577

van Wijk, J. J., & van Selow, E. R. (1999). Cluster and calendar based visualization of time series data. *Proceedings of IEEE Symposium on Information Visualization*, 4–9. 10.1109/INFVIS.1999.801851

Vijayakumar, C., Damayanti, G., Pant, R., & Sreedhar, C. M. (2007). Segmentation and grading of brain tumors on apparent diffusion coefficient images using self-organizing maps. *Computerized Medical Imaging and Graphics*, *31*(7), 473–484. doi:10.1016/j.compmedimag.2007.04.004 PMID:17572068

Vincent, E., & Laganiere, R. (2005). Detecting and matching feature points. *Journal of Visual Communication and Image Representation*, *16*(1), 38–54. doi:10.1016/j.jvcir.2004.05.001

Vincent, E., & Laganire, R. (2001). Matching feature points in stereo pairs: A comparative study of some matching strategies. *Machine Graphics and Vision*, *10*, 237–259.

Vondrick, C., Khosla, A., Malisiewicz, T., & Torralba, A. (2013). Hoggles: Visualizing object detection features. In *Proceedings of the IEEE International Conference on Computer Vision* (pp. 1-8). IEEE.

Wang, B., Zheng, H., Liang, X., Chen, Y., Lin, L., & Yang, M. (2018). Toward characteristic-preserving image-based virtual try-on network. In *Proceedings of the European Conference on Computer Vision (ECCV)* (pp. 589-604). Academic Press.

Wang, F., Guo, Q., Lei, J., & Zhang, J. J. I. C. V. (2017). *Convolutional recurrent neural networks with hidden Markov model bootstrap for scene text recognition*. Academic Press.

Wang, Q.-F., Yin, F., Liu, C.-L. J. I. t. o. p. a., & Intelligence, M. (2011). *Handwritten Chinese text recognition by integrating multiple contexts*. Academic Press.

Wang, T.-Q., & Liu, C.-L. (2018). *DeepAD: A Deep Learning Based Approach to Stroke-Level Abnormality Detection in Handwritten Chinese Character Recognition*. Paper presented at the 2018 IEEE International Conference on Data Mining (ICDM). 10.1109/ICDM.2018.00176

Wang, C.-W., Jeng, J.-H., Yang, W.-S., & Hsieh, J.-G. (2016). PCA image coding with iterative clustering. *Multidimensional Systems and Signal Processing*, *27*(3), 647–666. doi:10.100711045-015-0357-0

Wang, H., & Brady, M. (1995). Real-time corner detection algorithm for motion estimation. *Image and Vision Computing, 13*(9), 695–703. doi:10.1016/0262-8856(95)98864-P

Wang, J., Chung, Y., & Chen, S. (2004). Shadow detection and removal for traffic images. *IEEE Int. Conf. on Networking, Sensing and Control,* 649-654. 10.1109/ICNSC.2004.1297516

Wang, W., Zhang, J., & Shen, C. (2010, September). Improved human detection and classification in thermal images. *IEEE International Conference on Image Processing* (pp. 2313-2316). IEEE. 10.1109/ICIP.2010.5649946

Wang, X.-Y., Wang, T., & Bu, J. (2011). Color image segentation using pixel wise support vector machine classification. *Pattern Recognition, 44*(4), 777–787. doi:10.1016/j.patcog.2010.08.008

Wang, Z., & Bovik, A. C. (2001). Embedded Foveation Image Coding. *IEEE Transactions on Image Processing, 10*(10). PMID:18255485

Wang, Z., Bovik, A. C., Sheikh, H. R., & Simoncelli, E. P. (2004). Image quality assessment: From error visibility to structural similarity. *IEEE Transactions on Image Processing, 13*(4), 600–612. doi:10.1109/TIP.2003.819861 PubMed

Wang, Z., Lu, L., & Bovik, A. C. (2003). Foveation Scalable Video Coding with Automatic Fixation Selection. *IEEE Transactions on Image Processing, 12*(2). PMID:18237905

Wang, Z., Song, Q., Soh, Y. C., & Sim, K. (2013). An adaptive spatial information-theoretic fuzzy clustering algorithm for image segmentation. *Computer Vision and Image Understanding, 117*(10), 1412–1420. doi:10.1016/j.cviu.2013.05.001

Ward, J. H. Jr. (1963). Hierarchical grouping to optimize an objective function. *Journal of the American Statistical Association, 58*(301), 236–244. doi:10.1080/01621459.1963.10500845

Ware, C. (2004). *Information Visualization: Perception for Design.* Morgan Kaufmann.

Ware, C. (2008). *Visual Thinking: for Design.* Morgan Kaufmann Series in Interactive Technologies, Paperback.

Watanabe, K., Takahashi, S., Takagi, Y., Yamada, M., Mekada, Y., Hasegawa, J., . . . Miyazaki, S. (2018). *Detection of Characters and their Boundary from Images of Modern Japanese Official Documents using Fully CNN-based Filter.* Paper presented at the 2018 Nicograph International (NicoInt). 10.1109/NICOINT.2018.00024

Weigel, M., Meinel, M., & Fiedler, H. (2015, October). Processing of optical telescope observations with the space object catalogue BACARDI. In *25th International Symposium on Space Flight Dynamics ISSFD* (Vol. 19, p. 23). Academic Press.

Weike, L., & Sei-Ichiro, K. (2017). *Radical Region Based CNN for Offline Handwritten Chinese Character Recognition.* Paper presented at the 2017 4th IAPR Asian Conference on Pattern Recognition (ACPR). 10.1109/ACPR.2017.76

Wells, D. C., & Greisen, E. W. (1979). FITS - A Flexible Image Transport System. In Image Processing in Astronomy (p. 445). Academic Press.

Wibowo, M. A., Soleh, M., Pradani, W., Hidayanto, A. N., & Arymurthy, A. M. (2017). *Handwritten Javanese character recognition using descriminative deep learning technique.* Paper presented at the 2017 2nd International conferences on Information Technology, Information Systems and Electrical Engineering (ICITISEE). 10.1109/ICITISEE.2017.8285521

Wijaya, S. H., Afendi, F. M., Batubara, I., Darusman, L. K., Altaf-Ul-Amin, M., & Kanaya, S. (2016). Finding an appropriateequation to measuresimilaritybetweenbinaryvectors: Case studies on Indonesian and Japaneseherbalmedicines. *BMC Bioinformatics, 17*(1), 520. doi:10.1186/s12859-016-1392-z PubMed

Wikipedia, The Free Encyclopedia. (2020). BI-RADS. https://en.wikipedia.org/wiki/BI-RADS

Wikipedia, The Free Encyclopedia. (2020). Random Sample Consensus. https://en.wikipedia.org/wiki/Random_sample_consensus#cite_note-1

Wikipedia. (2020). *Corner Detection.* https://en.wikipedia.org/wiki/Corner_detection

Willigan, G. W., & Sokol, L. M. (1980). A two-stage clustering algorithm with robust recovery characteristics. *Educational and Psychological Measurement, 40*(3), 755–759. doi:10.1177/001316448004000320

Willis, A., & Sui, Y. (2009). An Algebraic Model for fast Corner Detection. *2009 IEEE 12th International Conference on Computer Vision,* 2296–2302. doi:10.1109/ICCV.2009.5459443

Wong, M. A. (1982). A hybrid clustering method for identifying high-density clusters. *Journal of the American Statistical Association, 77*(380), 841–847. doi:10.1080/01621459.1982.10477896

Wong, S. T. (Ed.). (2012). *Medical image databases* (Vol. 465). Springer Science & Business Media.

Wu, D., Wang, R., Dai, P., Zhang, Y., & Cao, X. (2017). *Deep strip-based network with cascade learning for scene text localization.* Paper presented at the 2017 14th IAPR International Conference on Document Analysis and Recognition (ICDAR). 10.1109/ICDAR.2017.140

Wu, P., Huang, Z., & Li, D. (2017). *Research on the character recognition for Chinese license plate based on CNN.* Paper presented at the 2017 3rd IEEE International Conference on Computer and Communications (ICCC). 10.1109/CompComm.2017.8322820

Wu, P., Wang, F., & Liu, J. (2018). *An Integrated Multi-Classifier Method for Handwritten Chinese Medicine Prescription Recognition.* Paper presented at the 2018 IEEE 9th International Conference on Software Engineering and Service Science (ICSESS). 10.1109/ICSESS.2018.8663789

Wu, Y., Shivakumara, P., Lu, T., Tan, C. L., Blumenstein, M., & Kumar, G. H. J. I. T. o. I. P. (2016). *Contour restoration of text components for recognition in video/scene images.* Academic Press.

Wu, Y.-C., Yin, F., Chen, Z., & Liu, C.-L. (2017). *Handwritten chinese text recognition using separable multi-dimensional recurrent neural network.* Paper presented at the 2017 14th IAPR International Conference on Document Analysis and Recognition (ICDAR). 10.1109/ICDAR.2017.22

Wu, C.-H., Lai, C.-C., Chen, C.-Y., & Chen, Y.-H. (2015). Automated clustering by support vector machines with a local-search strategy and its application to image segmentation. *Optik (Stuttgart), 126*(24), 4964–4970. doi:10.1016/j.ijleo.2015.09.143

Wu, G., Tang, G., Wang, Z., Zhang, Z., & Wang, Z. J. I. A. (2019)... *An Attention-Based BiLSTM-CRF Model for Chinese Clinic Named Entity Recognition., 7,* 113942–113949.

Wu, Z., Lin, G., Tao, Q., & Cai, J. (2019, October). M2e-try on net: Fashion from model to everyone. In *Proceedings of the 27th ACM International Conference on Multimedia* (pp. 293-301). ACM. 10.1145/3343031.3351083

Xiang, Z., You, Z., Qian, M., Zhang, J., Hu, X. J. E. J. o. I., & Processing, V. (2018). *Metal stamping character recognition algorithm based on multi-directional illumination image fusion enhancement technology.* Academic Press.

Xiang, T., & Gong, S. (2008). Spectral clustering with eigenvector selection. *Pattern Recognition, 41*(3), 1012–1029. doi:10.1016/j.patcog.2007.07.023

Xiao, X., Yang, Y., Ahmad, T., Jin, L., & Chang, T. (2017). *Design of a very compact cnn classifier for online handwritten chinese character recognition using dropweight and global pooling.* Paper presented at the 2017 14th IAPR International Conference on Document Analysis and Recognition (ICDAR). 10.1109/ICDAR.2017.150

Xin, M., & Wang, Y. (2019). Research on image classification model based on deep convolution neural network. *EURASIP Journal on Image and Video Processing, 2019*(1), 40. doi:10.118613640-019-0417-8

Xu, X., Zhou, J., & Zhang, H. (2018). *Screen-rendered text images recognition using a deep residual network based segmentation-free method.* Paper presented at the 2018 24th International Conference on Pattern Recognition (ICPR). 10.1109/ICPR.2018.8545678

Xu, L., Wang, Y., Li, X., & Pan, M. J. I. A. (2019).. . *Recognition of Handwritten Chinese Characters Based on Concept Learning., 7*, 102039–102053.

Xu, R., & Wunsch, D. II. (2005). Survey of Clustering Algorithms. *IEEE Transactions on Neural Networks, 16*(3), 645–678. doi:10.1109/TNN.2005.845141 PMID:15940994

Xu, X., Xu, S., Jin, L., & Song, E. (2011). Characteristic analysis of Otsu threshold and its applications. *Pattern Recognition Letters, 32*(7), 956–961. doi:10.1016/j.patrec.2011.01.021

Yampolskiy, R. V. (2011). Behavioral, cognitive and virtual biometrics. In A. Salah & T. Gevers (Eds.), *Computer Analysis of Human Behavior* (pp. 347–385). Springer. doi:10.1007/978-0-85729-994-9_13

Yampolskiy, R. V., & Govindaraju, V. (2008). Behavioral biometrics: A survey and classification. *International Journal of Biometrics, 1*(1), 81–113. doi:10.1504/IJBM.2008.018665

Yampolskiy, R. V., & Govindaraju, V. (2010). Game playing tactic as a behavioral biometric for human identification. In L. Wang & X. Geng (Eds.), *Behavioral Biometrics for Human Identification: Intelligent Applications* (pp. 385–413). IGI Global. doi:10.4018/978-1-60566-725-6.ch018

Yang, D., Gan, J., Wen, B., & Xu, T. (2017). The Algorithm for Extracting Elements of National Costume Based on Region Growing. In Proceedings of the 2017 2nd International Conference on Control, Automation and Artificial Intelligence (CAAI 2017). Atlantis Press, doi:10.2991/caai-17.2017.71

Yang, F., Jin, L., Lai, S., Gao, X., & Li, Z. J. I. A. (2019). *Fully convolutional sequence recognition network for water meter number reading.* Academic Press.

Yang, Y., Li, D., & Duan, Z. J. I. I. T. S. (2017). *Chinese vehicle license plate recognition using kernel-based extreme learning machine with deep convolutional features.* Academic Press.

Yang, T., Long, X., Sangaiah, A. K., Zheng, Z., & Tong, C. (2018). Deep detection network for real-life traffic sign in vehicular networks. *Computer Networks, 136*, 95–104. doi:10.1016/j.comnet.2018.02.026

Yang, Y., & Huang, S. (2012). Image segmentation by fuzzy c-means clustering algorithm with a novel penalty term. *Computer Information, 26*(1), 17–31.

Yanushkevich, S. N., Stoica, A., Srihari, S. N., Shmerko, V. P., & Gavrilova, M. L. (2004) Simulation of biometric information: the new generation of biometric systems, in *Proceedings of International Workshop Modeling and Simulation in Biometric Technology*, 87-98.

Yao, J., & Zhang, Z. (2004). Systematic static shadow detection. *Proc. 17th Int. Conf. Pattern Recognition*, 76-79.

Yarlagadda, S., & Zhu, F. (2018). A Reflectance Based Method For Shadow Detection and Removal. *IEEE Southwest Symposium Conference on Image Analysis and Interpretation (SSIAI)*, 9-12. 10.1109/SSIAI.2018.8470343

Yatsuyanagi, H., Fuchida, M., Okayasu, K., & Nakamura, A. (2017). *Development of a specific word recognition system for the visually handicapped—Character recognition based on dataset generated from font data.* Paper presented at the 2017 IEEE/SICE International Symposium on System Integration (SII). 10.1109/SII.2017.8279305

Yazdani, S., Yusof, R., Riazi, A., & Karimian, A. (2014). Magnetic resonance image tissue classification using an automatic method. *Diagnostic Pathology, 9*(1), 207. doi:10.118613000-014-0207-7 PMID:25540017

Yi, J. S., Kang, Y., Stasko, J., & Jacko, J. A. (2007). Toward a deeper understanding of the role of interaction in information visualization. *IEEE Transactions on Visualization and Computer Graphics, 13*(6), 1224–1231. doi:10.1109/TVCG.2007.70515 PMID:17968068

Yi, Y., Hengliang, L., Huarong, X., & Fuchao, W. (2016). Towards Real-Time Traffic Sign Detection and Classification. *IEEE Transactions on Intelligent Transportation Systems, 17*(7), 2022–2031. doi:10.1109/TITS.2015.2482461

Yoneyama, A., Yeh, C., & Kuo, C. (2003). Moving cast shadow elimination for robust vehicle extraction based on 2d joint vehicle/shadow models. *IEEE Conference on Advanced Video and Signal Based Surveillance*, 229–236. 10.1109/AVSS.2003.1217926

Zaklouta, F., Stanciulescu, B., & Hamdoun, V. (2011). Traffic sign classification using K-d trees and Random Forests. *The 2011 International Joint Conference on Neural Networks*, 2151-2155. doi: 10.1109/IJCNN.2011.6033494

Zaklouta, F., & Stanciulescu, B. (2014). Real-time traffic sign recognition in three stages. *Robotics and Autonomous Systems, 62*(1), 16–24. doi:10.1016/j.robot.2012.07.019

Zayene, O., Amamou, S. E., & BenAmara, N. E. (2017). *Arabic Video Text Recognition Based on Multi-Dimensional Recurrent Neural Networks.* Paper presented at the 2017 IEEE/ACS 14th International Conference on Computer Systems and Applications (AICCSA). 10.1109/AICCSA.2017.126

Zeng, X., Xiang, D., Peng, L., Liu, C., & Ding, X. (2017). *Local discriminant training and global optimization for convolutional neural network based handwritten Chinese character recognition.* Paper presented at the 2017 14th IAPR International Conference on Document Analysis and Recognition (ICDAR). 10.1109/ICDAR.2017.70

Zeng, X., Ding, Y., & Shao, S. (2009, December). Applying image warping technique to implement real-time virtual try-on based on person's 2D image. In *2009 Second International Symposium on Information Science and Engineering* (pp. 383-387). IEEE. 10.1109/ISISE.2009.9

Zhan, H., Lyu, S., & Lu, Y. (2018). *Handwritten digit string recognition using convolutional neural network.* Paper presented at the 2018 24th International Conference on Pattern Recognition (ICPR). 10.1109/ICPR.2018.8546100

Zhang, B., Hsu, M., & Dayal, U. (1999). *K-harmonic means - A data clustering algorithm.* Academic Press.

Zhang, H., Liu, D., & Xiong, Z. (2017). *CNN-based text image super-resolution tailored for OCR.* Paper presented at the 2017 IEEE Visual Communications and Image Processing (VCIP). 10.1109/VCIP.2017.8305127

Zhang, J., Du, J., & Dai, L. (2017). *A gru-based encoder-decoder approach with attention for online handwritten mathematical expression recognition.* Paper presented at the 2017 14th IAPR International Conference on Document Analysis and Recognition (ICDAR). 10.1109/ICDAR.2017.152

Zhang, J., Du, J., & Dai, L. J. I. T. o. M. (2018). *Track, attend, and parse (tap): An end-to-end framework for online handwritten mathematical expression recognition.* Academic Press.

Zhang, J., Li, Y., Li, T., Xun, L., & Shan, C. J. I. S. J. (2019). *License plate localization in unconstrained scenes using a two-stage CNN-RNN.* Academic Press.

Zhang, T., Cheng, L., & Ma, F. (2014). A modified rough cmeans clustering algorithm based on hybrid imbalanced measure of distance and density. *International Journal of Approximate Reasoning, 55*(8), 1805-1818.

Zhang, X.-Y., Yin, F., Zhang, Y.-M., Liu, C.-L., Bengio, Y. J. I. t. o. p. a., & Intelligence, M. (2017). *Drawing and recognizing chinese characters with recurrent neural network*. Academic Press.

Zhang, Y., & Huang, C. (2019). *A Robust Chinese License Plate Detection and Recognition Systemin Natural Scenes*. Paper presented at the 2019 IEEE 4th International Conference on Signal and Image Processing (ICSIP). 10.1109/SIPROCESS.2019.8868545

Zhang, C. Q., Zhang, Y. N., & Zhang, C. M. (2012). Surface Constraint of a Rational Interpolation and the Application in Medical Image Processing. *Research Journal of Applied Sciences, Engineering and Technology*, *4*(19), 3697–3703.

Zhang, H., Sun, K., & Li, W. (2014). Object-Oriented Shadow Detection and Removal from Urban High-Resolution Remote Sensing Images. *IEEE Transactions on Geoscience and Remote Sensing*, *52*(11), 6972–6982. doi:10.1109/TGRS.2014.2306233

Zhang, T. Y., & Suen, C. Y. (1984). A fast parallel algorithm for thinning digital patterns. *Communications of the ACM*, *27*(3), 236–239. doi:10.1145/357994.358023

Zhang, W., Fang, X., & Xu, Y. (2006). Detection of moving cast shadows using image orthogonal transform. *International Conference on Pattern Recognition*, 626-629. 10.1109/ICPR.2006.441

Zhang, Y., Gao, S., Zhang, C., & Chi, J. (2009). Application of a bivariate rational interpolation in image zooming. *International Journal of Innovative Computing, Information, & Control*, *5*(11), 4299–4307.

Zhang, Y.-J., & Liu, Z.-Q. (2002). Self-Splitting competitive learning: A new on-line clustering paradigm. *IEEE Transactions on Neural Networks*, *13*(2), 369–380. doi:10.1109/72.991422 PMID:18244438

Zhang, Y., Wu, H., & Cheng, L. (2012). Some new deformation formulas about variance and covariance. *Proceedings of 2012 International Conference on Modelling, Identification and Control*.

Zhao, N., Zhang, Z., Ouyang, X., Lv, N., & Zang, Z. (2018). *The recognition of RMB serial number based on CNN*. Paper presented at the 2018 Chinese Control And Decision Conference (CCDC). 10.1109/CCDC.2018.8407694

Zhao, F., Xie, X., & Roach, M. (2015). Computer Vision Techniques for Transcatheter Intervention. *IEEE Journal of Translational Engineering in Health and Medicine*, *3*, 1–31. doi:10.1109/JTEHM.2015.2446988 PMID:27170893

Zheng, J., Fuentes, O., Leung, M. Y., & Jackson, E. (2010). Mammogram Compression Using Super-Resolution. In J. Martí, A. Oliver, J. Freixenet, & R. Martí (Eds.), Lecture Notes in Computer Science: Vol. 6136. *Digital Mammography. IWDM 2010* (pp. 46–53). Springer., doi:10.1007/978-3-642-13666-5_7

Zhou, X.-D., Wang, D.-H., Tian, F., Liu, C.-L., Nakagawa, M. J. I. t. o. p. a., & Intelligence, M. (2013). *Handwritten Chinese/Japanese text recognition using semi-Markov conditional random fields*. Academic Press.

Zhuang, H., Li, C., & Zhou, X. (2018). *CCRS: web service for Chinese character recognition*. Paper presented at the 2018 IEEE International Conference on Web Services (ICWS). 10.1109/ICWS.2018.00010

Zoghlami, I., Faugeras, O., & Deriche, R. (1997). Using geometric corners to build a 2D mosaic from a set of images. In *Proceedings of the Conference on Computer Vision and Pattern Recognition*. IEEE Computer Society. 10.1109/CVPR.1997.609359

Zulkifli, N. A., Karim, S. A. A., Shafie, A., Sarfraz, M., Gaffar, A., & Nisar, K. S. (2019). Image interpolation using rational bi-cubic Ball. *Mathematics*, *7*(11), 1045. doi:10.3390/math7111045

Zuo, L.-Q., Sun, H.-M., Mao, Q.-C., Qi, R., & Jia, R.-S. J. I. A. (2019). *Natural scene text recognition based on encoder-decoder framework*. Academic Press.

About the Contributors

Muhammad Sarfraz is a Professor and Director of MSIT in the Department of Information Science, Kuwait University, Kuwait. His research interests include Computer Graphics, Computer Vision, Image Processing, Machine Learning, Pattern Recognition, Soft Computing, Data Science, Intelligent Systems, Information Technology and Information Systems. Prof. Sarfraz has been keynote/invited speaker at various platforms around the globe. He has advised more than 110 students for their MSc and PhD theses. He has published more than 380 publications as books, journal and conference papers. Prof. Sarfraz is member of various professional societies. He is the Chair and member of the International Advisory Committees and Organizing Committees of various international conferences. He is also Editor-in-Chief and Editor of various International Journals.

* * *

Samsul Ariffin Abdul Karim is a senior lecturer at Fundamental and Applied Sciences Department, Universiti Teknologi PETRONAS (UTP), Malaysia. He has been in the department for more than ten years. He obtained his B.App.Sc., M.Sc. and PhD in Computational Mathematics & Computer Aided Geometric Design (CAGD) from Universiti Sains Malaysia (USM). He had 20 years of experience using Mathematica and MATLAB software for teaching and research activities. His research interests include curves and surfaces designing, geometric modeling and wavelets applications in image compression and statistics. He has published more than 135 papers in Journal and Conferences as well as ten books including five research monographs and three Edited Conference Volume and 20 book chapters. He was the recipient of Effective Education Delivery Award and Publication Award (Journal & Conference Paper), UTP Quality Day 2010, 2011 and 2012 respectively. He is Certified WOLFRAM Technology Associate, Mathematica Student Level. He has published four books with Springer.

Abderrahim Bajit was born in Khémisset, Morocco, in June 1969. He received a B.S. degree in Electronics in 1989, an Aggregation degree in Electronics, an M.S degree in Computer Science, Telecommunications and Multimedia ITM in 2004, and the Ph.D. degree in Mobile TV coding and transportation in Mohammed V University of Rabat and the National School Of Telecommunications Systems, INPT Rabat respectively in 1993, 1998, 2004 and 2011. Since 2011, he works as a professor of higher education at the National School of Applied Sciences ENSA of Kénitra in the Department of Electrical and Automotive Engineering where he teaches on-board computer and real-time embedded systems applied to automotive and industrial fields. At this moment, and in the frame of a research project, our laboratory has begun the implication of the artificial intelligence AI in the autonomous driving vehicles

ADAS and its impact on road safety adapted specifically to Moroccan citizens and intelligent cities for energy management and low consumption aim.

Michael Burch works as an assistant professor at the Technical University of Eindhoven. He is interested in information visualization, visual analytics, data science, and eye tracking.

Youssef Chouni is one of the young leaders in Moroccan born in 1985 in Oued Zem. He holds a baccalaureate in mathematical sciences, has a computer engineering license with honors graduation and Masters in business intelligence with honors graduation. Youssef is a PhD student and professor of Informatics, actor activist for more than 10 years, founding member of the Civil Alliance of Youth for reform in Morocco in 2012, president of the Moroccan Coalition for young researchers. He participated in many of the dynamics; national and international programs: Program "SANAD" to support young people, organized by the USAID, Program "Arab young volunteer for the best future" organized by PNUD, Program "Regional Partnership for Culture and Development" organized by USAID, Monitoring of public policies, organized by the National Democratic Institute, Program "RAED" leadership for sustainable development. Its goal is to leave a positive mark on histoir their country with a change toward the good of the Moroccan society.

Mohit Dua is PhD in Computer Engineering from National Institute of Technology (An Institution of National Importance),Kurukshetra, India. He did his B.Tech. degree with Hons. in Computer Science and Engineering from Kurukshetra University, Kurukshetra, India in 2004 and M.Tech degree in Computer Engineering with distinction from National Institute of Technology(An Institution of National Importance), Kurukshetra, India in 2012. He is working as Assistant Professor in Department of Computer Engineering at NIT, Kurukshetra, India with more than 14 years of academic and research experience. He is a life member of Computer Society of India (CSI) and Indian Society for Technical Education (ISTE). His research interests include Pattern Recognition, Image and Speech processing, Theory of Formal languages and Statistical modeling. He has published more than 50 publications in various reputed international journals/conferences.

Roman Durikovic is a full professor at Comenius University in Bratislava, Slovakia, heading the Computer Graphics and Visualization Group. He was an invited professor at Tokyo University Japan, (until 2011), associated professor at Comenius University in Bratislava (until 2010), professor at The University of Aizu, Japan (until 2005), invited researcher at Kyushu University, Japan (until 1999), research assistant at Hiroshima University (until 1998). He studied Numerical Analysis and obtained his RNDr. in from Comenius University in Slovakia 1989, Ph.D. in Computer Science from the Hiroshima University in Japan 1996. He spent a research visit at Groningen University, Netherlands and University of Utrecht, Netherland (1991).

Mohammed Erritali is a Professor in the Department of Computer Science at the Faculty of Science and Technology of Beni Mellal at Sultan Moulay Slimane University, Master in Business Intelligence. he has a master's thesis offering research contributions on the topic of information systems security based on cryptography. While the research topic of his doctoral thesis focuses on the aspects of communications and security ad hoc vehicular networks.

Marina Gavrilova is a Full Professor in the Department of Computer Science, University of Calgary. Dr. Gavrilova's research interests lie in the area of biometric security, cognitive sciences, pattern recognition, social networking and cyberworlds. Prof. Gavrilova is the founder and co-director of the Biometric Technologies Laboratory, with over 200 journal and conference papers, edited special issues, books and book chapters. Prof Gavrilova is a Founding Editor-in-Chief of Transactions on Computational Science Journal, Springer. Prof. Gavrilova appeared as Invited Keynote and Invited Panelist at many key international events. She has given invited talks at DIMACS, Bell Labs; Microsoft Research, Redmond; Samsung Research, South Korea; CERIAS Purdue University, DRDC Canada and at numerous universities worldwide.

Abdul Ghaffar is member of Informetrics Research Group, Ton Duc Thang University, Ho Chi Minh City, Vietnam; He has taught Mathematics to post-graduate, graduate and undergraduate classes side by side with notable engagements in research work, assessment and evaluation; teachers' training and administration. His areas of interest include Computer Aided Geometric Design, Multiresolution in geometric modeling, special function, and Subdivision scheme. He has participated in several conferences and seminars in Pakistan and abroad. He is member of various professional societies including Pakistan Mathematical Society. He has the distinction of winning the Research Productivity Award for the year 2012-13 from the Pakistan Council for Science and Technology.

Enrique Herrera-Viedma's main research interests are in the fields of: linguistic modeling, fuzzy decision making, aggregation, consensus, information retrieval, recommender systems, digital library, web retrieval, web quality, social networks, blockchain and bibliometric.

Gee-Sern Jison Hsu received the dual M.S. degree in electrical and mechanical engineering and the Ph.D. degree in mechanical engineering from the University of Michigan, Ann Arbor, in 1993 and 1995, respectively. From 1995 to 1996, he was a Post-Doctoral Fellow with the University of Michigan. From 1997 to 2000, he was a Senior Research Staff with the National University of Singapore, Singapore. In 2001, he joined Penpower Technology, where he leads research on face recognition and intelligent video surveillance. In 2007, he joined the Department of Mechanical Engineering, National Taiwan University of Science and Technology, Taipei, Taiwan. His research interests are in the areas of computer vision and deep learning, particularly face recognition, and license plate recognition. Prof. Hsu received the best/outstanding paper awards in ICMT 2011, CVGIP 2013, CVPRW 2014 and CVGIP 2018. He is a senior member of IEEE and a member of ACM and IAPR.

Ichrak Khoulqi is a PhD student in computer science at University Sultan Moulay Slimane especially in laboratory of treatment of information and the aid of decision.

Uwe Kloos is a Professor for Computer Graphics and Visualization, Reutlingen University.

K. N. Pavan Kumar is currently pursuing his M.Sc. from the University of Calgary, Canada in the Biometric technologies laboratory. He received his B.Sc. degree in Information Science and Engineering from the Sir M. Visvesvaraya Institute of Technology, Bangalore in 2015. He has published journal and conference papers in the areas of deep learning and online behavior recognition.

Tobias Lampprecht received a bachelor's degree in media and communication informatics and is currently studying in the master's program Human-Centered Computing at Reutlingen University. In addition to software development and information visualization, he is interested in topics related to computer vision and IoT.

Peilin Li received Bachelor of Engineering in mechanical design manufacturing and automation from Shanghai Tong Ji University in China of P. R. in 2002 and Master of Engineering in advanced manufacturing technology from School of Advanced Manufacturing and Mechanical Engineering (Now named as School of Engineering) at University of South Australia in 2007. He has completed Ph.D. degree in 2014 with the School of Engineering under Division of Information Technology, Engineering and Environment at University of South Australia sponsored by the scholarship of University of South Australia President's Scholarship and Australian Postgraduate Award. His current research interests include the algorithmic methods and machine learning in image processing for machine vision and its applications.

Marek Mauser received a bachelor's degree in media and communication informatics and is currently studying in the master's program Human-Centered Computing at Reutlingen University. In addition to software development and information visualization, he is interested in topics related to collaboration and providing solutions in Office 365.

Melody Moh obtained her MS and Ph.D., both in computer science, from Univ. of California - Davis. She joined San Jose State University in 1993 and is currently Professor and Chair of the Dept. of Computer Science. Her research interests include cloud computing, mobile, wireless networking, security/privacy for cloud and network systems, and machine-learning applications. She has received over 550K dollars of research grants from both NSF and industry, has published over 150 refereed papers in international journals, conference proceedings, and as book chapters, and has consulted for various companies.

Mihir Narayan Mohanty is currently working as a Professor in the Department of Electronics and Communication Engineering, Institute of Technical Education and Research (FET), Siksha 'O' Anusandhan (Deemed to be University), Bhubaneswar, Odisha. He has received his M. Tech degree in Communication System Engineering from the Sambalpur University, Sambalpur, Odisha and obtained his PhD degree in Applied Signal Processing. He is the fellow of IE (I), and IETE. Also, he is the member of many professional societies including IEEE, IET etc. He has 25 years of teaching and research experience. He has published more than 300 papers in different Journals, Conferences including Book Chapters. He has authored two books. He is the successive reviewer of manuscripts from IEEE, Elsevier, Springer, IGI Global etc. His areas of research interests include Applied Signal and Image Processing, Speech Processing, Antenna, and Intelligent Signal Processing.

Suhaib Musleh is a teacher of Information and Communication Technology (ICT) in the schools of Ministry of Education, Kuwait. Currently, he is a graduate student pursuing his Master program in Computer Science, Kuwait University, Kuwait. He graduated from Zarka Private University, Jordan with a bachelor's degree in Computer Science. His research focuses on digital image processing and related applications. He participated in Conferences and Seminars and presented in subjects related to image processing and multimedia forensics. Suhaib likes to participate in creative workshops, conferences, and meetings related to his area of expertise.

Kottakkaran Sooppy Nisar received an M.Sc. degree in Mathematics in 2005, M.Phil. degree in Applied Mathematics in 2008 and Ph.D. degree for his research with the Department of Applied Mathematics, Faculty of Engineering, Aligarh Muslim University in 2011. He is working as an Associate Professor, Department of Mathematics, Prince Sattam bin Abdulaziz University, Saudi Arabia. His current research interests are Special Functions, Fractional Calculus, Approximation Theory (Statistical convergence), SAC-OCDMA code networks, Machine learning, Mathematical Physics, Fluid Dynamics, and Mathematical Modeling. He has more than 300 research publications in highly reputed international journals. He is also the author of some books and book chapters.

Hazem Raafat received the B.Sc. degree (Hons.) in electronics and communications engineering from Cairo University, Egypt, in 1976, and the Ph.D. degree in systems design engineering from the University of Waterloo, Canada, in 1985. He was an Associate Professor with the Department of Computer Science, University of Regina, Canada, where he also held a joint appointment with the Electronics Information Systems Engineering Department. He is currently Professor of Computer Science at Kuwait University. His research interests include data mining, computer vision, pattern recognition, multiple classifier systems, and natural language processing. He is a member of IEEE and ACM.

David Salb received his B.Sc. degree in medical engineering from Hochschule Furtwangen University (HFU), Germany. He is currently working towards his M.Sc. degree at the Faculty of Computer Science at Reutlingen University. His work focuses on computer vision for medical imaging.

Afza Shafie is a Senior Lecturer at the Fundamental and Applied Science Department in Universiti Teknologi PETRONAS. Her area of interests includes statistical and mathematical modelling especially in the field of Oil & Gas Exploration and Recovery. She is actively involved in the STEM initiatives to raise awareness and interest among the primary and secondary school students. She has secured numerous local and international funds for her ongoing research. Her works have been published in several Q1/Q2 and indexed journals.

Jiri Silha is employed as a researcher at Comenius University in Bratislava. During his employment at the Astronomical Institute of the University of Bern AIUB in 2013-2017 he was working and managing several different ESA studies dedicated to space debris research and SST applications. Currently, he is involved in the space debris research performed at Comenius University, with focus on observations planning, acquisition and processing. His research interests are in space debris photometry, light curves and colors, image processing algorithms testing and validation, minor planets photometry. Silha co-authored the book *From Space Debris to Cosmology* written in English.

Madeena Sultana completed her PhD in Computer Science at University of Calgary in April 2018. She is a recipient of the prestigious Vanier Canada Graduate Scholarship (2014 - 2017) and Alberta Innovates Technology Futures Scholarship (2014 - 2016). She worked as a Postdoctoral Associate at Cumming School of Medicine of University of Calgary for a year. Madeena co-authored over 30 scientific articles in peer-reviewed journals, conferences, and books. Her research interests include Biometric Security, Machine Learning, Data Science, Human Behavior Analysis, and Digital Image Processing. She is currently employed as a Defense Scientist by DRDC Canada.

Sanjida Nasreen Tumpa is currently pursuing her M.Sc. from the University of Calgary, Canada. She received a B.Sc. degree in Computer Science and Engineering from the Military Institute of Science and Technology (MIST), Bangladesh in 2014 and an M.Sc. degree in Computer Science and Engineering from Bangladesh University of Engineering and Technology (BUET), Bangladesh in 2019. Sanjida Nasreen Tumpa joined as a faculty member of the Department of Computer Science and Engineering, Military Institute of Science and Technology (MIST), Bangladesh in 2015. She served there for 4 years 6 months. She has published over 15 conference papers, in addition to a book chapter.

Huub van de Wetering works as an assistant professor at the Technische Universiteit Eindhoven. He is interested in information visualization and visual analytics.

Orly Yadid-Pecht received her B.Sc. from the Electrical Engineering Department at the Technion - Israel Institute of Technology. She completed her M.Sc. in 1990 and her D.Sc. in 1995, respectively, also at the Technion. She was a National Research Council (USA) research fellow from 1995-1997 in the areas of Advanced Image Sensors at the Jet Propulsion Laboratory (JPL)/ California Institute of Technology (Caltech). In 1997 she joined Ben-Gurion University in Israel, as a member in the Electrical and Electro-Optical Engineering departments. There she founded the VLSI Systems Center, specializing in CMOS Image Sensors. Since 2009 she is the iCORE Professor of Integrated Sensors, Intelligent Systems (ISIS) at the University of Calgary, Canada. In 2014 she received the iCORE/ AITF Strategic Chair position in Integrated Intelligent Sensors (I2Sense).

Svetlana Yanushkevich is a professor in the ECE Department at Schulich School of Engineering at the University of Calgary. She directs the Biometric Technologies Laboratory at the University of Calgary, the only research facility dedicated to the biometric system design in Canada. She received her Dr. Sci (Dr. Habilitated) degree from Technical University of Warsaw in 1999. She was with West-Pomeranian University of Technology, Szczecin, Poland, prior to joining the ECE Department at the University of Calgary in 2001. Dr. Yanushkevich contributed to the area of artificial intelligence for digital design and biometrics since 1996. Most recently, she and her team have developed novel risk assessment strategies based on machine reasoning, with applications to biometric-enabled border control, forensics and healthcare.

Nur Atiqah Zulkifli has obtained her MSc from Universiti Teknologi PETRONAS (UTP) under the supervision of Dr Samsul Ariffin Abdul Karim and Dr A'fza Shafie. Her research interests include image interpolation and curve modeling in computer aided geometric design (CAGD).

Index

Recommended Reference Books

Premier Reference Source

Cases on Immersive Virtual Reality Techniques

ISBN: 978-1-5225-5912-2
© 2019; 349 pp.
List Price: $215

Critical Explorations

Cloud Security
Concepts, Methodologies, Tools, and Applications

ISBN: 978-1-5225-8176-5
© 2019; 2,218 pp.
List Price: $2,950

Premier Reference Source

Smart Devices, Applications, and Protocols for the IoT

ISBN: 978-1-5225-7811-6
© 2019; 317 pp.
List Price: $225

Premier Reference Source

Innovative Solutions and Applications of Web Services Technology

ISBN: 978-1-5225-7268-8
© 2019; 316 pp.
List Price: $215

Premier Reference Source

Code Generation, Analysis Tools, and Testing for Quality

ISBN: 978-1-5225-7455-2
© 2019; 288 pp.
List Price: $205

Research Insights

Ambient Intelligence Services in IoT Environments
Emerging Research and Opportunities

ISBN: 978-1-5225-8973-0
© 2019; 200 pp.
List Price: $195

Ensure Quality Research is Introduced to the Academic Community

Become an IGI Global Reviewer for Authored Book Projects

Premier Reference Source

Emerging GIS Applications for Emergency and Disaster Management

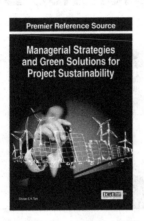

Premier Reference Source

Managerial Strategies and Green Solutions for Project Sustainability

Premier Reference Source

Comparative Approaches to Using R and Python for Statistical Data Analysis

Premier Reference Source

Solutions for High-Touch Communications in a High-Tech World

The overall success of an authored book project is dependent on quality and timely reviews.

In this competitive age of scholarly publishing, constructive and timely feedback significantly expedites the turnaround time of manuscripts from submission to acceptance, allowing the publication and discovery of forward-thinking research at a much more expeditious rate. Several IGI Global authored book projects are currently seeking highly-qualified experts in the field to fill vacancies on their respective editorial review boards:

Applications and Inquiries may be sent to:
development@igi-global.com

Applicants must have a doctorate (or an equivalent degree) as well as publishing and reviewing experience. Reviewers are asked to complete the open-ended evaluation questions with as much detail as possible in a timely, collegial, and constructive manner. All reviewers' tenures run for one-year terms on the editorial review boards and are expected to complete at least three reviews per term. Upon successful completion of this term, reviewers can be considered for an additional term.

If you have a colleague that may be interested in this opportunity, we encourage you to share this information with them.

IGI Global's Transformative Open Access (OA) Model:
How to Turn Your University Library's Database Acquisitions Into a Source of OA Funding

In response to the OA movement and well in advance of Plan S, IGI Global, early last year, unveiled their OA Fee Waiver (Offset Model) Initiative.

Under this initiative, librarians who invest in IGI Global's InfoSci-Books (5,300+ reference books) and/or InfoSci-Journals (185+ scholarly journals) databases will be able to subsidize their patron's OA article processing charges (APC) when their work is submitted and accepted (after the peer review process) into an IGI Global journal.*

How Does it Work?

1. When a library subscribes or perpetually purchases IGI Global's InfoSci-Databases including InfoSci-Books (5,300+ e-books), InfoSci-Journals (185+ e-journals), and/or their discipline/subject-focused subsets, IGI Global will match the library's investment with a fund of equal value to go toward subsidizing the OA article processing charges (APCs) for their patrons.

   Researchers: Be sure to recommend the InfoSci-Books and InfoSci-Journals to take advantage of this initiative.

2. When a student, faculty, or staff member submits a paper and it is accepted (following the peer review) into one of IGI Global's 185+ scholarly journals, the author will have the option to have their paper published under a traditional publishing model or as OA.

3. When the author chooses to have their paper published under OA, IGI Global will notify them of the OA Fee Waiver (Offset Model) Initiative. If the author decides they would like to take advantage of this initiative, IGI Global will deduct the US$ 1,500 APC from the created fund.

4. This fund will be offered on an annual basis and will renew as the subscription is renewed for each year thereafter. IGI Global will manage the fund and award the APC waivers unless the librarian has a preference as to how the funds should be managed.

Hear From the Experts on This Initiative:

"I'm very happy to have been able to make one of my recent research contributions, 'Visualizing the Social Media Conversations of a National Information Technology Professional Association' featured in the *International Journal of Human Capital and Information Technology Professionals*, freely available along with having access to the valuable resources found within IGI Global's InfoSci-Journals database."

– **Prof. Stuart Palmer**,
Deakin University, Australia

For More Information, Visit: www.igi-global.com/publish/contributor-resources/open-access or contact IGI Global's Database Team at eresources@igi-global.com.